The Winnipeg Connection:
Writing Lives at Mid-Century

The Winnipeg Connection:
Writing Lives at Mid-Century

edited by
Birk Sproxton

Prairie Fire Press, Inc.

Prairie Fire Press, Inc.
Artspace
423-100 Arthur Street
Winnipeg, Manitoba R3B 1H3
www.prairiefire.ca

Prairie Fire Press, Inc. gratefully acknowledges the financial assistance of The Winnipeg Arts Council, The WH & SE Loewen Foundation, The Winnipeg Foundation and the Assiniboine Credit Union.

Cover and interior design: Tétro Design Incorporated
Cover photograph courtesy of Robert E. Wanner
Typesetting and layout: Heidi Harms

Printed in Canada by Hignell Book Printing for Prairie Fire Press, Inc.

Library and Archives Canada Cataloguing in Publication Data

Main entry under title:
The Winnipeg connection : writing lives at mid-century / edited by Birk Sproxton

Includes bibliographical references.
ISBN-13: 978-0-9731608-1-9
ISBN-10: 0-9731608-1-0

Canadian literature (English)—Manitoba—Winnipeg—History and criticism.
Authors, Canadian (English)—Manitoba—Winnipeg—Biography.
Canadian literature (English)—20th century—History and criticism.
Authors, Canadian (English)—20th century—Biography. I. Sproxton, Birk

PS8133.W55W55 2006   C810.9'9712743   C2006-904019-2

For Lorraine

Acknowledgements

This project has gathered many supporters over the course of its preparation. Thanks go to the contributors for their insights and commitment to the book. Thanks also to my three student research assistants. Mark Johnston helped in the early stages, Karl von Tettenborn then took over for more preparatory work, and subsequently, Marion Swainson Allred worked many months to help bring the project to life. The people at Prairie Fire Press have been unstinting in their support and courtesy over the long gestation period. Janine Tschuncky, Andris Taskans and Heidi Harms have gone beyond duty to make this book possible. Heidi deserves double mention for shepherding the manuscript through the production process. Thanks to Karen McElrea for proofreading the galleys. I also wish to thank my family and especially my wife, Lorraine, to whom this book is dedicated. And there is always Winnipeg, a character unto herself.

Contents

The Winnipeg Connection:
Writing Lives at Mid-Century

Introducing **The Winnipeg Connection:**
A Series

*T*he *Winnipeg Connection* began in the afterglow of the special issue of *Prairie Fire* published in 1999 to coincide with the Pan-American Summer Games. We called the issue "Winnipeg in Fiction," a collection designed to celebrate Winnipeg's history as a place of writing. That summer Winnipeg was alive and bristling with good feeling about herself as she welcomed visitors from across the Americas. The special issue sold out quickly, and we realized we had tapped into a widely shared interest in the city's writing life as it emerges in English-language fiction. With fifty contributors in all, including striking art work and an intriguing batch of archival images selected by Louise Jonasson, the book-size magazine offered a visual as well as verbal feast. For visitors and Winnipeggers alike, "Winnipeg in Fiction" served as a healthy introduction to Winnipeg's literary and artistic life.

Some time later, the idea for *The Winnipeg Connection* began to brew. Then I approached the *Prairie Fire* people with a proposal to focus on Winnipeg at mid-century, especially the 1940s and 1950s. These were crucial years, I argued, for the emergence of an internationally acclaimed contingent of writers—Margaret Laurence, Adele Wiseman, Patricia Blondal, Jack Ludwig and John Marlyn among them, a group aided and abetted by Malcolm Ross, James Reaney and many others. This was a time when Winnipeg once more remade herself as a vital hub of the literary arts. She had reached pre-eminent status through her many newspapers and the early-twentieth-century writing of Ralph Connor and Nellie McClung. In the World War II era Winnipeg's output and influence reached new heights, as the list above suggests.

As *The Winnipeg Connection* assumed imaginative shape, and long before I began to approach contributors, I gained considerable impetus from informal sources. A lunchroom table conversation in Alberta comes to mind, people gathered with bag lunches, coffee, bagels. The conversation turned to Winnipeg. Someone directed a question to me, "Why does Winnipeg have so many fine writers?" I was pleased by this turn and gave a quick response.

"Well," I said, "first of all, Winnipeg is an island." Winnipeg people, I went on to say, have a habit of making their own culture; they know they are physically distant from other metropolitan centres; they do not depend on others to make culture for them. Someone mentioned Carol Shields, and the conversation turned to other writers, to Margaret Laurence and Robert Kroetsch, Miriam Toews and David Bergen.

"Winnipeg is an island"

The island metaphor is consistent with geographer Desmond Cole's description of the country as a string of island cities, Canada as archipelago.[1] But the island metaphor seems rooted in a felt reality. I think of another conversation, this time from the early 1970s. The setting was a graduate class at the University of Manitoba conducted by Margaret Stobie. We had asked her about the Manitoba Theatre Centre (MTC). What impulses led to its founding? Stobie spoke as one involved in that founding. She said people realized they had choices to make if they cared about theatre. They could flit off to New York and London, or they could make their own theatre. The choice was stark and clear.

Obviously, they chose the latter course, to the great benefit of Winnipeg and the country as a whole. Led by John Hirsch and Tom Hendry, MTC became a powerful force, and similar regional theatres sprang up shortly after. An island, we might say, encourages co-operation and the emergence of a distinctive culture, especially when the people are diverse in background. The ongoing daily drama of clash and negotiation becomes part of a city's living habits, a pulse at the heart.

Sand and Sandbox

At the same time, no city is an island entire of itself; there are always hooks and links to other places, some far, some near. As I was on my deck scratching notes one evening, my wife, Lorraine, came outside to join me. She carried a letter she had written as a girl to her father. She was giving him instructions about what she needed at the lake. She wanted him to bring a doll, not the big doll, but the one with the napkins that looked like (and then a drawing of two rectangles). He was to bring the napkins too. She had to stop there, she said, because she was going to "the sand." On the back of the envelope, no doubt to guarantee her older sister wouldn't get her teenaged hooks into the letter, Lorraine had written the words "Very Private."

The letter is dated 1953, and it speaks volumes. Intertwined with the spidery handwriting of a girl is the culture in which she grew up. There was the train she and her mother and sister had taken to the beach while her father worked in the city; though separate, they were joined by a quick and reliable mail system, and always in their lives was the twin presence of sand, drawing children out of the house, and lake, drawing families out of the city, by train or by car.

For many middle-class people, this little story captures the rhythm of a life. The city was not for them an island, any more than it is now, but a central place with satellite communities connected by train and by highway. The train and the highway both shrank the distance between Winnipeg and Winnipeg Beach. This small domestic episode suggests an element of pastoralism in the many-textured network of the city's life. You might hear the rush and rumble of the city all around you but the peace of the lake always beckons. The gestures of everyday life inevitably carry the aura of other lives elsewhere.

The network metaphor—or it is a hubbub?—hints at larger, more dramatic social changes already underway at the time. In speaking of the influences that mark her writing, Adele Wiseman, in conversation with Wayne Tefs, describes playing at home in her yard. "[W]e were the only house on the block . . . where there was a swing . . . and a sandbox which meant the neighbouring kids came to us, we weren't to disappear from sight. . . . [The] constant flow of language, it was . . . encircling us. . . . [M]y mother's past . . . was to me another life of my own, a kind of past into which I explored, just as I explored the future. . . ."[2]

An Electric City

Such a constant flow of language calls to mind networks of electronic media and Marshall McLuhan's remark about how a new medium or technology effects cultural change. The "content," he says, "of any medium is always another medium." McLuhan proposed a new way to think about messages.

> For the "message" of any medium or technology is the change of scale or pace or pattern that it introduces into human affairs. The railway did not introduce movement or transportation or wheel or road into human society, but it accelerated and enlarged the scale of previous human functions, creating totally new kinds of cities and new kinds of work and leisure. This happened whether the railway functioned in a tropical or northern environment. . . . The airplane, on the other hand, by accelerating the rate of transportation, tends to dissolve the railway form of city, politics, and association, quite independently of what the airplane is used for. (141)

In *The Winnipeg Connection*, contributors address shifts in scale and pace and pattern, though they may use different words and various tones of argument. They speak of a city in the process of transformation, with an emphasis upon the ongoing process of change rather than any fixed outcome or product. A city is a place of movement.

Winnipeg at mid-century was moving from a railway city, in which she held pre-eminence in the Canadian West, to an airplane city, a city with new politics and associations. A 1949 song composed by Vida C. Fritch called "Manitoba Calling" speaks of the city's self-image in the immediate post-war. On the back cover sheet under a large headline, "Manitoba Welcomes You!", a series of paragraphs proclaims the virtues of the province and its capital city.

> [Winnipeg] is noted for its Hydro-Electric System, the cheapest electric power in North America, developed on the Winnipeg River. Winnipeg is the greatest grain centre on the American continent. The largest music festival in the world is Winnipeg's proud boast. On the Canadian Pacific grounds stands the "Countess of Dufferin," Winnipeg's first locomotive which arrived in 1877 by barge.

This post-war boosterism is warm-hearted, though we may now be inclined to read it in the context of the Cold War. The boom years have since faded away, and an ironic self-awareness seems to settle in.

As an example of this irony, I think of Esther Warkov's stunning paper sculpture "Empress of Rust," a title surely chosen to recall the name of Winnipeg's first locomotive. From the Countess of Dufferin to the Empress of Rust. So the city has moved. Warkov sees the railway form of city rusting away around her, capable of its own beauty, but rusting nonetheless.[3] By contrast, as a major writer of the mid-century era, Margaret Laurence in "North Main Car" imagines the city's transit system as a vehicle for positive social change, a democratic vehicle giving space to all who board.

The Winnipeg electrical system, "cheapest electric power in North America," allowed a new way of life to emerge. Winnipeggers enjoyed a grid capable of changing ratios of night and day, and shrinking the world via the new technology of TV, to a global village, to use McLuhan's phrase. The living world was brought into living rooms, cheaply.

Television brought home what the movie houses and radio had made available earlier. In *The Winnipeg Connection* the dance of continuity and change can be sampled by moving from the article on film by Gene Waltz to pieces on radio and television by Chris Dafoe and Howard Curle respectively. Walz recounts the distribution across North America of a film based on "If Day" in Winnipeg, a depiction of what might happen if Nazis gained power. Books were burned, elected officials were herded onto buses en route to "incarceration," swastikas blotted out Union Jacks. The film was released across the continent on February 26, 1942. For a time, Winnipeg was at the centre of the continent. Yet by the end of the 1950s the rise of television, as Howard Curle argues, challenged the power of movie houses and radio stations. A new pace of life began to take hold, though newspapers continued to be very important.

Writing Lives at Mid-Century

Winnipeg's pre-eminence as a writing place has a long foreground. By the late 1890s, Winnipeg produced dozens of newspapers, a reflection of the city's diversity. Over time, Winnipeg papers became known for their vitality and journalistic excellence. Frank Underhill, writing in the *Canadian Forum* in 1933, referred to the *Winnipeg Free Press* as "the only newspaper in Canada which exercises anything approaching to a national influence . . ."[4] A decade later Bruce Hutchison also stressed the central role Winnipeg played in the country's intellectual life. His tone seems to belie the distresses of war. "[T]he spirit of Winnipeg," he wrote in *The Unknown Country* (1942), "is the true hope of Canada—the forward look, the broad, worldwide feeling, the pioneer spirit, the willingness to gamble. It is no accident, therefore, that Canada's best thinking in the last twenty years has come out of such a place" (218). In 1948, when the second edition appeared, Hutchison saw no reason to change his opinion.

Hutchison identified the source of this "best thinking" to be a uniquely gifted individual, John W. Dafoe, editor of the *Winnipeg Free Press*. Hutchison called him "the greatest Canadian of his time," one whose ideas were taken up, later, across the country (213).

The medium provides a message. In the climate of ideas engendered in part by the newspapers, many writers were nourished, however indirectly. Among them was Miriam Waddington, for example, who left the city in the late thirties but was forever marked by Winnipeg. Dorothy Livesay also influenced Winnipeg, as evidenced in her memoirs, especially *A Winnipeg Childhood* released by Peguis in 1973 and expanded as *Beginnings* in 1988. Her influence goes much beyond her substantial poetic accomplishments. Livesay's brilliant essay "The Documentary Poem: A Cana-dian Genre" continues to spark debate about the impulse to documentary, an impulse informing thinkers from Norman McLaren to Glenn Gould, an impulse that informs this present book.[5] Another kind of writer was also nourished in Winnipeg. Marshall McLuhan, English professor and media guru, was educated at the University of Manitoba (he took his MA in 1934). Excellence generates excellence. "I keep coming back," Northrop Frye writes, "to the feeling that there appears to be such a thing as an imaginative continuum, and that writers are conditioned in their attitudes by their predecessors, or by the cultural climate of their predecessors, whether there is conscious influence or not" (250).

"An imaginative continuum"

Certainly J.W. Dafoe did not act in isolation. No writer does. I prefer to see him as part of a culture with lines of filiation and affiliation. His grandson Christopher Dafoe, himself a distinguished journalist and historian, carries on the family line, and Chris Dafoe's contribution to *The Winnipeg Connection* speaks not of solitary toil but of creative co-operation in the radio days before the dominance of television in popular culture. These lines of continuity give a culture a unique shape.

The continuities are not easy to maintain. Writing requires commitment and sustained effort. Contemporary novelist Margaret Sweatman, herself descended from a novelist, makes the point in an engaging way, via Stanislavsky. The challenge for making a culture, she argues, is to create an unbroken line, whether in an individual play or in a larger cultural setting.

> Working as a writer, it's easy to feel disempowered, colonized, without a role to play because there's such a small audience. It can happen on a larger cultural scale, one or both. Unbroken is a powerful word. So is its counterpart: broken.

A challenge for writers, even in relatively peaceful times, is to establish and maintain unbroken lines to the past and into the future.

Sometimes the lines need to be drawn taut and plucked so they sing. A line I find to be especially resonant begins in the Canadian issue of *Time* for December 29, 1947. In a brief piece called "On the Verge," we find this note. "In Winnipeg last week, the University of Manitoba's Chester Duncan, lecturer in English, told the Winnipeg Poetry Society: 'Our well-known laconicism is not always concealed wisdom, but a kind of dumbness, a frustration, a between-ness. We are continually on the verge of something but we don't quite get there. We haven't discovered what we are or where we're going and therefore haven't much to say'" (quoted in Kenner 203).

As a specialist in the work of W.H. Auden, Duncan must have enjoyed the irony in finding his remarks on poetry making their way into the cultural record in this way. Auden asserted that poetry makes nothing happen, but comments on poetry evidently do. Or at least Chester Duncan's comments do.

In 1948 Hugh Kenner subsequently quoted Duncan's lines as epigraph to an essay called "The Case of the Missing Face." In this piece Kenner argues that the Canadian artist must turn away from the habit of looking at bush and rock to look in the mirror. "The primary critical question in Canada today is whether it is yet safe to cut the umbilical cord to the wilderness: whether it is time to conduct a new raid on the inarticulate" (207). The Group of Seven, Kenner goes on to say, found "the Canadian

Image" to be "faceless" (208). Now, post World War II, artists must look more searchingly. Implicit in severing the cord to the wilderness that Kenner recommends is a turn to the cities, the great magnets of human activity.

Interestingly, at just this time Margaret Laurence attempted to give a face to Winnipeg in her long poem "North Main Car," reprinted in this volume. From Duncan to Kenner to Laurence runs an unbroken line. When Laurence imagines a face for her (temporarily) adopted city, she addresses the lack Kenner speaks of; furthermore, she anticipates our ongoing interest in the character of Winnipeg.

Still later, in 1977, to show the persistence of the connection, Duncan's metaphor of the margin appeared again, this time in an essay by Marshall McLuhan. Always interested in margins, McLuhan called his essay "Canada: The Borderline Case." First, he summarizes Duncan's main point concerning Canadian identity, and then offers his own twist.

> Duncan found the key with "between-ness," the world of the interval, the borderline, the
> interface of worlds and situations. It may well be that Canadians misconceive their role
> and opportunities and feel the misguided urge to follow the trendy ways of those less
> fortunately placed. The interface is where the action is. No need to move or follow, but
> only to tune the perceptions on the spot. ("Borderline" 233)

"The interface is where the action is." The sentence has a nice McLuhanesque ring to it, yet in the days of the DEW Line (first established in 1957) and other radar stations strung across the Canadian North the theme would have carried an ominous undertone. Canada surely would entertain the action if the Soviet Union and the United States started to exchange intercontinental ballistic missiles. The threat of nuclear war marked the 1950s, as Jack Bumsted argues, reminding us that the fifties were not only a time of euphoria. But the nuclear threat changed. By 1977, McLuhan could speak with enthusiasm about Canada's position in the electronic world. "Today, when the old industrial hardware is obsolescent, we can see that the Canadian condition of low-profile identity and multiple borders approaches the ideal pattern of electronic living" ("Borderline" 248). McLuhan's optimism brings the dark undertones of the 1950s into relief.

The Scene of Writing

In this book Winnipeg figures as a seat of composition. You read of James Reaney riding down Pembina Highway on a bus, teasing *Alphabet* into life. You read of Patricia Blondal, elsewhere yet connected, pushing words through and into and against the pain of loss and the enticements of death. She refused to go gentle into that good night. Her measured stabs at an invading cancer in a piece published here for the first time bring to light the scene of writing as life, every word a triumph against the encroaching night. You read of John Hirsch, freezing and burning in downtown Winnipeg, coaxing a theatre into life. You see Jack Ludwig in the sweat-shop of the Ryan Building clacking at a typewriter with a bare bulb hanging over-head. You imagine Margaret Laurence shaping a radio play, a long poem, a documentary on North Winnipeg. You might see her holding a ruler steady on her page, drawing vertical lines in the margins, and you think of the multiple margins she uses twenty years later, in her 1969 novel *The Fire-Dwellers*. She works by day as a journalist but clearly she is determined to explore the possibilities of literature.[6] You hear of Chester Duncan, surely a gentle man, skewering radio listeners across the country with his irony and wit. You imagine young Dave Williamson approaching Adele Wiseman, book in hand, seeking the autograph of the Governor General's Award-winning novelist. All this, and more, in a scene marked by the relentless push of Red River floods, the fear of polio, the enduring pain of the Holocaust, the threat of nuclear war. A war to end all wars. And yet, persistent, the writing, the writing.

"Where is here?"

The Winnipeg Connection addresses Northrop Frye's famous comment, "It seems to me that Canadian sensibility has been profoundly disturbed, not so much by our famous problem of identity, important as that is, as by a series of paradoxes in what confronts that identity. It is less perplexed by the question, 'Who am I?' than by some such riddle as 'Where is here?'" (220)

By the 1940s, amidst much profound disturbance, Winnipeggers had a pretty good idea of where "here" was. They knew the city was connected with the country at large. Winnipeg was connected with the larger culture by the two national rail lines and by the energy and intelligence of Canadians.

A city is and is not an island. A city is a node in a network, a junction, perhaps an intersection. A conjunction teasing us to make connections. Winnipeg becomes a letter in an alphabet, a book in your hands.

A Biography of a City

The Winnipeg Connection attempts the impossible. It presumes to present a biography of a city, as if we were writing the biography of a real-life person. Cumulatively, the book gets at the "character" of Winnipeg. Given that any attempt to compose the character of a city will necessarily be limited, I have chosen to stress writing lives. *The Winnipeg Connection* therefore presents a partial biography of the city.

This book is partial in both senses, for I have an enduring fondness for Winnipeg with her refusal to disappear into the ever-lurking underground sea, for her ongoing commitment to a vital arts scene, especially to those I know best, the arts of writing. Writing lives, I say with a short "i," because for me and many others, it is as if writing were itself a character living in Winnipeg. The character named Writing lives in the city. It is no accident that James Reaney started his little magazine *Alphabet* in Winnipeg. Think of the traditions we hint at in "Winnipeg in Fiction," stretching from Ralph Connor and Nellie McClung to Margaret Laurence and Adele Wiseman to Robert Kroetsch and Carol Shields to David Arnason, Margaret Sweatman, Tomson Highway, Dennis Cooley and Di Brandt, to name only a few; or think of the honours accorded to dramatist Ian Ross, novelists Miriam Toews and David Bergen, and the continuing successes of Winnipeg publishing houses, or *Prairie Fire* magazine, *Mosaic* and *Border Crossings*. The list does go on.

World War II signalled a new political and cultural moment, a moment this book examines. Incomplete as such books must be, *The Winnipeg Connection* demanded to be written. We have with us still some of the leaders of those days and we have tried to tap their knowledge. And we turned to younger generations as well. We determined to make it the work of many hands; hence we included the best of relevant pieces from the "Winnipeg in Fiction" issue. Then we added more new documents, articles and personal essays. The overall result is a new and enlarged introduction to one phase of Winnipeg's cultural history. Many hands and many sources make this a rich book.

An Emerging Poetics

A new era calls for new reading habits. In her "Note" to "Winnipeg in Fiction" Carol Shields speaks of her novel *The Republic of Love*: "As a reader, I like to be firmly placed in time and space, but it nevertheless surprised me how distressed some Winnipeg readers were by these altered elements [of street names and neighbourhoods]. My intention had been to produce a sense of the city, while at the same time indicating that the Winnipeg that blinked from the pages of my novel was a fictional structure, my own invention" (19). Shields wrote this in 1999.

Her theme is a recurrent one. Here is Adele Wiseman, in an interview with Wayne Tefs, challenging readers to acknowledge the power of invention. She speaks of her novels, the Governor General's Award-winning *The Sacrifice* (1957) and *Crackpot* (1974).

[P]eople bug me a lot for not naming Winnipeg specifically. Neither novel is a sociological novel and I figure, oh God, if I name Winnipeg then they will start looking for streets and stuff and they won't look at what I'm really trying to say. And the other thing with Winnipeg is, I couldn't call it Winnipeg [in *The Sacrifice*] because I had a hill. I had a hill because when I left college I was lumbered with my education and I had this whole symbolic framework . . . and I needed that hill so what I described was Brandon, Manitoba, where my sister had learned to be a lab tech in her early days at the mental hospital . . . . that's when I first learned that there really were hills in the world. (Wayne Tefs, interview, 5-6).

Similarly, in a 1961 interview, Margaret Laurence (called Mrs. Lawrence with a "w") spoke of her concern about readers. "She cited Patricia Blondal, the Souris girl who died at 32 after writing a novel about Mouse Bluffs, a fictitious Manitoba township. A lot of people thought that Mrs. Blondal had written about Souris and its people. 'This is very unfair,' she said. 'She was a far more creative writer than that, and Mouse Bluffs was a literary production of imagination.'" (Colin Godbold, *Winnipeg Tribune*). The theme is common. The challenge is to recognize the transforming power of imagination.

"To remember, to celebrate"
As this book unfolded, many writers contributed to its shape. One four-cornered conversation connected me with Patrick Friesen, Andris Taskans, and Robyn Maharaj. Patrick spoke eloquently about the need "to remember, to celebrate those who came before us." He hoped it might be possible to have "a festival of Winnipeg as source of creativity, as catalyst." He alluded to the creative spirit that people sense in the city, a quality he linked to unique "power" sites in Native culture around the city (personal communication, April–May 2004). We hope the book will open up conversations and generate other books and prompt ongoing discussion. What makes Winnipeg a writing centre?

Multiple Points of Entry
One pleasure of a book made by several hands is that it allows many points of entry. You may wish to begin anywhere, at the beginning, for example, or at other points midstream. The book announces itself as an ordinary book, bound between covers, but in your hands it can become a mosaic, with many pieces to catch your reading eye. For those who prefer a straight-ahead reading, as well as those who select and dip, the challenge will be to shift gears, to speed up and slow down according to the pace and grid of the piece you are reading. Nevertheless there is a thread here, a through line. Pieces are clustered, roughly, into two groups. First come those pieces concerned mainly with the 1940s, and then those concerned mainly with the 1950s. You will sense

the movement. Everywhere, though, you are likely to be reminded of the backyard sandbox Adele Wiseman speaks of, where the voices play and run and overlap and call to mind the past and hint at the future. And in the grid of past and present and future you find at mid-century in a mid-continental city writing lives, writing lives.

NOTES

1. Quoted in Gerald Friesen, "Defining the Prairies: or, why the prairies don't exist" in Wardhaugh, 13.
2. See Typescript of Interview with Adele Wiseman, in David Arnason fonds, University of Manitoba Archives and Special Collections, Canadian Writers Symposium, mss. 111, Box 1, Folder 22, 2.
3. For a photograph of the piece, see the "Winnipeg in Fiction" issue of *Prairie Fire*, 36-37.
4. See Frank Underhill, "J.W. Dafoe," rpt in *Malcolm Ross, Our Sense of Identity*, 156.
5. See Livesay's essay in Eli Mandel's *Contexts of Canadian Criticism*, 267-281.
6. For a recent account of Laurence's journalism, see Donez Xiques, *Margaret Laurence: The Making of a Writer*, chapter 6, 135-150. In one of her 1947 newspaper columns, Laurence praises Sinclair Ross and his *As for Me and My House* as having "done more" to "intensely portray people and their environment" than does W.O. Mitchell in *Who Has Seen the Wind* (quoted in Xiques 141).

WORKS CITED

Frye, Northrop. "Conclusion to a *Literary History of Canada*." *The Bush Garden: Essays on the Canadian Imagination*. Toronto: House of Anansi, 1971. 213-251.

Hutchison, Bruce. *The Unknown Country*. Toronto: Longman's Green, 1942.

Kenner, Hugh. "The Case of the Missing Face." *Our Sense of Identity: A Book of Canadian Essays*. Ed. and with an introduction by Malcolm Ross. Toronto: Ryerson, 1954.

McLuhan, Marshall. "Canada: The Borderline Case." *The Canadian Imagination: Dimensions of a Literary Culture*. Ed. David Staines, with an introductory essay. Cambridge: Harvard University Press, 1977. 226-241.

———. "The Medium is the Message." *Contexts of Canadian Criticism*. Ed. and with an introduction by Eli Mandel. Chicago: University of Chicago Press, 1971. 140-153.

Ross, Malcolm, ed. *Our Sense of Identity: A Book of Canadian Essays*. With an introduction. Toronto: Ryerson, 1954.

Tefs, Wayne. Interview with Adele Wiseman. David Arnason fonds, University of Manitoba Archives & Special Collections, Canadian Writers Symposium, mss. 111, Box 1, Folder 22, 1-15.

Xiques, Donez. *Margaret Laurence: The Making of a Writer*. Toronto: Dundurn Press, 2005.

Wardhaugh, Robert. *Toward Defining the Prairies: Region, Culture, and History*. Winnipeg: University of Manitoba Press, 2001.

TRICIA WASNEY

Making Way: Loss and Transformation in Winnipeg's Urban Landscape— a Miscellaneous Photo Album

T he character of a city is shaped by what has been built and remains visible and also by what has been lost. Loss is embedded both in physical evidence and in discrete traces that remain in memory only. In this way loss is also about fullness; large and overstuffed with the knowledge of the past as well as the possibility of the future. To lose is not necessarily to forget, although to forget a little is necessary to move on. In "Funes the Memorious," Jorge Luis Borges writes of a boy who recalls everything, who "remembered not only every leaf of every tree of every wood, but also every one of the times he had perceived or remembered it." The details of his remembering are so overwhelming that he finds comfort only in complete darkness, quiet, solitude and, finally, death.

A city, too, can remember only so much. Layers accumulate; memories ebb or hold fast.

There are many kinds of loss: sudden and unexpected devastation caused by natural forces or outside influences; intentional undoing to replace the old and outmoded with the shiny and new. In between are many more variations of loss that come about from a combination of forces and result in changes both in habits and habitat. Loss is always transformative. Something always replaces what used to be, whether deliberately built or overgrown, slyly. The old makes way for the new.

The mid-twentieth century was a tumultuous time. Winnipeg, like many other cities, was affected by major global events like the Great Depression and World War II. The city was transformed by loss and by the social shifts that followed. A post-war housing shortage and significant changes in transportation had a considerable impact on our landscape and our habits. The increase in automobile use precipitated the need for wider streets and better bridges. It also spawned a culture where the car became much more than a conveyance; people not only drove cars to newly developed suburbs and malls, they were also served food in their cars and watched movies from them (now we can watch movies inside them). Air travel was accessible to many with the invention of the jet engine and its refinement. Television became enormously popular; attendance at movie theatres declined. Architecture dramatically changed and Winnipeg began to adopt new designs. Several major fires destroyed buildings and altered the activities housed within them. Winnipeg suffered a devastating flood at exactly mid-century. The result was that the landscape was carved into, pushed up and reconfigured to make sure the floodplain we chose to live on did not act like one anymore. Artists and writers shaped the cultural landscape; literary figures who continue to loom large rose out of this period. The form of the city continues to undulate as we build, undo, remember, forget.

The following photographs were chosen to capture moments of transformation in landscape and architecture that reflect some aspect of social change in Winnipeg in mid-century. In *Ways of Seeing*, John Berger writes that "the relation between what we see and what we know is never settled." With countless photographs at our disposal we choose only some to depict our reality. It is possible to conjure many histories, many stories from photographs. This is one small depiction of loss and transformation.

WORKS CITED

Berger, John. *Ways of Seeing*. New York: Viking Penguin, 1977, 7.

Borges, Jorge Luis. "Funes the Memorious." In *Labyrinths: Selected Stories and Other Writings*. Ed. Donald A. Yates and James E. Irby. Trans. James E. Irby. New York: New Directions Publishing, 1964, 65.

ARCHIVES OF MANITOBA. WINNIPEG—BUILDINGS—MUNICIPAL, NO. 57 CIVIC AUDITORIUM 11, 5138.

Construction of the Civic Auditorium, 1932. A number of public works initiatives, such as this one, were undertaken during the Depression years in Winnipeg as relief works projects. The building cost an estimated $1 million to construct. Designed for multi-use by the community, the Civic Auditorium for a time housed The Winnipeg Art Gallery until it moved in 1970 to its present location in the acclaimed building designed by Gustavo da Roza. The Archives of Manitoba is now located here.

ARCHIVES OF MANITOBA. FOOTE COLLECTION 2359. PHOTO BY L.B. FOOTE. N3000.

VE Day, corner of Portage and Main, May 7, 1945. The war, and its end, had a huge impact on culture, economics—every part of life.

UNIVERSITY OF WINNIPEG ARCHIVES/WESTERN CANADA PICTORIAL INDEX (WCPI) (50522). WINNIPEG ARCHIVES.

Osborne Street Bridge, Winnipeg, c. 1937. Workmen breaking up concrete counterweight into pieces that could be loaded and carried away. Photo by Foote.

Horse-watering trough on the south side of Osborne Street at Strad-
brook Avenue in Winnipeg, which was removed prior to construction
of the present fire hall and widening of the intersection, 1950.

Main Street Bridge under construction, September 8, 1931.

Last run of the streetcar in Winnipeg on Portage Avenue, September 19, 1955.

The interior of Uptown Theatre, Academy Road, being renovated to make way for a bowling alley with 30 lanes, 1960. Despite financially and socially troubled times (or perhaps because of them) the Uptown Theatre was designed in 1930 as a whimsical escape by Winnipeg architect Max Blankstein and built by local Allied Amusements Limited. "While Hollywood produced sensational and spectacular films featuring glamorous actors and set in exotic locales, the theatres themselves were also a set for this fantasy world. Movie houses became exotic replicas of mosques, temples and palaces . . . in the case of the Uptown Theatre, the architecture recalled a Moorish palace of Spain." By the late 1950s, however, the advent of television drastically reduced movie attendance. The fantastical interior of the Uptown was gutted in 1960 to make way for the decade's new pastime: bowling. Its use as a bowling alley continues to the present and the building's exterior remains relatively unchanged from the original. (*1985: The Year Past, Report of the City of Winnipeg Historical Buildings Committee.* Urban Design Branch, City of Winnipeg, Department of Environmental Planning, 22.)

ARCHIVES OF MANITOBA. FRANK HALL COLLECTION 57. PHOTO BY A.H. NEG. #367.

North Main Drive-In Theatre, May 1952. The use of the car as an entertainment centre rose in the 1950s; drive-in theatres became popular and the first A&W Restaurant in Canada opened in Winnipeg in 1956.

Smoke and flames rising from the Arctic Ice Co. building at 156 Bell Avenue, September 5, 1948.

UNIVERSITY OF MANITOBA ARCHIVES AND SPECIAL COLLECTIONS. WINNIPEG TRIBUNE COLLECTION, PC18/3024/18-2314-52.

Furby Theatre fire, 599 Portage Avenue, 1952.

UNIVERSITY OF MANITOBA ARCHIVES AND SPECIAL COLLECTIONS. WINNIPEG TRIBUNE COLLECTION, PC18/3024/18-2314-4.

Fire at Manitoba and Imperial Hotels, 509-517 Main Street, across from City Hall, March 4, 1954.

Manitoba and Imperial Hotels fire, March 4, 1954.

Time Building Fire, 333 Portage Avenue, Dismorr Building in flames, June 8, 1954. Winnipeg's largest and most destructive fire occurred during a rainstorm with 100-kilometre winds. Five years later, on June 20, 1959, Winnipeg received the first emergency number in North America (999, later changed to 911). (Text source: The Fire Fighters Museum of Winnipeg.)

St. Boniface Cathedral, December 24, 1956. Built in 1908, the St. Boniface Cathedral, Manitoba's best example of French Romanesque architecture, was almost completely destroyed by fire in 1968. Winnipeg architect Étienne Gaboury later designed a new chapel in its place, incorporating the remaining façade. The cemetery contains the graves of historic Manitoba figures such as Louis Riel and his grandparents, Marie-Anne Gaboury and Jean-Baptiste Lagimodière. The cathedral was designated a provincial heritage site in 1994.

St. Boniface Cathedral in flames, July 22, 1968.

ARCHIVES OF MANITOBA. FLOODS 1950 — 344.

The flood of 1950 devastated the City of Winnipeg, damaging and destroying thousands of homes and businesses. More than 80,000 citizens were evacuated and a state of emergency was called. The river crested on May 19, 1950 at 30.3 feet above datum. A total evacuation of Winnipeg was to be ordered at 32.5 feet. The St. Boniface Cathedral is seen in the background in this image of a flooded Water Street looking east.

Construction of dike in St. Vital, Winnipeg, 1950. A system of dikes was created to protect areas along the Red and Assiniboine Rivers during the 1950 flood. Later, the Red River Floodway, also called Duff's Ditch, after Premier Duff Roblin, was created to divert floodwaters around the city. A public work of massive scale, the floodway is 47 kilometres long and the amount of earth excavated in its creation was approximately half of that of the Panama Canal.

Wildwood Park, 1950 Flood. Wildwood Park was Winnipeg's first fully planned suburban development. Created following World War II in the 1940s by developer Hubert Bird and GBR (Green, Blankstein, Russell) Architects to accommodate the post-war housing shortage, the development was inspired by the famous Radburn model in New Jersey. Wildwood Park reversed the concept of private/public space by having houses front onto a shared park with vehicular access restricted to back lanes. The area's houses were heavily damaged during the flood of 1950, but the community spirit the development was built upon, and which still remains today, restored the area through the concerted efforts of residents and the developer.

Wildwood Park, 1950 Flood.

ARCHIVES OF MANITOBA. FLOODS 1950 16. N16103.

St. Mary's Academy, 1950 Flood.

UNIVERSITY OF MANITOBA UNIVERSITY RELATIONS AND INFORMATION OFFICE COLLECTION. WINNIPEG TRIBUNE COLLECTION, PC80-181-2.

John A. Russell Building, University of Manitoba, Fort Garry campus. Although the international modernist style of architecture originated in pre–World War II Europe, it wasn't until the 1950s that the design took hold in Canada. The Russell Building was built in 1959 as the home of the Faculty of Architecture and named for its progressive Dean of Architecture, John A. Russell. The Russell Building was among the first, and finest, examples of modernist architecture in Winnipeg.

View of Winnipeg Airport, looking north from Winnipeg tower. Winnipeg Flying Club seen in foreground. Photo courtesy Nelson Harvey, 1941.

May 8, 1963. Construction of a runway at Winnipeg International Airport. Operating since 1928, the Winnipeg International Airport was known earlier as Stevenson Airfield. The first jet arrived in 1955. In the early 1960s the passenger terminal was constructed and runways were expanded.

CHESTER DUNCAN

CHRISTOPHER DAFOE

Radio Days: Remembering Chester Duncan

One Christmas in the 1940s my parents presented me with a crystal set and earphones. We had several conventional radios in the house, the one in the kitchen perpetually tuned to the CBC and the one in the living room capable of calling in stations from as far away as Schenectady, but my crystal set transformed the commonplace, turn-the-knob science of sound broadcasting into a form of dark magic. Connected to my bedsprings by copper wire, the "cat's whisker" touching the crystal, this odd little device somehow plucked voices and music out of thin air. When I took off the earphones and raised the "cat's whisker," the room fell silent, but I knew that all around me, unheard for the moment, but subject to my command, the music was still playing and the voices were still speaking in all the languages of the world.

I had no idea then and I have no idea today how those sounds were plucked out of the vibrating air and conveyed to me out of nowhere via the crystal set and earphones. There was, of course, a detailed tutorial, with informative diagrams, on radio transmission in our copy of "The Book of Knowledge," but, being a romantic even then, I was inclined to reject the scientific and embrace the magical.

Adding to the enchantment was the fact that the music and the voices I heard on my crystal set, not to mention every sound made on Earth from the barking of a dog to the sound of ice breaking on the Red River in the spring, were believed to reverberate eternally through the universe. Far out in space, in harmony with the music of the spheres, sounds first heard by me on my crystal set continued to resound long after they had faded from memory back on Earth. A CBC news report read by Lorne Greene one gloomy night in 1941 is still echoing far beyond the Milky Way, Wayne and Shuster are playing to an empty house out there beyond Jupiter and commentaries spoken by Chester Duncan of Winnipeg over thirteen seasons of *Critically Speaking* are still bouncing off passing asteroids almost a lifetime after the program signed off for the last time. The transient sounds of our planet may be repeated far out beyond the planets, but here on Earth the word, once spoken, vanishes into the ether and in time the speaker, too, grows old and disappears. The voice that uttered the words may occasionally survive on recording tape or on an old transcription disc in the sound archives, but it is all too easy to forget the speaker after the radio has been switched off and the program that provided the stage upon which the performing voice once flourished has closed down. Time goes by and the voices and lively minds that once charmed a nation often pass into undeserved obscurity.

Chester Duncan first came to national attention with his astute and witty arts commentaries on a once-popular CBC radio program called *Critically Speaking*, a Sunday afternoon review of cultural matters directed to listeners in a country that still thought of itself as "young" and still spent a lot of time wondering about its "identity."

Looking back over more than half a century it may be difficult for Canadians of today to understand the important role played by CBC radio in its early years as a beacon of hope and warmth to isolated clusters of educated citizens and artists scattered over the broad expanse of the snowbound Dominion. It was still early days for Canadian culture. Only a supply of novels sufficient to fill a small shelf were published each year, Drama was kept alive by the regional Little Theatre groups, the Dominion Drama Festival, Andrew Allen's *CBC Stage* and regional drama programs such as *Prairie Playhouse* out of Winnipeg. Regional symphony orchestras were just getting started, augmented by CBC "house" orchestras across the country. Few beyond sign painters and commercial artists made a living in the visual arts. At the Ryerson Press Lorne Pierce struggled to keep poetry alive with a series of inexpensive chapbooks that did not sell briskly in the few surviving bookstores. Aspiring singers from across the land such as Lois Marshall and James Milligan got their chance on CBC radio's *Singing Stars of Tomorrow*. Opera came from New York on Saturday afternoons, introduced by Milton Cross and Deems Taylor.

Programs such as *Critically Speaking* on the CBC network provided a sort of national campfire around which the scattered bands of book readers, theatre and music lovers, radio listeners, film buffs and gallery-goers could gather to warm their hands and find assurance that Canadian Culture was, indeed, alive, more or less kicking and destined to survive against all efforts to shut it down. Those wolves we heard howling in the darkness around the campfire might well be driven off if Vincent Massey would only finish his report.

The CBC played a large role in Chester Duncan's life, and his association with the Corporation's Winnipeg outpost, as performer and commentator, began in the very early days of national broadcasting and the not-always-successful effort by the CBC to unite Canada by making it possible for region to speak to region.

He was born in Strasbourg, Saskatchewan of Scottish parents in 1913. The family soon moved to Winnipeg, then Canada's third city, and Duncan would spend the rest of his life there. By 1943 he was teaching English at the University of Manitoba and his broadcasting career was already in full stride.

Through the Great Depression he had been making a hit-or-miss living as a musician, playing at lunches—once treating the startled members of a service club to an entire Haydn symphony as background music—and as piano accompanist at concerts and choral events. The call to teach at the University of Manitoba, as a result of a wartime shortage of teachers, came, he later wrote, "quite unexpectedly."

His career as a university lecturer began in "Lucky Jim" fashion. "I had," he later recalled, "about six weeks notice that I was going to teach at the university, and I spent the six weeks in a frantic preparation, for lectures on Chaucer and Addison, who came first. When I walked into my first lecture theatre I was about as sick and nervous as it was possible to be. I was laden with books and notes which I found difficult to carry in my weakness. I started at a terrific rate and in fifteen minutes it was all over. The lecture period was fifty minutes long, but I had used up all my golden words in fifteen! Everything I knew about English literature from Chaucer to Eliot I had lavished on this class and I had seven more lectures to go that week . . . Never mind: ten years later I was going great guns with repetition, jokes, improvisation, free amateur philosophy, scraps of highly coloured information, confidence and roll calls. It's amazing how long a roll call can take when you haven't prepared anything." (38)

In characteristic self-effacing style, Duncan later recalled that his broadcasting career got started almost by accident in the 1940s. He had been asked, with several other members of the Winnipeg musical community, to take part in a CBC radio panel discussion at the old CKY studio on Portage Avenue East.

"As it happened," he recalled years later, "my little speech in the symposium on 'Music in Winnipeg' was the least bad of the five that were heard, since I rushed at the script in fine style and gobbled it up just as if it were good. Anyway, since nothing disastrous happened, and the others were so terrible, the producer, who was Thom Benson, said afterwards that I had something. He and everybody else who said this—that I had a *certain something*—found it very difficult to say exactly what I had; for *certain*, of course, here means *uncertain*. But who was I to care what it was, so long as I had it and could broadcast it. But it was strange to have no visible qualifications except a mystery that no one could define or even find." (85)

Soon Duncan became a familiar figure at the CBC Winnipeg studios in the Telephone Building, not only participating in commentaries and panel discussions for Talks and Public Affairs but serving as piano accompanist in vocal recitals, performing as a solo pianist and occasionally contributing incidental music to radio dramas. His academic colleagues, of course, regarded all this as a form of "slumming" and offered satirical comments on the extra "public money" that made it possible for him to buy a new coat or take a special holiday while ordinary, non-broadcasting members of the faculty struggled along on inadequate academic salaries.

Producers at CBC Winnipeg continued to agree with Thom Benson that Duncan *had something*, but opinion was still divided on just what "it" actually was. One lady producer, he recalled, "in discussing this mystery with a mutual friend, went on to list all the things that as a broadcaster I didn't have—things like voice and bounce and personality and so on . . ." (85) This may have been the same producer I overheard remarking to a sound technician after one of my early morning movie reviews: "My God, he's pompous!" As Chester once remarked, "They do it to keep us humble."

Mysterious or not, Duncan's microphone success in the Prairie Region led to an offer in 1950 to be a regular contributor to the Sunday afternoon national network program, *Critically Speaking*, reviewing radio and, later, television as well as movies and books. "I must admit," he later recalled, "that on *Critically Speaking* I took advantage of a microphone to be harder on some people than I would certainly like them to be on me, and as a result I gained a reputation for the kind of scathing wit that people enjoy, so long as they aren't the object of it. This kind of thing is especially attractive to people who basically hate the arts. But what I found more interesting and a little frightening was that even when I said something directly and innocently, listeners immediately took it for irony. When I praised something, they rarely believed it." (86)

Duncan, who was actually mild-mannered, non-confrontational and generally cheerful, was soon admired from coast to coast as an acid-tongued and wickedly amusing wit, like the fictional broadcaster and monstrous clapperclaw Sheridan Whiteside in the popular stage play *The Man Who Came to Dinner* by Kaufman and Hart. People expected him to be amusing and madly clever and he later wrote of a hostess in Vancouver who, frustrated by his failure to sparkle as expected, cried, "Please, Mr. Duncan, say something witty!" (87)

I felt I knew Chester Duncan long before I actually met him. My aunt Elizabeth Dafoe was head librarian at the University of Manitoba and at family dinners in the late 1940s I frequently heard her speak of the popular and amusing Professor Chester Duncan, a friend and colleague at the university. As she reported on his astute comments about current literature and his trenchant and funny observations on contemporary life, I felt, even as a relatively young boy, that here was a person worth knowing and I felt certain that he had been allowed to read the copy of *Ulysses* I had learned she kept secure in a vault in her office, to be perused only by qualified persons, of whom I was not yet one.

At about this time, or possibly a bit later, I began to join my parents beside the radio or alone in my room with my crystal set to listen to *Critically Speaking* and I was interested to discover that one of the regular commentators was the very same Chester Duncan. I looked forward to the day, not too far distant, when I would attend his lectures at the university and, with luck, become acquainted with this amusing and learned man. In the event, it was an older brother who attended the Duncan lectures, my entry to the University of Manitoba having been blocked, *inter alia*, by my inability to master long division and fractions. My brother used to regale us at the dinner table with examples of Chester Duncan's wit and wisdom, his cutting criticisms of term papers, his views on English poetry, his insights into the novels of Hardy and Joyce and commentary on the Irish playwrights.

It was around this time—the middle 1950s—that I began to realize that there was far more to Chester Duncan than the literary opinions and the classroom wit. He was a composer and musician as well, heard regularly on CBC radio, as accompanist and piano soloist, performing his own works and the works of others, old and new. It soon became clear that his composition and his work as a performer represented the very essence of Chester Duncan and that, in the best of all possible worlds, his name and work would become known far beyond Winnipeg. He was a sensitive and inspired accompanist for both singers and instrumentalists and his abilities as a solo performer were impressive. He gave the North American premiere of the Gordon Jacob Piano Concerto No. 2 on CBC radio and was heard regularly as a soloist with the CBC Winnipeg Orchestra. In a series of radio programs with names such as *Sharp, Flat and Natural, Listening with Duncan* and *Duncan's Diary*, he adroitly combined entertainment and instruction.

In *Duncan's Diary* Chester often posed as an aged and indignant fuddy duddy deploring the decline of the nation's God-given "mediocrity and normality." Canadian writing, for example, was displaying distressing signs of improvement. "There are a few Canadian books," he complained, "like Charles Cochrane's *Christianity and Classical Culture* and Northrop Fry's book on Blake, which have achieved some sort of highbrow reputation abroad, and they are actually read by many university students in Canada, sometimes with great excitement, so we can be glad that Canadian students have a unique trick of forgetting all they've learned a few months after graduation." (149)

Like many of the wise, Chester often elected to use humour to make a serious point. To a stern British critic who had heaped scorn on "artists who outlive their usefulness as performers but are unable to give up because of pride," Chester Duncan offered the following gentle response:

> But can we say sensible, reasonable things to musicians who give their farewell recitals again and again until they become a laughingstock to the many and creatures of pathos to the few? Singers when the voice has gone, rheumatic violinists, poets to whom the Muse no longer comes—these should no doubt never hesitate to enter the valley of change and humiliation. Oh, sure. All that is unconditionally demanded is heroism and poise and wisdom. Time to go—no longer willing to believe the flatteries of yesterday. Time to take sad stock of one's colleagues' quizzical glances or deprecating coughs. Time to hear the faint hiss from the cutting of the laurels. Time to say, like Henry James, when Death approached to lock his silver throat: 'Ah, at last—the Really Distinguished Thing!' But many have difficulty recognizing anything, let alone the End of the Game. (166-7)

Talking of games, was Chester Duncan a sports enthusiast? Many of his friends were aware that he owned and often used a miniature pool table, but few could say that his was a familiar figure in the stands at Winnipeg sporting events. While others froze in the rain or falling snow on autumn afternoons and evenings, Chester, we imagined, was at home reading a book or playing his piano. Nevertheless, no Canadian sports writer, as far as I know, has better described the epic quality of the modern sporting life than Chester did in a radio essay entitled, simply, "Football":

> On those aching late-fall afternoons the game will be a folk-epic, the tone clearly *Beowulf*. Crouched on the blasted heath in the wind and rain and snow, great blocks of sympathies, called football players, are now engaged in savage struggles to the death. In doing so they have all our love and hate. With equal skill, they break hearts and legs and records. There may even be a chance this year to break the roughing record. Things may even go so darkly, beautifully, tragically, that along with the usual number of concussions and separated shoulders there may be a chance that some of the key players in the league will be destroyed so that they can never play again. "Heart and head shall be keener, mood the more" in the league of thunder, as a broken member of the opposing team is carried as a ruined hero from the field. A terrible beauty is born, and he has played his part. In these Rites of Fall there is a mythology, complete with gods—some have got broken—violence, lyricism, cold and dirt. (100)

Friends of the CBC sat transfixed by their humming radios, their tea cooling, biscuits untouched, as Professor Duncan expanded on his dramatic theme: "And so in the epic games of Autumn down they will go into the dark, to the fate of an unchangeable score. Games are often called classics, but they are romantic too in their aspiration toward unattainable touchdowns, and in the end, with wild passing to the final fling, courting defeat like a lover." (111)

Another radio series consisting of lecture/recitals given in the 1960s enhanced his reputation as critic and performer. Off the air, he was a busy member of Winnipeg's musical community, appearing as accompanist to singers and choirs in the Manitoba Musical Festival, serving as piano soloist with the Royal Winnipeg Ballet and as a member of the Hidy Trio.

His own work, in individual compositions for instruments, settings of poetry for voice and in incidental music for plays and dramatic poems, indicated that he was singularly gifted and worthy of being placed near the first rank of Canadian artists. There were vocal settings of Yeats and Housman and incidental music for plays, including Shakespeare's *The Winter's Tale*, "The River Child" by James Reaney, Margaret Stobie's "Pleasant Plains" and W.H. Auden's "For the Time Being" and "The Ascent of F6."

Growing up during the Depression, coming to maturity in the years before and during the war, and the immediate need to earn a living to support his family in the years thereafter may have made it impossible for him to follow all his dreams, but his accomplishments were great, although curiously under-appreciated. "I have found," he once wrote, "that it is much easier in Winnipeg to get an audience to hear how wittily unsuccessful you are as a composer, than to manage an actual performance of your work." It was a problem that would persist: "Being a composer in Winnipeg is almost a contradiction in terms, or like that old school problem in physics: is the sound still there if no one hears it?" (67) In another essay on the life of a composer, one section set off by stars consisted of only the following sentence: "Winnipeg can break your heart." (78)

I finally came to know him in the 1960s when he wrote occasional music criticism for the *Free Press*. We worked together as reviewers on a CBC Winnipeg version of *Critically Speaking* called *The Passing Show*, and as writers and presenters on a program of English poetry and the music it inspired called *Enter the Musicians*, presented first in the Prairie Region and later on the National Network. We had old friends in common, including the radio producer Jeffrey Anderson, who did much to keep Duncan in front of the microphone, and the critic Ken Winters, and it was in these years, after a long wait, that I began to enjoy first-hand contact with a man I had admired for much of my life. Working with Chester in the studio made you try harder and reach farther. He set a standard that, on most occasions, you could only aspire to, but his example made you want to keep on improving. With Chester, hard work could be a pleasure, although he occasionally felt inclined to cast a cold eye on some of the studio highjinks of his younger colleagues. He could bring you up short when it was needed, but my memories of those studio sessions in the sixties are dominated by laughter and good talk. So, in the end, he became one of my teachers after all and, even now, I often hear his voice admonishing me when I am about to go too far off course or urging me on when I am about to take the too-easy way. He taught me as well the importance of a sense of humour and the stimulating quality of laughter.

He was a small person, always well turned out and with a voice so high and light that many of us had the disconcerting experience when calling him on the phone of mistaking him for his wife, Ada: "Is Chester at home, Ada?" A brief, electric silence, then, a bit testily, "This *is* Chester!"

His interests were musical and literary, but there were surprising sides to him. He once told me that he loved taking the car out onto Pembina Highway, pointing it in the direction of the US border and stepping hard on the gas. He found it restful to watch the fields and farms speed past him.

Once you knew him it was impossible not to like him and it seemed unlikely that someone so pleasant and friendly would have any enemies. He had at least one, however. The Irish novelist Shaun Herron, author of *The Whore Mother* and *The Bird in Last Year's Nest*, who was my friend and colleague for several years at the *Free Press*, had it in for Chester and nobody knew why. Shaun seemed to find it difficult to write any article on any topic without pausing in the middle to make some slighting and usually out-of-context reference to Chester Duncan. Chester was perplexed. "Why does he hate me?" he asked me one day. As they were both friends of mine and because I thought they would probably like one another if given a chance, I decided to bring them together and make peace. My project failed dismally. I did manage to discover the cause, such as it was, of Shaun's annoyance with Chester. Years before, while giving a lecture at the university, Shaun had said something harsh about the poet Roy Daniells. Chester, always a loyal friend, had risen to defend the poet and there had been a sharp exchange. Shaun, a true son of Ulster, had never forgiven Chester. They both attended the farewell party when I left for Vancouver in 1969, but I noticed that they sat at opposite ends of the room.

A year or two before his death in 2002 I received a note from Chester saying that he and Ada had enjoyed reading a recent article of mine in the *Free Press*. "It gave us the midnight giggles," he wrote. I have never received a sweeter or more satisfying compliment and the thought of Chester and Ada laughing merrily in the dark over my little joke enchants me still.

As an essayist, Chester was among our best and his 1975 collection called *Wanna Fight, Kid?* remains a book to cherish. At the time of its publication Robert Fulford noted that "Chester Duncan writes with such charm and wit, and with a marvelously confident sense of his own inconsequence. He is the perfect Canadian. If this country were sane there would be a Cult dedicated to Chester Duncan."

He should have written and published much more, although he seems to have been troubled by persons from Porlock and by what he once described to me as a maddening and inhibiting worry about exact word meanings, a form of writer's block in which you wonder if the words you have written actually mean what you think they mean. He need not have worried. He wrote like an angel.

During his final years I often got the impression that Chester felt that he had not been given his just due, especially as a musician. He had often joked about the seeming indifference of the greater audience, but there was clearly a hurt behind the self-directed mockery. I fear that he was right about that. Winnipeg can break your heart. So can Canada. This inattentive country too often ignores its best or too soon forgets those it once applauded and loved. His legacy should be part of our national treasure, but it may be that some of his finest performances, spoken and played, are still moving outward through deep space, the lost, reverberating echo of those forgotten radio days singing on through the starlight.

NOTE
All quotations are from *Wanna Fight, Kid?* by Chester Duncan (Winnipeg: Queenston House, 1975).

Aesthetic

So I must try another poem
To ease in part in print the usual blow
Which, daily now, with a clinical insistence,
Reaches for the clock, prepares the
Complicated apparatus which, set,
At last will click and chime.

Neat and calm deliberation,
Invariably on time, drives the last stake
As the prepared and waiting engine whistles, overwhelms
The charming impossible victim.

For improvisation these matters are just a little slick:
The odds are a shade absurd.
Approach, draw back, promise, retreat,
Until you have him tucked, propped,
Pinned to a crumbling dyke,
Then laughing strike.

Taut, nerved, dead behind a wall,
A dead man's body hidden in the long grass:
That it seems is both the Future and the Past,
While Art receives her necessary gall.

Poem

Finally, I suppose, everything fails,
Night falls and the appalling black-out
Spurns even the live Destroyer
With his healing hurt.

In one sense you see we're out,
Game's up, the string's short, the ink's dry
Long ago; but yet out of it all
There's a clean gain of a kind.

Be faithful then, everyone,
To the single treasure;
Heart calm, eye's strong in the parting,
Straight in the loss.

There's a twist can be given the ending
Which having no substance needs no excuse,
Carries no weight or needs none
As day follows day

As far as eye can see,
Each with its rim, its form, its static whole, —
Like an ageless dull succession of dry cells
But polished now.

Moviemaking in Manitoba:
The World War II Era

In Manitoba—as in much of Canada—moviemaking for the first seventy years of film history (1895–1965) was nothing like the glamorous, heroic affair epitomized by Hollywood studio productions. Only one theatrical feature was made in the province during this entire period. In the summer of 1920 Ernest Shipman blew into Winnipeg, raised a quarter of a million dollars in local capital, and produced *The Foreigner* based on a best-selling novel by a hometown literary legend, Charles William Gordon, under his pen name "Ralph Connor."[1] Aside from this and a modest student production in 1939 called *And So to College*, nothing that was committed to celluloid here ever challenged or even modestly mimicked the Hollywood model.[2] If you wanted to be a moviemaker in Manitoba, you devoted your energies to newsreels and industrial films or you moved to Ottawa and joined the National Film Board of Canada. Fortunately, enough people pursued both opportunities that Manitoba has a more substantial presence on movie screens than its size, resources and location might warrant, and an influential cadre of moviemakers to its credit as well.

Newsreels and "industrials" (i.e., industrial films; also called sponsored, institutional, or promotional films) are the most overlooked and underprivileged branches of moviemaking. Newsreels are considered by some to be "mere journalism," the raw material for films rather than actual films themselves. They were usually filmed by "stringers," people with their own movie cameras who were paid for each submitted and acceptable piece of footage rather than by salary. Their work was anonymous, usually unacknowledged in the credits. Industrials are even lowlier because of their association with strictly commercial objectives. Commissioned by corporations, government agencies, or institutions, they are made to sell products, clarify procedures or processes, build or modify images and identities, or influence public attitudes. Because they are "client-driven," functional and quickly outdated (i.e., quaint and somewhat disreputable), most of them have either disappeared forever or been relegated to the dusty recesses of various archives.[3] And the moviemakers who fashioned them have rarely been given their proper recognition. In Manitoba four makers of newsreels and industrials stand out: Angelo Accetti, Ken Davey, Frank Holmes and George Cotter.

These four men were practical, unpretentious movie artisans, often self-taught and working virtually alone. Moviemaking for them was neither a glamorous nor a particularly lucrative business. In fact, it often was not a business at all. During the Depression and World War II, production opportunities, money, equipment and film stocks were particularly scarce. None of Winnipeg's moviemakers could count on a steady income; they all took on other jobs.

This is not to say that they were amateurs or that they weren't alert to the latest developments in their craft. Because they were isolated and independent, they often had to build things from scratch or invent processes from the barest of outlines: Ken Davey built his own film processing lab, Frank Holmes designed his own studio inside a truck, and George Cotter's inventions were used by Marlin Perkins, the long time American television star of *Mutual of Omaha's Wild Kingdom*. Clever, competitive, toughened by the conditions of the times, with an unshakable belief in their own talents and contributions, these four men embody a certain kind of archetypal prairie resourcefulness and persistence. That they all worked mainly outdoors and usually alone is a tribute to their hardiness, a throwback perhaps to the pioneering spirit of the Canadian frontier. They succeeded against disheartening odds.

Pioneers and first stringers
The first resident Canadian to make films in Canada was a Manitoban. James Freer (1855–1933) was a British newspaperman who left England in 1888 and settled in the southwest corner of the newly demarcated province. In 1897, from his farm south of Brandon, he made a series of short "home movies" about life on the Canadian prairies: *Premier Greenway Stooking Grain; Harvesting Scene, with Trains Passing By; Arrival of CPR Express at Winnipeg; Cyclone Thresher at Work*, to name a few. He took these movies back to his native England on lecture-screening tours intended to promote the Canadian west to prospective immigrants. After two tours of England, in 1898 (titled "Ten Years in Manitoba" and sponsored by the Canadian Pacific Railway) and again in 1902 (sponsored by his friend and neighbour from Brandon, Clifford Sifton, Federal Minister for Immigration), Freer "apparently abandoned film production, though he continued running his film shows"[4] in Manitoba. He moved from Brandon to Eriksdale, Manitoba in 1901 and then into Winnipeg in 1917, where he became staff editor for the *Manitoba* (later *Winnipeg*) *Free Press*, working with legendary editor

John Dafoe. Whether Freer made any more films or passed on his equipment and his expertise to others remains a melancholy mystery.

Even more mysterious than Freer are the original newsreel-makers of Manitoba. Next to nothing is known about them—neither dates of birth or death, years of employment, nor specific films. All that exists is a list of twenty-one "CAMERAMEN IN WESTERN CANADA, EARLY 1920'S" found in the New York City files of Fox Movietone News[5] for 1921. Three of the men on this list have Winnipeg addresses: J. [John] Herron, Angelo Accetti and P.F. Brown. Herron ran a still photography business called Reel Craft Studios on Sargent Street in Winnipeg's west end for only two years (1921, 1922); after this he disappears from the city directories. So too does Brown, who is listed in 1920 as an optician. By far the most productive of the early stringers in Manitoba was Angelo Accetti (d. 1955), a massive (300-lb.) but energetic man who, it seems, also went by the name of A.C. Angelo. From his studio in the French and Belgian quarter of St. Boniface, Manitoba, he supplied Fox Movietone News with a steady stream of filmed material on everything from burning buildings to blizzards, from visiting royalty to dog shows and sports events, from floods to flowering gardens.

Although the newsreel footage of Manitoba from Accetti's era (1920–1954) that is archived is mostly anonymous, it is likely that most of the footage is his. Existing records (i.e., forms entitled "Cameraman's Title and Dispatching Sheets," which had to accompany all footage sent to Fox's New York City offices) indicate the breadth of his news interests. In 1929 he sent 100 feet of film on Scandinavian immigrants leaving a train in Winnipeg that includes "several shots of odd types" and notes that it is "the best class of immigrants that have come to Canada for many years." Another 100 feet of "undeveloped super x panchromatic stock taken in good light" was submitted to Fox on the arrival of the St. Boniface Seals hockey team when it returned home with the Memorial Cup in 1938.[6]

Accetti was even far-sighted enough to hire airplanes to film scenes in Manitoba from the air. As enterprising as he was, however, Accetti could not survive on newsreels alone. He made most of his money providing "promos" for local movie houses. He began with three-by-four-inch glass slides and then moved on to 35mm moving picture advertisements that were inserted between the usual weekly fare. By 1930 he was calling himself a "movie-maker" on his stationery, a producer of synchronized and talking pictures, commercial films and film titles. He had also moved into a "laboratory" in the former Film Exchange Building at 361 Hargrave Avenue in downtown Winnipeg, taking over from Charles Lambly, who had moved to Vancouver after struggling to make ends meet in Winnipeg for almost five years.[7]

Fox's records indicate that Accetti was submitting material exclusively to them. But Accetti did not have exclusive filming rights to Manitoba. Associated Screen News (ASN), a Montreal film lab founded by the Canadian Pacific Railway to reproduce prints of Hollywood movies for the Canadian market, periodically sent cameramen west to collect footage for its homegrown newsreels and the Canadian Cameo series. ASN was responsible for the most widely screened newsreel about the province during Accetti's era.

On February 19, 1942 several communities in Manitoba, including Winnipeg and Selkirk, staged an "If Day." In an elaborately orchestrated effort involving politicians and the press, law enforcement officers, businesses, church groups, the military and ordinary citizens, events were staged to show what purportedly would happen if Nazi troops were to take over the province.

ASN sent veteran cameraman Lucien Roy from Montreal to capture the event on film. According to an article in the *Winnipeg Tribune* (February 26, 1942), Roy had been a regular visitor, "coming here a half dozen times a year shooting scenes which have appeared in newsreels. Last year he filmed the flood which inundated city streets." He was also collecting footage of women workers in the machine shops of Trans-Canada Air Lines at Stevenson Airfield.

On If Day, Roy filmed Premier John Bracken and his cabinet as they were marched out of the Legislature, Mayor John Queen and city council being arrested, a clergyman being removed from All Saints Church,[8] and citizens rousted from the Charleswood bus or reading posted Nazi warnings and a special issue of *Das Winnipeger Lügenblatt*. The Canadian troops who played the Nazi soldiers seemed to take particular delight in their film roles; they burn books, confiscate furniture, scatter a paperseller's bundle of *Tribune*s, and take over the Great-West Life lunchroom with broad smiles and exaggerated gestures. The completed newsreel, titled "Winnipeg Shows What It Would Be Like If . . ." and narrated by Lowell Thomas, was released in four separate versions throughout the US and Canada by Fox Movietone News, Paramount News, Metrotone News of the Day and Universal News. The newsreel inspired similar events at other cities and prompted articles in US news magazines *Life* and *Newsweek*. It put Winnipeg on the cinematic map.

"Film Production for Business"

Few people in Canada can boast of a career in movies as long as that of Francis J.S. (Frank) Holmes (1909–1991). Inspired by scenic movie promos for Ford Motors and Robert Flaherty's *Nanook of the North*, Holmes made his first commercial motion picture when he was just sixteen.[9] It was a short, silent movie, a kind of travelogue for the

North Country Tourist Association. He spent his seventeenth birthday in Fort Nelson on Hudson's Bay on a similar project, a seventy-seven-minute silent film called *Sea Port of the Prairie*. That was enough to get him a job as a stringer for Fox Newsreel Presentations (the silent film predecessor to Fox Movietone News). Holmes's initial assignment took him to Red Lake, Ontario for the 1926 gold rush there, working on 28mm film with four perforations on one side and one on the other.

Thus began a forty-year career as an independent film producer, a career that reached its zenith in May, 1958, when a Hollywood trade journal called *The Professional Cine Photographer* featured Holmes in a pictorial of his "mobile movie studio." Typical of many early independent filmmakers, Holmes was a one-person crew, and he designed and outfitted his mobile studio by and for himself. Inside the panel truck were equipment lockers, developing, printing and editing facilities, "Magnasync 16mm magnetic film recording equipment," dual turntables, a six-channel consolette for the mixing of music and sound effects, and "a narrator's booth with floating floor, and double walls lined and interlined with fibreglass" to provide "the maximum in extraneous sound reduction for voice recording. . . . In the truck he range[d] Canada from coast to coast shooting documentary and commercial pictures for a wide variety of clients."[10] On the outside of the truck, above his name, he advertised "Film Production for Business."

Chief among Holmes's clients were United Grain Growers, Hudson Bay Mining and Smelting, Wawanesa Mutual Insurance Corporation, The National Grain Company and various provincial government departments. His specialty was films for agribusiness. *Prairie Conquest* (1952) is one of the more interesting titles in this regard; it is a visual history lesson focusing on wheat, starting with the introduction of Red Fife in 1842 and Marquis in 1909, and including the evolution of grain-farming machinery from scythes to threshers, binders and reapers, the role of the railroads, and an inside look at a grain elevator.[11]

More typical is *Victory Over Weeds* (1956), one of fifteen chemical weed-control films Holmes made over the years, and *The Magic of Milk* (1960), an examination of a day in the life of an efficient dairy farmer. As cinematic documents of the social attitudes of their times, they are paeans to the wonders of modernism: machinery and chemicals. More revealing are two half-hour films made for Wawanesa Insurance. *Unlimited Horizons* (1967) and *The Great Potential* (1968) are clearly intended to extol the virtues of family farm-life and reverse the tide of migration from rural Canada to the cities.

Beyond the Steel (1953) is probably Holmes's best film because it is such a matter-of-fact account of a truly unique and remarkable event. Between 1950 and 1953 the entire town of Sherridon, in northern Manitoba, was moved to Lynn Lake, a distance of 250 kilometres. The move was primarily accomplished during the winter. Virtually every building in town—houses, a church, school and bank—plus supplies to build a railroad and establish a new nickel mine were mounted on sleds and pulled by bulldozer over snow and ice-packed trails. At the climax of this twenty-minute film, one of the Caterpillar tractors and its load break through the ice and have to be salvaged by crane. Like most client-driven films, it is clearly intended to celebrate the accomplishments of the firm that commissioned it, in this case, The Patricia Transportation Company. The film is presented, however, with minimal fanfare and no sound-track superlatives. Its value today far supersedes its promotional intention.

Holmes himself felt that his finest film was one he made for Ducks Unlimited in 1958: *Each Year They Come*.[12] This story about waterfowl conservation for the benefit of duck hunters features outstanding wildlife footage and a rather clumsy insert of puppet animation "in the round." The film won numerous citations, among them one from the Canadian Film Awards as "one of the best, perhaps the best, waterfowl film [sic] ever made in Canada."[13] To capture the close-up nature footage, Holmes designed a special "turret blind," a foot-controlled, rotating, fabric-covered dome inside which Holmes sat with his specially designed Cine-Special camera. This fascination with the mechanical aspects of the film business and a kind of ad hoc resourcefulness are things he shares with many other early filmmakers.

Holmes never achieved the stature of his hero Robert Flaherty nor did his films have the impact of his other favourite, *Grass* by Ernest Schoedsack and Merian Cooper.[14] His films, from the vantage point of the end of the century, are polished but with a bluntness and earnestness that are slightly clumsy. And his jack-of-all-trades attitude to directing caused him to overvalue his role as a composer, singer and animator in a few of his films. Still, as records of how things looked from the 1930s to the 1970s in rural Canada, his films are unique and irreplaceable; he ranks with Evelyn Cherry and Dick Bird as the three major mid-twentieth-century film chroniclers of the Canadian west.

Films for business, for sport, for television
Frank Holmes made a fairly regular and respectable living from his filmmaking. He was a shrewd businessman, confident enough in his abilities to demand a professional's wages; so he also could afford the best in equipment. In this he is the exception to the rule of Manitoba filmmakers. Ken Davey (b. 1915) is more typical. His accomplishments may be more modest, but his impact was far greater. And his career is more illuminating.

Davey got interested in films when he switched, in 1933, from grinding lenses in the optical department at The Bay to selling and repairing cameras in the photographic department.[15] Part of his job required that he serve as projectionist for the hundreds of Hollywood movies (most of them one-reelers of *Our Gang* and *Laurel and Hardy*), which The Bay rented out to churches and clubs through its Kodascope distribution library. He quickly taught himself everything there was to know about cameras, film stock and projectors. He even remembers the time he projected the first sound motion picture on a Victor Animatograph with an accompanying record spun on a record player.

In 1934 Joe Ryan, the general manager of the Winnipeg Football Club, stopped into The Bay to visit his niece, a co-worker of Davey's in the photographic department. Ryan was looking for someone to film his team's games, something he and the players could show when they went to speak at various social events and gatherings. Before Ryan left the store, Ken Davey had volunteered to do the filming. He would use The Bay's equipment; Ryan would pay for the film stock. This was the start of over thirty-five years of sports filming by Davey, much of it unpaid.

Filming football games may seem like a simple operation now, but in the 1930s it was more than a mere technical challenge, especially given Winnipeg's ferocious and unpredictable football weather. Davey had to balance on the roof of Osborne Stadium, a slippery surface with a 30- to 40-degree slope. His camera took only 100-foot loads; he had to rewind the camera before every play from scrimmage and reload the magazine after only three minutes of exposure. At away games in Regina and Edmonton, he had to don a lineman's boots, hoist himself up a hydro pole on the sidelines, and strap himself up there for the entire game.[16] Many a game he had to strip the oil out of the film's gears and replace it with graphite to prevent the camera from seizing up. Frostbite was a constant occupational hazard.

The high point of Davey's early career as football documentarian came in 1935. That was the year the Blue Bombers got their nickname, and the year they won the Grey Cup, the first western club ever to do so. Winnipeg beat Hamilton 18-12 in Hamilton, and Davey captured the game in its entirety. It was the first Canadian championship preserved on film, a stirring contest highlighted by a 78-yard punt return by Winnipeg player-coach Fritz "The Golden Ghost" Hansen, which by itself justified the film's cost as it was "the theme of numerous stories, sketches, and paintings."[17] The footage was screened at the Walker Theatre in Winnipeg and at "Quarterback Clubs" around the province and was used as "ocular proof" of the superiority of the Bombers (and the West) as well as a celluloid signal of the emergence of a national interest in football.[18]

Screenings in movie theatres and at various social occasions were, in fact, of secondary importance. Davey's football newsreels quickly changed function. A certificate of merit awarded by the Blue Bombers to Davey in 1966 outlines his real contribution:

> In 1934 he took motion pictures of a home game played by the Winnipeg Football Club team. This was the first time in Canada that motion pictures of an actual football game were used for coaching purposes and was the most important innovation since the game originated.[19]

Not too many years later, Davey extended the range of films for scouting purposes by becoming the first person to film football games at night. He had heard about prefogging (the process of exposing the film slightly before actual filming so as to make it more sensitive) from a Kodak representative and experimented on his own until he got it right. Winnipeg dominated the nation's football wars through 1941 partly because of its film-centred scouting system; Blue Bomber players often grumbled that the films were "lie detectors."

At first these football films had to be sent to a lab in Toronto for processing. That changed in 1940 when Davey built his own "dip and dunk tank" and converted a projector into a printer.[20] He thus became the proprietor of one of the first film processing labs in western Canada. It not only reduced the one-week delay between filming and viewing, it allowed him the opportunity to do both other work and others' works.

In 1940 the Brier, Canada's national curling championship, was held in the Winnipeg Amphitheatre. Because of his experiments in prefogging, Davey was able to dispense with the klieg lights, banned because they melted the curling ice. Not only did he succeed in filming the first Brier competition in the West, he developed the footage overnight and took the rushes the next morning to show the president of MacDonald's Tobacco, the sponsor of the event. It was the 1930s equivalent of instant replay, a truly impressive feat. Davey later put the entire event together, from the opening through closing ceremonies plus all the games, into a filmed record of the occasion.

At the same time, Davey was making more conventional "industrials" for various Winnipeg enterprises. He made a series of twenty-minute films for Perth's Cleaners that showed how drapes were cleaned and carefully pleated, how shirts were pressed, etc. He made a documentary for the CNR on the resort and skiing facility at La Riviere, Manitoba. Most memorable was a series of films for Canada Packers. They were the first plant to can meat, and they used film to show that it was sanitary and safe. On one occasion he was filming when an unsuspecting employee doffed his rubber boots and waded barefoot into a pile of aging beef chunks.[21] Instead of recreating

Le sang des bêtes, Davey became adept at the kind of tactful, elliptical editing essential to promotional films.

All this changed in 1941 when he got a letter from Kodak conscripting all film for the wartime effort. During World War II very few filmmakers except for those who worked for the National Film Board or for provincial government agencies had access to film stock. Many of them, including Davey, were forced to abandon their film work. He had to sell his Cine-Special camera and rely on his display business for the duration of the war. He made floats for Victory Bond drives, supplementing his income by spray-painting Avro-Ansen Bombers.

After the war Davey returned to filmmaking and his life became more hectic than ever. By 1948 he was again filming all Winnipeg football games. In 1949 he got the contract to film the games of all four Western teams (Vancouver was not yet in the league). During the football season he spent most of his time either on a plane (Winnipeg to Calgary took eight hours) or in his lab (the teams demanded extra prints and next-day service).

This was the era of Winnipeg's great football coaches: "profane, loud, fiery" George Trafton (1951–53), scholarly Allie Shermann (1954–56), who later coached for the New York Giants, and the incomparable stoic, Bud Grant (1957–66).[22] Davey excelled as a football filmmaker because he was accepted as a member of the team and he was a fan who had an uncanny instinct for the game; he could tell what play was going to be called and claims he was right over 90 per cent of the time. He got so good at it that Coach Trafton would debrief with him for an hour after each game.[23] And he collaborated with Grant to make six coaching films for the Department of Education.

When television was introduced in 1953, it was inevitable that Davey got the contract to film the CFL game of the week. It meant that he had to master the new sound cameras and Zoomar lenses very quickly. More importantly, he had to rethink his approach to the game, for now he had to film the entire event, including the huddles, and do it in close-ups and mid-shots, not just long-shots.

In 1954, when television came to Manitoba, Davey added newsfilm processing for the CBC affiliate to his duties, and in 1960 for the CTV affiliate. He also did freelance news shoots for both local television stations and was a stringer for CBS, earning a commendation from CBS for his coverage of a spectacular downtown Winnipeg fire in June, 1954.[24] His series of films on Kids' Safety for CJAY-TV was filmed so convincingly (especially his drowning and bumper-shining accidents) that parents complained they were too scary.[25]

By the late 1960s Davey could see the writing on the wall: videotaped industrials and television. He tried his hand at television, doing a pilot for curling and one on the do-it-yourself craze. Then he turned his attention to a couple of industrials: *E for Efficiency* (1969) and *Cargo Carriers of the Seaway* (1970). His major task was converting his lab to colour processing for the 1967 Pan Am Games and for television. He shot all the preliminary footage for the games, and his lab did all the colour processing, becoming the first colour lab in western Canada. He sold it in 1970 and retired in 1975, although he has remained active in the business to this day. In 1967 he was made a life member of the Canadian Society of Cinematographers, one of his proudest achievements.

Ken Davey is like Winnipeg's answer to Budge Crawley but without the benefit of federal contracts and feature film opportunities. Their careers overlap substantially (Davey 1931–1970; Crawley 1939–1974). Like Crawley, Davey was a no-nonsense, blue-collar filmmaker who also provided processing and laboratory services. He is a blunt-speaking, unsentimental man who has few illusions about his work and is genuinely surprised that anyone besides his grandchildren would be interested in his career. In other words he is the epitome of what Rick Prelinger defines as the un-egotistical maker of ephemeral films.[26] His films are time-bound and made-to-order. Much of the footage did not outlast its immediate usage, and even he does not remember titles or dates anymore. What remains is only now being recognized for its uniqueness and quirky charm.

Films about nature

Because of his recent series of nature shows on the Discovery Channel, George Cotter (b. 1915) is probably Manitoba's most famous, and most unlikely, independent filmmaker. Cotter was born in the northern outpost of Cumberland House, Saskatchewan into a family that can trace its connections to the Hudson's Bay Company back to that organization's origins 300 years ago.[27] Raised among the Cree and taught to survive by trapping and hunting with a bow and arrow, Cotter came to Winnipeg during the Depression and did not take up a movie camera until the Red River flood of 1950, when he filmed a skunk, a squirrel, two rabbits and some mice stranded together on the first tee-box of a flooded golf course.[28] That slight but striking piece of footage launched a hobby that would ultimately lead to an award-winning if late-blooming career.

Entirely self-taught, Cotter took his Christmas bonus from a local lumberyard to make his first professional film, *Wildlife Surrounds Us*, in 1954. Several years later, encouraged by the National Film Board that all the footage he had shot over the years could be turned into good films, he sold his interest in the lumberyard and turned to filmmaking full time. Relying exclusively on a hand-wind, 16mm Bolex camera with a 100-foot load, Cotter returned to the wild reaches of the three Prairie provinces that he knew so intimately in his youth. His wife Sally was his constant companion and assistant until her sudden death in the fall of 1994.

Whether they are careful studies of wildlife (*Prairie Giant*—about a species of Canada Goose once thought extirpated) or films about the techniques of survival (*You Bet Your Life* and *Wild Beauty*—about twenty-eight different edible plants in Manitoba) or the beauties of the rugged North (*Winter Gallery*), Cotter's films are neither as sentimental nor as sanctimonious as many nature films tend to be. His films do not preach, yet he is concerned that "soon there won't be any wildlife. People are draining swamps like they are going out of style. I can see the end of wildlife. We are trying to take (film [of]) everything we can get."[29] But George Cotter is not a wholesale preservationist. He must be the only naturalist who has regularly enjoyed shooting, cooking and eating cedar waxwings for dinner. This is not a typical latter-day eco-saint.

Nor is he an overly sophisticated cinematographer. A two-time winner of the Wildlife Filming Award presented by Wildlife International Incorporated, Cotter has made his mark because of the ease, immediacy and clarity of his vision. He cites *Wilderness Trails* as his best film because the lighting and focus were so precise that it could be blown up from 16mm to 35mm for theatrical release without a reduction in quality; he also likes the fact that it was so full, "a grab-bag" of impressions and insights.[30] Cotter eschews montage effects and intrusive close-ups, relying on patience and first-hand knowledge of his subjects for his effectiveness. In his classic 1973 film *Great Grey Owl* he spent two months in a camera blind within metres of his subjects to examine this elusive provincial symbol.

Cotter is probably more widely known for his disarmingly simple one- and two-minute nature documentaries called *Cotter's Camera on Canada* and used by television stations for many years in lieu of advertising. These documentaries and the longer films he made over the last forty-five years, as well as much new and unused footage, served as the raw material for the twenty-seven-episode series *Cotter's Wilderness Trails* that began airing on the Discovery Channel during the 1996–97 television season. Although George Cotter started late, he has outlasted all his contemporaries. He is the last of a dying breed, the true, old-fashioned independent filmmaker, making the films he wants to make and selling them personally across the country.

The biggest and the busiest

After World War II, Phillips Gutkin & Associates (PGA) was among the biggest and busiest animation companies in North America. The fact that they accomplished this in Winnipeg, a city of maybe 300,000 people on the bald-headed Canadian prairie, speaks volumes about the creativity and can-do stubbornness that characterized all independent Manitoba filmmakers.

In 1948 John Phillips and Harry Gutkin formed a partnership to provide live-action industrial films and print advertising for western Canadian businesses. Their first venture was a movie for the co-ops that were so important to western Canadian development. *What's Co-operation All About?* was a twenty-minute promo, half animation and half live-action. Rudimentary in design and structure, the movie is significant mainly because it forced PGA to invest in a historic animation stand.

The specifications for the stand came from the National Film Board. That's more ironic than it appears. At the time the NFB was justly famous for Norman McLaren's cameraless (and, therefore, non-animation-stand) films. The stand was then built by a local mechanic for Trans-Canada Air Lines (now Air Canada), Harold Rasmussen. Sturdy and reliable as a DC-3, the stand would be crucial to PGA's main claim to fame—hundreds of animated TV commercials.[31]

John and Harry were quite an unlikely pair. Gutkin, from Winnipeg's ethnic North End, was a commercial artist and part owner of a publishing firm. Phillips was the son of a renowned Canadian painter, a quiet man from the WASPish south end of town, who left a job as layout man and fashion photographer for the Eaton's catalogue, subcontracted to the graphic arts company Brigden's of Winnipeg Limited. The Canadian equivalent of the great Sears and Montgomery-Ward catalogues, the Eaton's catalogue was one reason that post-war Winnipeg was the third largest advertising centre in North America. It was a good time and, oddly, the right place for PGA to get into the animation business.

When CBC television became a coast-to-coast operation in 1954, PGA had already done some local animation ads. So Harry Gutkin took a sample reel to Toronto to impress the Libby's Foods' executives who had just agreed to sponsor National Movie Night on CBC television. With an amusing storyboard for "Quality Control Cops," PGA got their first big break.

The ad proved more expensive than PGA had estimated. With no lab facilities in Winnipeg, many flights had to be made across North America to complete the soundtrack, the editing, the final print, and even the live-action "sandwiches" inserted between the animation sequences.

To complicate matters, a fast-talking "Hollywood producer" convinced PGA to substitute milk for tomato juice in the black-and-white product close-ups. A budget-busting trip to New York to mask and recolour each individual frame of the insert saved the account.[32]

The golden age of PGA was between 1954 and 1960. The company was making between 15 and 30 TV commercials per month. Major accounts included Windsor Salt (whose "Wacky Bird" was Gutkin's favourite creation), Esso Oil, The Bank of Canada, Simonize Wax, Blue Ribbon Tea, Kellogg's Cereals, Chrysler Canada, Kraft Foods, and Libby's. Most of these were exclusively Canadian ads; Kraft, Libby's and Windsor Salt spots also appeared on American television.

Although all ads were done in the spare UPA (United Producers of America) animation style popular at the time, PGA still needed between twenty-five and thirty animators working full-time to keep up with the pace. Some of the animators came right out of local art schools and apprenticed on the job. Among those who worked at PGA and went on to even better things were Barrie Nelson (who later set up his own animation operation in Santa Monica, California), Barrie Helmer (John Phillips's brother-in-law, who was recruited from the NFB), Jeff Hale, Jan Kamienski (who became a noted political cartoonist), and, perhaps most famous of all, Winnipegger Bill Mason (whose canoeing and wolf films—especially *Cry of the Wild*—were among the best-selling NFB documentaries of all time).[33]

PGA is also where Charlie Thorson ended his long career in animation. He spent three months here in 1956, drawing the "fuzzy bunnies" and other cute animals he perfected as a character designer at Disney, MGM, Warner Bros., Fleischer, Terrytoons, Columbia, and George Pal Studios in the 1930s and 1940s.[34]

Most of PGA's talent, however, was imported from Europe. And this, plus a feature article in the prestigious Swiss magazine *Graphis*, led to a proposed transatlantic alliance with John Halas and Joy Batchelor, England's premier animators of the time.

Harry Gutkin met John Halas in New York City in 1960, and the two worked out a plan to alternate production of a weekly cartoon. PGA created a pilot from a series of children's books that Gutkin had published and one of his animators, Ray Darby, had created before PGA was founded. The series was to be called *T. Eddy Bear*. The pilot was then included on a demo reel with Halas and Batchelor's famous *Hamilton the Musical Elephant* and a handful of commercials from both companies.

Although the menagerie of animals was cute and kooky and the UPA-style animation colourful and inventive, the sample vignettes were uninspiring. *T. Eddy Bear* never found a buyer. It was the beginning of the end of PGA.

With production costs rising and profit margins evaporating because of costly trips to labs outside of Winnipeg, PGA struggled throughout the swinging sixties. Twenty-second animated commercials took over 300 person-hours to complete; the average contract was for $5,000 to $6,000. Live action could be done for about one-tenth of that.

The *coup de grâce* came from the CBC. Canada's government-sponsored TV net-work ruled that it would no longer accept animated ads for products aimed at children. The CBC was convinced that, "Animation was like a Trojan horse that secretly worked its way into children's minds."[35] Cereal ads for Coco Puffs and Rice Krispies were the first to go. Everything else that was animated was somehow suspect.

So, in 1966 PGA merged with another local ad agency, Brigden's, and reluctantly abandoned animation for print advertising. Luckily, they found a local buyer, Kenn Perkins, for their trusty animation stand. That meant that animation in Winnipeg did not come to an abrupt end.

The National Film Board (NFB)

As a teenager in the 1930s Stanley Jackson once flew with Angelo Accetti while Acetti filmed Winnipeg from the air. The plane ride convinced him to become a moviemak-er, a dream that was realized in 1942 when he joined the NFB in Ottawa. When he arrived there, he was greeted by what was then a standing joke: "Not another Winnipegger!" Obviously an exaggeration, the joke had some basis in reality; people from Winnipeg were playing crucial roles at the NFB from its beginnings in 1939—and even before. Throughout the 1940s the NFB became the main option for young Manitobans with movie aspirations and national/social ideals.

Four Manitobans were instrumental in the establishment and early successes of the NFB: Ross McLean, Sidney Smith, Joseph Thorson and Gordon Adamson. McLean was a founding member of the National Film Society in 1935. In 1938, when he was staff secretary to the Canadian High Commissioner to London, Vincent Massey, he convinced the Liberal government to hire John Grierson to study the sorry state of Canadian film. Grierson's report became the basis for the National Film Act of May 1939, which created the NFB. When the first person approached to be the Canadian Film Commissioner rejected the offer, Grierson was persuaded to accept. He appoint-ed Ross McLean as Deputy Film Commissioner; when Grierson stepped down, McLean became his successor.[36]

Sidney Smith, president of the University of Manitoba, also served as the presi-dent of the National Film Society from 1937–45, the organization that championed the making and distribution of Canadian films for educational and cultural purposes. His organizational skills, political savvy and lobbying expertise provided the ground-work for the NFB. Joseph Thorson, Manitoba Member of Parliament and Minister of War Services in the Mackenzie King government, oversaw the wartime NFB and pro-moted one of its early films, *Iceland on the Prairies*. A fellow Icelandic-Manitoban, Gordon Adamson set up the alternative film circuits that gave Canadians an opportunity to view their country's films. Largely shut out of movie theatres, NFB films were shown in factories, community centres, schoolrooms and church halls, non-theatrical circuits established by Adamson through his contact with educational agencies, labour groups, provincial governments and interested citizens. He also instituted the practice of discussion trailers, which ensured that NFB films would not only be widely seen but also debated.

It was *Iceland on the Prairies* that brought the first of seven Manitobans to the NFB in the pre-television era: Margaret Ann Bjornson. She was hired at the urging of Joe Thorson to provide research on that film. Her efforts landed her a full-time position as a researcher, editor and chief assistant to Stuart Legg on the *World in Action* series. Although none of the films she worked on were about her home town and province, she was the unofficial social arbiter of the NFB; her parties and get-togethers eased the way for the other Manitobans attracted to the NFB.[37]

Chief among them was Gudrun Bjerring Parker. An early film directed by her, *The People's Bank* (1943), focused on the importance of a credit union in the town of Starbuck, Manitoba. It quickly established her progressive and Prairie populist credentials. *Listen to the Prairies* (1945) underlined her commitment to culture and the arts. It captured the choirs, individual singers, musicians, audience and judges of the annual Winnipeg Music Festival (as well as the city itself and the surrounding farmland) in such a graceful and convincing way that few have ever noticed that it was shot without sync-sound after the competition was concluded. The response to the film was so positive that it was released in a shortened, theatrical version titled *A City Sings* (1946).

Just how important it was to have a moviemaker of Gudrun Parker's calibre, who was knowledgeable about the city and its people as well as sympathetic to its culture and traditions, can be seen from the lacklustre films about Winnipeg made at this time by outsiders. *Ukrainian Winter Holiday* (1947), also called *Ukrainian Christmas*, is a dull, by-the-numbers NFB portrait by Chicago "anthropologist" Laura Boulton. *Call For Volunteers* (1941) was an early, perfunctory effort by Graham McInnes that details the efforts of women's volunteer work during the war, work that was so groundbreaking and effective that "the Winnipeg Plan" was copied around the world, partially due to the wide distribution of this film.

In 1950 Gudrun Parker returned to her hometown to help her husband Morten Parker, another Winnipegger and University of Manitoba graduate, on *City in Siege* (1950), one of the most famous movies in the history of the province. *City in Siege* documents the 1950 Red River flood; it emphasizes the co-operation of the citizens, personifies the river as a rampaging enemy, and presents the battle in the style and tones of a World War II propaganda film. After this the Parker duo collaborated on social action films and cultural subjects (she directed the award-winning films *Opera School* and *A Musician in the Family*, and together they made *The Stratford Adventure* about the construction of the Shakespeare theatre and its first stage production). Gudrun also turned her attention to films for children, young mothers and teenagers, including the *What Do You Think?* discussion series on current social/moral issues.

Two other Winnipeggers who joined the NFB during the war and right out of university were Stanley Jackson and Grant Munro. Although neither one of them made films in or about Manitoba, both went on to long and distinguished careers at the NFB, Munro primarily as an animator, working extensively with Norman McLaren, and Jackson as a director and producer.

The most influential and arguably the most gifted Prairie moviemaker of all time joined the NFB in 1952 after graduating from the University of Manitoba. Roman Kroitor made his directorial debut with *Paul Tomkowicz: Street Railway Switchman* (1954), an engaging portrait of an about-to-retire labourer whose nightly job is to keep Winnipeg's streetcar tracks free of ice and snow. The Ukrainian immigrant and his city take on mythic dimensions. Streetcar passengers hardly take notice as he totes his broom, salt-bucket and lantern down the wide, snowy expanses of Portage Avenue while musing: "Winnipeg, after Paris, is a small, small village. Winnipeg, can put him in a wheelbarrow and wheel him away."[38]

Paul Tomkowicz was a widely admired precursor of the direct cinema or cinéma vérité movement, and Kroitor went on to be one of the pillars of the NFB's fabled Unit B in the 1950s and 1960s. A firm believer in innovation, he quickly adapted the new lightweight documentary equipment of the television era, created *Labyrinth*, the revolutionary multi-screen Canadian exhibit at Expo 67, and co-founded the Imax Corporation, writing and producing its first effort, *Tiger Child*, in 1970. He was also instrumental in developing *Heartland* (1987), Manitoba's self-promoting Imax film, which he also produced.

Conclusion

In his memoir about the earliest years of the NFB, Graham McInnes confirms Winnipeg's reputation as a producer and exporter of talent: ". . . at that time Winnipeg furnished more than its share of writers, broadcasters, filmmakers, intellectuals and bright young men. Ottawa, indeed the East, was full of them." McInnes further notes: "There was something about the gateway to the Prairies and the long hard winters that fostered intellectual sharpness and a spare but trenchant vocabulary."[39] But attributing Winnipeg's contribution to the arts and national civil service to "the long hard winters" is undernourished as analysis.

Winnipeg in the first half of the twentieth century was a city of extremes. The Depression squelched much of the city's early bullishness; the straitened conditions of both world wars, especially the second, further diminished expectations and enthusiasms. What is remarkable about this era as it is reflected in the art and business of moviemaking is that it is by and large composed of second-generation immigrants whose parents were risk-takers and nothing-to-lose dreamers who had settled in a frontier boomtown but endured startling deprivations and hardships. Winnipeg's moviemakers were raised amid contradictions and extremes: not just bitter cold but also glorious sunshine; ethnic and geographic isolation mixed with cultural community and do-it-yourself culture; promise plus disappointment; local pride tempered by national frustration and resentment.

It should not be surprising that this environment nurtured such a disproportionate number of young, ambitious people who excelled at the NFB or that moviemakers who stayed here managed somehow to survive and prosper. Film, the very medium they chose, was a study in contradictions. It was the most sophisticated of the new technologies of modernity at the service of old-fashioned values. In addition, several local moviemakers seem to have adopted an attitude of "I'll show you!" (instead of D.W. Griffith's famous "I want you to see"). It's not an unusual sentiment in an area that feels distant from the centres of power, systemically disadvantaged or looked down upon. Film was a medium for communicating across vast distances, a medium for making a case. Film and Winnipeggers were a perfect fit.

NOTES

1. *The Foreigner* was also called *The Crucible* or *God's Crucible* in pre-production. Shipman, the movie and local investors' hopes disappeared quickly from Winnipeg. If the movie was released elsewhere, it may have been under an alternate title; it is now presumed lost.
2. A few international movies were shot in the province during this era or contained second-unit or stock footage of local landmarks.
3. Some rescue work has been done on industrial films in the US. See: Rick Prelinger, *Ephemeral Films 1930-1960*, CD-Rom (New York: The Voyager Company, 1994).
4. Peter Morris, *Embattled Shadows: A History of Canadian Cinema 1895-1939* (Montreal: McGill-Queen's University Press, 1978), 30.
5. I am grateful to Bill O'Farrell for providing this information.
6. Again, I am grateful to Bill O'Farrell for providing this information.
7. Lambley was a highly regarded commercial artist and film technician who made an animated film (now lost) about Romulus and Remus in 1925 and specialized in making movie trailers. This part of his business prospered in Vancouver when he hooked up with (the now immensely profitable) Lion's Gate Films there.
8. Interestingly, it is a clergyman rather than a rabbi who is arrested, and a church is closed, not a temple or synagogue.
9. Francis J.S. Holmes, personal interview with the author, July 2, 1985.

10. *The Professional Cine Photographer* (May, 1958), n.p.
11. Less than a dozen of Holmes's films are at the National Film, Television and Sound Archives in Ottawa. Some films and outtakes are in the Manitoba Provincial Archives.
12. Holmes, personal interview.
13. Promotional flyer, Francis J.S. Holmes.
14. Holmes, personal interview.
15. Ken Davey, personal interview with the author, February 11, 1996.
16. Hal Sigurdson, "A True Impact Player." *Winnipeg Free Press* (November 22, 1993): D-13.
17. Vince Leah, *A History of the Blue Bombers* (Winnipeg: Winnipeg Blue Bombers Football Club, 1979), 43.
18. Davey's film of the 1939 Grey Cup game and several of his other films are in the Manitoba Provincial Achives. Unfortunately, his film of the 1935 game is lost. For more information on Davey check the Canadian Society of Cinematographers' website: www.csc.ca/news for November, 1998 and November, 2001.
19. Davey, personal interview.
20. Davey, personal interview.
21. Davey, personal interview.
22. Leah, 152.
23. Davey, personal interview.
24. Davey, personal interview.
25. Davey, personal interview.
26. Prelinger, *Ephemeral Films.*
27. His family crest (with the motto Dum Spero Spero—while I breathe, I hope) can be seen at the end of "Cotter's Camera on Canada."
28. I am grateful to filmmaker John Whiteway for sharing his information on George Cotter with me.
29. Kevin Prokosh, "An Obsession with Wildlife." *Winnipeg Free Press* (July 3, 1986): 85.
30. George Cotter, personal interview with the author, September 30, 1997.
31. Harry Gutkin, personal interview with author, October 28, 1995.
32. Gutkin, personal interview.
33. For more information on Mason, see my essay "A Motion and a Spirit: Bill Mason's Nature Films" in *Border Crossings* 8.2 (Spring 1989): 37-40.
34. For more information on Thorson, see my *Cartoon Charlie: The Life and Art of Animation Pioneer Charles Thorson* (Winnipeg: Great Plains Publications, 1998).
35. Gutkin, personal interview.
36. Gary Evans, *John Grierson and the National Film Board* (Toronto: University of Toronto Press, 1984), 51 ff.
37. Graham McInnes, ed. Gene Walz, *One Man's Documentary: A Memoir of the Early Years of the National Film Board* (Winnipeg: University of Manitoba Press, 2004), 155-58.
38. For more information on the film, see Rick Hancox, eds. Jim Leach and Jeannette Sloniowski, "Geography and Myth in *Paul Tomkowicz*: Coordinates of National Identity" in *Candid Eyes* (Toronto: University of Toronto Press, 2003), 13-30.
39. McInnes, 153.

A Note on Sinclair Ross
and the City

Nothing but wind and horses, his mother used to say. She'd come from Edinburgh, Scots Presbyterian through and through, and she spoke more than a little scornfully—in a "dismissive tone [that] rankled a bit," Ross has written ("Just Wind and Horses," 96). She was an unrepentant termagant, but she spoke a little proudly too. According to Ross this is what she said when she'd show around a copy of some journal in which one of his stories had appeared. That's all they're about, she'd snort. And in a way she'd be right. The old prairies were there in wind and horses.

Ross himself was a musician who had studied piano for years and he was a sophisticated writer who knew a lot about art. He was in many ways an urbane man. He worked for years in Winnipeg and for many years he lived in Spain and Greece. He read French and Spanish. He had an eye for painting, an artist's eye for concrete image, and he himself painted. And yet in his best work he wrote about the rural prairies. Most often he wrote about disappointed lives, or (in comedy, in poignancy) the fantasy lives of kids and the occasional adult (often as they circulated around horses). The Ross characters were situated typically on farms or in small towns, hardly a theatre or an art gallery in sight. He produced stories that were staggering for their depiction of loneliness and grief and (for his young characters, often) their touchingly kept sense that something, something rare and special, might happen in their lives. They inhabited an agricultural world, one in which few could find or contemplate, and fewer still would risk, life as artist or intellectual, those largely urban occupations. Ross, himself, did most of his writing while he lived in larger cities from which he expressed the unspoken disappointments of those living in the rural parts of the Prairies. He confessed once in a characteristically brief statement that, though he wrote most of his short stories and *As for Me and My House* while he was living in Winnipeg, "I was looking back, and drew on Manitoba not at all." "I always say that when I write I like to feel

Saskatchewan under my feet. I do. I feel 'safer'" ("On Looking Back," 94). He wrote while he was in cities, but they hardly figured in his most impressive work.

There are few cities in his prairie work (which is his best writing), then, not directly or immediately, that is. They are seldom mentioned in those books, and when they do appear, they are either unnamed or fictively named. Almost never, if ever, are they described. They exist out there, somewhere, in an almost phantom world of wish and memory. They figure most often as site of something "more" for his characters, an indefinable place where stirrings for a larger life might be realized or other ways of conducting their lives might at least be contemplated. They symbolize hope for something new perhaps even more keenly than regret for something lost.

Many readers will know of the Bentleys in *As for Me and My House*, Philip and his unnamed wife, who struggle in a blighted small town to lead a tenable existence. It's the Dirty Thirties. In Ross it's almost always the Dirty Thirties, a drought-stricken period which has so taken hold of the Saskatchewan imagination it has become a durable and an informing myth in his home province. The two principal characters have come from the city, which remains anonymous, though as university city it vaguely hints of Saskatoon. This city, like other of Ross's cities in his best-known work, is held in almost oneiric suspense inside a highly realist text. Because urban centres remain vaguely "out there," we have only an uncertain sense of those places as informing the lives of characters in his prairie settings.

The city in Ross is often the source of music—classical music, or jazz and swing. It figures for Mrs. Bentley as a place where her hopes to perform as classical pianist found their earliest and strongest expression. Music that speaks powerfully to Ross's characters often finds its source and its viability in the city, which is strangely distant, even though it cannot be far from the small town in which the Bentleys live. For Mrs. Bentley that music is residual, something she carries with her, in memory, and that she puts into spasmodic practice. She relishes moments of transport in occasional muted outbursts. Music for her is situated as "then" and "there," music in its fullest and most fulfilling expression, that is. "The musician in me dies hard," Mrs. Bentley laments in the first pages of her book (12), which we know as the novel *As for Me and My House* and which, she has told herself, is her personal journal. The passion lives on in her romantic understanding of playing as occasion for releasing pent-up passions.

The music Mrs. Bentley has brought with her represents for her self-assertion. She performs at one point in an avowed attempt to regain the attention of her estranged husband, whose affections she won when he first heard her performing at a recital. She also plays the piano on at least one occasion to compete for the loyalties of her foster son, Steve; and she performs vindictively, without fully admitting to her motives, in seeking to woo the family friend, Paul. "My fingers grow stronger" (188) in playing, she writes, and further observes that practising the piano, the "only thing that really mattered for me, . . . made me self-sufficient, a little hard" (22). She names her frustrated attempts to bring the piano into gratifying sound as an act that seeks god-like creation. It is, or could be, she believes, a matter of bringing surd matter into animation: "I can't make it respond to me, or bring it to life" (34). In striking sound from the instrument, she would hope to enlist it as ally in conflict with the citizens of the small town. "I must play the piano again," she, in a "combative mood," thinks, "play it and hammer it and charge with it to the town's complete annihilation" (18). Music from the city, music that is part of the larger metropolitan worlds Mrs. Bentley once conceived of entering, is now something she seeks to preserve in perpetuation of that world but more particularly in resistance to her enforced residence. She wants to believe that a bit of the city—embodied in a music that is at times uplifting and at times fortifying—lives on in her determined playing.

There is local music, too, which is either dance-hall music, or church music, or a classical repertoire that signals a veneer of respectability among those women who act as cultural custodians, woodenly preserving some remnants of a better existence as it occurs in the cultural centres of the world. The respectable music tends to be a little stodgy, at least as it exists under the jurisdiction of local matriarchs who in Ross are comically armed with metronomes, steely wills, and a dead certainty that they are fighting a battle to hold a beachhead of urbanity in the hinterlands. The dance music is akin to something that exists elsewhere, perhaps, but it also finds provocative and moving local expression. It offers in Ross the most vital and the most possible meeting of the urban and the rural. Ross perennially names it as enticing and dangerous, near but also a bit out of reach for most of his characters.

One of the most touching scenes in *As for Me and My House* occurs when Mrs. Bentley stands in a dark garden one night listening to the sounds of a band playing somewhere across town. From the garden, in the night—place and time of permission—she listens to the saxophone that was "wavering and slender like a fine thread of light" that she receives as "poignant and mellow." She hears in "the drum throb" something that she feels as "zest and urgency." The moment is made all the more poignant when her husband comes out to find her listening. They wait in the garden as the band plays a foxtrot, then a waltz. Philip, restrained and halting, then turns to his wife and says "I suppose, if we knew how, we could dance a little just ourselves out here" (64). The dance they cannot join Mrs. Bentley is able to enter, later, at a ranch, when a gangly young cowboy takes her in his arms. It is, I suppose, a version of "the better dance" the young men offer to Mrs. Bentley when they are driving by on the night she is listening to the band. She is "Lonesome," as they name her, in the permission of the night and the summons of the music. Her figure is replicated across Ross's short stories, in "The Painted Door" especially. In that story a frustrated and neglected farm wife, defying the inevitable storm of gossip that will follow her actions, finds brief pleasure in dancing with a charmer on the make. What that music and that dance can mean to her becomes clearer as their public embrace later is recapitulated privately in her bed when her worn and unfestive husband is away.

For Philip the city means a source of books and learning, a place where he might read and write, somewhere he possibly could (in the ending of the novel and in Mrs. Bentley's mind) re-enter as keeper of a bookstore. Philip's artistic impulses as a visual artist are in their own way indebted to a prior or an anticipated urban life and are no less suppressed in the prim and pinched town in which the Bentleys find themselves entrapped. His art, cosmopolitan in its own way, shows awareness of what is happening in art elsewhere, in Europe, and is responsive to those currents. The very name of their dog, El Greco, attests to that line of influence, as does Mrs. Bentley's description of the night as high and swirling—high and swirling as it is in Van Gogh's paintings, perhaps. Philip's art is something he characteristically hides and even guards jealously, resenting its discovery and resisting its display. It represents for him a furtive life and a tie to city life somewhere over the horizon, beyond Horizon, whose citizens scarcely notice it or appreciate it.

Ross establishes the power and the risk of those ties for Philip when he writes a scene about the arrival of art supplies from some unnamed city. Mrs. Bentley has ordered them discreetly wrapped in plain brown paper, so that they will escape the notice of the townspeople. Philip lingers over them, feeling their heft and brush, as he savours the magic of their names. He allows himself a ripple of exhilaration, evidently, one so small and so constrained it is hardly evident. The makings for art are spirited into the midst of a hostile camp of the puritanically and the practically minded. The city and its contraband goods are smuggled as illicit pleasure past customs.

The city for both of the Bentleys, then, hovers somewhere on the margins of their memories and drifts across their dreams. It is a site for something they there had once begun, and that has since become frighteningly receding, and (depending on how you read the end of the book) even more unattainable in their futures. And yet it is named as an elsewhere in whose ambit a life in art and books is at least thinkable.

The most recurrent sign of the city in Ross, however, is music. In *Whir of Gold*, one of Ross's least-known books, the city (the novel is set explicitly in Montreal) is named as debilitating. It is a hard and unwelcoming world in which the main character, Sonny McAlpine, seeks to find himself, as a down-and-out clarinet player. Sonny grew up on a Saskatchewan farm but, under the iron tutelage of Dorothy Whittle (shades of Ross's own mother?), he comes heroically to win a musical competition as classical pianist in an event that is rendered (defensively?) almost Dickensian. Sonny himself, like Mrs. Bentley as a young woman, perhaps like Ross himself when he studied classical piano, had felt for the music "an urgency—something that whipped and tugged, kept flashing signals from the other side, as if I were a stray" (76). The adjudicator, who has "an overwhelming English voice" (74), tells Sonny to shake off the provincial limits of his birth. "Above all, get away" (75) to "London" if possible, he urges, though the kid fears he may get no further than "Winnipeg" or "Regina" or "Saskatoon" (76), if he gets anywhere at all. For the worldly adjudicator, Sonny supposes, the small towns that speckle his world must have appeared as "one of the lonely, false-fronted Main Streets that he had wondered at through a train window or seen from his plane like a litter of boxes tipped out by some other plane" (74). Raw, lacking in grace or imagination, crudely oblivious to something other, anything more, they are marked as lacking any semblance of art and stand as culturally barren alongside the artistically enabling places from which so confidently the adjudicator comes and to which he so summarily beckons the farm boy. The advice, or the manner of the advice, may to our ears sound as much condescending as helpful, but it does point nevertheless to a world in which aspirations might be met—its music "something to compensate for wheat and windy bleakness" (21).

Sonny McAlpine is not quite so sure about his options. For him life as a classical pianist seems to be scarcely tenable, and he becomes drawn to what in Ross is a frequent alternative. Infatuated with a neighbouring musician who plays the clarinet, he soon takes up life in a local dance band, his newly defined role leading him to Montreal, where he flounders. Ross constructs this city as goal of both shining promise and place of ruined dreams. Good things can happen here for a musician, but so can dereliction and loneliness. "I put my clarinet to my lips," Sonny says. "Top form: notes silver-clean through the squalor—both the world and I restored" (53).

Music, inasmuch as it exists as urban prospect, or as it arrives from the city, however obliquely mediated by its large and stolid small-town champions whom Ross pillories, speaks of a larger life. That's what the city exemplifies, and it is what Ross's sensitive young kids and mothers, hopeful of something finer for their children, dare to imagine. Perennially the farmer father/husband is a blocker, scornful of music as diversion and of musicians as unmanly. Musicians generally are physically unproductive and fail in ways a farmer would find appalling. (And how often have we read that narrative in Prairie writing: the sensitive kid, incipient artist, raised as ineffectual figure in an uncaring or uncomprehending world?)

"Cornet at Night," one of Ross's most impressive texts, develops that narrative in a moving way. A young farm boy, sent to town to find help to get off the harvest, brings back a young musician. The young man's otherworldliness fascinates the boy, but it is clear the cornet player is eminently unsuited for the work. He is coded as "other" and unfit for life in a rural economy, as even the infatuated boy has realized from the outset. The cornet player, presented as citified and eastern, is, by the father's estimate, "effeminate." He is quite likely, also, judging from the suggestive terms with which Ross describes him, homosexual, as often in Ross musicians are (among them Benny Fox in Ross's remarkable last novel, *Sawbones Memorial*). Their sexuality is marked as aberrant and abhorrent in rural areas and as possible in any conspicuous way only in the more accommodating and anonymous city, site of greater permission or tolerance.

To no one's surprise the cornet player is sent on his way. Before he goes, however, he plays for the young boy. His music transfigures the young farm kid who, years later as narrator, describes it in highly lyrical (and sexual) terms. He writes as an adult who keenly remembers the magic of that night. The visitor's horn and his playing are overwhelming for the boy, and they speak of a reach in life that takes his breath away. The cornet gleams in the August sun "like pure and mellow gold" (46) and the boy can feel its presence, even in its case, "as if it were a living thing" (47). Its very existence quickens the boy, the day, the fields. When the musician agrees to play, the boy sees the cornet "glow and quicken," hears its sounds as "piercing, golden as the cornet itself, and they gave life expanse that it had never known before." The boy listens, stricken, as the notes float up and hang "clear and visible" in the air, then appear "bright through the dark like slow, suspended lightning" (49). The boy's parents, though angry about what has happened, find that in spite of themselves, they too are suddenly stirred by what they hear. The father is brought suddenly to startled hearing when for a brief sharp moment the music touches him. The mother too is stirred by what she hears. In a way, without realizing, they have been waiting for an expression that might lift them from their denied lives—from what the narrator calls "the clumsiness and crudity of life" (51).

What we hear so often and so movingly in Ross is a yearning for something more in lives so pinched that the artistically inclined characters want more than anything the best that the city signifies—a flare of colour, a moment of sudden beauty, a sense of life that is rich and involved. They want a chance to splash through the theatres of their lives. That hopefulness finds further expression in Ross, as it does in Margaret Laurence, in the trains that cry in the long prairie nights. There's nothing more lonely, Rachel Cameron says in Laurence's *A Jest of God*, nothing more painful, than hearing the trains that call out in the night, on their way to somewhere. Only the loon with a voice so indescribable it sends shivers through you—only it, Rachel thinks, can match the sound of a train at night. Only a train or, later in the history of small prairie towns, only a silent bus, can carry you away. Rachel, with her mother in tow, glides out of town and into the night:

> We watched until the lights of the town could not be seen any longer. Now only the farm kitchens and the stars are out there to signpost the night. The bus flies alone, smooth and confident as a great owl through the darkness, and all the passengers are quiet, some of them sleeping. (*Jest*, 208)

Rachel Cameron on her way to join her sister, Stacey, in Vancouver, where Stacey fights with her own demons, remembers the call of the train when as a young girl she heard it in the deep prairie nights:

> Those damn freight trains—I can still hear them, the way they used to wail away far off at night on the prairies, through all the suffocating nights of summer when the air smelled hotly of lilacs, and in winter when the silence was so cold-brittle you thought any sound would crack it like a sheet of thin ice, and all the trains ever said was *Get on your way, somewhere, just so something will happen, get up and get out of this town.* (*The Fire-Dwellers*, 33)

Had Stacey or Rachel been born earlier, she might have headed out on a train, ridden as Hagar Shipley did, a train into her departure, out past the farms that were "lost and smothered," past the frozen blue landscape "and the breath of barking dogs [that] gushed white and visible into the dry air snapping with cold":

> Winter was the right time to go. A bell-voice, clear in the cold air, cried "All aboard!" and the train stirred and shook itself like a drowsy dragon and began to move, regally slow, then faster until it was spinning down the shining tracks. . . . I could see on the hill brow the marble angel, sightlessly guarding the gardens of snow, the empty places and the deep-lying dead. (*The Stone Angel*, 142-3)

The escape in its "spinning" and "shining," and in its fairlytale train that rouses like a dragon, bears all the symptoms of Hagar's longing for romance and release.

Ross's characters are no less responsive to the whistle. Mrs. Bentley, and her rival, Judith West, wander the railway tracks, restlessly walk them to the outskirts of town, to the risked edges of their lives. Judith West, to the scandal of the town's ladies, earlier and on her own has heeded the summons: she has "been heard singing off by herself up the railroad track as late as ten o'clock at night. Naturally people talk" (16). It is not clear whether the dismay is caused by Judith's timing or her behaviour, but her impulses seem to be occasioned, or to be permitted, by the location.

At one point when the two women have been idling beside the tracks, Mrs. Bentley suddenly becomes alarmed at her awareness of Judith's sexuality. Then a handcar appears with two men aboard, two swarthy men. The workers "stopped when they saw us, and one of them called out did we want a ride. I looked at Judith, and dared her, and she said all right, we'd go" (102). The nature of the risk and the extent of the women's nerve becomes even more apparent when upon arrival in town they are greeted with raised eyebrows and arch comments about the "cure" they have effected (103). The ride they accept, somewhat giddily, has got to remind us of the ride Mrs. Bentley earlier had declined when she listened to the dance music and the young men who had called into her night garden.

Judith West, who for Mrs. Bentley disturbingly embodies something primal in the prairies, is drawn from the sheer darkness of the farm to "the bright little sprinkle" of lights that mark Horizon, and then, once she has moved into town, she soon is making excuses to greet the train, what for her is a modest and portable version of the city, when it comes in. "It always excited me, the glare of the headlight, the way the engine swept in steaming and important, the smoky, oily smell.... When it was gone I'd stand by myself on the platform watching the green tail light disappear past the elevators, listening to the whistle, two long, two short at every crossing" (75). Ross attributes to the train an unspeakable melancholy for characters stranded outside their dreams, but he constructs it too as emblem of a mysterious and distant life beyond the reach or the knowing of his characters. And so Mrs. Bentley too stands deeply shaken as

> The train pulled slowly past us. There seemed something mysterious and important in
> the gradual, steady quickening of the wheels. It was like a setting forth, and with a queer
> kind of clutch at my throat, as if I were about to enter it, I felt the wilderness ahead of
> night and rain. (172-3)

The pages of Ross's fiction are peppered with scenes in which characters long for contact with the world from which the train comes and into which it recedes. Philip Bentley, his wife wistfully conjectures, must as a boy have been stricken at its coming and going: "A train still makes him wince sometimes. At night, when the whistle's loneliest, he'll toss a moment, then lie still and tense. And in the daytime I've seen his eyes take on a quick, half-eager look, just for a second or two, and then sink flat and cold again" (39). He must have been impressed seeing the passengers, she imagines, with "the glamour of distance about them, because they came out of the unknown" (41). Whenever he dreamt of creating something, he, she feels certain, herself knowing the feeling, would have experienced the heart-wrenching force of the train always "roaring away to the world that lay beyond" (43)—to places where magical things happen and where wishes find shape.

I have been working for fifteen years now on a series of poems inspired by *As for Me and My House*. I have not felt any great fidelity to the details of the book, and I have written even less of the city than has Ross. What I have retained, I think, is the aching that his characters feel so often for something just beyond their lives, a belief that over there, somewhere, there must be, has to be, a land of joy, nearly inaccessible, a place they hardly dare imagine. For Ross this place usually is an unspecified city. In *the bentleys*, the interminable series I have been writing, Mrs. Bentley and the other characters look not to the city but to the garden she believes must be found beyond their lives, usually in BC. In *the bentleys* the figures look out from a dry and blighted prairie, stand in desiccated yards, the sounds of trains and dreams of boats raining through their heads, their days and nights filled with longing for music and water and green spaces.

WORKS CITED

Laurence, Margaret. *The Stone Angel*. 1964. Toronto: McClelland & Stewart, 1995.

————. *A Jest of God*. 1966. Toronto: McClelland & Stewart, 1988.

————. *The Fire-Dwellers*. 1969. Toronto: McClelland & Stewart, 1991.

Ross, Sinclair. "On Looking Back." *Mosaic* 3.3 (1970). 93-4.

————. "Just Wind and Horses." John Metcalf and Leon Rooke, eds. *The Macmillan Anthology*. Toronto: Macmillan, 1988. 83-97.

————. "Cornet at Night." *The Lamp at Noon and Other Stories*. Toronto: McClelland & Stewart, 1968. 35-51.

————. *As for Me and My House*. 1941. Toronto: McClelland & Stewart, 1989.

————. *Sawbones Memorial*. 1974. Toronto: McClelland & Stewart, 1978.

————. *Whir of Gold*. Toronto: McClelland & Stewart, 1970.

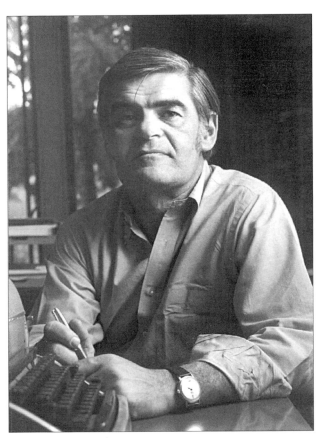

JACK LUDWIG

Star Chamber Day in the Committee Room

I'm not sure you'll want to read beyond what I have to confess here and now: I was *expelled* from a University, the University of—o I mustn't say its real name—let's call it the University of M: I became a person expulsed, deepsixed, chucked, jettisoned.

I'll pause to allow a swift departure by the shocked.

You few still with me in spite of your shudders mustn't think the UofM issued the pariah tag whimsically or that I had not incurred the justifiably righteous wrath of the pure of heart. I'll try to fill you in on the episode. Don't be surprised if I at times whisper.

The French critic Sainte-Beuve wondered how many *I*s would die before the mobile being who bore his name was laid to rest: the implication, *numberless*. The writer of fiction or chronicle prefers to think *few*, even *none*. With luck each consecutive early *I* is somehow available for reawakening. To Proust past time was sealed, in jars, each containing an intact *I*, intact epiphanic moments only a *chance* sensuous reverberation—a sound, flavor, feeling, image—could quicken; a mere act of *will* could not. His character Marcel bends to tie a shoelace, is suddenly overwhelmed by a childhood memory of his grandmother leaning over to help; a sealed time jar springs open and for the very first time Marcel *feels* the absence of that grandmother, *feels* his loss, truly *mourns*.

Unlike a proper Proustian *recherche*, this attempt to replicate in the 21st Century a moment in the 20th Century past was *willed* though I suspect something about the here and now echoed earlier feelings, earlier thoughts. Perhaps the flourishing of flat-earth theory irrationalities to our south—raging manipulated political shrillness, faith-based science, "creationism"—woke sympathetic vibrations in memory's tuning fork.

Think of this as a *willed* tuning of two musical instruments.

We have to go back to a tremulous moment in mid-*20th* Century— the time jar is labeled *World War II*: I'm at that UofM, in fourth year, Literary Editor of the University newspaper, Editor of the special annual *Literary Supplement*. Our editorial offices are a kind of hangout, Pat Blondal was a classmate of mine, it's where I first meet a talented student at United College, the "Peggy" later known as Margaret Laurence.

We get submissions—poems, stories, criticism, one act plays, radio scripts, travel pieces, touched-up term papers, jokes, limericks, cartoons, drawings. We have a board. Every piece of writing is passed around, read, reread, winnowed, art work is looked at, considered, the short list grows shorter and shorter. Much disagreement. A final selection is made.

I'm also one of two Arts representatives on the student governing body, the other Arts representative is Albert C. Hamilton, the popular elected President of the UofM student union, a good person.

For some reason Arts students, particularly those in literature, languages, philosophy, history often encounter polar hostiles of *The Incipient Classes*, incipient lawyers, incipient engineers, bankers, stockbrokers unsurprisingly located in the nurturing Faculties of Law, Engineering, Commerce. Arts people are much inclined to argue, sometimes vociferously, ofttimes invite controversy by picking on Prime Ministers say, Premiers, establishmentarians, authoritarians, majoritarians, broad spectrum philistines, guardians of privilege and power nobly serviced in the past by Chaucer, Molière, Voltaire. Pre-professionals aspiring to lofty niches often side with The Powerful and in doing so seem to undergo a crucial transference, become as vigorously paranoid as their role models.

All this of course by way of prelude.

In the *Literary Supplement* we published a poem, "Atrocities," anonymously—the author preferred it so; *Incipients*, others perhaps, found it scurrilous, disloyal, even *subversive*. Arts students clearly didn't understand *our country was at war*! What what, publish a witty ironic snide uppity poem when the entire world's in a state of chassis? In drastic times why care a fig about freedom of the press, *freedom of expression, freedom of thought*?

It's quite possible too that particular *Incipients*, members of the University Students' Union representing the staunch and upright Faculties didn't much prize the existential recognition Arts people conferred by way of individuated disparagement at contentious meetings. It's even conceivable they were looking for a way to get even.

And lo, *deliverance*, "Atrocities," a poem that suggested vicious ugly actions in wartime weren't an Axis monopoly and, in addition, took a whack at meretricious "Bible thumpers." It was a poem about attitudes, stances, nothing in it questioned the necessity of secrecy and security in wartime. The instant, and *orchestrated*, response was impressive, a splatter of gung-ho genuflectives, *disloyalty in wartime, giving aid and comfort to the enemy*—jingoistic cliches are mother's milk to true believers.

Shock and dudgeon were a fine beginning but to get even properly required *action*! *Hup hup quick* off went *annotated* copies of the poem to the RCMP, University President Sidney Smith, local newspapers, various prominently positioned puffers. The *Winnipeg Free Press* promptly printed a flounce denouncing irresponsible under-graduate fulminations *in wartime*! *Hup hup quick* this too was annotated, delivered to the RCMP.

Incipients pushed all the right buttons: hanging judges bayed, grainbrokers trembled, unsurprisingly the University administration quaked, caved, buckled, O, and the Communists, free now of their early pact with you-know-who, brayed like colony-deprived Victorian Imperialists. If any thinkers shared the ideas put forward in John Stuart Mill's *On Liberty*—one assumes there must be a few in a first-class University—they, for some reason, took the monastic vow of silence.

A few relevant family details: my mother's youngest sister was having a baby, in Edmonton, my mother went to help. We decided to cheer her up in the midst of the worrying War with a surprise, paint the house, build new cupboards, &c. I went off to stay with my Aunt Lillian. And *hup hup quick* the RCMP came acalling, an un-uniformed investigative Inspector—not Peter Sellers, not Clouseau—a putative professional set about briskly, questioning painters, plasterers, carpenters. None had a clue *where* I was, *who* I was.

Aha! *Fled*! *In hiding*!

One of the little kids next door overheard the questioning man in fedora and raincoat, told him I was just over at my Aunty Lil's on Bannerman.

A car drove up. Man in fedora, raincoat.

"You responsible for this?"

Held up the poem, every other word underlined.

"Had it analyzed, experts say language of this poem and comm'nist peace pamphlets thrown up on steps of City Hall in 1935 are exactly the same."

"Sir," I stupidly said, "in 1935 wouldn't any current student at the University be about thirteen or less? And aren't comm'nists our allies now?"

"Don't act smart with me, young feller, who should I believe, trained *experts* or you?"

It's wartime. Maybe the military and the RCMP have proscribed chronology. Proscription was in the air. The pronunciation "comm'nists," for example, was a signature of that most enthusiastic proscriber, J. Edgar Hoover, head of the publicity-wise Communist-sniffing American FBI. Yes, a Yank: ideological hysteria has no difficulty crossing sovereign borders.

"*You* write that poem?" Inspector asked.

I shook my head.

"Somebody did. *Who*?"

"Anonymous.'"

"You actin' smart again?"

Clearly not.

"Don't you go nowheres, young man. I'll be back. Better be ready to tell me who."

A seepy uneasiness took me over, this man, sans red coat, was an *Inspector* in the world-famous RCMP! International snoopdom had probably been alerted, perhaps I was under surveillance at this very moment, my Aunt Lillian too. I hesitated to call anyone from a home phone, in search of a "safe house" took myself to the noisy raucous technologically unbuggable Marlborough Hotel beerparlor, a preferred University R&R oasis. The usual resident noisy UM spigots harangued around wet tables loaded with O'Keefes, Labatts, Molsons. Sitting among them, significantly quieter than the rowdies, was my fellow Student Union rep, Bert Hamilton.

Not a fedora in sight, no raincoats, no trenchcoats, only hordes of loud happy bareheaded drunks in Navy, Army, Air Force uniform.

Over the din I whispered my RCMP tale, Bert had his own story to tell: President Smith had called, wanted to see us both in the morning.

Oho! RCMP Inspectors move quickly!

We went. The President, like that RCMP Inspector, had a theory. Not 1935 *peace* pamphlets but *1944 anti-war* pamphlets linked up with the anti-war sentiments of the poem. *And* the President *knew* who had written both. *Refugees*. We were being asked to confirm. This by President Sidney Smith, a fair man we liked and respected, neither crank nor crotcheteer.

I did, at the time, wonder why Albert C. Hamilton was being brought into this discussion of a specific *publication* problem? He had no editorial connection with the *Literary Supplement*, no responsibility for anything that was printed, so why include him? My guess was the President wanted a calm popular *student* voice to join his in urging a *student* editor, me, to name *the refugee* before the RCMP, who always got their man, entered stage left.

No no, you didn't mishear, I did say *refugee*. Were you perhaps wondering *refugee from what*?

Permit me to *fake* a digression: wartime Canada, as you may or may not know, had (I must whisper it) *internment camps*, such things are of course necessary in wartime. By now most Canadians have heard about the scandalous mistreatment of interned Japanese British Columbia residents (among them Canadian *citizens*) during World War II. But we had internment camps in other parts of the country as well, Red Rock, Ontario, for instance, The University had not too long ago admitted a group of German refugees released from Red Rock. Now you're wondering what were *refugees* from Nazi Germany doing in a *Canadian* internment camp?

To continue the phony digression: most of us at the University knew or knew about these liberated German refugees, some were in our classes. All of them had escaped from Germany, from concentration camps or impending Nazi catastrophics; world and national humanitarian organizations had worked hard to get them out of Europe and into Canada, but on their arrival many were taken into custody as "enemy nationals" and interned in Red Rock—alongside Nazi war prisoners, Nazi spies, North American Bundists, Italian fascists.

These refugees had lived under Hitler since 1933, had thought themselves finally free of *arbitrarily imposed incarceration, racial, religious and ideological persecution,* the very last place they expected to encounter it again was in their *emancipating refuge,* Canada.

The internment experience embittered them. It had taken Canadian and world organizations a long time to rescue them from imminent danger and almost as long to get them *out* of Red Rock; they were back in a university world from which they had been barred. A happy-ending story, or more delusion about Canada as a sanctuary?

What what, refugees *embittered*? Well now, wasn't this palpable motive for writing anti-war pamphlets *and* an anti-war poem? Such was President Smith's reasoning; if followed up on, some poor blameless refugee would be hauled in to face inquisitors inside *and* outside the University.

In the Arts Common Room we had heard refugees tell of being hunted, caught, beaten, imprisoned, of parents killed, of houses torched. They, as Hannah Arendt pointed out, had *no juridical identity* in Nazi Germany, they didn't exist, their deaths would have gone unrecorded. In the Common Room of our Canadian university they not only existed but were recognized as people of *the resistance,* true *freedom fighters.* We could not allow anything ugly to happen to them—again.

The obvious solution? I would ask the author of "Atrocities" to release me from my guarantee of anonymity. A pressing human "good" outranked the abstract principled other.

The author of "Atrocities," as we shall see, had an even better solution.

Bert and I left the President's office on a gorgeous spring day, walked along the river, quickly agreed the only way to get everyone off the refugees' backs was to *disclose.*

Disclose what?

Was the author of "Atrocities" the comm'nist pamphleteer the RCMP's experts came up with? The embittered German refugee of the President's deducing?

I offer a few hints:

1. the author of the poem was as far from being a "foreigner" or "refugee" as President Sidney Smith himself

2. the author was, like President Smith, a full-blooded white anglo-saxon Protestant Canadian

3. if the German refugees were the President's *most likely* suspects, the author of the poem—along with the President himself, the Prime Minister, *and* Winston Churchill—would be *least likely*

Prepare for an irony, dear reader, and please pity poor University President Sidney Smith: he was on the verge of giving *us* the name of the refugee who wrote "Atrocities" while sitting only a few feet away from the *poem's actual author* and—good grief!—the student on campus he justifiably most admired, University Undergraduate President Albert C. Hamilton!

Which was why, when our pastoral walk along the river ended, Bert Hamilton came up with *his* solution, go right back, *tell all.*

President Smith's openmouth astonishment on learning *un*German *un*refugee Albert C. Hamilton wrote "Atrocities" was not recorded on any EKG, radar detector, Geiger counter, Richter scale, a pity. Neither was his sigh of relief at being rescued from perpetrating an embarrassing injustice.

To go with Bert's owning up I took sole responsibility for the poem's publication, which cleared everyone else on the newspaper and *Literary Supplement* staff.

It wasn't over, of course. Consequences followed, interpretations abounded. The RCMP could call it a score—the person who wrote that openly subversive blasphemous poem *proved* himself comm'nist. The *Incipients* had skewered *two* Arts representatives, a serendipitous *double coup*! And since, as their annotations had proved, the poem was *seditious* and *blasphemous*, shouldn't these two be sent to Stony Mountain, say, or Red Rock?

More was to come: Bert and I were asked to appear, separately, before the Faculty Disciplinary Committee. Its make-up was a mystery, so too its *wartime* powers.

When I was called in the first person I saw was a bland forgettable English professor war had metamorphosed into a dapper uniformed army *Major* in charge of the
campus COTC; the University's affiliated Colleges were represented by an Anglican
priest from St John's, a Jesuit priest from St Paul's, a Mother Superior from St Mary's
along with a United Church Warden, a French speaking priest and nun. The devoted
brought missals they read throughout the hearing, others tapped unopened Bibles,
paid small attention to questions or answers.

I knew it would be unwise and impolitic to pick up a sketchpad and play
Daumier, Hogarth: the costumes, postures, facial expressions, gesticulations of this
picturesque dramatis personae begged for capture, particularly after an unexpected
perhaps uninvited guest, Manitoba's Chief Justice Dysart, Chairman of the Board of
Trustees and alleged champion of "the lash" and "the noose" popped in to make sure
the Committee did its firm patriotic duty.

Questioning was left to two Deans, Armes and Saunderson, good people, who
asked first whether I had any brothers in the army (I had a brother in the Air Force),
and next whether anyone close to me had been killed or wounded in the war: my
cousin Jimmy Chess (we were both named after a mutual greatgrandfather) was a
20yearold aerial gunner killed during the early days of the Battle of Britain.

A hit, a hit, a palpable hit! Psychological pay dirt. Clear and convincing motive for
publishing an anti-war poem! Bert in his turn was asked more or less the same questions, came up with a similarly incriminating *motive*—his father had been incapacitated during World War I.

The subject of *free speech, freedom of the press* somehow never came up, neither in
this *University* committee nor, as I've already mentioned, anywhere else on campus.
The *Incipients* had everything right: in wartime civil liberties didn't count for much.

Each of us in his turn was sent out of the room while the Committee deliberat-
ed—at least *three* minutes in my case. Unsurprisingly we were both found guilty—
of what? "An act prejudicial to the University," language *gobbly* and *gooky* but decisive, final: both of us were expelled from the University, allowed to take final exams
but not get results or degrees until one of several conditions obtained: for Bert, who
was in Fifth Year Honors, both results and degree would be withheld until he was
either

a. honorably discharged (from the navy) or

b. killed in action.

I—classified "physically unfit" by the army—would not be admitted into Fifth
Year Honors, my BA degree was consigned to academic escrow (but for some
unknown reason conferred even before I got my exam results).

The "*b*" clause in Bert Hamilton's "sentencing" was fortunately never invoked: Albert C. Hamilton was honorably discharged an officer in the navy, given his exam results and BA Honors degree; went on to a University of Toronto MA, Cambridge University PhD, a most distinguished career as Professor of English at the University of Washington, James Cappon Professor at Queen's University, Fellow of St John's College at Cambridge, a renowned Renaissance scholar, a recognized expert on the works of Edmund Spenser.

Before I try to reseal this time jar let me add that many of the interned refugees never could erase the hideousness of their Red Rock experience, some ultimately left Canada, I'll mention only one, Harry Seidler, a brilliant student in the Faculty of Architecture who went on to an internationally acclaimed architectural career—living in Australia.

Some years after Bert and I had been turfed out I met former President Sidney Smith in Ottawa, in the Parliamentary dining room—he was now a federal cabinet minister. He was apologetic, slightly embarrassed by the whole episode he put down to *wartime hysteria*. When I later published a celebration of John Stuart Mill's *On Liberty* (a book I strongly recommend to everyone living in our *21st* Century), I sent him a copy. I somehow neglected to do the same for the RCMP or any of *The Incipients* on the University Students Union.

This time jar is now sealed.

Introduction to the paperback edition of **Confusions**

I wrote *Confusions* in the reading rooms of the New York Public Library, in various apartments scattered around New York City and New York State; it contained stuff I had jotted in notebooks years earlier, while in Massachusetts, California, Minnesota, Puerto Rico; but the novel proper was written during a long hot summer in—of all places—my home town, Winnipeg. It was done in a rush and sent off, ten or so pages at a time, to a guy who was interested in my work and wanted to see the book completed that very summer. He was a book editor then, perhaps, just doing his job, but his style was not job-like. Every batch of manuscript I sent Kildare Dobbs was read and commented on immediately. Having him plugged into what I was up to was invaluable. In spite of the number of novelists and writers who come from Winnipeg not much actual writing is done there. A few people around town care about fiction as a going thing. Some care about it without knowing they care about it.

Take my cleaning lady in the Ryan Building. I don't know her name but I can tell you this woman was the kind of critic to make a writer sweat. There I was—you see it? Seven storeys up, half a deserted floor to myself—the only other occupant on the seventh a distributor of jockey shorts. The Ryan Building was a relic of sweatshop Winnipeg, slantfloored, filmwindowed, paintpeeled, barebulblit. Say you put a desk down in the middle of Maple Leaf Gardens, in summer I mean, at night. That was my station in the Ryan Building, using furniture my uncle and I picked up from the Great-West Life Insurance Company who were abandoning their old off-Main Street offices and moving across the way from the Legislative Buildings on Osborne, easy walking distance for its lobbyists. Everything was for sale—hundreds of desks peeling aluminum paint, swivel chairs, typist's chairs, executive chairs, conference tables, corner tables, low and high tables—everything, regardless of size or condition, going for a democratic five bucks. The desks had to be approached through hat-trees tangled together with massive wooden antlers, a thousand desk trays evenly distributed between in's and out's. Auctioneers and dealers filled the old offices, kneedeep in a despair of wastebaskets, a solidity of filing cabinets, a pride of bronze lions, a bubble of watercoolers, an illumination of desklamps. One table, one chair, one wastebasket, three trays and I was in business meagerly, apologetically, occupying just enough space to bleat my squatter's rights. An amphitheater yawned beside me, behind me, in front of me, ominously empty, taunting my imagination to people it, and be quick about it.

So into this came my cleaning lady. I alone, all all alone, choosing to work late, when the hour was for cabdrivers, picked-on cops, Chinese restauranteurs, pimps, hookers, charladies. And John Hirsch. Three or four blocks from the Ryan Building Hirsch was trying to establish repertory in Winnipeg; his Dominion Theatre was at least as bad as the Ryan Building, with nostalgia added. The joint had flopped as a movie house, died as a vaudeville caper, and failed miserably in a dozen prior theatrical tries. So who has to take this thing on but lean, lank, lanceless Hirsch, crazy with unbased optimism, bent with complaints, double-bent with lamentations, Don Quixote with the added misfortune of being a Hungarian. In that ugly building he sweltered summers and winters wrapped himself in mufflers and sweaters, poor fleshless rake of an Oblomov, teeth chattering because several of his committee couldn't raise the few lousy bucks needed to heat the whole building. Across the street from him, elegantly cuffed cheery grainbrokers opened windows in winter to rid their chambers of a surfeit of heat; in summer airconditioners cooled their deliberations. Off Portage Avenue, Doris Day danced her brand of manic death in theatrehouses controlled by thermostats suited to all seasons. Hirsch that particular summer choked on pre-World War I dust curling up from shredded rugs his actors caught heels in working their way to the stage. He was doing some kind of theatre-under-the-stars carnival as part of his gigantic program to housebreak three generations of Winnipeg Philistines.

My ally.

Well, then, I'm finally at work, my first night, and it's fairly cool, the tailors and cutters and machine-operators and seamstresses don't fill the street below with joshing and wolf-whistling and the discreet punctuation of smashed milkbottles. I've read the *Free Press* and the *Tribune* and wonder how it is possible for a reasonable guy like me to be such a dreadful chauvinist once I cross the border into the United States. I read the papers and there's the Canada I know is real. So why do I lie so incredibly to any Yank who'll give me half an ear? Distance, I tell myself. But that doesn't explain the jingo behind my pushing the genius of McKenzie King. Distance might have made me less critical, maybe even uncritical, but I am clearly a revisionist full of tricks, apologetic, and double-take. If Canada were half what I pretend it is, I wouldn't have to pretend anything at all.

My window is open. The screen has holes in it. My lamp is instantaneously webbed with swiftly orbiting insects. My nostalgia doesn't extend to the Manitoba mosquito; not one seems to be bothered by the fact that my blood by now is probably part Yankee.

She entered the room, then, the cleaning lady, fumbled at the door with a ring of keys, opened it, smothered an "oh!," pushed in foul-smelling pail, backed in herself, mopping harder than the floor deserved. She muttered something about my lamp; but since it was once the property of the Great-West Life Insurance Company I felt they were the ones to seek satisfaction for her remark. She obviously had difficulty seeing the floor, or figuring out my small lighted pool in one tiny corner of the enormous space, Melville Bartleby, or Kafka clerk, staged by Beckett, lit by Cocteau. I obviously failed as burgher and businessman, having far too few obstacles to offer her or her broom.

Whistling, murmuring, she backed my way, swinging that mop like an old-fashioned ice-cleaner, circles widening. Her course took her rearward round three sides of my desk. I smiled. She glanced at me over her shoulder. I smiled again. She sniffed. The mop moved back and forth, enough to qualify for minimum compensation but not at all committed to my floor. She examined paper, looked under the table carefully, the broom in idle. She checked out my eyes, stationed herself behind me to see what I was looking at. Walked carefully round one way, then back, round the other.

"O.K.," she said, sighing, "where is it?"

"What?"

"What you're puttin' down on this here machine, where is it?"

"It's nowhere—"

"You don't understan', maybe. I mean where's the think you're copying? The words you puttin' down on paper—don't you understand me? I mean where are they?"

"In my head."

"How do I know that?"

"I'm telling you—"

"You still don't understand—I mean how do I know the ones you got in the head and the ones that get down on paper is the same?"

"You don't know. I mean you do know—I tell you—"

"Maybe I don't make myself so clear, eh? Let's put it another way—How do you know the ones you got in your head and the ones that get down on paper is the same?"

"They have to be," I said. "Without them being in my head there wouldn't be anything to put down on paper."

She looked at me scornfully, urged her mop into a wider swath.

Her head went down, she concentrated on dustballs spotted by my lamp. Two or three times I caught her glancing quickly up to see if she could catch me at my secret copying. She brushed a paper down from the table—in case it was covering the thing she searched for.

Whistling she shuffled across the floor, slammed the pail against a far wall, and began sloshing water into a corner. The room smelled of the Red on the hottest August nights, when everything that could has decayed. Swabbing and grunting she advanced closer, unmistakably spying. The circling routine was repeated. She couldn't keep her mind on her mop; my ankles were soaked through the socks.

She stationed herself behind the typewriter, resting on her mop. She was younger than I thought. And fatter.

"Let's put it still another way," she said patiently, "I mean like how if you ain't copyin' do you know if you got it right?"

"I'm making it up—I'm the only judge—"

"No no—you ain't followin'; I mean you got a supervisor or something? Like who in the morning'll check your work for the mistakes?"

"I do that myself."

"Ho—that ain't really checkin'. I can tell you the girl at the jockey shorts went to Success—that's the very best business school, now ain't it? She checks herself like you do but I couldn't begin to tell you how many times her boss goes over the same stuff and finds plenny mistakes."

She gave me twenty or thirty seconds to come clean.

"I mean—like the girl she can check back—I mean the salesman he give her a pencil thing, what do they call it—copy of order?"

"Right."

"Well so she matches what he got and what she got and if they ain't the same somebody done a mistake, see?"

"Yes—"

"Well?"

"I sometimes copy something I wrote out first in a notebook."

"Yah, but you wrote it."

"Yes—"

"Well if you wrote it one place and then wrote it another, and you got nobody after you, why would you look for a mistake in the first place? Everybody got to have a supervisor mister. I mean I don't do your floor and my super gets in at eight you can bet I'm gonna hear about it."

"In my way I try do the same –"

"Yah, yah, but you don't really succeed, now, tell me the truth, do you?"

Shaking her head, whistling the shrill superiority of her way over mine, she rode her mop and broom out of my darker loft.

I had read Eliot. I had read the new Critics. I had studied Frye, pondered Edmund Wilson, Eric Auerbach, none so unsettling, none so tough as she. In Winnipeg how does one *know* the Massachusetts or California in his head *is* the one demanded by his type on paper?

She had unnerved me.

She was no believing Yank ready to accept my Canadian bushwa. No sophisticated litterateuse blinking a bluestocking O.K. at everything understood.

Everybody got to have a supervisor, mister.

She was too tough to accept something so vague or fanciful as *my conscience is my supervisor, Bessie.* My standards; my taste; my sense of reality; my loyalty to the art; my imagination. They clearly ordered this matter better in the jockey shorts enterprise.

My lady of the pails filled this head with doubts.

I'm still working on the problem. A small practical portable built-in supervisor would be a true breakthrough in the arts. Fiction, she tried to convince me, needed it most.

I wrote *Confusions* surrounded by this cleaning lady. Never having attended Success, I couldn't really make it with her on the highest levels. But we became quite close. She was from the small town of Macdonald. She told me tidy little local tales. Necrophilia. Sadism. A suggestion of cannibalism. Child abuse, ritual murder. Each tale sent me into a spin. Her I checked out. Pushed aside *Confusions* and spent hours in the *Free Press* morgue. I always found a rough 'copy of order.' Her stories were unbelievably true. They played counterpoint against *Confusions*. Here I was writing a lark of a book about the mad phoniness of American life dedicated to the motto *Second Things First.* Three nights a week the cleaning lady came in with her unknowing "yes yes but." I would be derailed, though temporarily. I thought of writing two books simultaneously, and wish now I had done so. Companion volumes. *One flew north, one flew south, both flew out of the horse's mouth. Mine* would have begun:

I sing confusion, I, Jack Ludwig, myself confused, or, to put it another way, a come-home Winnipegger. Half my adult life I lived in Canada, the other in the U.S.A., is it any wonder that when I say *I'm going home* I don't know where I'm heading?

It might have been a fairly good sequel or prelude to *Confusions.* The tough job would have been to get the cleaning lady's tales in—and in the best possible order.

So what you have here, dear reader, is—I confess—but half a novel; and it's an unsettled question if half a novel is better than none. My cleaning lady is the other half. Or your cleaning lady. Your newspaper's morgue. Or you.

Just as two halves make a city. My half, the Winnipeg I come back to after having left it; John Hirsch's half, the Winnipeg he never saw nor knew about it but which, now, years after that long hot summer, did let him build what he was once madly dreaming. Are there only thirteen ways of looking at a blackbird? Maybe that's what I should have told the cleaning lady; that what I have in my mind is an endlessly complex blackbird whose contradictory shapes and faces make endless possibilities for fiction; or should I have told her that if I were lucky I would take from this mind something as real, as rattling, as murky as that greasy-sided, gray-watered, mop-shredding pail and cast it ringing, and thirteen-dimensional for ear and eye—even ones as tough as hers—to embrace?

Satire is a grappling hook thrown up the high wall of the everyday world; once we climb up we may lose sight of the means that took us up. And once up there we may find our task and targets changed. We may never want to do anything but describe pails and charladies.

Confusions I say is such a grappling hook. Cherished, first novel, and all that. It made me look on absurdity among pails and refugees, the arts and charwomen. My writing life began, of course, when I wrote it. For me it was an exciting beginning. And when I climbed that wall I flushed out ten times a brace of blackbirds.

But more about them later.

The Riverworlds of Jack Ludwig:
An Interview

In October 1999, Jack Ludwig was a guest of the Winnipeg International Writers Festival. There he read from a draft of "Ysak's Fable," his first novel since *A Woman of Her Age* (1973). Originally from Winnipeg's North End, Ludwig was an English professor, edited literary magazines, wrote three novels and numerous award-winning short stories and penned several books of literary sports writing. In no particular order, of course.

ARIEL GORDON: Tell me, what is it like being back in town for the Festival?

JACK LUDWIG: It's great to be back. I must say that there's a kind of dislocation—partly from what Portage Avenue looks like now and the way Portage Avenue was impressed on my old image of the city. I haven't been back in the city for about fourteen years; the Forks didn't exist when I was last here. But yesterday I did something I'd wanted to do for a long time, cross the Redwood Bridge again. I did that a lot when I was a child, and always felt the river's strength and power and loved its beauty. Water is a dominant force in this city. In order to get onto the bridge, though, I had to pass the ugliest stretch of unnatural unpastoral franchise stuff—Kentucky Fried Chicken is ubiquitous, it even slimes the approach to this wonderful river. Once past the west side's cookie-cutter set, and on the bridge, look down: leaves still on the trees add colour to the banks, a strong northward motion in the Red. Urban blight's washed away. There's my lovely old river.

AG: What parts of Winnipeg are most vivid for you, what are your physical memories of the city?

JL: The vital north section, and Fort Garry, notably the university. There's a river world out at the university, a river world in the North End. A kind of continuity. River water to me was always threatening. When I was about seven the older brother of somebody in my class drowned in the Red. Ice was starting to break up; he tried to step, leap, fly across the river soaring from floe to floe. The river at break-up is fabulous, *yearly*. A loud echoing sundering crack, ice, solid, miles long, heaves, breaks wide open. Gaps look inviting, simply jump from floe to floe, just don't stop. To some kids the whirling turmoil acts like a challenge, even a dare. Those gaps get wider, the surfaces wetter, but there's no turning back. They found that drowned boy, swept all the way to Lockport. And I learned my lovely pacific fleuve could be murderous. The epigraph to my new novel, "Ysak's Fable," in *Prairie Fire* ("Winnipeg in Fiction," Volume 20, Number 2) tries to capture the irony and complexity of an antediluvian, geologic Lake Agassiz overrun by a modern city.

AG: I wanted to talk about the North End a little. In some people's conception, the North End has become mythologized, almost sentimentalized.

JL: At my reading at the University of Manitoba I tried to make a distinction between sentiment and sentimentality, between remembering and flabby nostalgia. Do you know the late Chris Farley's shtick on *Saturday Night Live*, "Hey, remember . . . Hey remember when?" If one says "yah," then what? That kind of remembering is mindless, pointless, meaningless. True remembering fixes on a moment in the past, resurrects its dynamics, drama, complexities. Proust understood this best: memory preserves the past like an insect in amber, only something unwilled—a sound, a flavour, smell—releases that moment, changes mystery into revelation. The past is *experienced* in the present; everything is fresh and new. The act that brings Marcel's grandmother's death into the present is his bending down to tie his shoes, something she once did. A unique "jar of memory" is opened; he mourns his grandmother for the first time. Sentiment is awakened, not self-indulgent sentimentality, not time-killing nostalgia.

AG: You've lived all over the world—what about the North End except by virtue of having lived here and grown up here, what "busts out"?

JL: In T.S. Eliot's misreading of Joyce, archetypes are essential, forms from the past are needed to give shape to the—yawn yawn—diminished present. If Joyce writes a book called *Ulysses*, the character that represents Ulysses has to be a pitiful reduction of heroic Ulysses. But in Leopold Bloom Joyce has created a new "archetype," a wondrous mock hero for a world that has no other kind. Before I'd read Homer or really much of anything at all I encountered people in this city who remain fixed in memory, whose voices still sound in my ear, whose gestures still dance before me. These people to me were truly mythic; they needed no Ulysses, Job, or Jonah to give them shape. They were unique—unmanufactured, requiring no *prior* literary sanction. Those people taught me that possibility is never exhausted. Someone unique and wonderful can spring up—or be *imagined*—in the twinkling of an eye.

AG: Would your impression of this place, this very sensual image of who you are and what your surroundings are, have been the same if you'd grown up somewhere else?

JL: I have no idea. There were people of deep feeling in this city, with distinctive voices, cadences, fixes. This to me has always been a place of passion. And political ferment. And pressing economic realities. And, of course, those two rivers. When I was growing up I rarely encountered anybody who couldn't be politically located—wild-eyed Stalinists, theoretical Leninists, Trotskyists, Trotskyites, anarchists, Bundists, Nazis, fascists, every variety of European nationalist.

AG: So, at what age did you have to declare your allegiance, as it were?

JL: I never did. I've never been a joiner. That's why university fraternities seemed particularly absurd. I've been writing manifestos all my life, I think, but nobody was ever pressed to sign on. Allegiance to ideas is different: here and now, as then, I "declare . . . [my] allegiance" to fairness, justice, redress. In the opening pages of *Above Ground* (1968) the character Joshua is pristinely ignorant, the world's a blank. He has to learn to read its signs; everything is new and astonishing. My allegiance, like his, is to people, to places in space.

AG: You did join one community, the literary community.

JL: I'm part of the literary community because I'm a writer, a person committed to a writing life. I probably could have done other things but I knew very early that no matter what else I might do I would have to be somebody who wrote.

AG: Joining a community is more deliberate than that, I think. You can be a writer in isolation and publish and not be a part of the allegiances and support networks that are formed at things like literary conferences.

JL: That's true. I've helped found literary organizations, started school magazines, edited literary magazines without ever becoming part of this or that literary movement. I owe allegiance to my children, my grandchildren, to friends and family still living, and to those who are dead. One of my tasks as a writer is to preserve their uniqueness, celebrate them, allow them to break out of their Proustian jars.

AG: Why is it important for a writer to be involved in magazines?

JL: A writer is properly interested in writing—his own, her own, anybody's—and at the highest possible level. Talented people abound. They need encouragement; more than that, their stuff has to be published. That's what got me involved in magazines. When I was one of the editors of *The Noble Savage*, a mail truck dumped out tons of stuff. In the middle of one mass of manuscripts was something by someone called Thomas Pynchon, a section from what he turned into his wonderful novel *V*. There are a lot of talented people out there; it won't mean much unless their work is published.

AG: I wanted to ask you about the different phases of your career. You started out writing short stories, became a professor, founded magazines, went on to publish three novels, and got into sports journalism. Tell me about these phases—why did you reinvent yourself as a writer?

JL: In whatever I did—fiction, nonfiction—I wrote in the language of bustout, trying to write at the top of my bent. An editor used to journalistic stuff would balk, "Hey, what the hell is this?" The deal always was publish it as is. Or not at all. That particular exchange got tiring. Not very long ago I decided to bag non-fiction. Fiction is a way of telling it as it is. A true bustout.

AG: What did you do after 1976, after your last book, *The Five-Ring Circus*, was published?

JL: All kinds of things, above all, writing. And trying to absorb the double shock of my good Canadian friend and publisher, Jack McClelland, and my good American friend and publisher, Sam Vaughan, of Doubleday and then Random House, dropping out or being forced out of the publishing business. I properly trusted these two wonderful people; they were the dream publishers every writer wishes for, then their ventures ended. I haven't yet found their like. I hope I will. I've been working on novels and short stories I hope to publish in batches, leading off with the "Ysak's Fable" I read from at the Winnipeg International Writers Festival.

AG: When Margaret Laurence was writing about *Above Ground*, she said that the general theme was "a person who lives with the knowledge of the reality of death is a person who may be capable of living most fully." You were forty-six or thereabouts when you wrote *Above Ground*; three decades later, is this still something you subscribe to?

JL: What Margaret knew but didn't write about were medical predictions I would die at around the age of ten. That was then upped to fifteen. I've lived all these years under compound sentences of death. I would hope Margaret was right. That statement also applies to her.

AG: So what is survival to your characters? It seems to me that survival and making sense of it all become very important to the characters in your novels.

JL: It is. So is humour, so is the ability to recognize what is really happening, not take refuge in sentimentality or nostalgia. Another constant is a conviction that authority must be challenged—each and every day. I side with the powerless, the threatened, the coerced, with all those unable—for one reason or another—to say "fuck 'em."

AG: What's important to you now?

JL: Being engagé—work, family, love.

AG: Where would you put writing?

JL: That's the work, my work. I put it at the very top, it's a fix, a passion. I could no more think of not writing than of not hugging a child or grandchild.

Jack Ludwig's Winnipeg: Cold City, Warm People

N ear the end of Jack Ludwig's 1968 novel, *Above Ground*, his protagonist and narrator, Joshua, reflects sadly upon leaving his father's grave after the burial ceremony: "Burial should have covered both coffin and wound." I'm sure that many of us have felt similar sentiments after the death of a loved one. Inevitably, there are so many issues left unresolved, so many feelings and emotions left unexpressed, so many regrets. Such emotions, I think, are normal, and almost part of the human condition, but, should they be left unchecked, these emotions can transform into demons, jaundicing and perverting not only our memories of our loved ones, but also our thoughts and memories of everything surrounding our lives with those loved ones.

I was born and raised in Winnipeg, only three blocks north of the "Anderson Avenue perch" that Ludwig mentions in "Winnipeggers: Before and After *Dubliners*" as being so instrumental in forming his own perceptions of our mutual home town. I physically "left" Winnipeg some twenty-seven years ago, but the ghosts and demons of my rather unhappy childhood came with me and, rather than diminishing with time, were obstinately growing, thriving and multiplying in my mind. For several years I had told myself I would return to the old town, confront these ghosts and demons on their own turf, so to speak, and, like the audiences of the Classical tragedies of yore, experience a much needed catharsis. Finally, after much prodding from my wife (which culminated in her actually purchasing a plane ticket for me), I did return, only to find that the ghosts I had so long feared, the demons I had so long dreaded, had, like Hamlet's "solid flesh," melted, thawed and resolved themselves into a dew. The horrors were no longer there. The feelings of rage had, if anything, been replaced by a gentle sorrow. The place I had avoided for so many years finally came into proper perspective and I saw, perhaps for the first time, the vibrant, interesting city that no doubt played a huge role in forming my consciousness and perceptions. Again, Joshua's reflections after returning home near the end of *Above Ground* echoed my own feelings as I visited the old neighbourhood:

> I sat on the porch, lay on the couch to simulate the old seeing. The world outside was a door, a gate, a blank slide flashed on a screen while the show was preparing. No terror in it. No bad memory. The finite world fixed by the darkened houses across the street did not describe a universe which meant a thing to me. Two-dimensional memory, three-dimensional escape. (312)

It was, then, with a much more open mind, and with new personal perceptions of Winnipeg, that I began to consider Ludwig's portrayal of the Winnipeg that he knew. In her introduction to the McClelland & Stewart edition of *Above Ground*, Margaret Laurence comments on Ludwig's ability to "paint the picture of a specific place in incredibly few words, so that the reader can see and feel and hear the scene." Reading through the Winnipeg sections of Ludwig's novel, one almost walks the old neighbourhoods with Joshua, feeling the intense, oppressive heat, or the stinging, numbing cold. The sounds echo, rising and falling in the reality that belongs solely to memory; the smells waft and hang on the faint breeze, or are quickly dispersed by the stern north winds which have been gathering force unimpeded as they whistle across miles and miles of virtually surrealistic flatness. Joshua's initial meeting with the dark-haired, full-figured Zora ironically occurs on the night that he and Maggie announce their engagement and yet for me and, I would imagine, for many former and current Winnipeggers, the most memorable aspect of this encounter is Ludwig's wonderfully evocative description of a frigid winter night:

> Cold air stung my eyes.
> Tiny frost diamonds floated free of sidewalk cement. Heaped snowbanks shadowed the night in blue. A light fall had furred the lightpoles; snowstuck telephone cables looped over an icesheathed elm. Twigs cracked. In the cold clear air a freight shunting in the distant railyards sounded in the backyard. (93)

The novel's opening sentence not only hints that Joshua's romantic proclivities are part of his natural inheritance, but also that these proclivities will have to be exercised in a less than hospitable natural environment: "I was born in a cold city to a beautiful warm mother and a handsome father whose life began again every time he met a beautiful woman." The notion of the "cold city" emerges time and again as the novel progresses, taking such charming forms as the "rummy" who feigns illness every year so that he can spend the winter in the "Florida" of a nice warm hospital flat, or

Joshua's brother Gad, who adopts the name of "a boyhood hero, Scarface Al Capone" (30) and becomes Ruby Scarlatti so that he can pose as a Catholic and be admitted to the elite "Catholic Hockey League," or the character of Mr. Boyczuk, Joshua's neighbour, who enthusiastically pursues his perhaps unfortunate occupation as a fruit-tree grower, and who lovingly feeds his trees pigs' blood so that they might survive the harshness of the winter, and who is described as "rush[ing] the spring. Already digging. Storm-windows off" (40). In reference to this charming, enigmatic figure, Joshua says all it is necessary to say: "His trees bore fruit in summer."

Although the stereotypical picture of Winnipeg is one of deep-set, bone-chilling, unendingly cruel winters, Winnipeggers know that the summers can be just as extreme in the opposite direction. Memories of long, hot, humid summer days, days that almost force a trek to the beach, remain fresh in all Winnipeggers' minds. The hilarious account of Dobrushyn magnanimously offering Uncle Bim's relatives transportation to the beach, even though Bim and Dobrushyn carried on a life-long feud, perhaps indicates that the power of the weather transcends petty personal concerns. (Of course, Bibul, schoolmate of Joshua's and aspiring rabbi, will later drown in a YMCA pool, the last refuge from an unbelievably hot New York summer day). Other references to summer heat abound. Wilkoh Joe is described as having a face "burned red from the sun" (26), and almost his first words in the novel are "Terrible hot. I sweat" (27). Joshua's final image of his father, as Joshua, his wife and baby leave Winnipeg to start a new life on the West Coast, emphasizes the effect of the heat on both the land and its inhabitants:

> My father beside a burnt-out patch of brown grass, imprinting my mind and my imagination, his tanned hand waving, his tanned face under white hair, all of him bent, straightening up then, more and more land and less and less him in this rear-view mirror, till his image blurred away in a shimmer of heat. (46)

Perhaps in memory this intense, burning, intrusive summer heat tends to take precedence, but the other, gentler aspects of summer also linger, at times reasserting themselves in all their glory. As a child, I used to revel in the opportunity to "camp out" on our porch, a rare treat allowed by my rather stern grandmother only when the air in our old, stale apartment seemed even more old and stale because of the oppressive heat. Joshua mentions, in passing, that he also was allowed to sleep on the porch "on hot nights." Perhaps this was a more common event for some, I don't know, but I still vividly remember the sense of adventure and excitement I felt, being seven or eight, and camping "alone" (even though help, should it be needed, was only a shout away). Joshua also connects some of the most tender moments of his courtship of

Maggie with the warm and *gentle* summer. The first time he kisses Maggie, for example, occurs in "softest summer, and winged insects made soft whisperings around pendant streetlamps" (63), and their idyllic, overnight, lakeside lovemaking occurs on an August night, "when air was warm as a desert" (75).

Ludwig, then, very successfully evokes memories of these two extreme seasons, but for many Winnipeggers perhaps the transitional seasons of spring and fall are the seasons most cherished. After the desolate winters of Winnipeg, the traditional metaphor of spring representing growth and renewal becomes much more than a metaphor; it is a hope, seemingly futile in January and February, now realized, now brought concretely to reality by melting snow, burgeoning buds and greening grass. The scars of winter heal, the restraints of winter drop away, and life once again has meaning and promise. The young Joshua's description of his hospital environment, now somewhat revitalized by the season, captures this feeling:

> Soon it was spring. Free of bandages, strings, weights, pulleys. My scars were healing. A spring of nurses came to the ward. The man with the zither played recognizable Neapolitan tunes. The railroad foreman's daughter ran off with a jockey. The prison guard kissed his wife for one whole visiting hour.
>
> I loved a nurse whose hair smelled of the sea. (17)

If spring is a metaphor for growth and renewal, then fall must metaphorically represent impending death, and yet, for me, the memories of gentle fall days in Winnipeg, wafting breezes around my head; many-coloured leaves crunching under my feet and leaves clinging to half-bare trees, are pleasant memories indeed. I remember most vividly my father, a romantic and charming Irishman, every fall proclaiming "The melancholy days are here, / The saddest of the year," as he and I would walk for hours along the paths bordering the Red and Assiniboine rivers. Winnipeg is a city of trees, and hence a city of leaves. Joshua's description of scurrying home on a rainy fall night illustrates once again Ludwig's ability to evoke vivid pictures in a few words:

> Hurried home over damp leafpapered streets . . . , when the rain had stopped and air was warm. Red car lights winked off and on in standing pools glazing the streets. Tiny dark raindrops caught the light on leaves. Bark looked shiny, beautiful, fit to eat. (51)

Tom Russell, a contemporary folk singer whom I very much admire, has written a song entitled "Winnipeg." Perhaps predictably, the song begins with the line "How's the weather in Winnipeg?" and then continues to describe the more desolate aspects of a Winnipeg winter. The stereotype is clear; for most people, winter and Winnipeg are synonymous. Of course, any Winnipegger knows that weather and Winnipeg are synonymous, and that weather very much depends upon the seasons. Winnipeggers are, by necessity, acutely aware of the weather peculiar to each season, not just winter, and any accurate portrayal of Winnipeg must convey this notion. Ludwig, in Above Ground, is very successful in this regard.

But Ludwig not only describes the natural environment of Winnipeg, he also vividly describes the neighbourhoods in which Joshua grows to maturity, and the characters who frequent these neighbourhoods. Seeing that both Joshua and the young Jack Ludwig were incapacitated early in their lives due to serious hip injuries, it seems likely that Ludwig based many, if not all, of Joshua's early impressions of his neighbourhood on personal experience. Joshua speaks early in the novel of how, when he was carried to the verandah window, his world became essentially a "framed world," a world composed of "milkmen, breadmen, phonemen, deliverymen, neighbors" (20). Naturally, because of his incapacitation, the young Joshua became extremely sensitive to and aware of the scene passing outside his window. Like a viewer totally engrossed in a compelling play, Joshua became one with this world:

> I could almost see blades of grass lengthen. I knew every spill of tar on the road, the stain of dripping oil. I knew who had thrown what cigarette cardboard where, and what car ran over it when. I lived the routines of sparrows and robins, believed in their choices. I read wind in the motion of trees, rain in the darkening of clouds. A candy wrapper blown on stage was the gallop-past of a horse and strange rider. (20)

Eventually, Joshua's hip heals sufficiently for him to expand the horizons of his world, and he ventures outside the framed confines of the verandah. Descriptions of "peanut park," Joshua's elementary school (complete with bully), his high school, a Greek's street vendor's wagon selling fried potatoes and hot dogs, and a myriad of other things combine to produce a very vivid picture of North End Winnipeg in the nineteen-thirties. But perhaps most vivid is Joshua's description of the scene in the centre of town—Main Street:

> I came out one day and discovered a world. The city square. Politics shrilled there; the Salvation Army, pawnshops, beerjoints, a bank, a fourth-run moviehouse, a commercial hotel, three fleabag flops, the town's toughest newsie, his three vanquished rivals, a band of beggars, rummies, whores, pimps, chippies, gigolos, Seventh Day Adventists, Jehovah's Witnesses, pushers of *Pravda, Der Sturmer,* dope, nuns who were mendicants, riot-helmeted policemen, Chinese cooks, Negro barbecuers, Italian barbers, Jewish second-handclothiers, toughs, hoods, torpedos, rollersofdrunks, bookies, runners, marks,

retired railroaders, tourists, schoolkids, sometimes the Mayor, his council, taxcollectors,

landassessors, strikebreakers, lumberjacks, social workers, nymphs, dietfaddists,

psychologists, insurancemen, morticians, Don Giovannis, Faustuses, Medeas,

Cyranos, Tartuffes, Clytemnestras, punks, dolls, queans.

There I saw a husband swear at his wife.

There I saw a Communist blame the Depression on the bosses.

There I saw a young girl zip her dress half-down for one ready-made cigarette. The

second took her three-quarters down.

There I saw a drunk try to stop an oncoming police van with an arc of urine. A police-

man swung his nightstick. (49)

It is this image of Main Street, in all its tattered and frayed glory, in all its sordid and tacky vivacity, that lives on in the memory of all Winnipeggers of a certain age. As Ludwig himself says, "In the imagination Main Street is invincible, as impervious as Golden Boy, the Red River, the Thames, the Liffey, to the transitory encroachments of urban renewal" ("You Always Go Home Again").

In an interview conducted in the early 1970s, Ludwig comments that Winnipeg "stands as a metaphor of vitality" ("Speaking of Winnipeg"), and certainly this vitality, life and energy come through vividly as Ludwig describes Winnipeg during the Depression years. Ironically, perhaps, the vitality inherent in this description is matched only by a description of midtown Winnipeg during wartime:

Midtown swarmed with servicemen. A Ceylon airman with polished wood face

shone under a flashing yellow safety light at my car stop. I got off the trolley, three Aussie

airmen linked arms and swerved in front of the tram. The motorman clanged. A white-

helmeted head leaned out of an airforce patrol car to curse.

At the corner drunk sailors sank in snow. A Royal Navy hat lay upside down on a dirt-

crust bank. Cockney voices shouted. Someone started a Maori warchant. Harsh laughing

drowned it out.

Closer to the hotel I heard heavy boots crunch ice in rapid cracktroop beat, rattling man-

hole covers, scraping bare patches of cement. Gloved hands swinging, a sweep of maroon

berets headed for the beerparlor, their high paratrooper boots shiny brown and wet.

Khaki uniforms flowed into the hotel, and out, on two conveyer belts, palefaces in,

redskins out. Two sailors fenced in the middle of the street, clashing snowshovel on

snowshovel.

Under the hotel canopy an elegantly dressed man shielded a whitegowned woman

behind him while the doorman puffed his cheeks to whistle up a civvy cab. (110)

The irony in this description stems from the reader's knowledge that Winnipeg, at this time, is essentially "a mourning city." As the war drags on and casualties mount, Winnipeggers, initially so unaffected by the war, now daily hear news of loved ones who will not be returning, and the houses of the war dead are marked by Xs on the doors. The most feared person in the city becomes the telegraph boy, "who told of death [as he] passed frequently on his bike. He wore a uniform of charcoal, with shiny belted leather gaiters, and whistled tunelessly" (121).

And yet, the spirit and vitality of Winnipeggers remain, and that spirit and vitality, that essential joy in existence, is clearly reflected in the characters that Ludwig presents. Readers quickly get to know the irrepressible Uncle Bim, who is so full of life and energy that he makes all whom he meets "want to devour life" (6), and his own vital essence is so infectious that "He made you want to wrap your arms around spring greenness, imprison in your ear the cry of waking birds, love and be loved by a loving lovely girl" (6). Next, we encounter Bim's somewhat distant relation, but full-time feuding partner, Dobrushyn, who, despite his airs and delusions of grandeur, is still described as a man of "wit, . . . charm, . . . vitality, [and] . . . wise worldly ways" (24), as well as being a man of genuine culture and style: "He played the flute beautifully, and danced a dashing Russian waltz. He loved to give presents, flowers, chocolates, perfumes. He couldn't keep his hands off beautiful women." (26)

Other vividly realized, vital, life-embracing characters abound, but perhaps the most memorable of all is the incomparable Bibul. Schoolmate of Joshua's, peddler of fruit in a particularly downtrodden Winnipeg slum, and aspiring rabbi, Bibul is also a worldly-wise philosopher, scorning the abstract intellectualizing of his fellow students ("A lot them kids know about life" [66]), and realizing that one does what is necessary to survive. And so, without complaint, Bibul and his horribly (but humorously) dilapidated horse Malkeh, pulling an equally dilapidated cart full of dilapidated fruit, venture into the dilapidated neighbourhood of the dilapidated but formidable foes—housewives out for a bargain:

> Women old, women worn out, women in nightgowns at four in the afternoon, hair uncombed, feet in their husbands' wide felt slippers, hands deep in pockets. Into their slums Malkeh dragged that creak of a wagon, in front of houses that sagged against each other, crazy-angled, insubstantial as playing cards. Gates listed at the angle of Bibul's wagon; dry, cracking wood fences leaned in quits toward the ground, begging like bent old men in sight of their graves to be allowed to fall the rest of the way. Windows were tarpaperpatched, like pirate's eyes.
>
> The women waited behind doors. (68-9)

The description of Bibul duelling with these women, verbally ("Give here back them oranges. Shame! Where's restraint?" [69]) and even physically ("The whitehaired old lady reached for a fistful of cherries. Bibul's hand clamped on her wrist" [70]) is one of the highlights of the novel. Even though Bibul genuinely sympathizes with the terrible living conditions that these women endure, he realizes that he, too, must survive. His realistic philosophy is epitomized in his comment to one particularly aggressive potential customer: "Missus, my heart'll break better for your troubles if you don't steal plums while you cry" (70).

The death of Bibul is reported, largely without comment, in *Above Ground*, but in "Requiem for Bibul," the earlier short story upon which this portrait of Bibul is based, Ludwig says more about his feelings of loss over the disappearance of Bibul, characters like him, and the Winnipeg in which they lived:

> Through the streets old Malkeh drew that creaking wagon urged on by leather-capped Bibul, chrome-trimmed cars speed in unending gaggle, their sport-capped, stylishly-hatted drivers in control of power the equivalent of four hundred un-Malkeh horses. The Mayor tells Winnipeggers to "Think Big," bid for the Pan-American Games, hang out more flags and buntings. Slums like Bibul's "island" and the City Hall are fortunately doomed: Winnipeg is obviously a better place to live in.
>
> Who doesn't welcome prosperity?
>
> But the fact remains: I cannot find Bibul's like in Winnipeg today. . . .
>
> When the City Hall is torn down they will build Winnipeg a new one; but where, O where shall we find more Bibuls? (*Ten for Wednesday Night* 120)

The lament for a changing and changed Winnipeg articulated here is one that is probably shared by a number of present and former Winnipeggers, yet one can take some consolation from the point that Ludwig so strongly makes in "You Always Go Home Again" (*Mosaic* 107-11) The true reality, the authentic forms, dwell in the imagination, and ultimately "the imagination as memory won't settle for sentimental reminiscing, or self-indulging nostalgia." I realized after my last visit to Winnipeg that many of my personal ghosts, my personal fears, my personal antipathy towards the city, were largely the results of self-indulgence. My last visit to Winnipeg reminded me that my *spiritus mundi*, my storehouse of images, like Ludwig's, "feels most at home in Winnipeg—even now." My reading of Ludwig's *Above Ground* could not have come at a more appropriate time for me, and I thank him sincerely for sharing so many of his "images stored deep down inside."

WORKS CITED

Laurence, Margaret. Introduction. *Above Ground* by Jack Ludwig. Toronto: McClelland & Stewart, 1974. N.p.

Ludwig, Jack. *Above Ground*. Toronto: Little, Brown and Company, 1968.

———. Interview with Terry Campbell. In *Speaking of Winnipeg*, ed. John Parr. Winnipeg: Queenston House, 1974, 96-107.

———. "Requiem for Bibul." In *Ten for Wednesday Night*, ed. Robert Weaver. Toronto: McClelland & Stewart, 1961. Rpt. by Book Society Searchlight. Gen. eds. T.H. Cassidy and Hugh D. McKellar. Agincourt, 1967.

———. "Winnipeggers: Before and After *Dubliners*." In *A Political Art: Essays and Images in Honour of George Woodcock*, ed. William H. New. Vancouver: University of British Columbia Press, 1978, 3-14.

———. "You Always Go Home Again." *Mosaic* 3, no. 3 (Spring 1970): 107-11.

Russell, Tom. "Winnipeg." Perf. Tom Russell Band. *Hurricane Season*. Stony Plain, 1991.

reflections of

A. E. van Vogt

The Autobiography of a Science Fiction Giant
With a Complete Bibliography

Surrational Dreams: A.E. van Vogt and Mennonite Science Fiction

So also are the times of the Most High: the beginnings are manifest in wonders and mighty works, and the end in requital and in signs.
— II Esdras, 9:6

Science fiction is just fantasy wearing a tight girdle.
— Sam Merwin, Jr.

During the late forties and early fifties, this Manitoban was the most popular science fiction writer in the world, surpassing Isaac Asimov, Arthur C. Clarke and Robert Heinlein. His books have been translated worldwide and his reputation remains undimmed in Europe and South America. He is the acknowledged forerunner of SF giants like Philip K. Dick. His paranoiac storylines and exploration of interfaces between technology, mind and physiology presage cyberpunks like William Gibson, Bruce Sterling and Michael Swanwick. The movie *Alien* uses the plot of one of his most popular short stories. Yet today A.E. van Vogt is an obscure figure in Canada and the United States, not extensively discussed among the greats of the Golden Age of Science Fiction, an era he typified in many ways. His books still sell, but he's forgotten, critically. What happened?

He was born in 1912, just outside Gretna, Manitoba. Much of his childhood was spent in Neville, Saskatchewan, where his father practised law. The family moved, first to Morden and finally to Winnipeg, where he spent his teenage years.

He was a precocious child, skipping two grades and entering Kelvin Technical High School at age thirteen. Because of the Depression, though, he couldn't go to university. He worked at a number of odd jobs while refining his writing skills, selling romance stories, radio plays and articles at a number of outlets. In 1939 he met and married Edna Mayne Hull, a writer from Brandon. He tried to enlist for the war effort, but was rejected because of poor eyesight. After stints in Ottawa and Toronto, the couple moved to Los Angeles in 1944, where his career took off. He was a long-time resident of Hollywood and his last book was published in 1985.

That's the usual bio material. Van Vogt's early life and career are more interesting in light of one crucial fact: he was born Alfred Elton Vogt to Mennonite parents, not Dutch, as has been reported. (Calling himself Dutch wasn't exactly deceitful. It's common Mennonite practice, justified both by the broad usage of "Dutch" to mean anyone of Germanic origin—as in Pennsylvania Dutch—and the fact that many Mennonite families originated in the Netherlands. The Vogts, however, are not one of these; the name comes from Southern Germany and Switzerland.)

The "van" was added prior to World War II, no doubt to escape anti-German prejudice. The change was probably not Alfred's idea, at least not solely. His entire immediate family became "van Vogts" and his nephews and nieces have always known themselves by that name. The idea may have come from the agent's position his father Heinrich (later Henry) had once had with the Holland-America Line.

But does it matter? Dutch or Mennonite, what difference does that make for a science fiction writer, really? To answer that we have to speak of Prairie Mennonite life in general and make a number of inferences about that environment's effect on van Vogt in particular.

During the twenties and thirties, towns and farms in southern Saskatchewan and Manitoba seethed with conflicts and disparities. Some came with homesteading: the land was rich, but farmers contended with hail, flood, pests and finally, prolonged drought and avaricious corporate power. Others were peculiar to the time: the Prairies never really shared the twenties boom to the same extent as the East. The crash hit here even harder, coming on top of dry years and catastrophic soil erosion. Winnipeg's political climate was poisoned by memories of the disastrous General Strike of 1919, and trust of authorities was at a historic low. The grain belt was an ideological pressure cooker. The Canadian Commonwealth Federation, Social Credit Party and Ku Klux Klan were all organizing within the region. Van Vogt's work would embody this bubbling political cauldron.

Prairie Mennonites were a tough and peculiar breed, *Plattdeutsch* (Low German)-speaking Anabaptists whose origins lay in the civil wars of the Reformation. While many came of urban, burgher stock, most became farmers and ran small, rural businesses. Persecuted in the Low Countries, they'd been given land in Ukraine (which they called "Russia") by Catherine the Great, who needed hard-working settlers. They and their children prospered, often becoming wealthy landowners, *kulaks*, and exciting the envy and hatred of their Slavic servants and neighbours. They started arriving in western Canada during the 1870s and after World War I, in the wake of persecution.

Mennonitism had its own currents and tensions: while they were farmers with co-operative traditions, they could do sharp business, both among themselves and with others. Idealists and pacifists, charity organizers and contributors, they were shrewd, conservative traders, not averse to exploiting Anglo or Ukrainian unwariness. A clannish people whose views were shaped by a history of martyrdom and tyranny, they presented a united front to outsiders. Yet internally they were riven with doctrinal splits and formed new sects constantly.

Social life centred on the church, whose influence was augmented by radio broadcasts from Chicago's Moodie Bible Institute. Apocalyptic preaching was central to programs from this fundamentalist institution. Sermons by Moodie-influenced travelling ministers like N.F. Toews and J.J. Balzer were in much the same vein. The twenties and thirties were a golden age for this evangelical stream: it was an era of mass migrations, crop failures, unemployment and imminent war. Many couldn't find jobs or pay their mortgages, but they could get to church. Radio had a vast, new audience, eager, yet frightened, to hear what was going on in the world. To believers, news of calamities in Europe and in their new home were tidings of the Last Days.

At the same time Moodie sermons accented self-reliance and positive thinking. The twenties and thirties also saw the beginnings of what would become the motivational industry. One way self-help salesmen like Dale Carnegie and Earl Nightingale got their message across was through Protestant denominations, whose teachings stressed individual faith. Many inspirational tracts were written by clerics; "Acres of Diamonds," by Pastor Russell H. Conwell, was one of the most popular. The tone was upbeat, the message plain. Success and wisdom were the same thing, reached by simple means: following well-defined, numbered steps to clear goals. History and Freud were bunk; what mattered was do-it-yourself mental discipline.

Van Vogt's work is strongly imbued with millenarianism, Nietzschean elitism (in uneasy coexistence with populist idealism) and faith in new, superior ways of thinking. *Slan*, his best-known book, takes place after a cataclysmic war. Humanity is on the decline, technologically moribund, genetically increasingly sterile, impoverished and dispirited. The hero and heroine are Homo Superior, Slans, brilliant, telepathic mutants with superhuman strength and speed. Nine- and eleven-year-old Jommy and Kathleen are mercilessly hunted and marked for death by humans. How they triumph is a coming-of-age story told in plot reversals, chase scenes and conspiracies, marked by dark atmosphere and sudden, dizzy lyricism.

Ever the methodical do-it-yourselfer, van Vogt wrote *Slan* and his other fiction, not, as many writers might, by slowly groping toward his own approach, but by using an idea of plotting out of *The Only Two Ways to Write a Short Story*, a book by John Gallishaw he found in the Winnipeg Public Library. It's a sort of "Theory of Complication," in which a story is simply a collection of scenes, averaging eight hundred words per scene. As he explains in a lecture, later printed: "Every scene has a purpose, which is stated near the beginning . . . and that purpose is either accomplished, or not accomplished by the end of the scene."

And that's pretty much it, save that a story needs at least one subplot. He doesn't say so, but we're left to suppose that narrative depends on the impetus, variety and shock of its "complications" and conjunctions. The writer as crazed taxi driver, constantly pulling off near misses and high-speed turns while juggling china plates. He gets you there, but it's a memorable ride. Van Vogt seems to have developed, without aesthetic theorizing, a narrative futurism that depends on a poetry of disorienting juxtaposition, speed, power and technology (both physical and mental), rather than consistency and verisimilitude.

Mechanically, his novels' discontinuities stem from the way they were first published in pulp magazines like *Astounding Science Fiction* and *Amazing Stories*. Most are what van Vogt refers to as "fix-ups," discrete short stories loosely tied together with alterations and linking material.

So what's wrong with "complication"? It's a tad formulaic, but seems workable for writing multi-viewpoint serials, as indeed he was. What it doesn't talk about, and many have accused van Vogt of neglecting, is unities of form. SF was (and is) a conservative field in some ways. Critics wanted blue sky what-iffing anchored in logical chains of events, believable motivations and well-crafted storylines. Van Vogt, they said, gave you none of these. Further, they charged, he was skimpy on characterization, stylistically slapdash, cared little for building textured, nuanced worlds and hadn't a clue about real science.

A few of these cavils are dead-on. Some don't matter. Many are actually *strengths*. Critics and literary readers scorn van Vogt for his leaky constructions, but have never accounted for his appeal, particularly among younger readers. It's not, for example, violence; he isn't graphic and ten of his books don't stack up half the corpses of ten minutes at an arcade game.

What van Vogt delivers is paranoia and wonder, motifs of adolescence for which you and I, dear reader, are too sophisticated. Aren't we? *Slan*, for example, isn't really a tale of the far distant future, but a breakneck *bildungsroman* that pits the New, glowing, fragile and infinitely deserving, against the corrupt, piteous old of the (barely disguised) Depression:

The mop missed because he caught its shadow just in time to duck.

"Ten thousand dollars!" she screamed after him. "The radio said ten thousand. And it's mine, do you hear? Don't nobody touch him. He's mine. I saw him first."

. . . A fear came that he would be smashed by mops and hoes and brooms and rakes, his head beaten, his bones crushed, flesh mashed. Swaying, he rounded the rear corner of the tenement. . . . He felt . . . the turgid thoughts that streamed from them.

In all the fear and suffering there are luminous moments:

A thousand feet it reared and then it merged into a tower that soared another five hundred feet into the heavens. Stupendous tower! Half a thousand feet of jewellike lacework that seemed almost fragile, sparkling there with all the colors of the rainbow, a translucent, shining, fantastic thing, built in the noble style of the old days; not merely ornamental . . . it was ornament in itself.

Like that of many of his other books, *Slan*'s plot is tense, intricate and doesn't add up. There's just no logical way van Vogt's factions and characters would do everything they do. Yet his best books work, just as The Big Sleep works, when even Raymond Chandler couldn't account for some plot twists: by sheer paranoid drive. Van Vogt heroes are usually only one jump ahead of vast forces and murky cabals.

Persecution and embattlement motifs run throughout Mennonite history, from their sectarian origins, through the siege of Münster, the long sojourn in "Russia" and into the twentieth century. Partly this is the natural and indeed healthy tendency of people who, even in good times, had to contend with bands of marauding Cossacks and Tartars, and a not-always-friendly peasantry.

But there is a subtler, yet more pervasive, way Anabaptist society preserved its wary, even paranoiac isolation. Ask any Mennonite what distinguishes them and the phrase "in the world, but not of it" will come up. It sounds like a bromide; other denominations will say the same. But Mennonites have taken this creed quite seriously; being Mennonite is struggling to make peace with, or root out, "worldliness."

The central drama of this industrious, adaptable people is the conflict between the drive for self-advancement, on one hand, and an idealistic faith and communitarian ethos, on the other. The very qualities that made them desirable colonists led to schism and emigration, as hard work and enterprise inexorably tied them into the worldly power structure of their adopted lands. Time and again Mennonites have bumped up against the authorities, emigrated to Russia, to Latin America, to Canada, and why? To escape, not just persecution (minimal in the nineteenth-century Russian

Empire), but a more constant dread, assimilation by the polities around them, and with it, entanglement in the ways of the world.

There is a dualistic, even Manichaean, quality to the sectarian mind: Mennonite history is rife with schisms over doctrinal points that often seem insignificant to mainstream Christians, as believers struggled to maintain their own purity while guarding against agents of contamination, even (or especially) those most like them. With no centralized clergy, only schism or renunciation could resolve such quarrels.

Mennonite faith and unity, then, were constantly both strengthened and eroded from within and without, as friends and relatives were lost to the worldly (or the overly zealous) against the backdrop of a seductive larger society that could turn hostile at any time. Small groups of believers drew ever inward for their faith and resources.

And if there is one thing uniting van Vogt protagonists, Jommy Cross in *Slan*, Robert Hedrock in the Weapon Shop series, Nat Cemp in *The Silkie* and others, it's that they are embattled, pitted against vast forces, men fortified and separated by their superior knowledge and capacities. Their difference sustains van Vogt's heroes, even as they are persecuted for it.

These themes of alienation and battle against the odds tie in well with a lot of Boy's Own stories, including the one van Vogt read before he embarked upon *Slan*, E.T. Seton's *Biography of a Grizzly*, where a powerful bear wins out against human encroachment.

But van Vogt offers more to young readers: we all, especially as adolescents, deal with situations in which we can discern no good reasons for what people do, what life is. But we have to get through, somehow. We get help. We figure things out. We pretend. We dream: van Vogt's best work has an oneiric quality. But they are dreams of a very special kind, ones that insist, all evidence to the contrary, that actions, particularly the hero's actions, are logical, that seemingly disparate events are causally linked. Many van Vogt stories are wish-fulfillment *Measure for Measure* from the Duke's perspective; the hero succeeds, not through his trumpeted logic, but because he embodies a higher order.

It is this faith in a higher rationality (paranoia's flip side) beyond what the story's schema can really convey, a sort of surrationality, that marks van Vogt's work. Surrationalism informs the gadgets and "scientific" principles he invents ceaselessly, dreamily ignoring his editor John W. Campbell's pious exhortations that SF be based on sound scientific principles, dammit!, while keeping the firm jaw, clear glance and big jargon real scientists need.

Many van Vogt gimmicks have a homely touch; in *The Weapon Shops of Isher* a character winds up on a kind of temporal teeter-totter with a fortress the protagonists need to shift out of their time. Since his mass is so much less, he needs to go much further ahead and back than the building, on ever increasing swings. One of the book's dilemmas is what to do with all the "time energy" he accumulates. *Slan*'s disintegrator gun, ultra-tough "ten-point" steel and hypno-crystals are based on a plausible, wholly bogus, "atomic tension" principle of physics.

Van Vogt read and wrote when miracles seemed both near and just out of reach. Horses still pulled milk carts, but other galaxies had been seen, quantum mechanics formulated, neutrinos postulated and positrons found. Depression-era scientists made new elements and saw new worlds with electron microscopes. As a physicist, Campbell and other scientist-writers kept readers abreast of the newest wonders. The future was around the corner and had about as much truck with conventional wisdom as Schrödinger's Cat had with common sense.

A child of hard times, van Vogt lived at home till he was twenty-three. He got by as a clerk, thresher crewman, trucker and trapper. But his eyes were on the stars. In the fan clubs that sprang up as soon as Farnsworth Wright put out the first issue of *Weird Tales* in 1923, he was among his own kind, young men who couldn't wait for the Age of Miracles. When *Astounding Science Fiction*, the field's leading mag, did an audience survey they found their average reader was a young man in his late twenties, just short of a degree in science or a technical field. By and large, readers had little to do with organized religion or the humanistic ethos of mainstream literature. They worshipped instead, in David Hartwell's phrase, at the "Church of Wonder," setting their wildest imaginings, their fondest "scientific" misprisions in, say, 1994. Because *someday it might be true*.

Many van Vogt devices are straight wish-fulfillment; his stories are chockablock with infallible talking lie-detectors, immortal heroes, spy rays, instant hypnosis and faster-than-light travel. *The Weapon Shops* and its prequel, *The Weapon Makers*, have an immortal hero who founds a chain of gun shops to deal arms that only fire in self-defence. As such the weapon shops are a bulwark against tyranny and exploitation, usually in the form of the banks and bureaucracy of the Imperial House of Isher.

Critics have assailed van Vogt for anachronism and anti-democratic tendencies; his futures have a lot of autocracy and royalty in them, and often this is just a given. In *The Half Men* he attempts to explain that hereditary titles don't really mean much, but it sounds pretty thin in a story of struggle and romance between two space-going aristocrats. Keir Gray, the charismatic ruler in 1940's *Slan*, is a world dictator (and secret slan) with vaguely fascist overtones.

Partly this is just the self-invented hybrid form van Vogt works in: the Crypto-Fable of Science Miraculous. We usually stock fairy tales with princesses and potentates, not committee chairs.

But there is something to the critiques. Some central van Vogt concerns revolve around political authority and legitimacy. In *The Voyage of the Space Beagle*, Grosvenor, the young Nexialist (a van Vogt scientific generalist) is a typical protagonist: he overcomes SF-type crises with his new, better way of thinking. Grosvenor has the answers when the spaceship encounters hostile aliens. But he's a young practitioner of a novel, little-known discipline. Nobody listens. (*Voyage*'s popularity may be due, in part, to Grosvenor's resemblance to a young, socially marginal SF fan.)

Under repeated attack from without, the ship is also in danger from within, from a megalomaniac department head and repressed hostilities freed by aliens' psychic onslaughts:

> . . . two men were wrestling each other with a life-and-death concentration. They paid no
> attention to Grosvenor, but swayed and strained and cursed. The sound of their breath-
> ing was loud.
> . . . Whatever world of hallucination they were in, it had taken profoundly.

To avert bedlam and extinction, Grosvenor has to save the huge, bureaucratic hierarchy of the ship by gaining political clout and eventually taking over, which he does with a van Vogt combination of cunning, highhandedness and Weird Science. Time and again, van Vogt protagonists stand heroically between community and chaos, armed with their wits and magical powers. They are not, by and large, democrats.

To writers who lived through Depression poverty and social breakdown, there were two conflicting paths to salvation. One was mass action, espoused by socialists like Clifford Odets and Dorothy Livesay. The other was individualistic, exemplified on the one hand by Paris-based modernist explorers of Self, like Henry Miller and Ezra Pound, and on the other by prophets of technocracy like van Vogt, Isaac Asimov and Robert A. Heinlein, young men who wrote for pulps like *Astounding, Amazing* and *Thrilling Wonder Stories*.

Significantly, much of the SF scene revolved around Los Angeles, where van Vogt and E. Mayne Hull moved in 1944. In the mid-century, if New York was the New World, the broker between Europe and America, L.A. was the Future, free of history's entanglement, culture's *terra incognita*. In New York they read James Joyce, joined the Party and got analyzed. In LA they read palms, went to Hollywood parties and got tan. Angelenos could be *intellectuals* without joining the *intelligentsia*.

A socially conservative Mennonite, with his people's persecution-bred wariness of mass action, van Vogt was at home in LA, the ultimate individualist non-city. As a technical school graduate, he flourished in an environment that had no use for programmatic European culture. In this he was part of a long line of American intellectual tinkerers, autodidacts who grabbed onto whatever looked interesting to build their theories.

People who don't follow SF (in fanspeak, "mundane" readers) have a hard time crediting the intellectual ambition at home in even the cheapest Golden Age rags, with covers featuring Scantily-Clad Maidens Menaced by Bugeyed Monsters. Some of the prose is gawky, plots creaky, humour corny. But there are plenty of writers bursting with ideas, and they want to tell you all about them.

Here, too, van Vogt fits right in. As Algis Budrys, a writer and noted critic in the field, quipped: "Every time you open something new by Vogt, you think 'Uh, oh . . . he's read another book!'" Van Vogt leans toward right-wing, libertarian and populist theories; Korita, the anthropologist in *Voyage*, lectures everyone about alien cultures in terms straight out of Spengler's *Decline of the West*. *Empire of the Atom*'s plot comes directly from *I, Claudius*. In *The Anarchistic Colossus* Earth is a libertarian society under alien attack. When (rarely) van Vogt touches upon economics, he seems influenced by the Social Credit doctrine spread by the party of his Prairie youth. From *The Weapon Makers* on, van Vogt money usually comes in "credits."

Significantly, Ayn Rand's circle was on the ascendant in Hollywood, where she worked as a scriptwriter, when van Vogt got there in 1944. Her blend of right-wing romanticism finds many echoes in his work. The Weapon Shop series, particularly, embodies many Rand tenets.

Van Vogt was also interested in cybernetics and fringe science. In *Colossus,* peaceful anarchy is maintained through a system of "Kirlian" computers. In the foreword van Vogt acknowledges that according to some authorities Kirlian photography (which purportedly gives pictures of objects' and people's auras) has been discredited, but he doesn't buy that. His computers sense violent impulses before crimes take place and zap evildoers unconscious.

So it's not surprising, given his locale and preoccupations, that van Vogt espoused ideas that could be labelled surrational. The first was General Semantics, whose formulator, a Count Alfred Korzybski, claimed to have discovered a linguistic method by which people could liberate themselves from Aristotelian shackles. Null-A or $\overline{A}$, as its Polish inventor termed it, was designed to counteract what he regarded as Aristotle's primary legacy to Western thought: a bipolar, black-or-white value system. Korzybski's disciples argued that the gradient values described somewhat abstrusely in his book *Science and Sanity* would solve many of the world's problems.

For a time, Null-A was a runaway intellectual growth industry, especially in California. Believers testified that $\overline{A}$ had cured all sorts of things, from insecurity and drug use to homosexuality. Its faddish popularity may have been due to timing;

Korzybski became well known around the end of World War II, when many were weary of the all-inclusive antinomies that had ruled their lives for the past few years. To the Right, A̅, as well, offered an alternative to Marxist dialectics. To van Vogt it may have been a way of escaping the dualistic psychology of his sectarian background.

Having taken up the torch in 1945, though, with *The World of Null-A* and three years later, *The Pawns of Null-A,* van Vogt plunged back into Manichaean conspiracy. The protagonist of both books, Gilbert Gosseyn (Go Sane) is a typical hero: a man with preternatural powers (including a second brain and immortality via cloning) who is amnesiac and enmeshed in a cosmic plot of Byzantine complexity. He must find himself, thus saving Earth (and colonized Venus) from alien invasion, while preserving their A̅ utopias.

Critics and some readers complained that the books were confusing, plot-wise, which seems an odd charge to level at a writer whose most popular, acclaimed stories had never been bound by strict congruence. More importantly, there was a consensus that they lacked the emotional resonance that animated his earlier work; *Null-A* plot twists seemed arbitrary, motivations perfunctory, dialogue unconvincing.

Some of this may have been due to the enormous cultural sea change in the US and Europe at the war's ending. Roosevelt was dead, Churchill out, Stalin not Uncle Joe any more, nor yet The Enemy. Readers were looking for greater psychological complexity, more of the emotional grey-scale non-Aristotelianism pointed to, but that van Vogt didn't really explore.

But the books are a falling off. In his haste to move Gosseyn through the tangled, allegorical plot, van Vogt neglects two of his strengths. First, Gosseyn's foes aren't given enough time or weight, their plans not made sufficiently ominous to imbue the story with the paranoid drive of earlier work. Secondly, save some lick-and-a-promise touches, we get very few of the boldly drawn scenes of wonder that illumine his best stories. For all the frenetic pacing, Gosseyn might as well be shuttling between Burbank and San Fernando.

In the early fifties van Vogt fell under the sway of L. Ron Hubbard, a fellow writer in John W. Campbell's stable. Hubbard was a charismatic power monger with an interest in hypnotism and getting rich. To this end he concocted Dianetics, once described as "TM for engineers." Dianetics, which Hubbard promoted through *Astounding* (later *Analog*), was a hodgepodge of mainstream, abandoned and cultish ideas, positing the mind as an infinitely retentive system. Supposedly, the psyche remembered all experiences, whether one was asleep or awake when they occurred. Such traumas, some occurring before birth, impaired personal function by causing blockages, or "engrams" of neural passages. Dianetic "auditing" could, by inducing the sufferer to relive these painful experiences, "discharge" them, eventually getting rid of all engrams and leaving one a "clear."

Undoubtedly, part of Dianetics' appeal for van Vogt was its do-it-yourself aspect; friends could audit each other without using experts, at least early on in the organization's history. Then too, there was the idea of pre-birth experiences, which resonated with van Vogt's repeated theme of immortality.

From the fifties to the early sixties van Vogt produced little original material, though many of his "fix-ups" are from this period. Instead, he devoted himself to caring for his ailing wife (E. Mayne Hull died in 1975, after a long battle with cancer) and briefly running a Dianetics institute.

Dianetics had its problems; gradually Campbell and his circle were disillusioned. Hubbard abandoned it himself: when an income shelter scheme fell afoul of the IRS, he left the States, a wealthy tax exile. His decision may have been helped along by his third wife, the world's first "clear," divorcing him on the grounds that he was "hopelessly insane." To van Vogt's credit, he refused to convert to Hubbard's new cash cow, the Church of Scientology, regarding it as a falling away from Dianetics.

Van Vogt's later work was uneven. *The Silkie* (1969), his first entirely new novel since Dianetics, has bravura moments:

> Nat Cemp, a class-C Silkie, awakened in his selective fashion and perceived . . . that he was now quite close to the spaceship whose approach he had first sensed an hour before.
>
> Momentarily, he softened the otherwise steel-hard chitinous structure of his outer skin, that the area became sensitive to light waves in the humanly visible spectrum. These he now recorded through a lens arrangement that utilized a portion of the chitin. . . .
>
> There was a sudden pressure in his body as it adjusted to the weakening of the barrier between it and the vacuum. . . .

But in general, the later work suffers by comparison to the Golden Age novels, marred by shaky tone and flatly polemical narratives, using SF conventions as cardboard props to political allegories. Time and self-consciousness have outpaced the dreamer, displacing the wonder, the strangeness, at the core of van Vogt's best stories.

Mainstream criticism and opinion have always had difficulty, when not being flatly dismissive, with the SF strain van Vogt's work embodies, dismissing it as "juvenile." It's a revealing pejoration; we have nothing but scorn for the deep beliefs and appetites of slightly earlier selves, still unaccountably close to our present, exalted sophistication. A literary scene fetishizing "maturity" has good reason to scant the un-ironic marvelling, the breathless what-iffing of the pulps. Looked at too seriously, they expose the paper-thin assumptions of "serious" writing.

It's easy to belittle this work. Feminists could dissect van Vogt's dreams of mastery, his uncritical adoration of technology. (One might also trace E. Mayne Hull's contribution; van Vogt credits her collaboration on much of his work.) Anyone with politics left of Genghis Khan could poke gaping holes in the libertarian fantasy of *The Weapon Makers* and others. Van Vogt's panoptic worlds, their spy rays, hypnotic mind control and immortal, messianic heroes cry out for Foucaultian readings.

But consider: any Nintendo jockey or Dungeons & Dragons player knows van Vogt's blend of deep pessimism about present-day, unaltered humanity and visionary confidence in the strange brilliance of the Future. It's common, for "mundane" readers, to regard SF fans and such as dupes and accessories of technocracy, phallocentrism, or to say, tolerantly, "They'll grow out of it." But no popular art form as broad, various and persistent as space opera can be so tidily dismissed. It is the poetry of a powerful impulse in the world, one that brings us wonders and war. A.E. van Vogt's u- and dystopias, his glimpses of miracles, his surrational reveries speak to our deepest fears and aspirations.

NOTE

Researching this article presented certain problems, particularly in ascertaining exactly when Alfred Vogt started signing himself A.E. van Vogt. Mr. van Vogt, unhappily, died in 2000, due to advanced age. For the record, my sources were Mennonite Genealogy, Inc., which maintains extensive records on the Vogts and other Mennonite families, and the Winnipeg edition of Henderson's Directory, which shows the family changing names in 1939 and 1940.

There is another issue: One of the article's readers disagreed with my assertion that the Vogts were not Dutch, saying that all Mennonites passed through the Netherlands at some point. This is a common misconception: in point of fact there is a sizable minority of Mennonite families who were never in Holland. And even if the Vogts went through there, there is reason to doubt this claim.

For large numbers of Mennonites the Netherlands are a flag of convenience. In Europe, families who have lived elsewhere for centuries are still known by their place of origin; passing through Holland doesn't make anyone Dutch. One has to view the "Netherlands" assertion in light of two World Wars, particularly the Second, when atrocities against Mennonites and other groups made identifying yourself as German, to say the least, problematic (even if you had Prussian origins, as some Mennonites did). Many preferred the option of calling themselves Dutch. And again: virtually every Prairie Mennonite family passed through Ukraine, or "Russia," where they had lived for over a century. It makes as much sense, using the "Dutch" logic, to call them Russians (or Ukrainians). No one has, for some reason.

My thanks to Jeffrey van Vogt, Leslie van Vogt-Hamilton, Victor Goldman, Chester D. Cuthbert, Chris Petty, Audrey Poetker-Thiessen, Jack Thiessen, Mennonite Genealogy, Inc., Val Clemens, and Maurice Mierau: Mennonite Smart Aleck Extraordinaire.

Memoir of a Poet

In the later forties, as an undergraduate at the University of Manitoba, coming from a two-year spell in the army, I began, without thought of any career, but simply out of youthful exuberance and with a keen interest in literature, a sporadic spell of writing. Was it poetry? More a kind of inspired doggerel perhaps. My friends and I referred to it as "nonsense verse." Some of it found its way into print. As a result I found myself with, in that restricted world, a certain reputation. But in writing this memoir, I hope to impart more a sense of that time through my association with others who, then or later, played a role in the cultural life of Winnipeg, than to dwell on any accomplishment of my own. Still, in order to establish a perspective to which the reader can relate, I must recount my own individual experience and background.

Recently I dug out of the University of Manitoba Archives a copy of the first *Creative Campus* published in 1948, a literary magazine of student writing. It contained an essay by Adele Wiseman on a poem of Gerard Manley Hopkins, "That Nature is a Heraclitean Fire and of the Comfort of the Resurrection," short stories by Victor Cowie, Alvin Goldman and Hugh McPherson, a piece by Barry Broadfoot called "America," a poem by Abe Roytenberg (to mention only the people I knew) and two poems by me. I also contributed a review article on a then recent poetry anthology, *Other Canadians*, edited by John Sutherland and containing poems by Raymond Souster, Louis Dudek, Irving Layton, James Reaney, P.K. Page, Ronald Hambleton and some others.[1] This first issue of *Creative Campus* was edited by Alvin Goldman.

My article was an arrogant piece of writing, which often resembled a parody of T.S. Eliot at his most fastidiously pontifical. My judgment was immature and biased. My position was that some of these poets were too socially conscious and politically aligned. This was a period of studious aloofness on my part. Favourite characters in literature were Hamlet and Molière's Alceste. I felt poetry should shun ideologies and focus on symbolist imagery and formal structures. As Auden has aptly said, an opinion with which I agreed, a poet should produce poems that are "well made and show decorum." I was mainly interested in the French symbolists and Rilke. I did at this time get hold of another anthology of then contemporary Canadian poetry, *Unit of Five*.[2] It is significant that both of these anthologies contained only poets from eastern Canada, with the exception of P.K. Page. CanLit was just getting really under way, but the midwest had some catching up to do.

At that time I had not read and barely heard of such predecessors of my generation as Martha Ostenso or Frederick Philip Grove. And what contemporary Canadian writers were there at that time? Few who were yet widely known, unlike today's whole raft of widely recognized names. The only literary past I was aware of, except for Edgar Allan Poe, whose stories and poems I devoured when I was fourteen, was that of the British Isles and Europe. This bias was so ingrained that it showed up much later, while I was teaching at university in the mid-seventies. When Dorothy Livesay, then poet-in-residence at St. John's College, heard I proposed to teach a course in CanLit, horrified that I didn't know who Isabella Valancy Crawford was, she nixed the idea at once. In my undergraduate years I had been reading Annette von Droste-Hülshoff, among other German poets, but not, unfortunately, her Canadian counterpart. Of course I was familiar by the mid-seventies with current Canadian poetry and fiction; indeed, I included much of it in my first-year literature course, but I was certainly ignorant of most nineteenth-century Canadian writing.

The fact is, I was a colonial. This was due to my Anglo heritage. Confining as that sounds, it was a rich inheritance, and so not altogether negative. After all, it embodied my bona fide ethnicity. Therefore if I am to give an intelligible account of my association with literary life in the forties and fifties in Winnipeg, and my own particular orientation to what was going on, so much of which emanated from very different backgrounds, it is necessary that I refer to my own cultural reality.

Both my parents were readers and so our house was furnished with a fairly extensive library. My mother was a big fan of Dickens and Katherine Mansfield and was knowledgeable about the Bloomsbury Group. My father read Greek literature, Tolstoy and Proust in translation, as well as English authors such as Chaucer and Shakespeare. Our shelves contained the poetical works of Byron, Shelley and Keats. After reading such books as *The White Company, Arabia Deserta* and most of Edgar Allan Poe, I zeroed in on those poets and began writing poetry in their manner. In grade eleven at Kelvin High School (1942) I submitted an "Ode to Spring" to the school yearbook. It was not selected, and when I read the comments of the literary adjudicator to the effect that there appeared to be some still writing poetry in the outmoded manner of the early nineteenth century, I was mortified. But I got the point and moved on to Browning, whose poetry I had been introduced to in my English course.

My brand of colonialism went with being from the south end of the city. As everyone knows, Winnipeg contains a particularly interesting mosaic of ethnicity, still operative to some extent, but not as distinctively as in the first half of the last century. Then the north/south divide was crucial. South was mainly British in origin, with a smattering of Jewish families whose money came from the textile industry or the professions. In the North End, by contrast, Jews from Eastern Europe, Poles, Ukrainians and others lived cheek by jowl in an interaction of tension and exchange, which produced some remarkable individuals. Until I came to university, the North End was a foreign domain, which in my school days was represented by football teams from St. John's and Isaac Newton High Schools and the Daniel McIntyre Festival Choir, arch-rivals of us at Kelvin. It was to be my confrontation with this ethnic mix together with my experience overseas in the army that awakened me, and others, to a transforming world view.

The only contact I had with local writers in the forties and fifties was at the University of Manitoba. My only awareness of literary activity on the Winnipeg scene was confined to university life. There were no literary outlets as far as I knew in the forties, other than those provided by the student newspaper, the *Manitoban*, which was published twice a week and boasted a literary page; and the *Manitoba Arts Review*, a mainly scholarly publication put out twice a year; and then, beginning in 1948, the yearly magazine of student writing, *Creative Campus*. There were presumably similar publications at United College (later The University of Winnipeg). Margaret Laurence was an exact contemporary of mine there and was doubtless beginning her writing career in earnest at that institution. But I had no knowledge of her at that time, nor of anyone else outside of academe.

In my first year of arts at the University of Manitoba in 1943 I had met Jack Ludwig, who was a friend of my older cousin Alan Adamson. He was a formidable figure whose impression of physical presence went with intense intellectual energy. He was, at that time, the literary editor of the *Manitoban*. I was impressed by his musical criticism. He reviewed all the important musical events at some length and also the latest recordings. He proclaimed that a composer called Bartók was the fourth "B" and especially recommended his quartets.

One day in the fall of 1943 Jack Ludwig dropped into the junior division library where I was perusing a volume of A.E. Housman. After greeting me amiably he glanced with scorn at the volume I had laid down.

"Arthur, what is this nonsense? This is old hat. Have you read Eliot?"

I had never heard of T.S. Eliot, which indicates the isolation of even a moderately receptive mind such as mine in that place at that time. So I immediately got a copy of Eliot's poems from the library and a whole new world opened up. Soon I was aware of and reading W.H. Auden, Stephen Spender, C. Day Lewis and Louis MacNeice. But as yet, no Americans (except Eliot) or Canadians. My colonialism was not yet at an end.

In 1944 at the age of eighteen I enlisted in the Canadian infantry. I made it to the last troopship to the British Isles. I missed the war by a couple of weeks and was sent to the army of occupation in Germany in the spring of 1945 and spent a year and a half in West Friesland. Given the still very manifest desolation left by war in Holland and Germany, this year or more in the occupation turned my head right around. I escaped my surroundings and the alienation of army life by carrying a copy of Auden's *Poems* of 1930 in my duffle bag, which I read until I practically knew it by heart. When I returned to second-year Arts in 1946 I was a twenty-year-old would-be poet who imagined himself to be on the cutting edge. I wrote a poem I thought of as being in the manner of T.S. Eliot and read it at a meeting of the English Club, a group of the more serious English students who met periodically to discuss a paper presented by one of the participants. These meetings were held in private homes and presided over by one or more of the professors. My friend Ken Black was a member and also the editor of the literary page of the *Manitoban*. He took my poem and published it.

One of the professors who often attended the meetings of the English Club was Malcolm Ross, who was later general editor of the New Canadian Library series, which republished early classics of Canadian literature in paperback. I took his Milton course in my third year. A fine scholar, he was generous with his time and indulgent of youthful know-it-alls like myself. He gave me an A- for an extremely opinionated essay I wrote on *Paradise Lost*. Much later I corresponded with him and sent him the poetry I was writing at that time (the eighties and nineties).

Another professor who was an inspiration, to this youth at least, was Chester Duncan. In my fourth year I was assistant editor (my friend Tony Ensor was editor) of the *Manitoba Arts Review*, in which he published a fine essay on the poems of W.H. Auden. He lectured on modern poetry. I was especially impressed by his lectures on Yeats, who now became the focus of my interest in twentieth-century poetry.

In my third year I somehow became co-editor of the literary page of the *Manitoban* together with Meredith Robinson, later my colleague in the English Department. I began publishing some of my poetry under the pseudo-acronym "ZZ." I might have remained incognito but for the fact that Vic Cowie decoded the ruse and I gained notoriety. My smartass doggerel puzzled the philistines but apparently delighted the cognoscenti.

I was oblivious for a while of being what is now termed a WASP, as I was a callow youth, but in this milieu it was inevitable that I should sooner or later become aware of certain distinctions, however subtle. John Hirsch, for instance, would wryly refer to my background as "pukka sahib." No malice intended; it was good-humoured. But could such an attitude perhaps clarify to me at the time a quite inexplicable outburst from Adele Wiseman in the senior division library in my third year?

The library was then on the fourth floor of the Arts Building in Fort Garry (now the Tier Building). Entering it one morning in January or February of 1948, I saw Adele, whom I knew fairly well from classes we shared and from the English Club. Someone had recently given a paper there on Ezra Pound and in the following discussion there had been some reference to his and Eliot's alleged anti-Semitism. There was some comment as to how relevant this stance might be to the intrinsic value of their poetry. Could that have had any bearing on the mini-drama that now took place?

"So what's this, Adele?" I remarked. "What are you up to?" Looking at the paper she was writing I saw that it was an essay on Gerard Manley Hopkins. "Ah," I quipped fatuously, in my best Stephen Daedalus manner, "the priestly lyricist manhandled by God."[3]

She looked me sternly in the eye. "And what do you believe?" she quizzed, I suppose with Hopkins's stringent devoutness in mind.

I still had to play the wise guy. A couple of lines from Yeats that pretty well summed up my position came to mind. "What do we know but that we face / One another in this place?" I quoted.

There was a pause and then she slapped the table and pronounced loudly so that heads turned towards us.

"Sir! I am a Jew! That is what I am!"

I was taken aback. It had not been a hostile outburst, I felt; it was rather a forceful statement of position, a clarification, a putting of one's cards on the table, a clearing of the air and perhaps a tentative challenge. But more significantly, she was affirming her spirituality rather forcibly and bluntly in the face of my obtuseness, an affirmation made evident from her attraction to and sympathetic treatment of Hopkins's poetry and which here became an attestation to her own particular faith. I mention this incident because it made a big impression on me and I gave it a lot of thought.

"Okay, Adele," I said appeasingly. "Tell me about Hopkins. Tell me about the poem." At that time I had no appreciation of Hopkins whatsoever. After all, he was not accredited by Eliot, the high priest of modernism. Her enthusiasm for Hopkins left me cold. Which only goes to show that Adele was way ahead of me. It was much later that I twigged to what I had been missing.

"You can read my essay when I've written it," she said.

Perhaps I did when it appeared in *Creative Campus*. I don't remember. But fifty-five years later I read it and was impressed. The poem by Hopkins, "That Nature is a Heraclitean Fire," is among the greatest expressions of faith in all literature and a lyrical masterpiece. Adele's essay was an insightful and sensitive analysis.

About this time, I think in the early fifties, John Hirsch was contriving with his friend Tom Hendry to further the cause of drama locally. He started with puppets and would perform Punch and Judy shows in private homes. John gave the impression of someone charged with a special kind of electric energy. Normally, to be sure, he was perfectly composed and calm, but a latent tension could always be sensed. His features and at certain times his entire body were mobile when his interest was aroused. His dark eyes were alert behind horn-rimmed glasses. His facial expression, always arresting by its intensity, was subject to sudden changes, from seriousness and reflectiveness to a flashing out of indignation or gleeful amusement often accompanied by a sally of wit. His was a mercurial temperament and yet one was aware of an underlying hidden depth, as of deep water constantly in surface motion. I would think of Dryden's lines: "A fiery soul, which working out its way, / Fretted the fragile body to decay, / And o'er informed the tenement of clay."

I have known no one more persistently dedicated to the arts than James Reaney. Coming to the University of Manitoba English department in 1949, he was immediately the celebrated local poet. He had published a book of poems, *The Red Heart*. He was eventually to single-handedly edit and print on an old platen relief press, which he discovered in the basement of the old School of Art in the former Law Courts building, a literary magazine, *Alphabet*. He would go in the evenings by himself to the School and set type, every letter by hand, and after this laborious process, print the texts, page by page, manually, until late at night. As far as I know he had no grant or any remuneration whatsoever for this work. And this time-consuming effort went to produce not a literary masterpiece but simply a periodical. This gives you a measure of his dedication and his awareness (which has become so rare in our hi-tech times) of aesthetic quality, of printing as a true craft.

Every afternoon during term Jamie was to be seen at the Faculty Club listening to the afternoon broadcast on the CBC of a classical concert, marking papers or preparing a lecture the while. He is the only person I know who conscientiously read every word of *Finnegans Wake*. If there was art to be absorbed, Jamie would absorb it. Unlike most literati I have known, he was interested in painting, not as a practitioner, but as an appreciator. He was a devout follower of Northrop Frye and so, of course, he was a keen admirer of William Blake. I used to argue with him and Vic Cowie about Blake's negative judgment regarding Titian and Rembrandt. Blake claims that outline is the supreme criterion of good art. I tried to convince my opponents that there was as much outline in these two painters as in Blake himself, and in Michelangelo or Raphael, for that matter, whom Blake held up as models; it was simply more subtle. Although a devotee of Blake myself, I still consider him eccentric on this point.

Jamie had a keen appreciation of Winnipeg, in all its aspects, extending even to the orange streetcars and, later, buses, images of which appeared in his poetry. He had a curiously engaging morbid streak, which did not take the form of inward brooding in any sense, but rather as a quirky trait, which translated fittingly into his poetry. He lived in Riverview and as he did not (it seemed to me by principle) possess a car, he took the bus wherever he went. There is a large cemetery abutting Osborne Street with a stop at its midpoint, which he passed each day on his way to classes. He once remarked to me, "Arthur, I've noticed that whenever the bus stops at the cemetery a beautiful girl gets on. Isn't that extraordinary?"

"Naturally," I replied, catching on. "Vampires."

Jamie nodded musingly. Then of course he laughed.

It was in 1956, when I returned to Winnipeg after two years in France, a year in England, a year in Toronto at the Ontario College of Education and two years teaching at Ridley College in St. Catharines, Ontario, that I met George Swinton, who was teaching at the old School of Art, recently affiliated with the university. I took a night course and a summer course from him.

George was a very good painter, although most of his energy at this time went into writing a book about Inuit art.[4] George was one of the first to "discover" this art. He immediately saw Inuit carving as more than a mere craft or items of curiosity for an eager collector in Montreal, Toronto, Winnipeg or Vancouver. This was perceptive because Inuit art as we know it only came about by the intervention of the white man. Prior to that the carving of this ingenious people had been confined to small animistic icons and artefacts such as tools and utensils. Nomads can't carry around large pieces of stone, however aesthetically pleasing. George recognized that this art was significant in its own particular way and could not be judged merely as another "primitive" art form. He recognized each producer as an individual with a personal vision. Moreover, in his book he made his views widely known. This, I suppose, is what largely distinguished him from other pioneers in the area. He had a wonderful eye for the many various pieces being produced. There was not a uniform style, the carving ranging from "primitive" to more elaborate and even realistic work, especially as time went on. He perceived that white intervention, however well-intentioned, by promoting the carving (later drawings, prints and hangings) for the economic benefit alone of the Inuit, led to the production, in some cases, of souvenir-type junk, which was fine in that it sold, but unfortunately was also an inferior product. Some of the finest pieces George ended up owning, and which eventually found their way to the Winnipeg Art Gallery and other public collections, had actually been discarded as not salesworthy. It was largely due to George's initiative that Winnipeg ended up with the most significant collection of Inuit art anywhere, both in its art gallery and in private hands.

The fifties, for me, were not a time of much writing. I was teaching and had taken up painting in a rather desultory way. I began writing poetry again in the late sixties and seventies at the suggestion of some English department colleagues and particularly with the encouragement of George Amabile. I published a couple of books with Turnstone Press with my own illustrations, and in 1994 a very special book of poems, printed by Rinella Printers for Editions Ink Inc. in letterpress with illustrations from the original woodblocks, called *Bird, Beast and Lover* and limited to 126 copies, something known in France as a *livre d'artiste* but rare on this side of the Atlantic. I had also published in some periodicals, notably *Prairie Fire*, in several of the League of Canadian Poets' annual anthologies and in *Section Lines: a Manitoba Anthology* (Turnstone Press, 1988).

The forties and fifties were, for me, a time of discovery, of exciting associations with other creative persons, some of whom later made significant contributions to our cultural life; of witnessing important developments in our theatre, ballet, the visual arts and literature. It was the period in which our city came of artistic age, when the Royal Winnipeg Ballet, the Manitoba Theatre Centre and the Winnipeg Symphony Orchestra sprang to maturity. I shared the exciting moments of these developments. As for my undergraduate writing, it showed promise, possessing originality and imaginative audacity, but it was not by any means a fully accomplished performance. And so, dear reader, if you wish to find something of my poetic accomplishment, the fruit of those heady times, it is not easily available. It is to be found in the limited publications mentioned at the end of the previous paragraph. The forties were my salad days when I was green in judgment.

NOTES

1 John Sutherland, ed., *Other Canadians: An Anthology of the New Poetry in Canada 1940-1946* (Montreal: First Statement Press, 1946).
2 Ronald Hambleton, ed., *Unit of Five* (Toronto: Ryerson Press, 1944). This anthology contains poetry by Louis Dudek, Ronald Hambleton, P.K. Page, Raymond Souster and James Wreford.
3 See Hopkins's poem "Carrion Comfort."
4 George Swinton, *Sculpture of the Eskimo* (Toronto: McClelland & Stewart, 1972).

JAMES REANEY

Souwestoegg on Winnipuzz:
James Reaney's Winnipeg

The first professionally produced Canadian play I ever saw was *The Sun and the Moon* by James Reaney, at the Manitoba Theatre Centre in Winnipeg in 1973. This was when CanLit was just coming into being in our universities and still considered a Mickey Mouse option. All of us keeners in Honours English at Manitoba hugged away from it, and stuck to British and American, though even American was considered brash and loudmouthed and not really couth. Seeing a Canadian play on stage in the early seventies gave us all queasy shivers of familiarity and what I would call now a kind of shame, that feeling of being somehow found out, exposed, caught in the act, of existing in the public literary discourse that had until then completely absolutely excluded us. That felt safer. We understood we were readers of literature, critics in training, not ever its subject, never its authors. New Criticism, with its emphasis on the text, *sans* socio-biographical context, was then at its height. Archetypalist Northrop Frye ruled the halls of the University of Manitoba, through his numerous acolytes, as regally as he did Toronto. Literature was neatly divided into conceptual periods, Renaissance, Neo-Classical, Romantic, Victorian, Modern. Texts could be read, à la Frye, on predefined interpretive levels, literal, metaphoric, symbolic, anagogic. Through the veins of English literature flowed the ancient blood of the Romans and Hebrews and Greeks. We were not players on the stage of world history. We were its endline observers in a faraway country. We liked it that way.

Those of us with writerly dreams and murkily intuited creative manuscripts in the making bit our tongues, and hid them in mental caves and study drawers. Where did we get such self-important ideas from? There were no writer residencies, no visiting writers on our campuses, except as I recall, a youngish chain-smoking Mordecai Richler at the University of Manitoba's eclectic and energetic Festival of Life and Learning. The city was then beginning to pulse with the kinds of theatre and street and film festivals it has since become famous for. Creative writing classes were just begin-ning to be taught in Canadian universities. At Manitoba they were relegated to a minor category, over with CanLit. There were several published writers in our department, notably George Amabile and Ed Kleiman and Myron Turner, and even a composer, Chester Duncan. Myron Turner ran his own literary press, Four Humours. Turner and Amabile also published a semi-annual literary journal, *The Far Point*, which featured work by new Canadian writers, as well as established ones like Livesay and Ralph Gustafson; very few of its writers were local, very few of their works were set on the Prairies.

These professors taught British and American literature as well, and the gulf between their creative and critical work, and so between our own student efforts in these different directions, seemed unbridgeable and immense. Twice–Governor General's Award-winning poet and playwright James Reaney had taught creative writ-ing at Manitoba from 1949 to 1960, and his play, *Names and Nicknames*, had been per-formed at the Manitoba Theatre Centre in 1963, directed by John Hirsch and Robert Sherrin, and three years later by David Arnason's English class at Vincent Massey Collegiate. Frye himself was promoting new Canadian writing in his reviews, famous-ly collected in *The Bush Garden* (Anansi 1971). We were all reading Richler and Atwood and listening to Leonard Cohen in our dorm rooms. But mostly, we scribbled away in secret, hugging our sheaves of literary fragments surreptitiously under our jackets.

The Sun and the Moon embarrassed us with its familiarity, its small-town reli-giosity, and its symbolism, recognizably Frygian but applied so startlingly to a quin-tessentially Canadian setting. We discussed it in our Shakespeare and Victorian Lit classes, shivering over its invasion of our safe critical spaces with local contemporane-ity. Reaney's Mill Bank and United Church were set in anglo southwestern Ontario, far from our own much more sparsely settled but far more multicultural Manitoba prairie. His colourful Mrs. Shade and fair-minded Kingbird were allegorical figures in a metaphysical redemption story, a contest between good and evil, that evoked Blake and James Frazer's mythologies, rooted in other places and times. They were also, hilariously, uncomfortably, the kind of church-going, Bible-quoting people we might expect to meet on our Winnipeg and small town streets.

Did we notice then, as we can't help noticing now, the problematic genderedness of Reaney's implied metaphysical realms in *The Sun and the Moon*, the enlightened calm male sunny daytime realm chaotically impinged upon and enlivened by but ulti-mately prevailing against the energetic demonic female night realm? I took a course in "Literary Symbolism" with Frye at the University of Toronto in the mid-seventies. Frye persistently refused to address the possibly misogynist and anti-ecological bias in his equation of male with divinity and heroism and cultural enlightenment and female with nature, nightmare, chaos and darkness in his great symbolic code. Whenever challenged on this point by students, as he sometimes was then, though not as often as he would be now, he insisted on a metaphorical understanding of gender and culture and nature: we are all females, he would say, in relation to God, and all males in relation to the earth. Case closed. Reaney's characters are more nuanced, and certainly more fun, than Frye's metaphoric scheme allowed, but nonetheless Cixous's famous exposé of this pervasive Western binary as both misogynist and anti-ecological, and Adorno's warning that Enlightenment ideals are inextricably linked to fascism in their intent to dominate nature and designated groups of human beings, bear repeating here.

In 1960 Reaney moved to London, Ontario, to take up a teaching post at the University of Western Ontario, where he continued to produce prolifically and win more awards. That same year he wrote the poetic sequence "A Message to Winnipeg," which was later collected in *Selected Longer Poems* edited by Germaine Warkentin (1976, 30-38). A section of Part VI, "Winnipeg as a Chess Game," reappeared as a chant in his fierce dreamlike play, *Colours in the Dark* (first produced in Stratford in 1967 and published by Talonplays in 1969).

"A Message to Winnipeg" is the kind of "longer poem" (as he called it) you'd want to write when leaving a city, not when trying to live in it, with its alarming apocalyptic vision of the city's imminent doom: "Destruction cometh—a sucking cloud, / Your towers will tumble down / / Child's Restaurant will be consumed / Eaton's and Hudson's Bay / Grass will grow on your neon signs / And the rivers dry away," accompanied by loud warnings, "Leave the burning city / Leave this burning town"! There is no reason given for the poem's dire prediction, except Winnipeg's similarity to every other city, "the same as the London of the / Empire that spawned you, the Athens and Rome / that still / transmit some of their patterns to you sitting in the / swamp / at the forks of the river You are like Babylon and like / Nineveh You are any city." Reaney gives this fiery (and irresponsible, as it seems to me) doomsday message right after the marvellously conceived, humorous, site-specific line "Winnipeg is a loutish giant sucking a sugar beet beside / the two winding rivers."

The juxtaposition encapsulates precisely the best and worst of Reaney as he sounds to us now, several decades removed from the archetypalizing influence of Frye, forced to listen as we are to all too realistically conceived military doomsday rhetoric from trigger-happy presidents on a weekly basis, and hungry as ever for stories and images that reflect our own time and place with clarity and accuracy. Puckish humour, brash pronouncements, affectionate local colour and heavy-handed structural manipulation of plot in the name of a shadowy metaphysics that borrows heavily from fundamentalist Christianity while at the same time disavowing its influence, all these signature effects running through Reaney's oeuvre are present in this dramatic little sequence that nevertheless still delights with its provocative voice and vivid sense of detail, "ice glitter[ing] on the gargoyles and statues / High up on the 1913 boom business buildings."

Hard to believe now that it was for his interest in regionalism that Reaney was most criticized in the sixties and seventies, as can be seen from his own passionate defense of the same in an early seventies essay in *Maclean's*: "If, however, you go in for too much taking the Big Picture you miss something very valuable in the smaller picture" (Reaney 1971, 18). Terry Griggs, writing in 1983, repeats the anti-regionalist critical bias he was replying to in the *Maclean's* essay. Griggs defends Reaney against the charge of localism by championing his archetypalism: "Reaney mines atoms—small towns, children, the bare stage—to get at the giants lying foetal within" (Griggs 28), evoking the very kind of universalizing we have come to distrust now, in the age of cultural and economic globalization, which claims to act in the interests of all but so blatantly works for the few.

We long now, even in our psychological and ontological paradigms, for "thick" overviews rather than reductively "thin" ones, not because we're not interested in the "Big Picture" (or indeed inner giants) but because we don't, now, believe we can access them through confident universalist assertions (except tragically annihilating ones): that we must locate our theories in specificities of time and place and their randomly collected intertexts, and through meticulously open-minded proprioception, the "movement of life into language," to use Robin Blaser's phrase, and then work like hell at trying to understand how our theories might interface with others that began elsewhere (Blaser 10, cited in Dragland 220). Or to quote cultural theorist Eve Sedgwick, "[There may] be benefit in exploring the extremely varied, dynamic, and historically contingent ways that strong theoretical constructs interact with weak ones in the ecology of knowing—an exploration that obviously can't proceed without a respectful interest in weak as well as strong theoretical acts" (Sedgwick 23).

Margaret Atwood, who was interested in both Frygian archetypalism and Canadian regionalism but knew how to juggle them in a more sophisticated fashion than Reaney, wrote wittily and witheringly in 1971 of Reaney's *Poems*: "I have long entertained a private vision of Frye reading through Reaney while muttering 'What have I wrought?' or 'This is not what I meant, at all,' and this collection confirms it" (Atwood 114), though her criticism seems more directed at his clumsiness in melding the two than his interest in them as such: "If you can see a world in a grain of sand, well, good; but you shouldn't stick one on just because you think it ought to be there" (117). What she praises, on the other hand, is his "uniqueness, power, peculiarity and, sometimes, unprecedented weirdness." (I second the weirdness! You have no idea what is coming next in most of his poems and plays. Erin Moure is predictable by comparison. There is nothing else like it.)

Reaney's sense of apocalypse in "A Message to Winnipeg" borrows heavily from Eliotic motifs of modernity as wasteland, to describe the logical outcome of and just punishment for the sins of industrial overdevelopment of the recently wild prairie landscape. It also echoes what theologian Christine Keller calls the "apocalypse habit" of Western culture, rooted in its "master script," the Book of Revelation, which Eliot's modernist vision was not immune to. The apocalypse habit is pervasive in modern culture, notes Keller, in the positivist sciences as much as the nihilist humanities; it exhibits a tendency to respond to situations of dire need, such as the current eco-crisis, with unrealistic hopes of instantaneous large scale transformation, which flip inevitably, disappointed, into despair: "We wish for messianic solutions and end up doing nothing . . . If we can't save the world, then to hell with it" (Keller 14).

Reaney's Winnipeg poem captures the tone of environmentalist anxiety which has become endemic now, but was in fact rarely expressed in Canada in the sixties. He also catches the flavour of the Métis rebellion against eastern Canadian nationalist interests that have so coloured our cultural identifications in the West. He lets a grassroots sense of pro-trickster rebellion against bureaucratization come into his literary vision in a groundbreaking way. His Winnipeg is haunted by the ghosts of the defeated Bois-Brûlés; it is bogged down by the proliferation of factories and "Glittering / Hard merciless cars. Glittering hard merciless / Cars. Extremely useful, extremely depressing," where there were once "ravens in flocks" and an indigenous people "Who did what the stars did and the sun." And yet, paradoxically, the apocalyptic ending of the poem in the bombastic voice of the unnamed "Messenger" disturbingly resembles the very excesses he decries in the figure of "old Canon Bastion" who rides on the streetcar and "never understands but has a voice / Fit for anything in the King James Version."

Perhaps there is an element of revenge in "A Message to Winnipeg" for "the city," as Reaney complains in the preface, "where noone listened to the poet made up of one thousand rice paper Bible pages." Such lack of audience response, looking back, is not after all surprising in a city that didn't know itself yet, the way it does now, as a rich cultural site that not only spawns good writers who make their careers elsewhere (including such figures as Margaret Laurence, Adele Wiseman, Larry Zolf, Dorothy

Livesay, Sondra Gottlieb and many others), but as a place that sustains a large lively writing community, internationally renowned literary presses and journals and festivals, and Pulitzer Prize-, Governor General's Award- and Giller Prize-winning literary careers of the stature of Carol Shields, Robert Kroetsch, Miriam Toews and David Bergen. For Reaney, coming from Toronto with its much larger and more established cultural playing field, Winnipeg in the fifties must have felt small.

It was here, in strong-minded, multiculturally rich Winnipeg, that Reaney developed his localist vision, during his early academic and writerly years. Toronto may have instilled in him universalist archetypal ideas, and may have published his Governor General's Award-winning mythopoetic poetry collections, *The Red Heart* (1949) and *A Suit of Nettles* (1958); but it was in Winnipeg that he developed his own regionally flavoured symbolism. It was here, in conversation with colleagues and students at the University of Manitoba during the fifties, that he developed his sense of literary regionalism, as "an area of subtle zoning" of the "*here and now*," as he put it in the editorial of the inaugural issue of *Alphabet*, the literary journal he began editing there shortly before his move to London in 1960, which was to exert such a wide influence on the development of Canadian writing generally.

Among Reaney's students at Manitoba were Ed Kleiman, Jack Parr and Victor Cowie, themselves to became premier players in the Winnipeg academic and literary scene. Dick Harrison's influential book *Unnamed Country: The Struggle for a Canadian Prairie Fiction* (1977), which was one of the first booklength studies of Canadian prairie fiction, grew out of a dissertation supervised by Reaney. Harrison's study highlighted the multicultural character of western Canadian settlement, and referred (if too obliquely) to the presence of Métis and First Nations peoples in its cultural development. Later Reaney taught Cree playwright and novelist Tomson Highway at the University of Western Ontario. Highway acknowledges Reaney as one of the people who gave him "support, inspiration, faith and love" during the writing of his 1998 novel, *Kiss of the Fur Queen*, in which Winnipeg reveals a hellish face in its treament of indigenous citizens, worthy of Reaney's direst prophecies.

Reaney's influence on the development of regionally based writing in Canada and on prairie writing generally therefore deserves wider recognition. But so does the prairie's compelling influence on Reaney: the specificity of the local and the profound influence of particular landscape and region on cultural expression are pretty hard to avoid in western Canada, even though we have worked hard at cosmopolitanism and transnationalism in our ways. A debate like Griggs's, on whether regionalism matters as much as universalism, is simply unthinkable on the prairies, where cities are separated from one another by hundreds of miles, and where the landscape and harsh climate exert a strong unavoidable presence, indelibly marked by indigenous and multicultural mediations, both historically and in the present. It is intriguing to posit Winnipeg as the source and inspiration of Ontarian localist consciousness and pride, through its emissary Reaney, just as Reaney was the source and inspiration of western Canadian literary regionalism, through Northrop Frye. I think I will claim to do so here.

Alphabet No. 1 was published in September 1960 with a London address, but the editorial was signed "Winnipeg, July 1960"—it appears to have been mysteriously edited in Canadian Shield country en route. The inaugural issue included an evocative, beautifully written short story, "Crystal Pillow," by Ed Kleiman, set in the fictional town of White Horn, in Manitoba bush country not far from Winnipeg. The town boasts a small crystalline salt-bed in a circle of trees, mysterious reminder of a vanished geological age, and site of visionary glimpses of bygone times: an "Indian brave" leaping on a "fiery pony." The story concludes with a comical-satirical portrait of Winnipeg as "a sinking marshland filled with [dinosaurs]," which are, in the eyes of Billy, the protagonist, a rural visitor to the big city, high-rise buildings whose weight cannot be sustained by the swampy ground and which are doomed to sink "below the silencing muddy surface."

Reaney claimed Kleiman's story, in his editorial, as the inspirational text that motivated him to found *Alphabet*: "It was Kleiman's story I first felt I must see published; it was so imaginative and no one was doing a thing about it." The obvious symbolic and regional intertextuality between this story and Reaney's own "A Message to Winnipeg" bespeaks a rich cultural dialogue in the halls of the University of Manitoba's English department during the Reaney years. But notice the differences between Kleiman's vision of Winnipegian doom and Reaney's apocalypse: not only is Kleiman's more psychologized by being rooted in a suicidally inclined boy's vision, his ending for the city does not spell an ending for the environment and does not seem to be fuelled by fiery, angry gods, as does Reaney's, but rather by the city's own unsustainability in having been built on muddy ground. It's true: Winnipeg is built on a swamp; most house owners know what that means in terms of shifting foundations and basement flooding.

Kleiman comments on the source of the story as follows: "Of course I'd read 'Message to Winnipeg,' but am not aware of my story being influenced by his work. It was a period when many of us were taking teaching jobs in rural Manitoba, and I'd heard a story of a pupil taking his life. The story was haunting, and I began to wonder what could have been passing through that student's mind at that time and how he viewed his surroundings. All that concern gave way to a fictional communication with someone I'd never met and never would." He adds, "That ability to submerge one's self totally in one's material—and not let one's own personality get in the way—was a skill that Jamie's class helped us develop. Since then we've kept in touch and are always reading and commenting to one another about each other's work." (Kleiman, email to Di Brandt, December 12, 2004).

George Bowering has reflected wittily on the difference between Reaney's later souwesto-inflected regionalist aesthetics and the kind of local writing the TISH poets, under the influence of Olson's Black Mountain poetics, were developing on the West Coast in the sixties and seventies. The TISH poets, he observes, were interested in exploring place in the sense of *locus*, milieu, geographic site, while the "regionalists of London" led by Reaney, as he encountered them in the mid-sixties, seemed more interested in region as territory, as property, identifiable address. While the BC poets committed themselves to the notion of surface in writing—following among other things Robbe-Grillet's caution against depth because of its temptation to metaphorize nature out of existence under the pressure of unworldly metaphysics—Reaney and his gang were "intent upon exploring deep, well under the surface of the place where [they] lived]."

They did so, observes Bowering, not in order to lift themselves out of place or nature, but indeed to establish themselves more firmly in it, in the interest of "identification . . . and domestication. A sense of being capably at home, and glad of it." Souwesto regionalism thus becomes, in Bowering's definition, the "performance of a social consciousness." (It was Reaney, of course, who popularized the term Souwesto, for the very particular, mannered culture of the densely settled countryside southwest of Toronto, which produced Stephen Leacock and Alice Munro and Christopher Dewdney and Nino Ricci and Don McKay, and only much later non-anglo, non-European writers like André Alexis and Christopher Curtis. Though Reaney claims it was Greg Curnoe who coined the term [Reaney 1971, 18]).

We Winnipeggers took longer to come to our literary sense of the local and regional, beyond the pioneering efforts of Reaney and Kleiman, and writers like John Marlyn and Livesay and Laurence and Wiseman, who had after all gone elsewhere to write about our landscape and us. The Manitoba Writers' Guild was founded in 1981 by a small group of writers centered around the recently organized Turnstone Press and *Prairie Fire* magazine (then *Writers' News Manitoba*). There was similar organizational activity happening in Alberta and Saskatchewan in these years, with the establishment of presses like NeWest and Longspoon and Coteau and Thistledown and Red Deer, and literary magazines like *Dandelion* and *The Dinosaur Review*. Situated at the crossroads between east and west, densely settled Ontario and sparsely settled BC, we Winnipeggers looked in both directions for our bearings. Because we developed our sense of place during the seventies and eighties, under the additional galvanizing influence of feminism and multiculturalism, we did not share Bowering's West Coast sense of a lone (white, male) horse rider surveying an ineffable "phenomenal frontier" (Bowering 4, 6) even though we, like the BC writers, remembered the settler experience, and shared their sense of western alienation from the centres of power in the East.

For us on the Prairies, cultural activity did not happen in an empty landscape waiting to be discovered and explored by solitary wanderers, but rather in already well inhabited indigenous territory, Indian country and ethnically identified communities, Jewish, Ukrainian, French, Métis, Mennonite (often, and perhaps not coincidentally, with strong mother figures in them). Kroetsch's *Stone Hammer*, found on his father's farm, carries as much indigenous hunter/gatherer as settler/agricultural meaning, and his *Seed Catalogue* is as much maternally as paternally inflected. Patrick Friesen's and Kristjana Gunnars's and Eli Mandel's immigrant settler communities bear strong cultural markings that evoke old European landscapes and locate them alongside local indigenous rez communities, and are more akin to them in many ways than they are to the Canadian nationalism of anglo-derived communities in Ontario. Jan Horner's women are firmly embedded in family and neighbourhood. Anne Szumigalski's world is simultaneously domestic and wild-minded, surreal. Louise Halfe's *Blue Marrow*, sustained by Maria Campbell's trailblazing 1973 Métis manifesto, *Halfbreed*, boldly portrays Native women engaged in daring cultural reclamation acts, asserting their ancient Aboriginal and matriarchal clan rights in and against the invading white culture.

Like Reaney's regionalists, we were determinedly "we" rather than "I," to use Bowering's terms. Our domesticity was, however, is, wild-minded, Indian-flavoured, independentiste, forever western rebellious à la Riel, mistrustful of industrial eastern interests. Nevertheless we tended to see ourselves as more poststructuralist than phenomenologist, more performance poets in the Torontonian tradition than projectivists in the Olsonian, even though in so many ways we shared the proprioceptive aims of open field poetics. No doubt this had a lot to do with the affiliations of our leading regional mentors. bpNichol had grown up in Winnipeg, so was legitimately one of ours. Kroetsch had spent years in New York State, reading Heidegger and J. Hillis Miller and Derrida, before returning to the prairies to theorize his interests in local stories vis-à-vis the postmodern. Like them, Laurence and Wiseman had migrated east rather than west, while maintaining geographical loyalties in their writing. Livesay of course had lived a widely cosmopolitan life, in Montreal, Winnipeg, New Jersey, London, and Paris, before settling in Vancouver, and spanned a wide geographic and cultural intertext in her long and diverse career, which was reflected in the eclectic editorial policy of *Contemporary Verse II*, which she founded in Winnipeg in 1975, during a stint as writer-in-residence at the University of Manitoba.

Reaney's acerbic "Message to Winnipeg," relayed over his shoulder in a huff, so to speak, as he exited the prairies to take up adult abode in his childhood Souwestoland in 1960, unnervingly anticipates many of our later Manitoba literary trends. His collage portrait of the city is impressively diverse in its attentions, from factory to river to indigenous history to pioneer settlement to French and Métis presence to modern traffic to city politics. His amusing catalogue of citizens on the busy sidewalks of Portage Avenue between Eaton's and the Bay includes a dramatic range of character types which looks forward to both eighties-style identity politics and turn-of-the-millennium ecopoetics, marked by profession, psychology, ethnicity, family configuration, age, gender, even, remarkably, association with animals: "Doctor Horror, Assistant Professor Sulky, and Mother / Neurosis / Some Hutterites with geese under their arms, Father / Monster, / And the Sliver girls: Little Sliver, Just as little Sliver, / Sliver, / Old Spit, Young Kleenex and twenty-five Albanians."

Should we read Reaney's apocalyptic conclusion as a doomsday vision of the sort environmental activists are now predicting for us in the coming decades, if we continue in our escalating demands on the earth's resources? Part II, "Winnipeg Seen as a Body of Time & Space," suggests so: "Then on top of you fell / A boneyard wrecked auto gent, his hair / Made of rusted car door handles, his fingernails / Of red Snowflake Pastry signs, his belly / Of buildings downtown; his arms of sewers, / His nerves electric wires, his mouth a telephone, / His backbone—a cracked cement street. His heart / An orange pendulum bus crawling with the human fleas / Of a so-so civilization—half gadget, half flesh." The poem offers no alternative directions, however, admitting helplessly or even flippantly, "I don't know what I would have instead." The Messenger's exhortation to "leave the burning city" in Part VI offers no solution either, since presumably the citizens who left would have to congregate elsewhere and find or create similarly doomed conditions in another city.

As a displaced, homesick Winnipegger trying to live in Souwestoland myself this past decade, I can't help noticing how much more industrialized, how much more polluted, how much more car invested, how much more environmentally burdened the Souwesto landscape is than Winnipeg's, even though the latter is, to be sure, a bigger busier city than London or Sarnia or Windsor or Waterloo. Perhaps it was the proximity of the open prairie, and the recentness of agricultural settlement that tuned Reaney's environmental consciousness up to a higher frequency than seems to be the case in some of his earlier pre-Winnipeg writings, though the Great Lakes regions come under environmental scrutiny also, in his much earlier 1948 *Great Lakes Suite*: "Lake Erie is weary / Of washing the dreary / Crowds of the cities / That line her shores" (1976, V.16). Reading his "Message to Winnipeg" in the polluted air of Windsor-Detroit, as I am right now, I want to get up and wave fists and shout, Sarnia and Windsor will burn, are burning now, long before Winnipeg!

Interestingly, Reaney proposed regionalism as a solution to the problems of Souwesto über-industrialization: "At the present moment hopelessly uncontrolled and undersigned megalopolises are on the march. Politicians cheerfully prophesy that the Detroit complex will one day melt into the Toronto system at London, Ontario! Well, wonderful. And what kind of human rat will scuttle around in this huge maze of freeways and parking lots? Zombies don't know where they are; comforted by such phrases as 'global village' and 'you can't stop progress,' they cheerfully face the prospect of a world where all places are the same shopping plaza and all the shoppers are interchangeable units. For some reason or other I can't cheerfully face this prospect. One way to fight it is to 'know' where you are, and this means, among other things, your street, your apartment block, your window box, the faces of friends around you" (1971, 18).

This is the opposite solution to Bowering's, for whom cultivating cosmopolitan nomadism in sparsely settled areas offers a better guarantee against over-industrialization than does homemaking. Temperamentally, I am with him: like Bowering, I find Souwesto domesticity stultifying in its tameness, its large investment in factory life, its calm acceptance of shocking levels of air and water pollution. The easy skeptic's reply to Reaney's proposal of regionalism as a solution to megalopoli and overcrowding is that knowing where you are, where your street and neighbourhood are, doesn't stop the relentless march of "progress," doesn't stop the fields from being paved over, doesn't stop the excesses of petroleum culture from destroying what little natural beauty and untampered with ecosystemic vitality are left. Arguably it even enables further over-development, by providing the cultural locale that makes its horrors endurable.

The easy sceptic's reply to Bowering's alternative, on the other side, is that it applies only to the few, not the many, in its assumption of easily accessible, sparsely settled land; that cosmopolitanism depends on large city environments whose investment in environmental degradation is surely even bigger, or indeed directly related to, small town factory culture, if more buffered by niceties; and that urban nomadism encourages a good time for its privileged practitioners who can leave environmental troubles behind for the locally embedded to deal with. Bowering's vision of BC as sparsely populated and underdeveloped is, further, outmoded now in light of Vancouver's current population overrun and rural BC's overlogging.

What is striking, in light of the current eco-crisis, is Reaney's prescient rage about its coming horrors well before the topic became generally fashionable in North American lit circles, as it is beginning to be now. The "Lake St. Clair" section of the *Great Lakes Suite* declares humorously but emphatically, "I once knew a bear / Who swam in Lake St. Clair / And after the experience / Said, 'Hoity Toit / I don't like the way Detroit / Pollutes the air there.' Then after a while / He added with a smile, / 'And I don't like the way Windsor / Does, either'" (1976, IV.16). In "Yonge Street: A Denunciation of Toronto," Scene 15 of *Colours in the Dark*, the character PA curses "this street where it's increasingly difficult to find a green leaf" (1969, 80). Over and over, Reaney offers the Blakean adage of "Art as mentor of spiritual depths and heights, of rebirth, of combating the boredom of our capitalist, phoney paradise" (1990, 72), in ways that powerfully recapture the spirit of Romantic environmentalism, as recently explicated by Jonathan Bate (2000), but very pointedly set in the Canadian modern context.

What of Reaney's fanatical attachment to Frye's vertical levels of literary expression and interpretation and existential reality, in our own time which is so much more horizontally inclined, so much more trusting of contiguity than symbolism and metaphor, so much more materialist in its interests than archetypal and surrealist? A dedicated postmodernist like Stan Dragland has argued that while Reaney appears to adhere to premeditated and imposed formal structures rather than open-ended verse, he nevertheless is "formally eclectic and protean" and "restless" in meaning (Dragland 220). Less reserved in his praise, bpNichol enthusiastically highlights Reaney's alphabetic self-reflexivity, his concern "with language with the materials of language . . . [he] comes close to writing writing . . . [his texts] exist as real objects in the real world" (bpNichol 5).

To these postmodern defences of Reaney's admittedly old-fashioned sounding poetics (because of his penchant for rhyme and predictable rhythms as well as repetitive structural patterns) we can add his interest in the generation of experimental literary texts and performance pieces through arbitrary juxtapositions of myth with documentary detail, in ways that anticipate the new formalism in technique, if not in effect. We could argue that his failure to wed archetypes to realism convincingly in so many instances is precisely what interests us now, that his bipolar landscapes with their frightening figures of bears and interrogators and *danses macabre* on the one hand, and familiar realist details on the other, create a nightmarish and suggestive landscape that has impressive historical and psychological scope, unpredictable and often startling effects, and evocative prophetic vocality, of a sort that is often sadly missing in more fashionably circumscribed postmodern work.

I forgive Reaney his imminent Winnipeg apocalypse on these grounds. (Well, hey, who knows: Kerouac's little remarked passage on approaching the pollution haze of

New York from New Jersey in *On the Road* in 1955 now strikes us, post-9/11, with prophetic prescience: "When daybreak came we were zooming through New Jersy with the great cloud of Metropolitan New York rising before us in the snowy distance. Dean had a sweater wrapped around his ears. He said we were a band of Arabs coming in to blow up New York" [Kerouac 117]. Who knows which event Reaney's crazy Messenger had in mind in foreseeing the end of Winnipeg? Perhaps he was haunted by the spectre of nuclear holocaust as we all were in those frightening first decades after the invention of the bomb, before we had developed contemporary postmodern strategies of cynicism and detachment. Perhaps he was reviving an Ontario-inflected image of the Riel Rebellion along the lines of early Montreal in flames. Maybe he was thinking of eco-disaster, whose shape is not yet visible to us though its coming is known. Perhaps, simply, predictions of apocalypse are never wrong in the ultimate sense of predicting eventual mortality if not doom.)

Anyway, there is the possibility of reading the ending as ironic, a hallucination, a nightmare in the Messenger's head. After all, his vision of the burning city is interrupted by a "wise old idiot," a local guy, who reasonably protests, "But this city is not burning . . . And there's no war we've heard of." At this point, the Messenger "beats his brow," only to get dramatically swallowed up by the "stupid pavement," until "the Babylon becomes him" and the city "disappears." He himself, notably, does not disappear with it: on he gallops wildly, "Over the plain and under the sky," still shouting his unheeded message of "truthful fear." If Reaney meant to convey a general sense of anxiety and foreboding about the future, in a way that is becoming pervasive in North America and around the world now, using Winnipeg as reflective locus rather than specific source or target for this anxiety, then indeed we can embrace his portrait as an accurate one, as does the refrain of the poem's communal speaking voice, responding to the Messenger's unconfirmed warnings: "It's the sound of our hearts, say we."

And who else, after all, except perhaps Guy Maddin, has come anywhere close to the kind of inventive zaniness that characterizes Reaney's best work, which allows him to insert, in the middle of the dizzyingly unpredictable *Colours in the Dark*, set in Souwestoland but at any moment zipping out to other parts of the country or dramatically other psychic realms, the following marvellously nutty "Fantastia on the Street Names of Winnipeg"? Reaney's riff on our civic geography encouraged me to practise further nominal conjugations on our fair city's name in my title. I can't resist citing it here in full, in the name of (anti-apocalyptic) inter-regionalist cosmopolitan good fun:

I met a nun coming up Osborne Street

You met an Osborne coming up Fort Street

He met a Portage Fort coming down Main

She carried a Kennedy filled with Dagmar

It, Broadway, balanced its rows of elms

We are nothing but Pembina all that Wellington Crescent

You Assiniboine far too much about Gertie

They Corydoned their gay Oxfords and Ashes

  beg you Osborne. Portage your Main this conjugation.

To be a city system, Winnipegging the whole thing?

That's exactly what I Main Street South.

For Example:

I Winnipeg	We Winnipeged
You Winnip	You Winnipdown
He Winni	
She Winnipeggied	They Winnipugged
It Winned	

The Past Tense of To Winnipeg?

I'm not quite sure but I think that it would be—

I Winnipuzzed? (70-71)

Thanks to Birk Sproxton, David Arnason and Andris Taskans for enthusiastic advice and encouragement.

WORKS CITED

Adorno, Theodor and Max Horkheimer. *Dialectic of Enlightenment.* Trans. John Cumming. London and New York: Verso, 1979.

Atwood, Margaret. "Reaney Collected." *Canadian Literature* 57 (Summer 1973): 113-177.

Bate, Jonathan. *The Song of the Earth.* London: Picador, 2000.

Blaser, Robin. Introduction. *Particular Accidents: Selected Poems*, by George Bowering. Ed. Robin Blaser. Vancouver: Talonbooks, 1980 (10). Cited in Dragland. 220.

Bowering, George. *Reaney's Region. Approaches to the Work of James Reaney.* Ed. Stan Dragland. Toronto: ECW Press, 1983. 1-14.

Campbell, Maria. *Halfbreed.* Toronto: McClelland & Stewart, 1973.

Cixous, Hélène and Catherine Clement. *The Newly Born Woman.* Trans. Betsy Wing. Intro. by Sandra M. Gilbert. Minneapolis: University of Minnesota Press, 1986.

Griggs, Terry. "James Reaney's Giants." *Approaches to the Work of James Reaney.* Ed. Dragland. 15-31.

Halfe, Louise. *Blue Marrow.* Toronto: McClelland & Stewart, 1998.

Harrison, Dick. *Unnamed Country: The Struggle for a Canadian Prairie Fiction.* Edmonton: University of Alberta Press, 1977.

Highway, Tomson. *Kiss of the Fur Queen.* Toronto: Doubleday, 1998.

Kerouac, Jack. *On the Road.* Penguin, 1991, 2000.

Kleiman, Ed. "Crystal Pillow." *Alphabet* 1 (1960): 59-68.

Nichol, bp. "Letter re James Reaney." *Open Letter* 2/6 (Fall 1973): 5.

Reaney, James. *Colours in the Dark.* Vancouver: Talonplays/Macmillan, 1969.

———. "James Reaney's Canada: The Poetic Rubbings of a Defensive Driver." *Maclean's* (December 17, 1971): 18, 46, 51.

———. "Lake Ontario." *Contemporary Verse* 26 (1948): 9-10. Reprinted as part of The Great Lakes Suite, in *The Red Heart.* 43-48.

———. "A Message to Winnipeg." *Poetry* 62 (1960): 38-47.

———. *Names and Nicknames.* 1963. Vancouver: Talonbooks, 1978.

———. *Performance Poems.* Goderich, ON: Moonstone Press, 1990.

———. *The Red Heart.* Toronto: McClelland & Stewart, 1949.

———. *Selected Longer Poems.* Ed. Germaine Warkentin. Erin, ON: Press Porcepic, 1976.

———. *The Sun and the Moon*, in *The Killdeer and Other Plays.* Toronto: Macmillan 1962. 91-171.

———. *A Suit of Nettles.* Erin, ON: Porcépic, 1958, 1975.

Reaney, J. Stewart. *James Reaney. Profiles in Canadian Drama.* Toronto: Gage Publishing, 1977.

Sedgwick, Eve Kasofsky. "Paranoid Reading and Reparative Reading; or, You're So Paranoid, You Probably Think This Introduction Is about You." Foreword, *Novel Gazing: Queer Readings in Fiction.* Ed. Sedgwick. Durham & London: Duke University Press, 1997. 1-37.

Stingle, Richard. " 'all the old levels': Reaney and Frye," in Dragland. 32-62.

Before the Beginning:
We Were There

I n *What is a Canadian Literature?* (1988) and elsewhere John Metcalf declared that there was really no Canadian literary tradition as defined and illustrated by recent scholars and critics. In many skirmishes he has seemed to imply that little Canadian literature published before his arrival in Canada in 1962 was of much value, and that much of what followed was virtually worthless and would not have been published without subsidies or grants from the Canada Council or other granting bodies. (One assumes that what Metcalf wrote, edited and published is exempt from censure.) Several scholars of his generation have asserted confidently that there was no serious academic study or criticism of Canadian literature until Roy Daniells and George Woodcock founded the quarterly *Canadian Literature* and Reginald E. Watters published his *Check List of Canadian Literature and Background Materials, 1629-1950* in 1959, or until Carl F. Klinck and his colleagues published *Literary History of Canada: Canadian Literature in English* in 1965.

Many of us did not know this. There were fewer of us then than now. We responded to what we read as excitedly as did other generations, earlier or later, to what they read. We shared our critical appreciation in terms that were part of our experience.

It is undeniable, of course, that almost unimaginable changes in the writing, marketing, study, teaching and critical appreciation of literature in Manitoba and elsewhere have taken place in the decades following 1960. In the 1940s E.K. Brown's "Letters in Canada" section of the *University of Toronto Quarterly* filled only the last segment of the July number. Canadian poetry and fiction had a few pages each. There may have been one or two publications by western writers in each genre, but not always a Manitoban. Now "Letters in Canada" fills a whole issue of *UTQ*, and there are many quarterlies, regional and national, established and brand new, devoted solely to Canadian writing, both avant-garde and traditional. *Prairie Fire* is growing and maturing in all respects after twenty-five years of publishing and promoting Manitoba authors, and Turnstone Press has survived as a major publisher of Manitoba literature.

Back in the 1940s and 1950s Ryerson Press of Toronto published a handful of Manitoba poets (Mary Elizabeth Bayer, Thecla Bradshaw, Elizabeth Brewster, Michael Collie, Tom Saunders, to name a few), rarely more than one a year, in hardcover chap-book editions of 250 copies that sold for one dollar. Each launch was a real and singular, if unheralded, event. Rarely was more than one Manitoba novel a year published, nearly always in Toronto or New York, and never with the local fanfare that years before had always accompanied the appearance of a new Ralph Connor novel. However, in a period of about two weeks in the fall of 2003 McNally Robinson, at their Grant Park store alone, hosted book launches for thirteen of my former students, colleagues, or close friends, and that was just a fraction of their promotion calendar. Chapters and smaller stores had their own launch calendars. Most of these launches and signings were of Manitoba books, some of which a year later are still selling well and continue to receive international respect. In the 1940s no one could have envisaged the annual Winnipeg International Writers Festival and other celebrations in Winnipeg, let alone the constantly growing number of workshops and of university and college courses in Canadian literature and creative writing.

But yes, Virginia, there is a Santa Claus, and yes, the creation and appreciation and critical study of Canadian and Manitoba literature in Winnipeg did exist before 1960, often excitingly; before many of our living writers, teachers and critics were born.

One of the first poems I memorized in an early public school grade in Toronto was Wilfred Campbell's "Indian Summer"; several other poems by Confederation Poets that I enjoyed before I was ten years old are still vivid in my failing memory. W.J. Alexander's *Shorter Poems* (rev. ed. 1932), a major high-school text, had Campbell, Carman, Crawford, Pauline (as well as Samuel) Johnson, Lampman, two MacDonalds (J.E.H. and Wilson), Pickthall, Pratt and Duncan Campbell (along with Sir Walter) Scott. One of my compulsory first-year honours courses at the University of Toronto in 1940 was American and Canadian Literature, taught unforgettably by E.K. Brown and J.R. MacGillivray. In class we heard some of Brown's critical articles before anyone else heard them on the CBC or saw them in print as individual articles or collected in his book *On Canadian Poetry*, which appeared in 1943, along with the first edition of A.J.M. Smith's *Book of Canadian Poetry*. (Brown's *Rhythm in the Novel* appeared in 1950 and his biography of Willa Cather, completed after his untimely death by his friend Leon Edel, in 1953. All of Brown's books were reissued or reprinted in the coming years.) *David and Other Poems* (1942) appeared while Earle Birney was teaching us Old

English and Chaucer, and while Robert Finch's *Poems* (1946) did not appear until I was at Yale, I had read eleven of his poems in *New Provinces* (1936) before I took his course in Eighteenth-Century French poetry and heard some of his new poems in class.

In the Canadian navy I always had Penguin editions of Ralph Gustafson's *Anthology of Canadian Poetry* (1942) and *Canadian Accent* (1944) in my kit bag or my pocket (in greatcoat weather), and I remember the thrill of walking the streets of Halifax with the Collins White Circle Classics paperback edition of Hugh MacLennan's *Barometer Rising* in my hand as I traced the abrupt changes in architectural patterns indicating where the explosion had changed the cityscape instantaneously.

I still have a clearly etched memory of the national broadcast on CBC Radio of the oratorio on E.J. Pratt's *Brébeuf and His Brethren*, with music by Healey Willan, and with the voices of E.J. Pratt and E.A. Dale, among others, on September 26, 1943 (rebroadcast on April 11, 1944)[1]. I found it ironically significant, apart from the poem's intrinsic merit, that in the context of the apparently endless conscription crisis in Quebec, a Canadian epic by an English-speaking United Church minister, set to music by an Anglican, should glorify, among much else, the heroic faith of French-Canadian Catholics.

Of western Canadian literature I knew little as a child, except that Ralph Connor was one of my favourite authors—up there with Zane Grey. While selling magazines in the early 1930s, I thought that the fiction in the short-lived *National Home Monthly* from Winnipeg was far better than the stories in *Liberty* (only a nickel!), *Maclean's*, or even the *Saturday Evening Post*. But Winnipeg was not always enthusiastic about its own writers, who often made their reputations elsewhere first. Sinclair Ross wrote most of the stories later published in *The Lamp at Noon and Other Stories* (1968) and his best-known novel, *As for Me and My House* (1941), while working in a bank in Winnipeg. However, he kept very much to himself, and Bill Stobie may well be the only living Winnipegger who knew him well. To compound anonymity, Ross has said that Manitoba had absolutely no influence on him or his writing. (Manitoba writers such as Margaret Laurence have repeatedly said that Ross was a major inspiration for them.) Miriam Waddington and Dorothy Livesay, both born in Winnipeg, had moved away while still very young. They published all their poetry of this period and gained their reputations while living elsewhere. I have heard both of them express feelings of hurt that Winnipeg apparently did not remember them—until years later, when they wrote movingly about the depth of their Winnipeg roots.

Margaret Laurence, Adele Wiseman and Jack Ludwig fared better. While they wrote and published most of their work elsewhere, much of it after the decades of this survey, they had lived in Winnipeg until after graduation from university and were vividly remembered in the 1950s by their professors and fellow students, who kept in touch with them and spread word about their forthcoming publications to create a readership, eager, if small. Even so, widespread promotions were not for Winnipeg-gers. When I gave a paper on Margaret Laurence at the Association of Canadian University Teachers of English in Ottawa in 1967, it was well received, but many in the audience seemed not to have heard of Margaret Laurence, even though she had published six books, at least eighteen short stories, received the Governor General's Award for Fiction and several other prizes, and had been made an Honorary Fellow of United College. Like Adele Wiseman's *The Sacrifice* (1956), John Marlyn's *Under the Ribs of Death* (1957) has still not received the recognition it deserves, even in Winnipeg. (But when I first taught it, one of my students, on his own initiative, went out and photographed every location in the novel he could still find—fortunately before the razing of the Royal Alexandra Hotel and of whole blocks of slum housing on Henry Avenue.) Writers, like prophets, are not always recognized or appreciated in their own country.

When I came to Winnipeg to teach in a special Veterans session in the spring of 1946 at United College, I met Peggy Wemyss (who became Margaret Laurence) and Patricia Blondal, not veterans, but students who were keenly interested in literature and writing. In the near future they would be recognized as major novelists. At the time, however, the excitement was about Hugh MacLennan's just-published *Two Solitudes*. As a newcomer to Winnipeg, I was surprised and delighted to find Winnipeg mentioned in this Quebec novel. On pages 113–14, Dennis Morey is speaking to Kathleen Tallard, in Montreal:

> "Winnipeg could have been one of the cities of the world. Some of the world's best people live there. But of course, we're puritans. So the place is just Winnipeg. . . .
>
> "Imagine a flat plain," he said. "Not a narrow strip like you have here by the St. Lawrence, but hundreds of miles of prairie stretching in every direction as far as the eye can see. Imagine it green. Imagine above it a sky so blue your eyes can hardly bear to look at it, and cumulus clouds pure white. Imagine the whole sky seeming to move . . . . Like a great majestic bowl with the earth flat beneath it. Sky the giver, earth the accepter. Male and female . . ."
>
> . . . .
>
> "Now," he said, "imagine a building made of grey granite, reinforced with steel smelted out of the best Lake Superior ore. Imagine the building slim and light as a sword in front, long and light in profile. Imagine it six hundred feet high, towering off that flat plain, with set-backs like decks for gods to walk on and survey the earth. Imagine the sky blue and the white clouds moving past, so close to its pinnacle that you could stare up from

the ground and see the slender profile of that building and think it was moving, too. Imagine it"—he jerked the words out one by one—"clean-angled, balanced, slender, light—mercilessly right. And new, by God . . . like the country that made it! . . . Canadians would never permit such a building to exist."

A few years later when inexpensive reprints became available and I tried to put the novel on the Manitoba high school and the United College curriculum, I discovered that the whole episode containing this Winnipeg quotation was missing from available editions. The context of this conversation was an adulterous meeting, and the publisher Collins had taken so much flak that when Macmillan bought the reprint rights they excised the whole episode so that the novel would not be banned by school boards and libraries. I remember writing protest letters to both Winnipeg papers when even the bowdlerized versions of MacLennan's novel were under attack. Not until the appearance of the Laurentian Library edition in 1967 could readers again know that *Two Solitudes* mentioned Winnipeg.

Back in 1946 I was surprised to find that among the required texts in the first-year English course were translations of French-Canadian novels, Hémon's *Maria Chapdelaine* and Ringuet's *Thirty Acres*. In 1947 I returned to teach summer school at the University of Manitoba and found great excitement about the new English version of Gabrielle Roy's *Bonheur d'occasion, The Tin Flute*. When I came back to United to stay in 1953, I was delighted at the enthusiasm for Roy's *Where Nests the Water Hen* (1951), an enthusiasm that continued substantially for *Street of Riches* (1957) and translations of all the rest of Roy's books, many, of course, beyond our time frame. Colleagues in the French department and Franco-Manitoban friends were also devoted fans of the French originals of this expatriate, which brought their community so sensitively to life. One day, in 1954, I was talking with Father Gerald Lahey, dean of St. Paul's College, in the old Manitoba College building on Ellice Avenue, about curriculum proposals, when his secretary apologetically ushered in a woman. I excused myself and waited in the hall. When the woman left, I was invited back in, and Father Lahey said that his visitor was Gabrielle Roy's sister, Marie-Anna A. Roy, who was going around personally selling copies of her book *Le pain de chez nous: histoire d'une famille manitobaine*, which she had just published. She believed that Gabrielle had not told the whole truth about their family. (Little did I know that this direct marketing was or was to become a Manitoba pattern. Years later, passengers on the MS *Lord Selkirk II* were amazed to see Bill Valgardson hawking his books on the wharf at Gimli when the ship was docking or sailing—even when his works were in stores across Canada, his dramatized stories and novel were showing on TV and available in NFB cassettes, and his radio plays were being broadcast on CBC Radio.)

To return to the summer of 1947, in the old pre-fab Faculty Club on the University of Manitoba campus, Lloyd Wheeler introduced me to Paul Hiebert, who was even more irrepressible in person than in print, and was not to become over-familiar as a permanent guest on Don Harron or Peter Gzowski's CBC Radio morning programs until years later. However, that was the year Hiebert brought out *Sarah Binks*. I sent copies of it to several American academic friends as proof that we did have a distinctive Canadian literature.

The impact of *Sarah Binks* is hard to grasp today because the verse and criticism it satirizes have long been forgotten. The 327-page, beautifully bound volume *Manitoba Muses*, published earnestly by Isaac S. White in 1912, has this epigraph on the title page: "A man may muse here on earth's sod, / But inspiration comes from God."

White's epics "Gentle Joseph," "The Children of Israel in Egypt," and "Afflicted Job" are too massive to sample, but some stanzas from "The Maid's Reply" may reveal what God is guilty of:

"The Manitoba farmer's aim
    Is work, when he gets wed;
But women have themselves to blame,
    Who are so blindly led.
. . . .
"A man should have a thrifty spouse
    To comfort him through life;
But feeding pigs, and milking cows,
    Is not work for a wife.
. . . .
"The farmer oft will make a jest,
    And go off to his plow;
But would not give his wife a rest
    By milking of a cow. (259-60)

Here is Sarah Binks's "The Farmer and the Farmer's Wife":

The farmer and the farmer's wife
Lead frolicsome and carefree lives,
And all their work is but in play,
Their labours only exercise.

The farmer leaps from bed to board,
And board to binder on the land;
His wife awakes with shouts of joy,
And milks a cow with either hand.

Then all in fun they feed the pigs,
And plough the soil in reckless glee,
And play the quaint old-fashioned game
Of mortgagor and mortgagee.

And all day long they dash about,
In barn and pasture, field and heath;
He sings a merry roundelay,
She whistles gaily through her teeth.

And when at night the chores are done,
And hand in hand they sit and beam,
He helps himself to applejack,
And she to Paris Green.

In the paragraph of commentary that follows, Hiebert says: "Inspector Peeker, proba-bly the most outstanding critic in several school districts, says of this poem: 'The teachers of Baal and Cactus Lake have asked that this poem be put on the list of sup-plementary reading'" (64-65).

Not surprisingly, but sadly, Paul's later books, which he took much more seriously, *Tower in Siloam* (1966) and *Doubting Castle* (1976), in which he struggled honestly to reconcile his deep religious convictions with his faith in science, made no impact in comparison with *Sarah Binks* and its less successful sequel *Willows Revisited* (1967). Even to his closest friends Paul was and is humorist and clown.

In 1953, Lloyd Wheeler introduced me to the Poetry Society of Winnipeg. Today only a handful of members are left, but in the 1950s we flourished, with printed pro-grams, membership fees, and large attendance. In the fall of 1953 we packed the old Young United Church sanctuary with several hundred ticket holders to hear Roy Campbell, the then-famous South African poet. Not everyone was delighted, for some of his audience had seen poets before only in solemn sickly sepia daguerreotypes or engravings in the halls of older school buildings, and they were shocked to see a ruddy-faced performer who had obviously had a drink or two with dinner before giving his lively and articulate program of readings.

Other book lovers were a little baffled by Nicholas Monsarrat, whose novel *The Cruel Sea* (1951) was then famous. In addition to his appearance at the University of Manitoba, he spoke to the Three O'Clock Club and signed their guest book with an inscription in what seemed to be hieroglyphic. Because I was a naval veteran as well as an academic, I had been invited to provide the guest with male support on this otherwise all-female occasion. After a private chat about naval matters I confessed to him that I didn't recognize the language of his inscription. He said that he didn't, either. He had made it up because he thought it might keep people guessing.

There was no doubt about the reception of Leonard Cohen. In the late 1950s he read to packed audiences at United College and the University of Manitoba during the week, and then on Sunday afternoon he filled the old Dominion Theatre (long since replaced by what is now the Fairmont Hotel), performing with Lenny Breau, the great jazz guitarist, and a combo, who improvised accompaniments to Cohen's readings. This was before Cohen began releasing records of his singing. Decades later that afternoon is still a priceless memory.

Most of the time, before the Canada Council, the League of Canadian Poets, and The Writers' Union of Canada began arranging reading tours at little expense to host centres, we did not expect frequent visitors, and there were no writers-in-residence. Month after month the Browning Society, the Burns Society, the Dickens Society, the Poetry Society, the Winnipeg branches of the Humanities Association of Canada, the Canadian Authors' Association, the Classical Association, the Alliance Française, and other groups met with local speakers or writers, outside speakers being the exception. *Doctor* Leathers—word had it that everyone, even his wife, knew him only as "Doctor," but that is *un canard*, for I have heard Beatrice call him "Victor" many times—seemed to be present at every meeting of every literary association, diligently marking French exercises and tests throughout the speaker's presentation, and then proving that he had heard and understood every word by asking a crisply worded, relevant, polite question as soon as the chair invited the audience to respond. It is hard to do justice to the memory of this colourful, generous polymath.

United College had a long tradition of A.L. Phelps's English Club, which we revived in 1953 and which thrived for years, meeting monthly in faculty or student homes, as far as possible with students presenting papers for discussion or reading their own writing, and only occasionally with other authors, local or visiting. (Wives and mothers usually provided refreshments.) In 1962 Rudy Wiebe came to read from his just-published *Peace Shall Destroy Many* on the very day (or perhaps the day after) he had been fired from his job at the Christian Press for publishing a novel that some feared might discredit the Mennonite community. Adele Wiseman had left for England in 1956 when we had our first peek at *The Sacrifice*. Most of the group were Jewish students from the North End and, unlike Wiebe's community, they were delighted to encounter their neighbours, relatives and local shopkeepers in print, even if they did not all realize immediately the depth of the novel. (We had no Africans present when we looked at Laurence's "The Drummer of All the World" in 1956, and while Bob Hallstead and I knew we had a major author, Laurence did not make much of an impact on Winnipeg until her Manawaka novels began to appear with *The Stone Angel* in 1964. When Laurence or Wiseman made an infrequent appearance in later years it was always standing room only, no matter what the venue.) Patricia Blondal's untimely death prevented us from inviting her to a celebration of *A Candle to Light the Sun* (1960).

The English Club was always a group small enough to crowd into a modest living room. The Poetry Hour was a different matter. I believed that the oral dimension of literature was an essential part of it, and for more than two decades after 1953 we had a weekly noon hour, first in Convocation Hall, and later, in the 1960s, in one of the large lecture theatres in Manitoba Hall, devoted entirely to listening to poetry and prose, often with an audience of nearly two hundred. When visiting writers were available we tried to slot them into the Poetry Hour, but usually we had live readings by students and faculty, or excellent audio recordings that were increasingly available, or a combination of both. It was easy to provide recordings of Yeats, Eliot, Auden, Dylan Thomas, Frost, e.e. cummings and so on, reading their own work, and recordings of earlier poetry read by good actors and readers. Later, as they became available, we had recordings of Canadian writers when we could not afford live ones. In 1959 I sensed that most Winnipeggers hadn't really experienced the Beats, and I attempted a reading of Ginsberg's *Howl* and some Ferlinghetti poems, to the consternation and bafflement of more than one listener. In the 1960s Reg Skene developed one-hour readings of major Shakespeare plays, such as *Hamlet* and *Macbeth*, and his success emboldened me to direct readings of the Christmas dinner scene in Joyce's *A Portrait of the Artist as a Young Man* and one-hour versions of Milton's *Paradise Lost* and *Paradise Regained*.

For many years the Poetry Hour was the only noon-hour game in town, but as enrolments grew and timetables became more complicated, the Poetry Hour faded. Once, when Earle Birney was scheduled to read, I found that the philosophy department had booked Mircea Eliade for the same slot, and then learned that the students' association had booked Dick Gregory for that hour. From then on, visiting writers were usually invited to individual classes to avoid embarrassment. But while it lasted, the Poetry Hour met a real need. Years later, total strangers have come up to me in Safeway and said that while they were never in my classes, they still remembered the Poetry Hour.

In 1955 I could get good audiences for public lectures on regionalism and nationalism in Canadian literature. The publication of the first edition of Klinck and Watters's *Canadian Anthology* that year made it feasible to make a good honours course in American and Canadian Literature, even though full-priced trade editions of appropriate novels made the cost of texts almost prohibitive until Malcolm Ross and Jack McClelland launched the New Canadian Library in 1957, and Macmillan's Laurentian Library followed a decade later. By the mid-1960s full Canadian courses, both general and honours, were attracting waiting lists.

Credit courses in creative writing were not approved until the mid 1960s, but from 1953 on Bob Hallstead and I invited interested students to a weekly afternoon workshop with no text, no formal curriculum, no requirements or credits, no fees. Students took turns handing in, a week in advance, some writing, typed or handwritten, in multiple copies (no photocopies then, only carbons, dittos, occasionally hand-cranked Gestetner copies for those who could afford a stencil or two). A week later everyone present was invited to make comments or suggestions that we all discussed. Writers came as long or as often as they wished, and some continued with Bob or me with individual appointments. This is not the place to name names, but authors have spoken or written about what these sessions did for them. Of course, the weekly *Uniter* and *Manitoban* and annual publications such as *Vox* encouraged the development of writers.

Our small English department at United was part of the larger University of Manitoba English committee that planned curricula and set and marked examinations in a lockstep arrangement for the University of Manitoba and all the affiliated colleges. Of course there was friction and rivalry on occasion, but usually we were friends working together and learning from each other. Nuns in their habits, Jesuit and Anglican priests, a retired United Church minister, and a variety of near-hippies and neo-conservatives, from a variety of academic backgrounds, made a stimulating mix. My wife Margaret and I lived on Clare Avenue in Riverview. Bob and Anne Hallstead lived a block away on Clare. James Reaney lived with his wife, the poet Colleen Thibaudeau, a block over on Balfour, and Chester Duncan and his wife Ada lived just one block further, on Ashland. Our children went to school together. Jamie had already won two Governor General's Awards and was to win two more soon after he left for the University of Western Ontario in 1960, for work at least partly written in

Winnipeg. I was told by several people that they had seen him setting type by hand for the first number of *Alphabet* on the Winnipeg Transit bus going to Fort Garry. Colleen's poems were set to music by John Beckwith. The Reaneys hospitably hosted Norman Levine when he came through Winnipeg, and Norman wrote some unkind things about the occasion in *Canada Made Me* (1958), which offended all of us. Jamie's poem "A Message to Winnipeg" (1960) is a weirdly wonderful going-away present for any writer to give to a community.

Chester Duncan was as much pianist and composer as English scholar. He composed a musical setting for Auden's "For the Time Being," which a group of us put on in the Dominion Theatre, and which CBC Radio produced later for the national network. On New Year's Eve, 1957, I think, CBC TV Winnipeg presented a one-hour show entitled, if memory serves, "Thoughts for a Dying Year," for which Chester wrote the script and the music, played the piano and read the poetry. It is hard to imagine that happening today. (Orville Darraugh was usually the soloist in Chester's recitals, and he may have been on the program.) The CBC did a lot of local production then, and some us were invited to give broadcast talks as often as we had time and energy to do so. University colleagues performed Grove's *Settlers of the Marsh* as a radio play. In 1955 the Poetry Society asked Chester and me to judge a national poetry contest that attracted 550 or so paying entrants from all walks of life and from all over Canada— a humbling and revealing experience.

Ogden Turner and Bill and Margaret Stobie were active in the Winnipeg Little Theatre, out of which John Hirsch and Tom Hendry founded Theatre 77, which became the Manitoba Theatre Centre, and then Theatre Across the Street, which became the Warehouse Theatre. It was fun to see John Hirsch pushing a broom across the stage in a production of *Detective Story* that he directed for WLT. While John was busy developing professional theatre in Winnipeg, he took time in 1957 to help me devise a curriculum in English for an influx of Hungarian refugees who had been guaranteed entrance to the standard university programs without any requirement that they must understand, read or write English. Miraculously, some of them survived and went on to distinguished careers.

Malcolm Ross was at the University of Manitoba for only five years and left in 1950. In a deeper sense he never left. Margaret Laurence, Adele Wiseman and other students of his have repeatedly testified as to his scholarship, fairness and incredible helpfulness. I met him only briefly when I was in Winnipeg those two summers in the 1940s, but he became a friend, trying to get me back to Canada when I was teaching in the United States, always making helpful suggestions about many things. As editor of *Queen's Quarterly* he published Laurence's "The Drummer of All the World." He asked me to write an article on Canadian attitudes to American influence and sent me many challenging books to review. For years he was a regular and eagerly awaited contributor to the CBC Sunday afternoon program *Critically Speaking*, which was an intellectual blood transfusion for many of us, but which he hardly heard himself because CBC reception was abominable in Kingston in those days. His New Canadian Library was one of the most important resources ever for the teaching and appreciation of Canadian writing. His own scholarship was wise and original.

When I came back to Winnipeg in 1953 Tom Saunders, a United Church minister and chaplain, had already published two volumes of poetry, which at the time taught me more about life on the prairies than any other single source. He was to publish three more. Tom is in many ways a Manitoba version of Robert Frost. He was one of the first visitors to my office, asking me to read his poem-in-progress on the 1950 Winnipeg flood, which was eventually published in 1969, with illustrations by George Swinton, in *Red River of the North and Other Poems of Manitoba*. In addition to publishing his own poetry and writing on Frederick Philip Grove and Margaret Laurence, he served ably for fifteen years as literary editor of the *Winnipeg Free Press*. Not only did he have me write dozens of reviews, he did everything he could to promote good writing, especially by Manitoba writers. His wife Janet wrote regularly about children's literature before and after any of the Winnipeg universities had developed courses in it.

Here is the conclusion of Tom's "Winter Burial," originally published in *Horizontal World* (1951) and slightly revised when reprinted in *Beyond the Lakes* (1978):

. . . Someone had said "Come,"
And here we were. It was a thing to know
Just what to do. But here we were, half-numb,
And it a wind and thirty-five below.

The preacher spoke and prayed. His words were lost,
Tossed on the wind and hurtled God knows where.
But no one heeded. Suddenly he crossed
Back from the grave. We knew then that the prayer
Was ended. Quick, we took the spades and tossed
The frozen earth back in. In the chill air
The earth was hard and noisy with the frost. (43)

The thirty-page free-verse "Red River of the North," which I first saw when evidence of the power of the 1950 flood was still everywhere, is hard to sample today after decades of lulling security provided by Duff's Ditch, as the floodway is still called, for the poem's effectiveness is quietly cumulative. The poem traces the history of the Red in vivid vignettes from earliest geological times throughout Manitoba history until after the 1950 flood, raising unanswerable questions about the river's future. Here is part of serene section vi:

> brown
> unhurried
> the waters of the red
> ease by st. boniface
>
> the lyndale dyke
> flanks it to eastward here
> to south and west
> fort garry
> wildwood
> nestle like birds
> in their flat ground-nests
>
> st. vital's spread like a blanket
> out to dry
>
> to seine's mouth
> (past assiniboine)
> the river runs
> north through the heart
> of winnipeg
>
> through deeper slopes
> to lockport
> selkirk
> through a shallow bed
> reed-grown
> to reach lake winnipeg

it gropes
rather than flows
into the lake
(a seine of marshes
multi-home of birds)
a slough more than a river here
but still the red (9-11)

I mention one other memory. Before the Internet and before the founding and flourishing of many of our so-called learned societies with their annual conferences and their journals, a valued source of information about what was going on in the literary world was the publisher's representative. Many of these reps became our good friends, even if we saw them only twice a year at the most. They came ostensibly to bring news about their new texts and reference works, which they hoped we might adopt. But some of them were scholars and gentlemen who brought news of friends and trends and much more from all across Canada. Decades later I still remember with real affection Robin Strachan and Patrick Meany of Macmillan, and John Coutts of Oxford, to name three of many.

Certainly the 1960s brought a world of changes. Many of the new faculty who joined the universities were accomplished poets and novelists and generous teachers of good writing. Great new courses were developed, and all sorts of helpful texts and scholarly aids were available to support them. Newcomers to Canada from India, Ceylon (now Sri Lanka), Italy, the West Indies and the Caribbean, and other parts of the world we had known little of, enriched our literature unbelievably, and others made us aware of the richness of South American literature. First Nations' voices began to be heard at last. And a lot of Canadian-born writers too young to know about the Dark Ages that preceded them began writing and publishing.

However, I am not the only one still alive who is happy to borrow Wordsworth's words: "Fair seedtime had my soul . . . ."

NOTE

1. I am indebted to Marni Caliph of the CBC for verifying the exact dates, which I do not pretend to have remembered.

WORKS CITED

Alexander, W.J. *Shorter Poems*, Rev. ed. Toronto: T. Eaton, 1932.

Birney, Earle. *David and Other Poems*. Toronto: Ryerson Press, 1942.

Auden, W.H. *For the Time Being*. London: Faber & Faber, 1945.

Blondal, Patricia. *A Candle to Light the Sun*. Toronto: McClelland & Stewart, 1960.

———. *From Heaven with a Shout*. Toronto: McClelland & Stewart, 1962.

Brown, E.K. *On Canadian Poetry*. Toronto: Ryerson Press, 1943.

———. *Rhythm in the Novel*. Toronto: University of Toronto Press, 1950.

———. *Willa Cather, A Critical Biography*. Completed by Leon Edel. New York: Knopf, 1953.

Finch, Robert. *Poems*. Toronto: Oxford University Press, 1946.

Ginsberg, Allen. *Howl and Other Poems*. Pocket Poems No. 4. San Francisco: City Lights, 1956.

Grove, Frederick Philip. *Settlers of the Marsh*. Toronto: Ryerson Press, 1925.

Gustafson, Ralph, ed. *Anthology of Canadian Poetry (English)*. Toronto: Penguin, 1942.

———, ed. *Canadian Accent: A Collection of Stories and Poems by Contemporary Writers from Canada.* Toronto: Penguin, 1944.

Hémon, Louis. *Maria Chapdelaine*. Toronto: Macmillan, 1921.

Hiebert, Paul. *Doubting Castle*. Winnipeg: Queenston House, 1976.

———. *Sarah Binks*. Toronto: Oxford University Press, 1947.

———. *Tower in Siloam*. Toronto: McClelland & Stewart, 1966.

———. *Willows Revisited*. Toronto: McClelland & Stewart, 1967.

Klinck, Carl F. et al. *Literary History of Canada: Canadian Literature in English*. Toronto: University of Toronto Press, 1965.

Klinck, Carl F. & Reginald E. Watters, eds. *Canadian Anthology*. Toronto: Gage, 1956.

Laurence, Margaret. "The Drummer of All the World." *Queen's Quarterly* 63 (Winter 1956): 487-504.

———. *The Stone Angel*. Toronto: McClelland & Stewart, 1964.

Levine, Norman. *Canada Made Me*. Erin, ON: The Porcupine's Quill, 1958.

MacLennan, Hugh. *Barometer Rising*. White Circle Classics No. 75. Toronto: Collins, 1943.

———. *Two Solitudes*. Toronto: Collins, 1945.

Marlyn, John. *Under the Ribs of Death*. Toronto: McClelland & Stewart, 1957.

Metcalf, John. *What Is a Canadian Literature?* Guelph, ON: Red Kite Press, 1988.

Monsarrat, Nicholas. *The Cruel Sea*. New York: Knopf, 1951.

Pratt, E.J. *Brébeuf and His Brethren*. Toronto: Macmillan, 1940.

Reaney, James. *Selected Longer Poems*. Ed. Germaine Warkentin. Erin, ON: Press Porcepic, 1976.

Ringuet [Philippe Panneton]. *Trente arpents*. Paris: Flammarion, 1938. Trans. Felix and Dorothea Walter as *Thirty Acres*. Toronto: Macmillan, 1940.

Ross, Sinclair. *As for Me and My House*. New York: Reynal, 1941.

———. *The Lamp at Noon and Other Stories*. Introd. Margaret Laurence. New Canadian Library No. 62. Toronto: McClelland & Stewart, 1975.

Roy, Gabrielle. *Bonheur d'occasion*. Montreal: Beauchemin, 1947. Trans. Hannah Josephson as *The Tin Flute*. Toronto: McClelland & Stewart, 1947.

———. *La Petite Poule d'Eau*. Montreal: Beauchemin, 1950. Trans. Harry Lorin Binsse as *Where Nests the Water Hen*. Toronto: McClelland & Stewart, 1951.

———. *Rue Deschambault*. Montreal: Beauchemin, 1955. Trans. Harry Lorin Binsse as *Street of Riches*. Toronto: McClelland & Stewart, 1957.

Roy, Marie-Anna. *Le pain de chez nous: histoire d'une famille manitobaine*. Montreal: Lévrier, 1954.

Saunders, Thomas. *Horizontal World*. Toronto: Ryerson Press, 1951.

———. *Red River of the North and Other Poems of Manitoba*. Illus. George Swinton. Winnipeg: Peguis Publishers, 1969.

Scott, F.R. et al. *New Provinces: Poems of Several Authors*. Toronto: Macmillan, 1936.

Watters, Reginald E. *Check List of Canadian Literature and Background Materials, 1629-1950*. Toronto: Universiy of Toronto Press, 1959.

White, Isaac S. *Manitoba Muses or Gentle Joseph and Other Poems*. Toronto: Bryant, 1912.

Wiebe, Rudy. *Peace Shall Destroy Many*. Toronto: McClelland & Stewart, 1962.

Wiseman, Adele. *The Sacrifice*. Toronto: Macmillan, 1956.

Wordsworth, William. *The Prelude, or Growth of a Poet's Mind*. London: Moxon, 1850.

JEAN MARGARET LAURENCE

NORTH MAIN CAR
-Winnipeg- ("written in 1948")

morning, and the city's steel hulk
heaves, stirs itself, who has been
a lovely giant held by enticing night,
ungilding daylight, exploring now
her savagery and blemishes.

out of the north the streetcar crawls,
an outsize wood-and-iron worm.
people clamber aboard, still yawning,
an easiness in their faces
that the harsh day has not yet
pulled into tensions.

people have come from far off to this town,
from europe's handkerchief-sized farms,
from the winding streets of the world,
exchanging the known devil, the overseer's whip,
for another, sight unseen.

    "when we got on the boat, with our little luggage,
     a sailor said 'hello' to the baby, in english,
     and we knew we had left our country..
     we felt lost and stupid. and the small son
     cried sleepily, for we had walked,
     crossing three borders."

if the past weaves the future on its loom,
this city's tapestry should flower
from threads dipped in dyes of every land's sorrow,
deepened to wisdom, yet the bloodspitting
of race at race, breaks here and there the pattern,
letting the threads be torn and lost.

the car jolts sluggishly past fruit stores, where
prices are being stickily soaped on windows;
lumbers past avenues where houses are,
where tall gaunt houses, paint peeling,
crowd cottages like ancient swaybacks
among the young neat colts.
                    "St. John's Avenue..watch the door, there!"

(The young man climbs aboard, swinging his lunchpail)

Straight strong legs like living resilient steel,
And face moulded clean as fresh-cut stone..
Steve. Your last name does not matter..you are all names
And all races (whether you like it or not, it is so.)
In the packinghouse, you will put on canvas apron,
Heavy boots, get out throat-piercing powerful knives,
Go to the killing floor. A slaughter-house is a vast fantasia:
You can taste its rankness in your mouth at night..
The putridly pungent blood, turning to withered rot;
Nostril-cutting brine; hides, new-peeled; guts but recently stilled.
Well, it takes a strong man to work in a packinghouse,
You've often said, with a laugh, Steve, a little proud.
And each december layoffs are like bushfire:
Authority's logic.. "let stock pile up, its price will fall,
We buy cheap, sell dear, and profits mount."
(Should they care that your wife's eyes
Are fear-flecked when you tell her?)
Men standing night-duty on the picketline,
Shivering with cold and blowing on wind-cracked hands,

Have gained some ground..you have stood there with them,
And learned young that leisure is for the rich. The poor
Rise at six on workdays and make love on Sunday mornings.
Packinghouse workers die (you know the brief statistic)
Within two years of retiring..it is your cry, soundless,
Echoing through chilly corridors.. "our future is today!".

along main street, then, the car,
along the north town's spine.
the mushroom-growth of corner groceries
waken early, the slight-voiced bells on doors
herald the first customer, buying
a bread, one of the brown-bulging loaves
piled on wooden counters.
the car shudders to a stop; the driver is brisk.
                              "Mountain Avenue..Hurry it up!"

(The old man steps slowly aboard, quiet, scanning the people)

Abraham Greenspan, going to visit his daughter,
Has left his shop behind, with its spice-sweet pastrami smell,
And the oranges, tiny bright-globed suns, piled in the window.
His thin hands, grasping the cane, have touched
The spasm-pulse of years too gashed to tell..
There was a ghetto in Poland, years ago..he has felt
The monstrous whips dark-striping his flesh.
Perhaps the new world would be easier: he came to see,
And saw his children pointed at as yids.
Out of it all, a thought old as the talmud:
"You are a jew, therefore you live with suffering,
Are not the two synonymous as night and dark?"
When he was young, with veins on fire, he fought.
Always, beating against his nostrils, demanding only
Justice, was the sour smell of his people's blood
Being dredged from them through three thousand years.

Now he is seventy. He tires easily, and must watch his diet.
The soft black felt hat and grey wisps of beard
Frame the gentle dignity of deep-etched face. Only his eyes,
Alive, show that the outward fragility still sheathes a strength.
But last year at Hanukkah, festival of the lights,
The four boys seemed..indifferent, a little bored?
Glad, perhaps, to be going away again. They honor him..oh yes,
But the laws and faith no longer are the marrow of their bones.
What has a man got in the world but his sons after him?
No words can sense this mourning. Life goes on, though,
One tends the store, and walks a little to stretch old rusted limbs.
But still the hope persists, that some night,
The doors closed and the lamps lighted,
The sons of Abraham will gather as before.

till school enforces quietness at nine,
the boys shout (strident, talking big)
playing baseball on the streets,
and short-skirted girls skip rope
on sidewalks where mudpuddles spring up
like wet flowers, from the melted snow.
past drewry's brewery, the car groans to standstill.
                    "Redwood Avenue..Change for East Kildonan"

(Shopping bag in hand, the woman searches for fare)

Mrs. Riley is leaving the faded house
To fight pitched verbal battle with market gardeners
Over the price of carrots. She reads the magazines, mourns
Her lack of adventure, who for years has militantly rammed
Her floormop in poverty's peaked face.
Her hands are thick and red..they have washed many workshirts
And bathed many smooth-skinned squirming babies.
When she and Jim were married, they were both eighteen,
She with auburn hair and white body; he, six feet tall,

With corded-rope muscles and a job. During the depression, then,
Work gone, and four kids to be fed..holy mother of Jesus!
Those were the days when your belly was flat against your spine!
Now, the old man works in the needle trades,
The children are grown, and life is hushed.
Her solid square body in a greet [green] cotton dress
Spells weariness, but not defeat.
Mrs. Riley shifts weight from one hip to the other,
And wonders how in god's name the two of them will live
When (soon enough) her man's too worn
To be a profit to the men who hire.

creep along, morning streetcar,
past the shop with the fly-specked window
where the tailor's scissors fashion cloth
with expert snip..patterns are for fumblers;
he knew cloth long before he knew women.

in the small struggling houses here,
there is a newspaper, gazetska polska, perhaps;
the ukrainian word and the canadian tribune?
or the ukrainian voice and the winnipeg free press.
two voices, two sides of the great ravine.

my city, there is work for many
young printers' apprentices, learning the trade,
where so much is said on both sides,
and in so many tongues.

> "Alfred Avenue..Use both doors, please."

(Gripping a scuffed briefcase, the young man climbs aboard)

One day when Ben was five (youngster with wind-brushed hair),
The street's boys, mirrors of parental image, ukrainian and english,
Called him "lousy jew," bloodied his face, sent him seething

With anger and the first fear, to his father's store
Where knives shone under the dust, and doors were wide to the sun,
And big-bellied mixing bowls stood in a brown confusion.
Ben twisted under the counter and vomited into a pail.
At night his mother asked him, and he told her.
She took him in her soft full arms, called him schoen ingalah,
And said the goyim were like that. But he did not forget.
The city's conflicts shaped and scarred him through intense years..
He saw many wealthy of his race move from the district,
And cast their votes for aldermen who hated jews.
(Bargain prices: slightly tarnished social acceptance;
Durability unguaranteed.) Ben, at sixteen, had to work:
Once, seeing sweating hands held up for strike vote,
He knew he looked at workers' hands, no longer jew or pole,
But men resolved together. Slowly he understood:
Despite the everydays, the stones flung in the streets,
A man in the last-ditch stand, a man pressed to the ropes,
Cleaves to those who labor with him, of whatever race.
Ben's body shows thin in a grey trenchcoat;
The face is jagged, a sharp pencil-sketch of a face.
He works long for slim pay..an organizer doesn't join for cash.
At Ben's Bar Mitzvah (not so many years ago), the old man
His grandfather, said "perhaps this boy will help
To lead his people out of suffering." Somewhere along the way
All the oppressed became Ben's people. He must work for them
If he would work for himself and for his sons.
Someday man will be man, more merciful and just
Than any god. But now, the way..
Hard as unhewn granite, painful and sure as birth.

forward into the morning, the streetcar,
past the worn cafe, tired after the night,
where waitresses with passive shadowed eyes
leave for the meagre substitute for home, the narrow bed
under brown eaves. the city itself
has possessed and wearied them:

the night-throb of the cafe; the jukebox's false vigor;
and clumsy lovemaking among burned-out cigarettes.
hurry along, streetcar: inexorable timeclocks threaten,
clank in a rush past the delicatessen, where
in the savory-smelling kitchen, cabbage is being cut for borsht.
streetcar, rattle your bones along the track
to the ukrainian church, where cross and turret
gleam in the sun, and shame the old brown brick.

many churches and faiths are here,
the city receives them, it is big enough
(they say) for all. some go god's way,
and some lay up riches where neither moth nor rust
can corrupt, in the bank of montreal.

                    "Selkirk Avenue..Move along, please!"

(The large priest rings the bell and rises)

Father Konarski's solemn eyes withdraw
From the patch-quilt crowd bulging the car,
His glance goes past a soap ad to eternity.
The red face glows like an edam cheese,
Imagining the angels' approbation for his work
In leading his sheep stolidly to bear
Without rancour crowded houses and slight pay,
Or, if they must blame..blame jews and reds
(The source of the world's sores..step on them like ants).
Delicately the hands smooth the black cassock.
The altar and the bare, chalk-smelling schoolroom
Will embrace him, and stocky, high-cheekboned youngsters
Will be sponges to his fluid speech, as, prophet-like,
He offers for their loyalty the thirty-years-ago Ukraine,
Weaving enticing stories of that lovely land..
(Where peasant people starved in rank sod huts,
Working like oxen for the arrogant landlord;

Before, in simple desperation, they learned
To conceal guns in the tachanka; before
The icon's poison-fangs were drained..this
Was your paradise, father.) With ample piety
And force of hellfire in those pallid eyes,
Father Konarski goes to save his flock
From such a dreaded sin as minds' awakening.

people lean back on dusty wicker seats,
look through quavering windows, see the laundry lines
back of apartment blocks, where the overalls
and shirts go up, like tattered flags
waving brief victory over another week.
the manitoba maples' pale new leaves
like supplicant hands, reach out toward the sun,
and on front porches, women
come out from steamy kitchens,
yell at the kids to watch the cars.

away from the main street jostle
and the streetcar's iron jargon,
only a few blocks walk and you will find
the gathering places of each race:
like newspapers, two of most..
the vast community of strong slavic faces,
the ukrainian people, stand out here,
for nowhere but in the ukraine are there more.
the nationalists fly the flag
of the old old country above their hall:
laughter and beer-drinking: it is very gay
(and in the corridors the handsome lads
are jesting of the pogrom they will someday make).
walk further..in the ukrainian labor temple
race's bond is broadened to bonds of belief.
look at the boys, rough-voiced and energetic,
and the girls, their scrubbed triangular faces

and the living circles of their breasts.
these husky men and women and the old
with leathery, immutable faces, they believe
in the years to come that will belong to them.

"Stella Avenue..Use the rear door out!"

(The man with the flat plain face steps aboard)

Nick Hrynchuk, in grease-stained overalls, is bound
For the steel mill. He can work hard, this man
With the clay-red neck and shoulders muscled thick.
You would not think, seeing his laughter-knowing eyes,
That many nights he spends ploughing a difficult furrow
Through unyielding pages, tracing the contours of history
With slow stubbornness and a great need for the harvest.
His little rain-grey house is battered
Like a discarded packingcase (cramped, the family
Of six sleep in one room)..and to pay
For this shelter from weather, his wide-spanning hands
Work hard as any man's can, but the house remains the same.
His mind still gropes for explanations, painfully,
But in his life Nick Hrynchuk knows his kind should have
Brick houses and good gardens for their years of labor.

approaching the subway, the streetcar slows,
and devilish watches jerk to meet a dozen frowns.
city, your cheap blues-song,
with its ragged-jazz defiance, rubbing shoulders
with despair, shows in the leaning, the crippled lines
of buildings that crowd the railway tracks.

life is too thick, packed in as though inanimate;
here, the immigration hall (its children
play around that steel artery of the city,

the big trains clip past them);
here, the negro people, forbidden any homes
other than these shattered, rust-eaten shacks,
by tacit agreement of respectable landlords;
here, the people taste the grime-clogged smoke,
their throats are bitter with it always.

the subway inn, refuge of the city's driftwood,
and the empress hotel, once, perhaps, a lady,
now an old bedraggled harlot, close to collapse,
jealous of successors who have siphoned off the trade..
these take consolation from the corpse-faced houses.
they watch them greedily..they will seduce
some of the children who play beside the tracks.

                    "Henry Avenue..Move to the back of the car"

(The boy steps out, running slim fingers through blue-black hair)

As you swing your body, straight as a douglas fir,
Down the grey street, bend your artist's eyes, Takao Tamura,
To the thin dried grass like fine fingerbones
Clutching the treebase. Look keenly so your brush can tell
Of the black honeycombed snow now nearly defeated.
(Painted with deftness, april details may sell, Takao).
But if you want to eat, do not paint
Your father's patient face pierced with despair
When the little land in the Okanagan was wrenched away;
Himself (born in Vancouver), an "enemy alien"..
The homeless have no redress.
Do not paint (if you would make a living)
Your mother's hands, knotted like thorn branch,
Or her still, seamed face looking for the last time
At the sturdy apple trees that, like her children,
She had tended in all weathers and made grow strong.

picking up speed, the streetcar strains its ribs,
struggles past angular, tilted clothing stores
that elbow each other like eager salesmen.

out of the north town the car emerges..
the north town, shadows and lights, contrasts,
warring, stabbing each other, sweating,
yelling a greeting to the neighbor,
exploding with hot and nervous anger,
making the denim overalls for the prairie farmer,
slaughtering the stock in the packinghouses,
keeping the freight trains spanning a country,
living on one another's doorstep.

do you brawl together, you men of different tongues?
tomorrow you will suffer together, as you did yesterday.
can you not see it? in the mornings
jew and ukrainian, pole and english and negro,
wait shoulder to shoulder at the streetcar stop.
grit, whirling from the pavement,
blows in all men's eyes,
and in the winter, knifing frost has never cared
about the color of men's hides.

..where is the enemy, oh people?
is it here? is it that lithe negro girl
with legs like slight brown tapering pillars?
is it the italian child with eyes soft as a fawn's?
is it the russian mother, singing
the old songs of dusk to her child?
is it among us at all, that we should stab
blindly at each other?
when will the outer struggle call to our deepest energy?

those among us who cast the same stones at each other
as are cast at all by the immaculate who live

on the track's correct side..
you are betraying us.
those who bear inlaid on a silver cross
a heavy weight of hatred..
you are betraying us.
those in whose mimic mouths appears
their masters' bitter faith..
you are betraying us.
we are working people..life is not easy for us.
what room have we for strife among ourselves,
when all of us are human anthracite, consumed
to feed the fires for an owner's warmth?

"CPR Station..Hurry it up, we're late!"

the wheezing streetcar grinds to a stop;
surging movement breaks within, people push
desperately to the door; once out, disperse like dust.
individuals change to unsorted faces; briskness sets in.
here in the desperate traffic's thrust, the spinning minutes,
the crowd dissolves to one face..a young man, doubtful, eager,
a man who does not quite know yet his muscles' strength.

steve, your face is the face of my city,
dreaming about its many-textured past
and the promise of still-embryo years.
over a pint of beer in a north-end pub
let us talk, you and I, of ourselves,
let us trust one another (it is not easy), let us hear
the music of the ukrainian mandolins, let us get
the young jewish violinist to play for us
the Hatikvah, the song of israel's hope.
let us listen closely, as the old man with keen eyes,
bred in London's slums, tells us of his boyhood.
let us sit down with the negro lad
who knows in his heart the most real blues-song.

oh all of us have been separated long enough
by the cruel-crushing walls of race and creed
looming between us. let us take these old grey outworn blocks,
heave them apart, turn them around to the sun,
and see revealed the richness of our diversity,
the colors of speech and our songs' splendor.
let us build of these a new structure, a fortress
founded on common creed, our bond as workingmen:
a base against oppression, our first bastion of tomorrow.

Editor's Note: "North Main Car" is copyright © 1999 the Estate of Margaret Laurence. It is published here with the permission of Jocelyn Laurence. Every effort has been taken to preserve Laurence's punctuation (e.g., two dots for ellipses), spelling and stylistic innovations. The words "written in 1948" appear in Laurence's hand on the manuscript beside the title. The poem is signed Jean Margaret Laurence.

North Main Car:
A Context

F or Margaret Laurence's characters Vanessa MacLeod of *A Bird in the House* and Morag Gunn of *The Diviners*, as they set out from Manawaka, Winnipeg represents freedom. While we are given little information about Vanessa's experiences of Winnipeg, we share with Morag experiences more complex than mere freedom associated with university and the people she meets there. There are the experiences of uncertainty and loneliness, the discovery of delight in literature and a confidence in her own response to it, the discovery of a kindred spirit who shares her desire to be a writer, and the discovery of love. Laurence's memoir *Dance on the Earth* makes the reader aware that many aspects of Morag's life in Winnipeg are drawn from Laurence's own experiences there.

There are, however, notable aspects of Margaret Laurence's Winnipeg experience that do not appear in her fiction: the enriching experiences she had, after her graduation, as a reporter on the *Westerner* and the *Winnipeg Citizen*,[1] and as registrar at the YWCA. Of her time at the *Winnipeg Citizen* she says: "I wrote a radio column, did book reviews, and covered the labour beat, about which, at twenty-one, I knew absolutely nothing."[2] When discussing her job at the YWCA she mentions that "while [she] was there the Japanese Canadians were released from the camps and the Y formed a Teen Club for the younger ones."[3] The most telling remark about the importance to her of these experiences is the simple statement: "North Winnipeg in the 1940s decided a lot of my life."[4] It is therefore interesting that, despite the importance of these experiences and their undoubted influence on her attitudes toward life, she did not incorporate them as subject matter in her writing.

The discovery in the Margaret Laurence Collection at York University of the poem "North Main Car"[5] reveals that in 1948, when she was twenty-one or twenty-two, Laurence had used some of what she had observed in North Winnipeg as subject matter for her work. I have found no reference to the poem in any of the research I have done, but letters Laurence wrote to Adele Wiseman from England in 1950 indicate that she had submitted other poems to the *Canadian Tribune*. A poem that had been published presented a mother's response to the death of her sons in war and another one dealt with the revolt of the Italian peasants.[6] Her comments to Adele Wiseman indicate that while she wanted to write poems with serious content she did not want them to be works of propaganda. "I feel that a strictly propaganda poem is one where the propaganda matters more than the poem. A real poem, no matter how many flaws it may have, is one in which the idea and the form are inextricably united, the one impossible without the other."[7] While "North Main Car" contains a serious message, it also reveals the concern for the individual and the presentation of the dignity of the individual that are found in all of Laurence's work. Readers who now see this poem for the first time are more likely to be struck by the portraits of the characters she has created—the individuals who get on or off at the stops of the North Main car—than by the explicit message that ends the poem.

Because the poem contains such vivid portraits of individuals it seems strange that Laurence did not include these characters and their situations in works she wrote later, when she turned from the writing of poetry to the writing of fiction. It is perhaps worthwhile to remember that shortly after writing the poem she left Canada, first for England and then for Africa, and the immediacy of the African experience provided her with material for her writing. When she felt that she could no longer write from the perspective of an outsider observing African experience, she turned to her own experience and the experience of her ancestors as the source of the characters and themes she would explore through all the Manawaka works. However, that the subject matter that had been so important to her in the creation of "North Main Car" continued to be important to her is evident in an additional unpublished document that is in the Margaret Laurence Collection at York University.

In one of the accessions Laurence herself had prepared for the Special Collections is a folder titled by Laurence "Dance on the Earth."[8] Instead of containing notes for her memoir, which one might have expected to find in a folder with such a title, the folder contains something totally unexpected—a full chapter of an unpublished novel in Laurence's handwriting.[9] It is especially unexpected because it is known that Laurence destroyed drafts of her work. The title page with the words "Dance on the Earth" in capital letters and the words "a novel" crossed out makes clear that this is an excerpt from one of the novels Laurence had worked on after she completed *The Diviners*. On the next page the poignant words, "July 1983 I am not going to write this novel. Maybe this is a short story or maybe not," indicate that, whatever else was in the novel, this is something she thought should be saved.

There are indications in the chapter that within this novel Laurence had returned to the North Winnipeg experiences that had provided her with the subject matter for "North Main Car." The reader is able to deduce that as the narrator, Allie Chorniuk, traces for her granddaughter, Mairi, the line of descent of her female ancestors on her father's side, she will include information about Mairi's Ukrainian grandparents and great-grandparents, among them her grandfather Steve, who had been a Communist. The subject matter of the chapter also suggests that this telling of the story of mothers and grandmothers had led Laurence to consider her own female ancestors. She turned from the novel, which would have allowed her to use material from her North Winnipeg experiences, to the memoir, which allowed her to write about the three women she called her mothers and about herself as mother.

Letters to Adele Wiseman provide information about this movement from novel to memoir. In a letter of January 20, 1979, Laurence attempts to define the difficulties she was having with the novel. "Mostly, I *cannot* go back into Manawaka country, because that would be pushing it. The five books out of that territory were all necessary and demanded to be written, and together they form some kind of whole. But this time, I think I latched onto that background not because I really wanted to write out of it again, but as a kind of *refuge*, which isn't the right reason for doing anything like this. The revelation last summer that I wanted to attempt some kind of memoir also makes me question whether I *really* want to write *fictionally* about the Old Left in Wpg—I think I'd rather write what I truly know, which is my own (very limited) experience."[10] In a letter in 1981 commenting on her response to a book of poems which Andy Suknaski had sent her, Laurence develops this idea more fully. "His book of poems has confirmed in my own mind what I have always known, have fought against innumerable times but have always had to accept, finally—I cannot *ever* write about another cultural and ethnic background from the inside. It cannot be done, or not by me, anyway. I can write about my own, with *its* many variations. The others have to come in, but in ways other than *from the inside*."[11] She acknowledges that she had had this problem when she was writing about the Métis in *The Diviners*, and she is still confident she will be able to solve the problem in her new novel. However she says: "Actually, it was much more simple years ago when I didn't know as much as I maybe do now."[12]

Although Laurence says in her memoir that "North Winnipeg in the 1940s decided a lot of my life," the presentation of Winnipeg in her fiction appears to be based almost entirely on her experiences at United College. The discovery of the poem "North Main Car" and the chapter Laurence saved from one of her unpublished novels reveals

that, early and late in her writing career, she had used North Winnipeg as subject matter. We do not know whether Laurence was unsuccessful in attempts to publish "North
Main Car" and laid it aside. In any case, by the time she came back to the subject
matter of North Winnipeg she had become so aware of herself as an outsider to the
experiences of those she had depicted in "North Main Car" that she could not write
fictionally of such characters; she recognized that their story was not hers to tell. As
she had worked on the story of the wife and sister and mother of Steve Chorniuk,
perhaps the Steve of "North Main Car," "[whose] face is the face of my city," she had
been led to the story that was hers to tell, the memoir of her three mothers and of
herself as mother and writer, and as she told that story she could speak directly of
what Winnipeg in all its diversity had meant to her.

NOTES

1. Donez Xiques makes an important contribution to the study of Margaret Laurence through her article
   "Early Influences: Laurence's Newspaper Career," in *Challenging Territory: the Writing of Margaret
   Laurence*, ed. Christian Riegel (Edmonton: University of Alberta Press, 1997).
2. Margaret Laurence, *Dance on the Earth: A Memoir* (Toronto: McClelland & Stewart, 1989), 107.
3. Laurence, *Dance*, 108.
4. Laurence, *Dance*, 108.
5. The poem is found in the Margaret Laurence Collection, Accession 5, Box 1, File 18, Archives and
   Special Collections, Scott Library, York University. I wish to thank Jocelyn and David Laurence for
   giving me permission to examine the material in the Margaret Laurence Collection, and Kent Haworth,
   York University Archivist, and the staff of the Archives for all the help they gave me. A sabbatical leave
   from the University of Regina gave me time to examine the Margaret Laurence Collection thoroughly.
   Clara Thomas and John Lennox, at work themselves in the Special Collections, provided encouraging
   and stimulating companionship.
6. *Selected Letters of Margaret Laurence and Adele Wiseman*, eds. John Lennox and Ruth Panofsky
   (Toronto: University of Toronto Press, 1997), 35 and 37.
7. *Selected Letters*, 35.
8. The chapter of the novel is found in the Margaret Laurence Collection, Accession 5, Box 1, File 309, in
   the Archives and Special Collections, Scott Library, York University.
9. James King, in the Appendix to his biography of Margaret Laurence (*The Life of Margaret Laurence*,
   Alfred A. Knopf, Canada, 1997), includes transcripts of passages from this novel (which had been given
   to him by Laurence's family). This material is very valuable and gives more specific information about
   the possible structure of the novel and some of its concerns than does the chapter in the York University
   Archives. However, there is something special about the fact that the chapter in the York University
   Archives was placed there by Laurence herself, perhaps to reveal that she had been trying to work on
   other novels after *The Diviners*, perhaps because she felt that the subject matter of women dancing on
   the earth and sharing with one another the stories of what that dance on the earth had been was too
   important to be destroyed.
10. *Selected Letters of Margaret Laurence and Adele Wiseman*, 353.
11. *Selected Letters*, 377-78.
12. *Selected Letters*, 378.

MARGARET LAURENCE

The Dance Begins: Margaret Laurence and the *Winnipeg Citizen*

Margaret Laurence knew as a schoolgirl that she wanted to write fiction, but she also assumed that she'd have to make her living as a journalist. It wasn't until she was working for the *Winnipeg Citizen* in the 1940s that the course she thought her life was going to take changed. But while she was there, she also learned some valuable lessons that informed the rest of her life.

I discovered Laurence's buried journalistic past one winter day in 1977 while I was still a Carleton University student researching my journalism thesis on the *Winnipeg Citizen*, a co-operative daily launched in Winnipeg in the mid-forties. Laurence hadn't yet published her memoirs, *Dance on the Earth*, and none of her biographies had been written. I was cranking through the old newspaper's microfiche in the Manitoba Legislative Library when I stopped, mesmerized, on page 18 of March 1, 1948, the day the paper began. There, under the headline for a radio column, was her byline: "By Peggy Laurence."

Laurence wrote this column, *It's in the Air*, daily for five months, then weekly until September 22, 1948, but there was no glimmer in those early pieces of the powerful writing presence she was to become. In fact, those first ten paragraphs were a template of much that followed, in that they were simplistic and even a bit dull. The first six paragraphs featured comments on two Jules Verne shows, one of which the CBC had already aired, with the other playing on CKRC that night. The last four paragraphs described "What the Machine Has Done To Us," a drama about the impact of increased mechanization on farm work, which CKY's *Farm Focus* was also playing that evening. Sandwiched between *Today's Best Bits* and the day's *Radio Guide*, Laurence's light comments might have been essential reading in those pre-television days, but they were by no means captivating, let alone literary.

Still, as a young writer who had grown up in the town next to Laurence's Neepawa and had recently discovered both her writing and, through it, the fact that you could become a woman writer from our prairie corner, I couldn't believe Laurence had started her career at the *Citizen*, so I set out to interview her for my thesis. I wrote to her in care of McClelland & Stewart in late January 1978 and asked to meet with her to discuss her *Citizen* experience. She replied with great reticence from Lakefield. "I'm afraid I won't be able to help you with your research on the *Winnipeg Citizen*," her February 3, 1978 letter said. "It was a very long time ago and my memory is far from accurate. The reasons for the *Citizen*'s beginnings and failure are, of course, very complex and have much to do with the whole structure of Winnipeg and the diverse political life of the city. I wouldn't even attempt an analysis. I'm sorry about this, but I just would not be competent to undertake a comment, especially at this distance. Anyway, good luck."

Disappointed, I continued my thesis research but started asking Laurence's former colleagues what they remembered about her involvement in the *Citizen*. Eventually, the *Citizen*'s managing editor Bill Metcalfe said in our late February 1978 interview that he'd almost fired a reporter because a labour union she was covering complained she was a communist, but the firing was pre-empted when the reporter resigned. When he refused to name the reporter, his wife invited me to the kitchen to help her carry coffee and whispered, "Did you know that reporter was Margaret Laurence?" As soon as I returned to the dining room with his coffee, I asked Metcalfe if it was true. He insisted I turn off my tape recorder before confirming that his story was indeed about Canada's then pre-eminent novelist, Margaret Laurence.

Puzzled about why this allegation would be levelled against her, I kept asking other former colleagues about Laurence's involvement with the *Citizen* until I met her United College roommate, Mary (Turnbull) Mindess, in the spring of 1978. During our Winnipeg interview, Mindess relayed how Laurence had not only been a *Citizen* reporter and columnist, but how they had both worked as students for the *Citizen* coop when it started fundraising. Mindess encouraged me to contact Laurence again, which I did. Laurence replied by letter on July 26, 1978. "I still do not think I can be of very much assistance re: the *Citizen*," she wrote, "but I certainly believe the story should be recorded as much as it is possible to do so at this point. My memories, however, are not very accurate, but if you wish, I could see you on Wednesday Oct 11 or Thurs Oct 13 [sic] at my home in Lakefield." She provided her phone numbers, but before I could travel east, she visited Winnipeg in the fall of 1978 and invited me to interview her at Margaret and Walter Swayze's home.

I didn't realize then what a difficult time Laurence was having. A profoundly spiritual woman, she was still deeply wounded by some Lakefield fundamentalists' attempts to ban *The Diviners* from local schools two years earlier. Lyall Powers's 2004 biography, *Alien Heart*, states that she was struggling to write another novel, having said that her Manawaka series—and probably even her novel-writing career—was done. Walter Swayze recalled in another interview we did at his home in October 2003 that Laurence had asked him to drive her through Winnipeg's North End when she returned. He sensed that she was trying to write about the Winnipeg she may have experienced there in the forties.

When I met Laurence at the Swayzes' bungalow that fall, she struck me as a very shy woman, neither exuberant nor easily forthcoming around strangers. Her dark hair was closely cropped, her piercing eyes dwarfed by huge round glasses, and she was dressed like a small-town matron—in dark pants, blouse and a cardigan. Her prominent cheekbones were her most defining characteristic, a Celtic legacy that many still mistake as having native roots. But she soon surprised me by how quickly she seized on my simple reporter's questions as a way to reflect on her career trajectory. By then I had completed my Carleton thesis and started working for the *Winnipeg Free Press*, but I was still researching the *Citizen*'s story for my own interest. Her *Citizen* memories of three decades earlier were indeed as fuzzy as she'd warned in her letters, but there was no doubt that some parts of that experience had made a great impact on her and, despite her initial reticence to meet with me, she wanted to discuss them.

Laurence had been writing since she was a child. I've learned from her memoir, biographies and my research since I interviewed her that her stepmother encouraged her early writing. Laurence had won an honourable mention in a *Winnipeg Free Press* young authors story contest in 1940 and had been editor for two years of the Neepawa Collegiate's *Annals of the Black and Gold*, where she published many poems, articles and editorials. During the mid-forties, she also went on to study at United College, the liberal arts United Church college now known as The University of Winnipeg. While there, she published poetry, short stories and an essay in the University of Manitoba's *Manitoban* and United College's quarterly magazine, *Vox* , where she was also assistant editor in her final year.

By the time she graduated in 1947, her life was already transforming into its future shape. The seeds of her leftist passion for social justice had been watered by some of United's progressive teachers and students. She'd met her husband, Jack Laurence, a dashing veteran studying engineering at the University of Manitoba. They married that September, then moved into an upstairs apartment in Bill and Anne Ross's house in north Winnipeg. By 1948, Bill was provincial secretary of what was then called the Labour Progressive Party—the Communist Party was banned during the war—while Anne was head nurse of the inner-city Mount Carmel Clinic. It was a friendship Laurence would long retain.

Laurence first started working for the *Citizen* in the summer of 1946, just after the newspaper co-operative began fundraising to start the venture. The impetus for the new paper grew out of a November 1945 printers' strike against the *Winnipeg Free Press* and *Winnipeg Tribune*. The printers, members of the powerful International Typographical Union, were faced with the prospect of returning soldiers and wanted new contracts whereby they would be paid the same for a forty-hour week as they had received for forty-six hours. The publishers refused, and the union went on strike.

Harry Ferns, a United College professor, wondered if he could use this vacuum to start a progressive paper sympathetic to the city's unions and left-wing groups. He approached Dave Simkin, a North End printer, and they involved Jock Brown, the general manager of the relatively new farm machinery co-operative, Canadian Co-operative Implements Limited. Together they launched the *Winnipeg Citizen* publishing co-op in April 1946 and, supported by a board and an assortment of striking printers, unionists and students, set out to raise $150,000 in five-dollar shares and fifty-dollar loans.

Laurence and her friend, Mary (Turnbull) Mindess, were among the United College students who volunteered to help the *Citizen* because they knew of Ferns from United College. "I think," Laurence said in our interview, "most people came to the *Citizen* for the same reason I did, which was that we, that is a lot of us, were extremely young and very idealistic and we liked the idea. We thought that Winnipeg needed another paper. We liked the idea of a co-operative newspaper in which the shareholders would have some influence on the policy. I think many of us hoped that the policies of the paper would be, well, perhaps slightly more progressive than the policies of the *Tribune* or *Free Press*." While Mindess fruitlessly canvassed for shareholders in wealthy Tuxedo, Laurence was "a very lowly office worker" in the *Citizen*'s downtown office. "It was great fun working on it," she said. "I worked one summer when they were doing the organization for it and trying to raise funds, and I worked in the office. Really just folding things and putting them in envelopes, as I recall."

Laurence returned to school that fall and then graduated. By the time she married Jack in September 1947, she was working for the *Westerner* which, she noted in *Dance on the Earth*, she hadn't realized was communist until after she began. She was, however, already predisposed to Winnipeg's "old left" and United's social gospel philosophy, so she continued until early December, just before it folded. (Lyall Powers discusses Laurence's *Westerner* work and interest in the social gospel in *Alien Heart*. Donez Xiques also analyzes Laurence's early journalistic work in her essay, "Early Influences:

Laurence's Newspaper Career", in *Challenging Territory*.) Once done at the *Westerner*, Laurence returned to the *Citizen*'s organizing office, which by then had moved to Winnipeg's North End, the location from which the paper would be published.

Laurence told me she returned to the *Citizen* because all through high school and college she'd planned to be a journalist. "It never occurred to me that I might be able to earn a living from writing," she wrote in *Dance on the Earth*. Mindess said in our interview, "At that time, I don't think she ever thought of writing novels. She wanted to get into newspaper work." Laurence added in our interview that "Just before the paper started I worked at doing clerical work, just immediately before the thing started up. The reason I'd taken that job was because I'd hoped to get a job as a reporter once the paper got on its feet. I hated doing office work. I didn't do it too badly. I was a good typist. But that was the reason I took it, to get the foot in the door."

It was the right place at the right time and, just before the *Citizen* launched on March 1, 1948, managing editor Bill Metcalfe hired Laurence as one of his few, but eager, reporters. "It was really quite an interesting experience," she said. "There were some really experienced newspaper men like Bill Metcalfe. But an awful lot of us were enthusiastic youngsters who had to learn pretty quickly. There was a real sense of camaraderie because we were all so enthusiastic about the thing."

That was the beginning of "a very busy year" when she and Jack didn't see much of each other. "He was working during one summer," she said. "He was going to college taking civil engineering and working for the Prairie Farm Rehabilitation Administration, doing surveying. He had to get up about four o'clock in the morning to get out to work. The *Citizen* was a morning paper, so of course I worked nights. One thing I do remember is covering, I guess it would be '48 and there would be quite a bad flood that year—not nearly as bad as the great one of '50. But, I remember going out to someplace where they were doing a lot of sandbagging to try and prevent the houses from being flooded. And who should be there inspecting the sandbagging troops but the Governor-General, Lord Alexander."

Laurence's first signed article, however, involved another escapade, which drew on her true calling of writing from the imagination. "Café Mirrors Permanent; 'It's the Modern Touch'" was a short, sixteen-paragraph feature printed on page five of the March 2, 1948 edition, but she admitted in our interview that not one word was true. "I think people did a variety of things simply because there wasn't enough staff," she said. "I wrote a few feature articles, too. As a matter of fact, one of the very few times I actually cheated was—I never admitted this till now, but I'll tell you—it's so long ago I guess it doesn't matter. The city editor asked me to do a feature article on mirrors in cafés and restaurants. You know, how do people react when they walk into a café. Do they look at themselves, avoid looking at themselves, you know, this kind of stuff. He wanted me to go into cafés and ask people. Well, I could cover the stories all right. But I was really, despite a somewhat brash manner, a shy young lady, and I thought to myself, I can't bring myself to go into cafés and restaurants and go around and ask a whole bunch of strangers how they felt about the mirrors. So I simply sat down and made it all up." Surprised, I asked if it ran as the truth. "Oh, sure," she said. "He thought it was a good story. I guess my talents for fiction were apparent even then. In fact, I'd been writing stories and when I was at college, I'd been writing poetry. Dreadful poetry. But I had been writing stories nearly all my life. So it wasn't very much of a trick to sit down and do it fictionally."

Anyone who read this story would never have guessed it was fabricated or that the writer was to become an internationally recognized novelist. It started with a conventional lead: "Ever wonder who was the tired-looking individual behind the cafe counter, then discovered it was your own reflection? It happens all the time, according to Winnipeg restauranteurs." It then quoted a downtown café owner, some clients, and several waitresses. While the story was a pleasant piece of fluff, the only thing that would have twigged readers to Laurence's later characteristic style was her quickly paced quotes. One breakfaster ostensibly endorsed the mirrors, saying, "These mirrors are the smartest thing out. You can see every good-looking woman passing without having to turn around." Another waitress was "quoted" as saying the mirrors detracted customers' attention from the waitresses. "Some wise guy comes in, starts to make a crack, sees himself in the mirror, and combs his hair instead."

When asked if she ever invented any radio columns, too, Laurence laughed. "No, I never cheated on that one. I suspect I wrote a radio column on the basis of not many hours' listening. But I didn't cheat on that one." What she did remember was "it was the first year of my marriage. Really it was wild. I was writing a daily radio column. I don't know when I had time to listen to the radio, but I was writing this column. I did a number of book reviews. I would listen whenever I had the opportunity and then write just a comment on what was going on. Just a short little thing."

Having confessed why her column was so thin, she went on to explain how it also provided her with one of her most vivid memories from the *Citizen*. "One amusing story I recall has just in the last week had its finale," she said. "In this radio column— course I was a green kid of twenty-one, a smartassed kid fresh out of college, thought I knew everything. So I, at one time, wrote a review of a radio play which the CBC had broadcast from Winnipeg, it had been done here. I panned it—and, of course, what I knew about radio plays you could write on the head of a pin. I don't know what I said, I can't remember, but I said it was a pretty crummy play. So one of the actresses who had taken part was Helene Winston. I had not met her and, in fact, only met her a week ago. She phoned me up and bawled hell out of me. She said, 'You don't understand. We all worked hard on that play.'"

Laurence went on: "She was perfectly right. So, in the intervening years, I've sometimes thought I owe her a great deal because that was the first and the last time that I ever wrote a review frivolously. It taught me a lesson that everybody should learn when they're twenty-one, which is what you're reviewing is somebody's heart's blood. If you're going to pan it, there's more than one way. You don't have to stick a knife through the heart. Ever since, any kind of reviews that I've written, and I've written many, many book reviews—and some of them have been favourable, and some of them unfavourable—believe you me I write them seriously. So, what was funny was that sometime in the last few years, looking at *The King of Kensington*, in which Helene Winston is one of the chief actresses, I've often thought, you know, I'd really like to sit down and write her a letter. We had many mutual friends. Just a week ago, at last, I met her. So I said, 'At last, Helene, I can convey to you after thirty years both an apology and a thanks. My apology, thirty years late, for writing that dumb review and my thanks because you taught me a very valuable lesson.'"

Laurence continued the column until September 22, 1948, which may have been a little before she left the *Citizen*. She couldn't remember exactly when that was but Cynthia Wilmot, the freelance broadcaster who assumed the column, later remembered "Margaret wanted to be relieved" of that duty.

The end of Laurence's reporting career, however, actually arose from the labour beat she enjoyed covering. She'd been doing it, among other tasks, since at least April 1948. "For a time I was on the labour beat," she said in our interview. "Of course a lot of us were young, inexperienced reporters because the *Citizen* didn't have the money to get too many experienced ones. If it had not been for the kindness of some of those union men, I think I would have lost my job instantly because I knew so little about labour when I started that, I tell you, I picked up a lot very quickly. I remember covering union meetings and things like that, and going around to various union organizers' offices to get whatever low-down that happened to be going around. But, in terms of actual specific instances and events, regrettably it's gone. I just simply don't remember. I remember that a lot of the union men were extremely kind to a very green kid."

She did recall the unionists' discontent about the *Citizen*'s direction, a discontent they freely shared, as many were *Citizen* shareholders who had been told their five-dollar co-op shares bought them a say in the paper's direction. "There was an awful lot of arguing that went on," she said. "I wasn't involved with a great deal of it, but it was in terms of what the policy of the *Citizen* should be because a lot of the trade union men were involved and were shareholders. 'Course, because there were people of so many political and social opinions—it was a very wide range of opinions—so, naturally in a sense, everybody was constantly criticizing the *Citizen*'s policy because whatever it was it was wrong. You couldn't please everybody."

Laced through that discussion, though, was the rising fear of communism. During the late 1940s, the McCarthy era had not yet exploded into its legendary black-lists and recriminations, but there was growing concern about communists hijacking organizations. Managing editor Metcalfe, from a traditional *Winnipeg Free Press* and CBC background, was concerned that communists could infiltrate the *Citizen*'s co-op structure, since shareholders could become annual meeting delegates and then be elected to its board. He said in our interview that there were many who "wouldn't support the *Winnipeg Citizen* because it was too leftist or too communist." Meanwhile, the Communist Party's provincial secretary, Bill Ross, said in our August 1980 interview that his members had been invited to support the *Citizen* when it began and many bought shares, hoping the new paper would "give expression to the interests of labour and other democratic groups providing an alternative to the big business press." But, he said, they were soon disappointed, that it "developed into just another third paper without a distinctive pro-labour or anti-establishment editorial policy."

Not surprisingly, given the times, the *Citizen*'s senior staff was quick to react to any allegation that it, or anyone associated with it, was communist. When the *Brandon Daily Sun* printed an August 1948 editorial accusing the *Citizen* of being "a threatening daily newspaper devoted to communists and its menace quite openly," the *Citizen*'s staff immediately demanded an apology. That appeared in September. It was some-time after that that one of Winnipeg's key unions approached Metcalfe, complaining that his labour reporter was communist, and he knew he had to take action. "I know that this person was good, this person was a very good reporter," Metcalfe said in our interview. "But I eventually got a very strong complaint against this person from the Trades and Labour Council and you can't say the Trades and Labour Council would be ultra-rightists or anything like this. They said, 'Look, we don't want any part of that person again covering our meetings. That person is a communist.' And that was my first indication that she was a commie, or a fellow-traveller. And while I was debating what I was going to do, she up and quit."

Faced with Metcalfe's allegation when we met thirty years later, Laurence angri-ly defended herself. "I quit," she said. "One week before they were due to fire me, a member of the staff, who shall remain nameless, told me they were very unhappy because, after having been warned, I still continued to have lunch from time to time at a café across the street with a couple of friends of mine who were communists.

This, remember, was during the McCarthy era. So, I said, 'Great, if they're thinking of firing me, I quit, as of now.'" Upon reflection, she added, "Well, nobody was accusing me of anything. But it was a rather tense atmosphere. Also, my husband and I were in an apartment, the top floor of a house which belonged to Anne and Bill Ross. Bill was an organizer for the Communist Party, but the Rosses were close personal friends of ours. We were very happy in that apartment. But I suppose this was—well it sounds absolutely absurd now—in the days of the McCarthy era and some of that witch-hunt thing crept up to this country." Circling back to the topic later in our interview, she added, "Well, I don't know whether it was a week before they were due to fire me or whether they would have fired me. This was a rumour and I wasn't taking any chances."

Later in the interview, she re-emphasized her point by stating her political stance. "I was never involved with any political party," she said. "I never joined any political party in my life, to tell you the truth. But I was quite left-wing, and still am. I suppose I would describe myself more as a social democrat now than anything else. But there were a number of young people who had been students and so on, who were not at first actively involved but were really in a sense members of the 'old left.' We used to sit around and discuss how we were going to save the world."

Five months later, on February 9, 1979, Laurence was still reiterating her position as she wrote asking permission to quote the *Citizen* managing editor's comments from my thesis for her memoirs. "Of course I was no more a Communist than I was the Queen of Siam. It certainly goes to show the temper of those times," she said in her letter. When her memoir, *Dance on the Earth*, was posthumously published, she ended this tale with: "Years later, when a history was being written about the *Winnipeg Citizen*, the old-time Liberal editor was asked whether he thought Margaret Laurence was a Communist. He replied, 'Well, I don't know.' For the record, no, I wasn't. If I had been, though, it would not have been a disgrace to be among their number" (108).

Laurence left the *Citizen* well before Christmas 1948—and with her went her journalistic aspirations, at least the ones she had expected to shape her career. "I worked for the Hudson's Bay Company in the book department for a few weeks," she said in our interview. "Now, that was at Christmas 'cause I remember the terrible crowds." She then worked for the YWCA. "They needed a registrar and it was just my stroke of good luck" because it was a job "I really loved. All the little kids running in and out of the office all the time," she said. That, as it turned out, was also a better fit with what by then she knew was her real career goal, which had sharpened since her *Citizen* experience. "When I was working in the Y, it was a regular nine-to-five job. I had a lot more both time and mental energy to work at my own writing.

"My goal, after all, remained unchanged from about the time I was in grade three, which was to write fiction," she said. "It never occurred to me that I would be able to make my living from writing fiction. Indeed, it took me many years before I could. I thought the newspaper would in a sense be related to that. It really isn't. They're two different types of professions." Pondering it, she added, "Of course, this was really dumb. When young writers ask me today if I think that journalism is a good way of getting into the field of writing fiction, I say no. It's the worst possible way, because I believe that journalism is a very honourable profession, but it's a full-time profession.

"I discovered, after I had worked on the *Citizen*, that indeed if I really wanted to write fiction, the kind of job I should get was a nine-to-five office job that took as little of the mental processes as possible because when you have been tearing around covering news stories and sitting pounding them out on the typewriter, it's a very demanding job, and there really isn't much psychic energy left over for going home and writing a short story. But it proved, in my case, to not be the right kind of profession for me," she said. "However, I had to find that out. But it never had occurred to me, and in fact for several years I couldn't earn my living by writing fiction. I had to earn my living doing something. Journalism seemed to me to be for one who wanted to be a writer. One thing it did teach me, I must say, even though the style and everything in journalism is totally different than fictional writing, was to be concise and not too free with showing off the big words. So, I think I really did learn a lot, and it teaches you a lot about organizing your material and thoughts. So I think it was valuable in a sense. I wouldn't have wanted to go on working in journalism."

When Jack graduated in the spring of 1949, the Laurences left for England and Margaret never lived in Manitoba again. She eventually wrote many reviews and a number of essays and articles, some of which were collected in *Long Drums and Cannons* and *Heart of a Stranger*. She also wrote her translation of Somali poetry and prose, *A Tree for Poverty,* and non-fiction books, *The Prophet's Camel Bell* and *Dance on the Earth*. But, as she told Silver Donald Cameron in a December 10, 1974 letter in *A Very Large Soul*: "I'm not a good freelance journalist; I'm not a good literary critic or reviewer, although I've done all those things reasonably well. To earn bread, to keep the roof over the head. But my real work isn't there, as you well know" (57).

Margaret Laurence poured out her passion and her spirit in fiction. Writing in *Dance on the Earth*, she said, "North Winnipeg in the 1940s decided a lot of my life" (108). That was the time and place in which she consciously turned away from pursuing a journalistic career to create the kind of life that could feed her real writing soul, her fiction. But her months at the *Citizen* taught her some valuable lessons that she passed on in her reviewing and mentoring. And, while her *Citizen* tenure was undoubtedly formative for the freelance work she later did, all of us who have been influenced by Laurence and her writing should be thankful that it changed the course of the writing career she had anticipated. For who knows how Canada's literary history might have been altered if Margaret Laurence had followed many of her *Citizen* colleagues into a long career in journalism instead of creating her wonderful fiction.

WORKS CITED

Laurence, Margaret. *Dance on the Earth: A Memoir*. Toronto: McClelland & Stewart, 1987.

Wainwright, J.A., ed. *A Very Large Soul: Selected Letters from Margaret Laurence to Canadian Writers*. Toronto: Cormorant Books, 1995.

Flooding, Polio and Nuclear Bombs:
The Culture of Anxiety in Winnipeg
in the Early Fifties

T aken as a whole, the post-war years in Canada were good ones, of great prosperity and growth. Perhaps the most enduring picture of life in postwar
Winnipeg comes from Melinda McCracken's memoir, *Memories are made of this: What
it was like to grow up in the Fifties*, published in 1975. For McCracken, who graduated
from Churchill High School in Riverview in the class of 1957, the period was one of
adolescent good times and highjinks. Life consisted of school, attendance at extracur-
ricular organizations like Brownies and Guides, church and such neighbourhood
institutions as the Park Theatre, the Park Alleys and Ellett's Restaurant, which tempt-
ed "with visions of candy, sweets and fun" (45). According to McCracken, "There was
just too much of a good thing. . . . Life was stuffed with security. It filled the air around
you like cotton batting. You had no idea of what it felt like to need something. You
knew only good; you had no idea of what bad was at all." (65)

Despite the impression left by reminiscences such as those of McCracken, the
post-war period in Winnipeg was actually one of considerable levels of intermittent
panic and anxiety. The anxiety probably affected adults and parents significantly more
than it did children and especially adolescents. Three special situations were involved.
One was the flooding of the Red and Assiniboine Rivers, which could cause the greater
Winnipeg area high waters, considerable damage to property and, in the event of evacuation of the city, much disruption to normal living. According to McCracken, "For us
kids, the flood was a lot of fun. It was like a big blizzard that disrupted the whole routine of adult life. You didn't have to go to school at all, because the whole school was
full of water." But matters often looked more ominous for adults. A second situation
was the increased incidence of polio outbreaks, which were worse in Manitoba than
anywhere else in Canada. Ironically enough, the main hospital housing polio patients
in Manitoba—King George Hospital—was right in McCracken's Riverview. The third

situation was the threat of nuclear warfare, hardly distinctive to Winnipeg but regarded as quite serious by the media. Two of these three by menaces—flooding and polio—would be largely alleviated during the decades of the 1950s and early 1960s. The third would be dealt with by a different process.

1. Flooding

By the period after World War II, most of the population of the province of Manitoba, including the residents of the greater Winnipeg area, lived on a flood plain in the drainage basins of the Red and Assiniboine Rivers. Although these rivers, especially the Red, had flooded seriously on three occasions between 1826 and 1861, no further really disastrous inundations had occurred before 1948 because of a protracted period of relatively dry conditions in the region. Many inhabitants actually believed that development and settlement had resolved the flooding menace. Some argued the removal of the trees from the river banks had altered the climate, while others insisted that the ability to dynamite ice jams was responsible for the new flood-free conditions. In truth, Mother Nature was simply saving herself up for a series of major inundations.

The Red River flows across the bed of an ancient glacial lake into which it has not managed to cut deep channels. The shallowness of the channels of both the Red and the Assiniboine Rivers, combined with a relatively flat topography, means that when excess water overflows the banks of these rivers, it spreads quickly across the surrounding area. The relative absence of winter precipitation cuts down on the danger of spring flood. For Manitoba, the conditions for extreme flooding do not occur often. Usually over several years occur a series of heavy snowfalls, late melts, and quick runoffs, often exacerbated by substantial spring moisture. When the waters do overflow their banks in the valleys of southeastern Manitoba, they create a species of disaster quite different from those experienced by most people around the world.

Most natural disasters—flash floods, fires, earthquakes, hurricanes, tornadoes, even blizzards—happen suddenly, without much warning. Many people die because they cannot get out of the way quickly enough, while the survivors can do nothing but clear up the mess. Manitoba has these sorts of disasters, but Red River flooding—on one of the world's major flood plains—is different. It gives weeks of warning, so evacuation of people and livestock is possible. Loss of life is extremely low, and there is some opportunity, even encouragement, for residents to attempt to hold back the water with earthen dikes and sandbags. The result is a cliff-hanging situation that can extend for weeks while the water inexorably rises. Such an event is quite capable of exploitation by the modern media, which are drawn to the unfolding drama like moths to a flame. The event also produces an ongoing level of anxiety that can last for a relatively extended period of time, while the population fights the water and waits anxiously to learn whether this year is to be one of the "big ones." Before 1950, the residents of the river valleys of southeastern Manitoba could do little other than to accept stoically whatever Mother Nature unleashed. Flooding was an act of God and no human attempted to interfere in His divine plan. Everyone met the waters on equal terms. Disaster was a matter of the elevation of property and the height of the water.

The possibility of serious flooding had been virtually forgotten by 1948. More than thirty years had gone by without any sign of trouble from the rising water, and the flooding of 1916 had not been very serious. In that year, however, a cold winter and heavy snowpack met a sudden rise in temperature in mid-April. As well as causing high water on the Red and Assiniboine, the weather conditions created flash flooding on many streams in the province. Railway and telegraph lines were washed away. Despite constantly rising water, the Winnipeg city engineer refused to be panicked, apparently hoping that the reality would respond to the wish. It did not. The situation to the south of the city became the most serious it had been since 1916. On April 20, Mayor Garnet Coulter advised the residents of Winnipeg that the city might flood within three days. Seed companies remained open on Sunday to provide linseed to homeowners seeking to plug their drains against sewer backup, one of the most serious consequences of the high water. St Boniface began the emergency construction of a large number of huge earthen dikes. Kingston Row and Kingston Crescent were already under water.

As the waters crested in Emerson on April 25, the provincial cabinet finally met in emergency session to talk about flooding. It was possible to wait so long because the government had no plans for active intervention. It called upon the Canadian military. That same day, an emergency meeting was called by the Red Cross Management Committee of representatives from all sectors affected by the flooding. The meeting confirmed what everyone knew at the time. The Red Cross was the principal agency expected to deal with disasters. It would supervise evacuation and other flood relief efforts. Perhaps to its surprise, the Manitoba chapter also found itself responsible for coordination of all flood activities. Federal Agriculture Minister Jimmy Gardner made it clear in the House of Commons that flooding was a provincial responsibility. The province had insisted on gaining control of resources in 1930, Gardner noted, and one of those resources was water. In truth, despite Gardner's statements about provincial responsibility, flood-fighting was actually carried out solely by local municipalities, private charitable agencies, and the victims themselves, who were hastily throwing up dikes and sandbags from one end of metropolitan Winnipeg to the other. In an editorial on April 28, the *Winnipeg Tribune* sympathized with the flood victims, but held out no hope of aid beyond private charity and neighbourliness. The Winnipeg City Council voted to ask for an investigation of flooding by the International Joint Commission, which supervised waterways shared by the United States and Canada. Meanwhile, the Greater Winnipeg Emergency Flood Relief Fund was formally opened on May 4 to provide a central focus for private charity. The dikes did not always hold, but in 1948 mainly they did. On May 6, announcements were made from every church pulpit in the city of an appeal for emergency funds in the form of a door-to-door canvas. On May 14 the employees of Eaton's donated $2,000 to the Fund, and four days later more than 1,500 volunteer workers collected 60,000 contribution envelopes across the city. The fund stood at $11,500, and grew a bit beyond that figure before it was wound up.

In fits and starts, the reaction to the 1948 emergency produced a number of breakthroughs with regard to flooding by a people no longer content to trust in God for aid. Anxiety levels would be met with action. Attempts to coordinate flood fighting and relief appeared for the first time in Manitoba history, albeit by a private agency rather than by government. A large-scale campaign for financial assistance, admittedly also of a private rather than a public nature, was begun. Equally important was the beginning of a recognition of the possibility of flood control. In 1949, Winnipeg's city engineer W.D. Hurst told the civil bureau of the Winnipeg Chamber of Commerce that action could be taken to reduce the flood menace, including a series of levees and flood walls, several small dikes, and the construction of eight pumping stations to prevent sewer backup. The plan was initially rejected by City Council as too expensive, but was later in the year adopted in principle, although funding was not immediately available. Many citizens were not yet convinced that a recurrence of high water was worth protecting against. The flood of 1950 changed a good many minds in this regard.

By 1950, Winnipeg had gone nearly a century without major flood damage. In that year, however, a virtually defenceless city and valley faced high waters described at the time as "the most catastrophic ever seen in Canada." At its height, the floodwater covered an area 70 miles long and 5 to 30 miles wide, forcing the evacuation of most rural communities in the valley south of Winnipeg and coming within a few inches of producing the complete evacuation of the city's population. Manitobans were physically unprepared against the high water. No systematic flood control measures, except for a handful of dikes, had been put in place north of the 49th parallel. Moreover, none of the levels of government had given any serious thought either to flood fighting or flood relief. The lack of advance preparedness, perhaps more than the height of the water, was what made the 1950 flood such a disaster. Some sense of the feelings of the local population can be gleaned from Scott Young's 1956 novel *The Flood.*

As had always been the case, the standard response to the threat of flooding in the spring of 1950 was to deny the possibility. But the professionals were worried from the beginning, particularly when the situation deteriorated south of the border. By April 21 it was clear that flooding would be worse than in 1948, and volunteer organizations got on with the business of preparing for the impending disaster. Not until Friday, April 28, were Manitobans officially informed just how serious the situation had become, although anyone who read the daily newspapers could see the deteriorating direction in which things were moving. From early April to May 5, the growing menace of flood conditions had been handled as normal operations by the agencies of government, assisted by volunteer organizations coordinated by the Red Cross. Premier Douglas Campbell refused to declare a state of emergency until a meeting late on the evening of May 5, which carried over into the early hours of May 6, told him that centralization of resources and a declaration of emergency were absolutely essential. The Canadian Army was called in, in accordance with an earlier agreement, which called for the province to pay the costs of the intervention. Brigadier R.E.A. Morton of the Canadian Army assumed control of flood operations.

Premier Campbell formally wrote Prime Minister St. Laurent on May 7 to request a declaration of national emergency and assurance of federal funds "commensurate with our needs." In a cautious press release, Campbell warned Manitobans not to expect assistance with their private losses. That same day, Prime Minister St. Laurent told the House of Commons that federal aid would be based on the principles of the Fraser River Valley Flood in British Columbia in 1948. Under this earlier arrangement, the Dominion had assumed 75 per cent of the cost of flood fighting and 50 per cent of the cost of immediate relief. Rehabilitation costs would be negotiated later. Thus were the basic Dominion-provincial relationship and the basic principles of Canadian disaster relief well on their way to becoming institutionalized. Before the post-World War II period, Canadian disaster relief had not been based on any well-understood policies, and had been both casual and chimerical in its operation. The assumption of any financial responsibility for rehabilitation by federal and provincial governments was part of a new public attitude which was broadly related to the growth of the "welfare state" in Canada, although it has received little attention from those who have studied this growth. In this respect, Canada was clearly ahead of the United States.

The declaration of a state of emergency energized the volunteer effort, as increasing numbers of Winnipeggers joined rural Manitobans in leaving their homes. Neither in terms of loss of life nor extent of property damage was the Manitoba flood of 1950 a class-one disaster by international standards. On the other hand, the flood was great theatre. It was highly visual, full of human interest, and produced a series of cliff-hanging escalations in which the drama built over many weeks. The victims could be seen battling courageously against Mother Nature in very photogenic ways, particularly through the ubiquitous sandbagging of the dikes and the riverbanks. The world had time to hear of Manitoba's plight, and was able to follow its determined battle to hold back the rising waters.

One of the outstanding features of the 1950 flood was the creation of the Manitoba Flood Relief Fund, which collected the largest amount of money any peacetime Canadian charitable effort had ever raised in a single year. A public target of $10 million, originally intended as an impossible goal, was very nearly reached. Money was raised all across Canada, the United States and Great Britain. Although the extent of international contributions was impressive, over half the final sum recorded came from Manitobans who heeded the injunction to help others "hit harder" than themselves. Related to the extent to which Manitobans helped one another financially was the way they helped one another in other ways. Thousands of volunteers across the province fought the rising waters, and even more assisted with the cleanup. Thousands of houses had been flooded, often over the first-floor level, and the biggest structural problems were caused by water, mud and sewer backup. Many appliances were damaged and much furniture was ruined. Victims did not know about the financial implications of cleanup until mid-summer.

Along with the cleanup came a major effort of rehabilitation, financed in part by senior levels of government, which provided a precedent both for Manitoba and for Canada. On May 17 a joint federal-provincial commission was created to sort out the extent of flood damage and the amount of the federal contribution. It reported in early June, estimating the total costs of the flood at $26 million, which produced a federal grant of $12,500,000. Manitoba complained that this greatly underestimated the real costs. The main process of rehabilitation (never "compensation") ultimately took three forms: the provision of short-term necessities of life for flood victims, which was the responsibility of the Red Cross; the rebuilding or repairing of domestic and farm buildings, which was the responsibility of the senior governments; and the provision of domestic furnishings and furniture for flood victims, the responsibility of the Manitoba Flood Relief Fund. This rough division of responsibility among private charitable agencies, the senior governments, and the international flood fund would continue in existence in Manitoba throughout the remainder of the century, and would greatly influence disaster rehabilitation in other Canadian provinces as well.

The restoration of buildings was the responsibility of the Red River Valley Board (RRVB), established on May 31. The RRVB appraised damage to domiciles to restore them "reasonably to the same condition as existed prior to the flood." Very few flood victims had private insurance against flooding, and building rehabilitation was almost entirely in the hands of the RRVB, which inspected 2,371 premises in the Red River Valley and 342 buildings in greater Winnipeg. The Board did not operate on a replacement cost basis. Including garages and "unusual situations," 11,499 cases were eventually processed by the RRVB, for a total outlay of $11,007,697, an average of $957 per case. While many victims were unhappy with their settlement, most understood that before 1950 they would have been left completely to their own devices.

The success of the Manitoba Flood Relief Fund in raising money made it possible for the fund to become increasingly generous in its assistance. The Fund's Restoration Committee began modestly, but gradually expanded the scope of its efforts. Initially the Fund primarily assisted the needy, but it was soon replacing all articles of household use and ornament for all flood victims without insurance. Reimbursement levels were raised to replacement cost, and the difference between insurance company awards and the appraised value of personal goods was also compensated. Further expansion added extraordinary expenses, damage to private automobiles, and damage to residences not covered by the RRVB. Although its efforts were most generous, by mid-August the committee had paid off nearly all the domestic claims applicants for less than $2 million. Despite the Fund's best efforts to spend its money, it was eventually left with a $2 million surplus which became a "Canadian Disaster Relief Fund." Although governments had become involved, private humanitarianism was the difference between a very limited rehabilitation and a fairly generous one. Nobody talked about "compensation" for victims in 1950.

After the Great Flood of 1950, Manitoba began to take public action to protect against high waters. The first step was taken on July 8, 1950, with the creation of the Greater Winnipeg Diking Board by the province, in co-operation with the federal government and the flooded municipalities. The Board decided to extend to greater Winnipeg the flood control measures approved by the city of Winnipeg in 1950 but not yet implemented. In 1953 federal engineers in the Canadian Department of Resources and Development submitted a nine-volume report on flooding and flood control measures for the Red River Valley. The report rejected most flood control suggestions as impracticable or unsatisfactory. Most proposed remedies would have little effect on a flood as big as that in 1950, much less one bigger. The federal engineers did like the ideas of a detention basin at Ste. Agathe, a diversion of the Assiniboine River around Portage la Prairie, and the Greater Winnipeg Floodway, a 26-mile ditch to divert flood water at St. Norbert back into the Red River at St. Andrew's. The report sat on the premier's desk until 1956, when another flood menace (which did not materialize) finally forced the Manitoba government to create a Royal Commission on Cost-Benefit Analysis. The Commission reported in 1958 in favour of a number of engineering projects, especially a floodway. Construction on the floodway began in 1962 and was completed in 1968. Along with other flood protection measures, it defended Winnipeg against all but the worst possible flood. We came close to the limits of protection in 1997, but the system held in that year, at least for the city, and most Winnipeggers felt little sense of fear of floods, except from sewer backup, after 1970.

2. Polio

Polio, or infantile paralysis, was one of a number of airborne viral diseases that lurked around Manitoba to strike at people of all ages, but especially the young. One authority has described it as "the main plague of the post-war period." The incidence of the disease was extremely widespread, and experts calculated that only one in 10 cases was ever reported. As was later determined, the virus was intestinal and had to be ingested, but it could survive for 60 days outside the body. For most victims, the disease meant fever, headache and muscular pain that lasted for only a few days. Such a sickness produced immunity for the victim. Polio was an extremely scary disease because it caused epidemics. Moreover, the pathology of the disease was not clearly understood. What people did know is that while it attacked regardless of age, most of its victims were between the ages of 5 and 15. The disease not only produced muscle weakness and crippling consequences, but in the worst cases, breathing had to be machine assisted. The disease also result in produce large numbers of fatalities. There was no reliable form of treatment.

Polio outbreaks had occurred sporadically in Manitoba before the fifties. One epidemic had come in 1936, mainly in the southwestern area of the province. Medical emphasis in 1936 was upon early diagnosis and early treatment, including use of a "convalescent serum" made from the blood of victims and prepared by the provincial bacteriologist. In 539 cases where serum was administered, 404 individuals made complete recovery, 102 experienced residual paralysis and 33 died. In 1941 more than 2,000 cases were reported, although with only 20 deaths. Another outbreak occurred in 1947, when 59 cases, mostly of mild attacks, were registered. The 1947 epidemic was about equally distributed among Winnipeg city, the Winnipeg suburbs, and the countryside. Only two victims died, and very few had residual paralysis. Less than 20 per cent of victims exhibited later muscle weakness. A variety of protective measures had been developed around the world, including the administration of gamma globulin, but none seemed particularly effective. Treatment procedures instituted by Sister Kenny in Australia were among those that worked.

Scattered incidents of polio occurred in the province until 1952, when western Canada experienced a major outbreak as part of the worst polio year on record (the United States had reported over 40,000 cases by early October). Neither the city nor the province was adequately prepared. In 1952 the Winnipeg Municipal Hospital had only four tank respirators and four electrical circuits capable of supporting them. By July 15, 1952 Winkler reported 6 of the 22 cases. By August 21, 1952 a total of 220 cases had been reported in Manitoba, 33 of them in Winnipeg; and the final tally was 841 cases and 30 deaths. Never before had polio struck two years running, and most health officials expected 1953 to be a quiet year. Nevertheless, the *Winnipeg Tribune* on August 28, 1952 editorialized for more public information on the disease to "allay a great many unnecessary fears about the disease that are commonly felt by the public."

Nothing on record prepared Manitoba for the epidemic of 1953. By September of that year, Manitoba had recorded 1,995 cases, with 65 deaths and 1,083 instances of varying degrees of paralysis. Winnipeg had 676 cases, the surburbs had 392 and the remainder of the province 727. In comparison with 1936, when death struck just over 6 per cent of the victims and nearly four out of every five victims made full recoveries; or 1941, when only 20 deaths were recorded (about 1 per cent of those infected); in 1953 death came to 3.5 per cent of victims, while more than half of those infected experienced some form of paralysis and only 712 victims fully recovered. The incidence of fatalities in Manitoba was lower than in most other jurisdictions. The number of victims requiring iron lungs in order to breathe was up substantially. The iron lungs were concentrated at King George Hospital in Winnipeg, where 221 polio patients were housed by November 1953, 80 of them in iron lungs. This was the highest concentration of iron lung patients anywhere in Canada. In Winnipeg's hospitals as a whole, more than 90 patients were cared for in iron lungs. As early as September of that year the deputy minister of health pointed out that more than 200 polio patients at King George Hospital were being looked after by a nursing staff of only 267, working out to 1.3 nursing bodies per patient for each 24-hour day.

Not only was the number of victims up and the extent of paralysis greater in 1953, but the doctors had to report that they did not really know very much about the disease. They did not know where the virus went during non-epidemic periods, or how people became carriers. American researchers as early as 1941 had argued that infection from flies was probably responsible for the incidence of polio in warm weather, but eradicating flies was obviously impossible. The medical people suspected that spread was through nose and throat excretions, and that infectious periods seemed to last for about two weeks. A Greater Winnipeg Polio Prevention Committee inveighed against the pollution in Manitoba rivers, claiming the Red and Assiniboine Rivers were "little better than navigable sewers." The outbreak was met with various public precautions, including the closing of swimming pools and a ban on school sports when classes opened in September, but the provincial health authorities were reluctant to put drastic measures, such as closing schools, into practice for fear of causing a panic. Swimming pools were used by the Red Cross to provide programmes of hydrotherapy for victims. In Winnipeg gamma globulin was made available for inoculations, although nobody was yet sure of their utility. The deputy medical health officer reported that the spread of the disease was erratic, but that all areas of the province were about equally affected. In Canada as a whole, 1953 saw more than 8,700 cases reported, deaths of more than 400 and some form of paralysis for nearly 5,000 victims. Manitoba was the worst hit province, with one of every 330 Manitobans contracting the disease and nearly two-thirds of those infected experiencing some form of paralysis. Nearly one-third of the afflicted were over 20 years of age.

The handling of the 1953 epidemic became a highly contentious political question early in 1954, when C.C.F. leader Lloyd Stinson charged in the Manitoba legislature that the government had met the crisis in much the same way as it had handled the 1950 Manitoba flood: "in its characteristic slow and indecisive manner." Stinson claimed that the government was reluctant to spend money, especially on standby generators for King George Hospital and on increased nursing staff. He also complained that the distribution of gamma globulin was not well managed, and that the rich were able to obtain supplies from private sources. All these charges were denied by Health Minister F.C. Bell.

Not surprisingly, the epidemic of 1953 considerably speeded up emergency research seeking some kind of preventative solution in the form of a vaccine. The big breakthrough actually had come in 1952, when researchers had discovered that the virus struck first through the blood instead of through the nerves. Not until April of 1955 was the National Foundation for Infantile Paralysis at the University of Michigan able to report that a vaccine developed in Canada by Dr. Jonas Salk of Pittsburgh was both safe and effective. The vaccine had first been developed by Salk in a chemical medium produced at Toronto's Connaught Laboratories, the same experimental complex that had earlier been responsible for the development of blood plasma. Tests and trials on an emergency basis in 1954 indicated that the vaccine was extremely effective, and Dr. Salk predicted that it would prove to protect virtually everyone. The Canadian government embraced the vaccine and announced that enough supplies would be available by early summer to inoculate more than one million Canadian children, with the goal being vaccination for every child in Canada. As early as 1955, the incidence of polio in Canada dropped substantially. In Manitoba there were only 17 cases in that year, with no cases reported among the 50,000 school children in the province who received Salk vaccine shots. Nationally, only 20 deaths from polio were reported in 1955. Unfortunately, the United States was neither as swift nor as successful with its vaccination programme. One of the American laboratories producing the vaccine failed to separate totally the polio virus from its vaccine, and another vaccine researcher, Dr. Albert Sabin, insisted that the Salk vaccine was not sufficiently safe. As for Great Britain, it rejected the Salk anti-polio vaccine in 1955 as too dangerous, cancelling plans for large-scale tryouts. The Salk vaccine worked for Manitoba, however, although the full eradication of polio in North America did not occur until after the Sabin oral vaccine was used on a mass scale in the early 1960s.

The Cold War

The wartime alliance between the Soviet Union and the Western democracies had never been a comfortable one. There were numerous signs in the latter years of World War II that the Russians and the Americans were the emergent world superpowers, eager to carve up the world into respective spheres of influence. There were equally strong signs that the British and the French were simply not strong enough any more to count for much, and were satisfied to be allowed to participate in some of the major decisions. Countries like Canada found themselves virtually excluded from the process of making peace with the defeated enemies, as well as from most of the significant diplomatic maneuvering of the post-war years. Canada attempted to remain clear of commitments, like German occupation or participation in the Berlin blockade, when it was not part of the decision-making process. Towards the close of the war Canada tried to establish some diplomatic distance from the Americans in their continual arm-wrestling with the Russians. But the notorious "Gouzenko Affair" made it difficult for Ottawa to remain sympathetic with the Russians, and probably crystallized Canadian public opinion at the same time.

Part of the spinoff from Gouzenko was the growing awareness that the tight security connected with research on atomic energy carried out in Montreal had been breached. The Russians had received most of the results of Project Manhattan—the atomic-bomb development project at Los Alamos, New Mexico—which may have assisted them in developing their own atomic bomb, tested in 1949. As a result of these revelations, the Americans became even more secretive and possessive about their atomic energy research, and while the Canadian government complained about this policy, it accepted it because it "had no plans for military use of atomic energy." But

Soviet nuclear capability, which became a proven reality in 1949, meant that Canada was now geographically sandwiched between the two great superpowers who possessed atomic bombs capable of overwhelming destructive force. Neutrality was impossible, and so Canada was increasingly pushed into becoming a "Cold Warrior," often having to choose between the United States and Great Britain in the years immediately after the war. The process of polarization became exacerbated in 1950 when South Korea was invaded by North Korea, the Americans responded at the United Nations, and the Chinese entered the dispute. The attempt by American general Douglas MacArthur to obtain authorization for the use of nuclear weapons against the Chinese brought the nuclear threat to the fore. Fortunately he was denied by President Truman. As for Canada, it desperately sought volunteers for a "Canadian Army Special Force" composed of more than 10,000 men, more than 3,000 of them from Quebec. Eventually 20,000 Canadians served in Korea, with 1,557 casualties and 312 fatalities. Many of those Canadian soldiers came from regiments based in or trained in Winnipeg.

Obviously a good deal of disaster defence organization was associated with the 1950 flood, much of it organized by the Canadian military. But later in 1950 a number of experts were advocating civil defence planning for a major nuclear attack against Canadian cities and arguing that other emergencies could benefit as a byproduct. Lt. Colonel G.L. Morgan Smith of Prairie Command told a St. John Ambulance organizational meeting in Winnipeg in October 1950 that "a city that is organized for a major bombing attack would also be well prepared to cope with a Halifax explosion, a Red River Flood, or a Cocoanut Grove fire." Stories appeared in the Winnipeg newspapers in 1950 on emergency planning, not because of any immediate threat—they claimed—but "in recognition of the fact that Winnipeg has just set up the nucleus of a civil defence committee." A story in the *Tribune* advocated using basements as bomb shelters, although the author admitted there was no defence against a direct hit. The defence department in Ottawa issued pamphlets telling civilians what to do in the event of "A-B-C," an attack by atomic, bacteriological and chemical weapons, insisting the pamphlets were to prevent panic rather than to cause it. One of the 1950 pamphlets was entitled *How to Build a Bomb Shelter*. But Ottawa maintained that it would not spend anywhere near the money the Americans were talking about spending on civil defence in late 1950. Nevertheless, early in 1951 Ottawa and Washington signed a joint civil defence agreement.

In June of 1951, a newly appointed civil defence director for Greater Winnipeg, Major-General M.H.S. Penhale, entered town warning that "Winnipeg could prove to be a most attractive target for enemy planes" using the city as a secondary target.

Penhale set out to recruit 7,000 Winnipeggers for jobs as wardens, drivers, rescue workers, radio operators and engineers. The newspapers emphasized how useful such an organization would be in any disaster. Civil defence preparation—and spending—became a national political issue, with the Conservatives claiming that the Liberal government was not taking the job seriously enough. Mock air raids in Winnipeg were used in September of 1951 to help publicize the need for civil defence volunteers. Air raid sirens sounded and searchlights probed the skies throughout the city on the evening of September 26, 1951. The "raid" was a bit of a fizzle, however, because heavy rains cancelled a flyover by aircraft that was to be part of the simulation. General Penhale stepped up his campaign by public speaking engagements that claimed "there is an even chance of war with Russia and if that war comes there is a still greater chance North America will be A-bombed." The "experts" in both the United States and Canada emphasized that there was no defence against a nuclear attack. Material circulated by persons unknown, in Winnipeg and other Canadian cities, made fun of the air raid wardens as human hardware stores and, increasingly, civil defence preparations came up against hostility, black humour or public apathy. By 1954 Ottawa was allocating only $6.5 million of a $2 billion national defence budget on civil defence, and less than half of that was actually spent. The provinces and municipalities showed little or no interest in spending Ottawa's money.

A large part of the problem, of course, was that the experts kept insisting that the level of devastation involved in a nuclear attack was so high as to make the possibility of civil defence seem quite ludicrous. A 1954 story in *Newsweek* concluded: "If you live in a strategically important city, the odds against your survival in an H-bomb war would be about a million to one. If you live in the country, your chances obviously would be better. But wherever you live, much of what you live for would be destroyed." In 1957 the deputy federal civil defence coordinator for Canada, Major-General G.S. Hatton, told a local Kiwanis meeting that only 250,000 of the 5 million people in the largest Canadian cities would escape an H-bomb attack unscathed. Of the 5 million, 3,500,000 would be instantly killed and 1,250,000 seriously injured. Without fallout shelters, the Americans calculated that most of the population under attack would die. Even with shelters, only 60 per cent would survive. Virtually the only response possible to this sort of grim assessment was gallows humour.

Given the calculations of the effect of a nuclear attack, most Winnipeggers joined most Canadians and most Americans in thinking that the holocaust resulting from large-scale bombing would be a way of committing international suicide and therefore unthinkable. From time to time civil defence people would attempt to raise public awareness of the dangers. These forays were probably sufficient to keep a low level of anxiety alive, but not enough to encourage people to take serious steps to protect themselves.

Conclusion

The early fifties menace of flood, polio and H-Bomb existed as a sort of package, with overlapping parts. The same evacuation routes that were planned in the event of large-scale flooding were taken over as urban exits in the event of nuclear attack.

The three threats were often joined together in the media as examples of what a civil defence organization should be organized to fight. They were often brought up—singly or jointly—as illustrations of what governments, particularly the provincial government of Ralph Campbell, ought to be (and weren't) protecting Winnipeggers against. They were the problems, said some, that were not being sufficiently discussed. They were certainly part of a fifties in Winnipeg that was not all good and desirable; they were part of a culture of anxiety.

Crossing Portage and Main

I.

*city (OED): a large town; **city father**: a person [sic] concerned with or experienced in the administration of a city [a large town]*

I am a scholar of towns, let God commend that. To explain what I do is simple enough. A scholar is someone who takes a position. From which position, certain lines become visible.

— *Anne Carson, "The Life of Towns"*

René Descartes, who stands at the origin as paternal source of modern philosophy, might also be modernity's first city father. For he considered thinking, *res cogito*, the essence of what a person is and does, to have much in common with founding a town. Both kinds of construction—thoughts and towns—develop, he said, from a fixed and stable centre. From this Cartesian perspectival point, a single spectating eye/I supposedly looks out, surveying the uniformity of his own reason and the rationality of rectilinear space. Because the eye of such commanding vision is single (the gaze, for Descartes, is monocular, just as subjectivity is unitary), it follows that a sole author or city father is better than two. Both thoughts and towns must be built on this solid base. Whenever Descartes draws on the town-founding figure, he emphasizes the necessity of firm foundations, Jacques Derrida points out (1986, 17): the rational or load-bearing base is essential so that the edifice to be erected, the architectonic or architectural construction, can rise to a great height. Descartes's topography puts the human at the centre, as source and authority of vertical scale. The logic generates high/low, mind/body binary oppositions and, not the least, it secures a hierarchical distance between men and beasts.

I wonder whether modernity might have evolved differently had its founding metaphor been born in Winnipeg. How do we imagine René Descartes, even two hundred years after its publication, trying to write his *Discourse* at the corner that is now Portage and Main? Would Descartes have been inspired by the concept of stable and central perspective had his ocular position been taken, say, from a platform (afloat) on the Red River Settlement gumbo? The stories we tell about this glutinous "mixture of putty and bird lime" (Baker 5) are the stuff of which Winnipeg's cultural memory is made. Where the fur-runners' route down the Assiniboine met the one coming down the Red, the corner, it is maintained, no less the entire settlement, "was famous for its mud. In wet weather the few patches of wooden sidewalk, to quote a visitor, 'floated like barges.' Newcomers were told that if they ever saw a hat floating in the mud they were to throw it a line—there would be a man under it" (Artibise 56). Could architectural verticality have found philosophical bedrock in a quagmire that frustrated both foothold and fixed focal point? Think, for example, of the Royal Hotel—general store on the ground floor, lodging on the top—that Fort Garry merchant Henry McKenney built at Portage and Main in 1862:

> With much amusement and even jeers, the people from the Fort and the settlers from Point Douglas and points farther down the Red watched this building go up. It was much too far from the river, they said, and in the spring the land was so low, it was nothing but a swamp. Further cause for ridicule was found in the shape of the building, which being long and high—a second story was to serve as a stopping place—had to be shored up with timbers against the prairie winds. Noah's Ark was the name given to it, and it was predicted that its owner would have need for the boat which usually accompanied the toy ark of the day (Margaret McWilliams, *Manitoba Milestones*, qtd. in Artibise 11).

If, as Christopher Dafoe suggests, the building of McKenney's Royal Hotel was a "founding" moment, or metaphor, in the history of Winnipeg, then ours is a past informed more by the carnivalesque than by the *cogito*; more by "farce than fanfare" (32); more by "horselaughs" (32)—and horses—than by the man/beast binaries that were so important to modernity's philosophical (and city) father, Descartes. Indeed, the widths of the two famous thoroughfares, Portage and Main, were determined not by rational plan or interests of order, but by oxen pulling carts. "The wagons and carts tended to spread out to avoid the mudholes on the trails, thus inexorably widening the tracks to extraordinary dimensions" (Baker 5). After the oxen came horses, pulling everything from taxis to fire trucks. As it turned out, "Winnipeg was still a city of horses and would remain so well into the twentieth century, their pungent odor drifting on the winter winds, their droppings attracting flocks of sparrows, the clip-clop of their hooves a common sound on the streets of the city" (Dafoe 96-97).

Well into the twentieth century it was before Winnipeg, some say, surrendered its carnivalesque core, and its central corner, to the forces, and town-founding figures, of modernity. The date, February 27, 1979, was marked by another construction, that of the Trizec Building on the southwest corner of Portage and Main, and at the same time, by the closing of the corner to pedestrian crossing. As a result of the Trizec development, and following that, the demolition of the Child's building and construction of the TD Centre, Winnipegers were forced to descend through underground passageways merely to cross the street. Since 1979, this closure has remained in effect, with the exception of one day in 1991, a moment from Winnipeg's populist past, when three-time mayoral candidate Nick Ternette crossed the intersection with a band of demonstrators chanting "Tear Down The Winnipeg Wall." Trizec, David Walker argues in *The Great Winnipeg Dream*, was all about marketplace calculations and the politics of parking; it was a takeover of the corner by bureaucratic strong-arms. An architectural tower, Trizec, for Walker, represents capital-P corporate Power. As if the Cartesian figure, base/hierarchy, had the last word after all.

So as to let go of Descartes's metaphor with its topography of centre and vertical scale; and so as, after Foucault (see 1989), to relinquish a Cartesian relative, the metaphysical theory of repressive Power (the idea that power is a unitary, monolithic force imposed from above on below)—to figure things otherwise—I will approach Portage and Main not as a centre (of the city or of the continent) so much as an *intersection* (L. *inter*, between, and *seco*, to cut): a middle space (I am writing between father and son), differential and multi-layered, without centre or hierarchy, perpetually *crossed* by traffic—series, events, discursive processes—of all kinds. Basic to this metaphor of transfer is the infamous Red River gumbo that, in early Winnipeg, could not be transcended in favour of fixity and height: that muck is what informs my urban metaphor-cum-memoir here, the muck and the marks left in it by horses—in particular, by hooves belonging to the Winnipeg Electric Street Railway Company, since this is where my own story begins. Even in the 1880s, when the city moved from wagons and ox carts to public transportation, the first streetcars were powered by horses (twenty of them, housed in a barn on Assiniboine Avenue near the Portage-Main corner); those horses should have taught us that power *moves*, forever forges new pathways, shares with us a common milieu. Later, in the 1890s, when electric streetcars were introduced, their tracks ran alongside those of the horse-drawn cars. Like the meandering animal marks, the electric streetcar lines, cut into mud or paving stones, were anything-but-linear: grafts of transference, *transfer*, they, too, should remind us that movement, coming-and-going, and constant transition, are what all—architectonic and architectural—systems need to survive.

For most of the winter of 2003, I lived in Kamloops, British Columbia, high on a ridge overlooking semi-desert coulees, empty save for sagebrush and cougars who passed too quickly, or too slowly, for me to see. Though the view of the Thompson River valley was spectacular, and the people of Kamloops were equally so, I was often homesick for Winnipeg. Some days, on descending the canyon to the junction of Highroad and the Trans-Canada Highway, I would tell myself that one east turn would take me right to the corner of Portage and Main.

It has been said that all roads lead to Portage and Main, the so-called "gateway to the West," one of Canada's most important, and historically significant, crossroads, and a junction *crossed* each day by more than 160,000 people—now transported in vehicles, of course—coming and going to the Forks, the Exchange District, North Main, St. Boniface, South Main, Portage East and Portage West. Added to these riders are thousands of pedestrians who daily make their way underground, passing hurriedly between commercial centres, or leisurely shopping the subterranean mall. Whatever else it does, the topographical displacement of the corner—riders crossing on top; an interplay of bankers, merchants, tourists, shoppers, traversing the maze underneath—only adds to the dynamics of movement and transformation that have always characterized Portage and Main. Like the nineteenth-century arcades, with their passages and passageways that so fascinated Walter Benjamin and that provided him with a key to Paris as a "city on the move" (Benjamin 1999, 516; see also, Weber 2003), the dislocated Winnipeg corner remains a site marked, crossed, by recurrent movement. In change and movement, Benjamin suggested, a corner, or a city, finds its power to survive.

In an off-centre way, I grew up crossing Portage and Main: the corner has a strong hold on my childhood memories, and I guess that, as a writer, neither architect nor city planner, I remain drawn to affinities it suggests between text and intersection, both intensely overcoded and multi-levelled ("synchronic") networks. The photographic text is no exception. The one that accompanies this essay, with its Valentine wishes, appeared on the cover of the February 1950 issue of *WE*, the Winnipeg Electric Company magazine. Although I am only five years old in the photo, I remember the dress I am wearing and, hidden behind the cardboard heart, my new black patent Christmas shoes. I can still feel my impatience at mother's hand on the brush in my hair, parting it where I do not want it parted, drawn off my forehead and bobby-pinned to one side. What I remember most about that mid-century morning, however, months before sandbags were needed at Portage and Main, is the unbounded excitement of riding a streetcar to work with my dad. We took many such rides, sometimes on electric streetcars of the sort that Albert W. Austin introduced in the 1890s to civic authorities who were so incredulous and "[f]earful of 'dangerous aerial wires suspended over the heads of righteous citizens'" that they insisted "the new system be tried out on the south banks of the Assiniboine River 'in the bush of Fort Rouge'" (Baker 12); and sometimes on the trolley buses that, in the 1950s, were servicing Corydon Avenue to the Cambridge loop near the outskirts—decidedly "in the bush"—to the house to which, from Fort Rouge, we (Mom, Dad and seven children) eventually moved.

Albert Austin knew something about the interpenetration of movement and power. He must have recognized early on that a transportation revolution was behind the relocation of the Red River Settlement from the Lower Fort to the Forks and the Portage-Main corner. In this perception, he was one of a few, for on arriving in Winnipeg in 1880 from established Toronto's paved sidewalks and streets, Austin encountered only inexorable mud and matching resistance to his preposterous proposal that public transportation could be made to work on such boggy streets. Nonetheless, his Winnipeg Street Railway Company began operation in 1882, as a horse-drawn system that ran four cars on a single short track north and south, back and forth across Main Street and Portage. Although, as transit historian John Baker points out, the Winnipeg Street Railway headquarter buildings were soon constructed just off Main on both sides of Assiniboine Avenue, with a two-storey roundhouse stable on the north side of Assiniboine and a car shed on the riverbank, only the horses were regularly sheltered in these facilities: "Most of the time it was wet and muddy. To avoid becoming trapped in the quagmire the cars had to be left on Main Street, except when they were actually being worked on" (10). A small Winnipeg Street Railway office building stood on the river bank beside the streetcar shed; in 1900, under a new franchise and a new name, and now running electric streetcars and its own steam-generating plant, the

Winnipeg Electric Street Railway Company moved its general offices to the Montgomery Building at Portage and Main (30). In 1912, construction began on yet another office building for what was now named the Winnipeg Electric Railway Company: the Electric Railway Chambers Building that still stands at 213 Notre Dame, just off Portage and Main.

It was in this fine example of Chicago School architecture—complete with Italian Renaissance façades and lion statuary at the top of the building—that the paths of my mother and father crossed. Peggy Vivian Monahan and Donald Ian MacDonald were products of Irish and Scottish labourers, as were the first settlers of the Red River colony: my father's father came west from Nova Scotia, with his bride, to work as a salesman for John Deere; my mother's side of the family, merchants of the Henry McKenney type, ran hotels close to Portage and Main (the McLaren, just north of the corner on Main; the Bell, also on Main; and the St. Charles on Notre Dame). Having been fortunate enough to attend both the University of Manitoba and the University of Toronto, my father took up his first permanent employment in 1939 in the Electric Railway Chambers Building. It was no mean place to start: by this time, the still privately owned Winnipeg Electric Railway Company, renamed the Winnipeg Electric, exercised control over much of the province's electric power generation business, having merged with such companies as Manitoba Power, Winnipeg River Railway, and Winnipeg River Power; and having developed major generating plants at Great Falls and Seven Sisters. The architecture of the Chambers building befit the heady prominence enjoyed by the Winnipeg Electric Company in those days—not primarily because of the structure's rectilinear and vertical emphasis, but rather for reason of its lights. At issue in power is pleasure, as architects Pratt and Ross were surely aware; power is not a rude force, Foucault pointed out, so much as "a process that spreads over the surface of things and bodies, arouses" (Foucault 1990, 72), and gives delight: the Electric R. Chambers Building, as if built on this very principle, was embellished with no fewer than 6,000 electric bulbs that studded the length of its columns and that, when the switch was turned, "lit the building in a magnificent dazzle. Clearly, electrical power was power indeed" (City of Winnipeg 3).

Dad joined the Winnipeg Electric Company as a personnel assistant, in which capacity he interviewed and then hired Peggy Monahan, a recent business college graduate who had suffered sorely during the Great Depression and was now very much in need of work. Mom was posted to the schedules department, where she studied track maps, synchronized the movements of streetcars, and charted shifts worked by their drivers. It was exhilarating, Mom once told me, to stroll down Portage Avenue from the Chambers Building and window-shop at Eaton's. Yet, having grown up for a time in Ste. Anne, Manitoba, Mom was not yet comfortable with big-city life: every day on her lunch hour, she rode the streetcar home, to 812 Garwood Avenue, for the chopped-egg-and-sliced-orange lunch her mother had waiting. Years later, my grand-mother, Nanny, would prepare the same lunch for me, and one of my most cherished childhood memories is that of enjoying my own chopped egg—with just a little but-ter, pepper and salt, one slice of brown toast—on her backyard swing.

Mom worked at the Winnipeg Electric until her marriage in 1941. Dad's employ-ment there was broken only by the war, after which he returned to become the com-pany's assistant manager of transportation, and this at another time of movement and change, when trolley coaches and motor buses were increasingly replacing street-cars, and when route expansion and rearrangement was constantly underway. In 1953, when the Winnipeg Electric passed from private to public ownership, Dad suc-ceeded C.H. Dahl as manager of operations; in 1956, he became director of the new multi-municipality transportation enterprise, the Greater Winnipeg Transit Commission. My memory of the Chambers Building dates to those mid-century years, its marble floors and mahogany doors still vivid images in my mind, as is its cage elevator, and what I took to be the quiet elegance of Mr. Dahl's office. In my view, the new Fort and Assiniboine Greater Winnipeg Transit offices to which Dad moved in the 1960s were no match for the Electric Railway Chambers, though the relocation allowed me, when I tagged along, to return to the site where the mnemon-ic car shed of my childhood had stood, the place we rode to one January morning in 1950 to take a Valentine photograph.

Why would I remember a car shed as fondly as I do, if not that its vaulting barn-like roof signaled an adventure to be had—of the sort we would have when we visited the real farm of Dad's friend in East Selkirk? As in that farm kitchen, so in the car shed, formality gave way, Dad greeting everyone by first name; sharing stories with machin-ists, painters, and bus drivers. When it was bitterly cold, as it was on that 1950 winter morning, the conversations seemed especially warm. After shedding a snowsuit and changing snow boots for shiny Christmas shoes, one could jump tracks; marvel at wheel guards, fenders, and rotary ploughs; be reassured by the sounds and smells waft-ing from the carpentry shop. Or, best of all, one could be hoisted onto a coach and left to wander its aisle alone, to sit in various seats and imagine passengers and voices. I realize now that even as I grew older, the interior of a bus continued to provoke such daydreams in me. During the 1960s, when he was director of Greater Winnipeg Transit, Dad's signature appeared on bus tickets and transfers: while riding coaches to and from the Cambridge loop, I liked to think of these as little texts signed with his name, and in an early take on what the signature entails, I liked to imagine the multiple tracks traced by their journeys back and forth, on foot and by bus. In Winnipeg, where over 80 per cent of bus transfers cross either Portage or Main, this interlacing movement of the signature said something to me about the corner as intersection.

A text, Elizabeth Grosz suggests, can be thought of "as a kind of thief in the night." For, as is the case here, a text "steals ideas from all around, from its own milieu and history, and better still from its outside, and disseminates them elsewhere." Like the corner I am approaching as itself a discursive site, a text "is not only a conduit for the circulation of ideas, as knowledges or truths, but a passage or point of transition from one (social) stratum or space to another" (Grosz 56). This, I think, is one lesson I learned from my dad and from the perspective he took on the city as a network that, on many levels, enables circulation or passage. As Winnipeg's first chief commissioner and a strong supporter of the Trizec development (although, in his indifference to the severity of Winnipeg winters, he wanted vehicular traffic to move underground and pedestrians to cross on top and to enjoy a European-style, street-level square), this was Dad's position on Portage and Main: "The area is serviced, the streets are there, so are the sewers, water mains, hydro electric distribution system, transit services and other necessary public facilities, and the costs of these services were incurred years ago so that large new capital investment for these purposes is not now required" (MacDonald 43). Late in his life, after he was partially paralyzed and left speechless by a stroke, and once we had learned to carry on conversations by way of hand-signs and maps, I realized that Dad had not lost his sense of the multi-layeredness of space, and of the necessity of forging linkages between its volatile strata: street surfaces, for instance (these should be no lower than sewers, the Winnipeg Electric Company learned during the 1950 flood) and service systems and, no less important to my father, flight paths and nesting habits of urban peregrine falcons. For my father at least, despite the many times I tried to locate one on a map or in my life, there was no such thing as a fixed centre point.

II.

The account of a city given by a native will always have something in common with memoirs; it is
no accident that the writer has spent his childhood there [. . .] The city as mnemonic for the lonely
walker: it conjures up more than his childhood and youth, more than his own history.
— Walter Benjamin, "The Return of the Flâneur"

In the first pages of introduction to his unfinished work on the passageways of Paris as key to a city that never stops moving (see "Paris, the Capital of the Nineteenth Century"), Walter Benjamin turns to a discussion of the photograph—and not incidentally so. For just as the arcades interrupt modernity with an entirely new kind of architectural construction, so photography appears as a break with the Cartesian philosophical tradition. How could Descartes's privileging of the individual—artist or architect—be sustained against the photograph's infinite reproducibility for commodity exchange; and how could his ideals of immediacy and presence withstand the absence announced by a photographic image? I am particularly drawn to Benjamin's positing of the photograph as the twentieth century's figure of knowledge—and of memory—insofar as it reminds us that the referent (including the one disclosed by an image) is not present but absent. This, for me, is the point of departure provided by the image that opens this essay: a photograph of my mother as a child I never knew; an image that recalls events, an individual and cultural memory, and not the least, a philosophical-architectural tradition, in which I have not partaken.

How does one approach a "metaphor-cum-memoir" of Winnipeg at mid-century when one was not born until the late 1960s? When I was educated, the metaphor of "centre," with its fixed point of perspective and its need for absolute ground and great height, had already given way; I was born, as it were, after Walter Benjamin attested to the Cartesian tradition's displacement. And while I was born before, not long before, the topographical displacement of Portage and Main, I have no memory of crossing the corner during the first eleven years of my life. This means that I have never *crossed* the intersection on which so much of Winnipeg's cultural memory is constructed. I suppose that the only way I can add to this reflection, then, is by way of a *post*-script, by way of memory that comes *after* and that begins by recording its absence from the centre and the event. Such might be the situation of a post-modern architecture.

Firstly, the absent corner: as crossroads, arguably the most famous in Canada, it has no place in my remembered life. Having never walked across the intersection of Portage and Main—although I have lived much of my life in Winnipeg, and am old enough to have memories of 1979—I am missing a necessary relation to the site. For the primal experience, and ultimately understanding, of space and of place is attained by the movement of one's body through it. In some fundamental sense, "place" only springs into existence at the instant of one's interaction with it; in this instant of mutual imprinting (and subsequent metamorphosis), place and person perform each other. It follows from this that the place, Portage and Main, may not even exist for me, as I have never crossed it, moved "through" it. The corner is absent for me, as much as is my mother's memory of the mid-century event evoked by the Valentine's Day photograph.

Secondly, the centre displaced: as an undergraduate and graduate student of architecture, I was taught, again and again, that in order to create a "city," one must, in the first place, put a crossroads on a landscape, mark out an intersection, give the city a heart. All else is supposed to follow from this initial cut, which is not so much the fixing of a centre as the enabling of passage: gathering, marketing, transporting, traversing, home. The demarcating of a centre, as crossroads, is done only in order to differentiate: differences, displacements, dislocations, transformations are what follow. The crossroads may not ultimately prove adequate to the actual creation and experience of place, but one thing is sure: the movement, the interaction, of beings through space requires a crossroads to occur; it needs a metaphorical, and literal, intersection. Strange thing, then, that in the city of my birth, where I have lived most of my life, the city my family has played a significant role in developing, the city I now attempt to approach as an architect, I have never experienced passage through the primary crossroads. I arrived not only after the paradigm of centre, the Cartesian model, has lost its foothold, but also, it seems, after the crossroads.

At the same time, and not unlike my mother, I somehow grew up on, or just off, Portage and Main. From the start, I was connected to the corner through my grandfather MacDonald's civic involvements before and after Trizec; and if only through the stuff of family lore, the hoteliers on my grandmother Monahan's side gave me links of another kind. But my first "direct" experience of the corner stemmed from a more immediate familial relation: for many years my father had an office on the twenty-eighth floor of the Trizec Building. As I remember visits to his office as a youth, and later as a young man, the view completely engrossed me, and for a long while, it gave me much to ponder about the questions of position and perspective. For one who grows up on the prairies, there is something both entrancing and unsettling about perspectival change, about what is encountered, figuratively and literally, in the simple act of looking down, particularly from a great height. Both estrangement and enticement: this was my first, bird's eye, response to Portage and Main. The corner altered, fundamentally, the relation to horizon, sky, and ground, with which, as a prairie person, I had been unwittingly encoded.

I rehearsed this experience again when I was living and studying architecture in Vancouver. It was a time when, you might say, I was supposed to be thinking of such things, yet I recall being completely taken aback by the subtle (and perhaps not-so-subtle) destabilization wrought in me by that urban landscape's constant sectional and elevational changes. The experience reinforced my sense of "outsider-ness" to the place, and as well, my sense of the "otherness" its environment had for me. I was, by virtue of those perspectival changes, elsewhere; not at home. Only when walking through False Creek Flats did I feel a temporary comfort, a trace connection return-ing—and this, I realized later, for the reason that I was looking neither up nor down at anything. I was on flat land again. Landscape, on that occasion, evoked a surpris-ingly powerful memory of "home-place," the prairie topography of my childhood sur-roundings, my lived relationship to horizon.

The view from the seemingly impossible height of my father's office building was, as I remember it, at once surreal and beautiful, and strangely detached. I could look down at Portage and Main through hermetically sealed glass from some three hundred feet above, but I could not walk across the corner as I could through False Creek Flats. The only way I could actually see the intersection was through an experience of "out-sider-ness" to the place. The experience is now daily reinforced for me, as I work near the corner, just off-centre from it, and were the intersection open to *flânerie*, I would walk through it, not once but several times, each day. With such passage blocked to me, I walk instead around and underneath the corner, my daily paths circumscribing, rather than crossing, Portage and Main. Were I inclined to map my movements, as Benjamin was wont to do his, the trajectories in question would extend to four dimen-sions, with the skein traced by these lines forming a web that, like the corner's concrete buffer walls, seals off the city's core. Even if I drive through the intersection, its block-ades, the bland universality of its multiple lanes of traffic, and its nondescript signage give no hint of the cultural significance of this piece of real estate. I know the corner exists: I have seen it from a perch on the twenty-eighth floor. And I have listened to stories my family told me.

To look from atop a thirty-storey tower is to gain a view of the city's edge, and beyond. From this rarefied vantage point, one appreciates the artificiality and arbitrariness of a gridded city, and the little notice the prairie takes of this. The grid itself, as organiza-tional device, is a hangover from modernity's trust in system and Cartesian ordering: the grid registers place and space as abstract, neutral, and uniform. The particular, what we have come to call the regional and the local, is mollified to the grid as universal ordering principle. Winnipeg is no exception. Apart from instances of property demarcation derived from an agrarian river frontage tradition, and apart from recent subdivision planning based on culs-de-sac and non-orthogonal layouts, the city's infrastructure—its roads, property lines, and service systems—is born of belief in the grid. From a certain point of view (which was probably that of my grandfather), this grid organization makes a lot of sense: it facilitates orderly and efficient routing of persons and services, no doubt an important goal. When we rely on the grid, however, without allowing for the particularity of a city's heart, interaction—such as happens at crossroads—does not readily occur.

What anchors a city such as Winnipeg to the prairie on which it is precariously adrift? What, aside from artificial lines on a grid or on a map, defines its particularity as place; what locates this city in the scalelessness of its surrounding wheaten sea? Some argue that technology now has the capacity to liberate us from the confines of particularity, from the necessity of proximate crossroads, as it were. In the global condition in which we find ourselves, however, we may still require, as communal beings, a locality; a mnemonic home place, not just a home page. No doubt, in the years since mid-century, the businesses and corporations that stack themselves along the edges of Portage and Main have been "liberated" from the need to be physically present at this, or any, centre: most of the transactions and informational dispatches that disseminate from these points in space are destined for elsewhere, and might just as well originate from elsewhere too. Thanks to information technology, the current business paradigm suggests diminishing reliance on the need to be *physically* present at a given corporate or community crossroads. Like the artificial lines of a township grid, which may have no relation to a particular spatial-temporal context or condition, street names and numbers have surrendered priority to the email address.

To the Winnipeg generation that follows those of my grandfather and my mother, loss of centre is more than metaphoric. Many of my contemporaries have left; many more are leaving. What they seek is not the so-called greener grass of suburban life, but another kind of urban core, one that, in Foucault's sense, "gives delight." What they flee, people and businesses alike, is Winnipeg's "loss of centre." While there have been efforts made in recent years to revitalize the core through development, encouragement of live-and-work models, tax incentives, and so on, the city's downtown streets remain all but empty after the end of a business day. We cannot assume that another topographical transformation of Portage and Main will return us to the optimism of mid-century Winnipeg. At the same time, we might be reminded that, as Benjamin suggested, a city finds its power to survive in movement and change. The latter term has everything to do with place-making: change, difference, *differentiation* of *this* particular place from the universal is the potential of crossroads happenstance. Such differentiation requires both figurative and literal intersections—storytelling as well as service-routing—and thus is the work of the cultural community at large; poets alongside planners, artists and architects crossing paths.

WORKS CITED

Artibise, Alan. *Winnipeg: An Illustrated History*. Toronto: James Lorimer and National Museum of Man, National Museums of Canada, 1977.

Baker, John E. *Winnipeg's Electric Transit: The Story of Winnipeg's Streetcars and Trolley Buses*. Toronto: Railfare Enterprises, 1982.

Benjamin, Walter. "Paris, the Capital of the Nineteenth Century. Exposé of 1935." *The Arcades Project*. Trans. Howard Eiland and Kevin McLaughlin. Cambridge, Massachusetts and London, England: The Belknap Press of Harvard University Press, 1999, 1-13.

———. "The Streets of Paris. (Convolute P)." *The Arcades Project*. Trans. Howard Eiland and Kevin McLaughlin. Cambridge, Massachusetts and London, England: The Belknap Press of Harvard University Press, 1999, 516-526.

———. "The Return of the Flâneur." *Walter Benjamin: Selected Writings Volume 2, 1927-1934*. Ed. Michael W. Jennings, Howard Eiland, and Gary Smith. Trans. Rodney Livingstone and others. Cambridge, Massachusetts and London, England: The Belknap Press of Harvard University Press, 1999, 262-67.

Blake, Herbert W. *The Era of Streetcars and Interurbans in Winnipeg: 1881 to 1955*. Winnipeg: Herbert W. Blake/Hignell, 1971.

Carson, Anne. "The Life of Towns." In *Plainwater: Essays and Poetry*. Toronto: Vintage Canada, 1995, 93-111.

City of Winnipeg Historical Buildings Committee. "213 Notre Dame Avenue: Electric Railway Chambers" (April 20, 1981): 1-12.

Dafoe, Christopher. *Winnipeg: Heart of the Continent*. Winnipeg: Great Plains Publications, 1998.

Derrida, Jacques. "Architecture Where Desire Can Live." *Domus* 671 (1986): 17-25.

Descartes, René. *Discourse On Method, and Meditations On First Philosophy*. Trans. F. E. Sutcliffe. New York: Viking Penguin, 1968.

Foucault, Michel. "Clarifications on the Question of Power." In *Foucault Live: Collected Interviews 1961-1984*. Ed. Sylvère Lotringer. Trans. Lysa Hochroth and John Johnston. New York: Semiotext(e), 1989, 255-263.

———. *The History of Sexuality. Volume 1: An Introduction*. Trans. Robert Hurley. New York: Vintage, 1990.

Grosz, Elizabeth. *Architecture from the Outside*. Foreword by Peter Eisenman. Cambridge, Mass.: MIT Press, 2002.

MacDonald, Donald Ian. "From the Gallery: City Hall." *Manitoba Business* (September-October 1979): 43-45.

Walker, David. *The Great Winnipeg Dream: The Redevelopment of Portage and Main.* Oakville, Ontario: Mosaic Press, 1979.

Weber, Samuel. " 'Streets, Squares, Theatres': A City on the Move—Walter Benjamin's Paris." *boundary* 2 (Special Issue: Benjamin Now: Critical Encounters with *The Arcades Project*) Vol. 30, No. 1 (Spring 2003): 17-30.

The Myth of McLuhan: Talks with an Elder of the Global Village

W hen I saw the title of the recently published book *Understanding Me*, I thought it put forward quite the promise—understanding Marshall McLuhan. Thirty years after having sat bemused in his classroom at the University of Toronto, I approached this book as if it proposed the impossible.

An obvious play on the title of his most celebrated book, *Understanding Media*, *Understanding Me* comprises the transcripts of eighteen previously unpublished speeches, lectures and interviews the communications guru gave between 1959 and 1979. Edited by Stephanie McLuhan and David Staines, and with a foreword by long-time admirer Tom Wolfe, this book covers the range of McLuhan's public career, from his early academic renown as an analyst of manipulative advertising through to his celebrity as aphoristic seer who claimed to see the newly emergent pattern beneath the chaos of the sixties and seventies. The book ends with his last taped speech, in which he cautions us to be alert to the evolutionary nature of media change, for cultural myopia at this crux-point in history could be cataclysmic.

McLuhan first gained prominence in 1951 with the publication of *The Mechanical Bride*, a dark study of the coercive powers of advertising. Then, intrigued by the writings of economic historian Harold Innis, he began to look at popular culture more broadly and to focus on the way the dominant media in any culture shape the entire outlook and mores of that culture. This study gave rise to dozens of articles and conference presentations focusing on the way the post-Gutenberg spread of literacy made the Western mind as lineal and bounded as words on a page; print *caused* the West to become nationalistic, industrialized, bureaucratic, isolationist. His book on the role played by media in the shaping of a culture's consciousness, *The Gutenberg Galaxy*, won him the Governor General's Award in 1962. This text drew a lot of attention (and some carping at his "pseudo-science"), but it was with the release in 1964 of

Understanding Media—a book announcing the emergence of a post-literate, tribal, audio-tactile Western mind—that McLuhan became a household name. By focusing primarily on the medium of television—not its apparent content, for it is the medium alone that is the message—McLuhan startled people by suggesting that as they watched *The Flintstones*, the medium itself was insidiously reconfiguring their entire approach to social values and even to reality. Over the next fifteen years, McLuhan released a spate of articles (for he was in high demand) and several more books (mostly co-authored), although these generally involved refinements of the groundbreaking ideas previously released. He had as many skeptics as he did acolytes, but he continued to be a major draw at any conference. He dedicated his last years to the search for perhaps the most important premises of all: the Laws of the Media, the knowledge of which may enable humanity to pilot its own evolution. Hence, the transcripts in *Understanding Me* offer an intriguing, if sketchy, twenty-year autobiography of a man whose ideas still percolate through cultural studies.

Anyone who is unfamiliar with McLuhan's writings and wants to learn more about his ideas may find this book tempting—like a "Marshall McLuhan's Greatest Hits." To be sure, in these transcripts he does discuss his famous distinction between hot and cold media, his suggestion of an emergent global village, and his musings on the features and future of a post-literate world. However—and as the editors concede—the very demands of a symposium address or a talk-show appearance do not allow him to establish clearly his full theory on the mythic nature of media, and thus a reader (and no doubt many of the original listeners) may find his discussion a bit recondite. In fact, it is apparent that his interviewers themselves were not fully grasping what he was saying, and some even ask him directly why he is so hard to understand.

Anyone who already *is* familiar with his writings may be better prepared to understand the ideas that are couched in his notoriously elliptical style and his puzzling aphorisms. Such readers, however, may find no new insights in this text, for his spoken material, especially that in his lectures, is intellectually quite consistent with that in the books published in his lifetime. Indeed, the very intent of these talks was for him to elaborate on or to focus on one aspect of the ideas presented at length in his texts.

And without seeing the full argument to buttress his claims, any critical reader of this book may be a bit put off by the breezy way in which McLuhan describes the new world created by the electronic media. Not everyone, for example, would simply take his word on the following: Nature ceased to exist on October 4, 1957 (because Sputnik was launched); the advent of TV orientalized the West; electricity is organic;

the viewer of TV is being X-rayed at all times; illiterate people cannot be religious; illiteracy is India's biggest asset; with movies, the viewer is the camera, but with TV the viewer is the screen; electric light (but not candlelight) is pure information.

Still, this is vintage McLuhan: glib, cryptic, even outlandish. But this is also the reason he was invited to talk to the corporate leaders of countless multinational firms and to appear on major American talk shows and even to do a cameo walk-on in Woody Allen's *Annie Hall* (in which, appropriately, he debunks a windbag boasting he understands McLuhan). Not many Winnipeg intellectuals find themselves the darling of the American media.

A cynic might say that McLuhan had crafted this persona of the tuned-in swami who talks in riddles, but I know that his public image was no pretense. The McLuhan of *Annie Hall*, the McLuhan of this book, is the same McLuhan who sat with a gaggle of grad students every Wednesday night in a war-surplus shed on the University of Toronto campus. His fame by the late sixties had earned him the position of director of the newly created Centre for Culture and Technology, which consisted of an empty building and McLuhan's mind. He worked on his books for much of his time, but he looked forward to his Wednesday nights. About twenty-five of us would gather in a carpeted corner of the building and he would show up, often with a friend passing through town, such as Malcolm Muggeridge or Tom Wolfe, and he would talk. And challenge us to challenge him. It normally wouldn't be easy to disagree with a publicly certified genius whose knowledge of literature and communications theory was encyclopedic, but such people also usually aren't prone to knock-knock jokes and groaner puns. With his beat-up cardigan and his slow, easy laugh, he was not so much the pedant as the good-natured uncle who tended to say things that didn't quite seem right but that very possibly might be—and if they were, then they were brilliant. Tom Wolfe likens him to Freud, who also had little empirical data to validate his provocative theories but who imagined a system that explained so much, and who even today is admired for where he was right.

He cautioned us students that his pedagogy was grounded in "probes" or conjectures as a means of expanding rather than repeating knowledge. We didn't have to accept the literal meaning of what he said, but he wanted us to see the direction he was probing. And in this, we had a privilege that the auditors of the speeches in *Understanding Me* did not: we could interrupt him and say, "Wait a minute—how can you say *that*?" Inside the back cover of my now yellowed notebook, I have found a lengthy catalogue of some of his classroom probes that certainly led me to say (at least silently), "Wait a minute." For example, Orientals don't dream; gravity is a form of acoustic space; Muzak comes in newspapers; an Arab would never understand a picture of a camel; fluorescent light inhibits speech; women's lib is caused by electricity.

A bit perplexing, to be sure (is this stuff going to be on the exam?), but in retrospect I can see the basic concepts he had framed through these highly reductive assertions. And I can see why he was making claims that he knew we would, by reflex, resist on the grounds of common sense. After all, would I have remembered a more muted, more abstract statement on communications theory? And would I have been as goaded to set aside common sense for a while in order to consider alternatives?

This is why the readers of *Understanding Me* may find themselves incredulous or even somewhat irked. They can't see the man with the wry smile and the beat-up cardigan. They have no clues to suggest that they should feel at liberty to regard his probes not always as statements of fact but as catalysts to new ways of seeing themselves. For example, it helps to read the following passage not as a statement of fact but as an invitation to consider the extent to which most people are blind to the cultural impact of such new technologies as satellites:

> What happened with Telstar was rather amazing in ways that people haven't noticed. When you put a man-made environment around the planet, the planet becomes an art form. Nature ceases to exist. Nature goes inside a man-made environment. . . . In the electric age, there is no more nature. The whole planet becomes programmed like a teaching machine. The whole human environment is now a teaching machine. The city becomes terrestrial in scope and the planet, in turn, becomes a global village. It is reduced by the speed of communication. Space is reduced to almost nothing. This kind of revolution is the one in which all of us are actually living, and it enables all sorts of things to appear and be noticed for the first time that had previously been unobservable. This principle is that, whenever a new technology develops, it creates a new environment for the whole culture, and that environment is totally invisible. (141)

Perhaps what stands out most in a contemporary reading of this book is McLuhan's prescience. Decades before semiotics and post-structural thought took academia by storm, McLuhan was articulating the same principles: a human mind is not an autonomous, self-determining entity, but rather is the semi-hapless product of the ambient technologies. The media through which the individual interacts with the empirical world inescapably structure the mind, both enabling and limiting that mind's operations. For five centuries, the lineality and sequentiality of print forged the logical, systematic Western mind. But today, the simultaneity and fragmentation and boundlessness of the electronic media produce unified, "Oriental" minds. McLuhan never saw MTV, but rock videos are veritable proof of his prognoses for the reconfigured Western mind. The kaleidoscopic barrage of fragmented images in these videos (pure medium, no meaning) perfectly attests to the power of a medium to rewire consciousness. That is, the very process by which the human eye reacts to the rapid-fire electron-dot image on a cathode ray tube renders the muscles less accustomed to, even less capable of, the lineal action needed for reading. For a TV-saturated generation, lineality just doesn't register in minds that have been wired for mosaic, as McLuhan was arguing thirty years ago. As the purest manifestation of the television medium, then, the high-speed cubism of rock videos is both a symptom and a cause of the cultural reordering that makes today's teens think and judge so differently from their counterparts of fifty years ago. And these massively popular videos will perpetuate in our culture the very biases and predispositions that the medium of TV engenders—until the next new medium goes to work on the next generation.

Also intriguing is McLuhan's vision of the Internet some thirty years before its actual emergence. Even at a time when computers were hulking boxes that half-filled a room, McLuhan foresaw in 1967 that "electronic information conditions" would soon result in making all information in the world accessible to everyone everywhere. He reasoned that just as tools are extensions of human hands, so digital information spread electronically is an extension of the neural system. The technical means of creating this capacity for vast and simultaneous chat in a global village would soon follow, he knew, for the medium would shape the minds which in turn would devise the hardware. That is, he foresaw this not in the sense that he could picture a software link among a web of computers, but in the sense that this new medium had already begun to "tribalize" the globe—to reinstate the values that go with an oral and tactile culture—by swathing it in a stream of information exchange.

McLuhan, to be sure, never openly passed judgment on the worth of these transformations. He simply pointed out that media constitute myth and myth generates values, and so evaluating one generation's values by the standards of outmoded myths is like judging Galileo against the axiom of a geocentric universe. As Wolfe suggests in his foreword, however, McLuhan—a convert to Catholicism—privately looked on the increasing sophistication of media as the God-ordained evolution of humanity up through a series of higher planes that will culminate in the unification of all human nervous systems within a homogenized global web. His frequent references in this book to the media-driven emergence of a "unified field" in a retribalized world smack of the same visionary ideal as that of Einstein, who strove to uncover a Unified Field

Theory, the core law that governs the universe. Perhaps McLuhan too felt that God does not play dice with the universe—there is a Master Plan, and the Internet he foresaw marks an important step towards its realization.

And as Tom Wolfe repeatedly asks: "What if he is right???" What if our culture has transformed to the point at which we need to understand the laws of media and become stewards of our own evolution or else risk apocalypse? As McLuhan told his students, "I don't know who was the first to discover water, but it certainly wasn't a fish." But unlike fish, humans are far too dangerous a species to be oblivious to the implications of the high-tech environment. The very possibility that he might be right means that his words are still important, his work still needs to be carried on.

Understanding Me, then, is a book that draws deserved attention to a man who is perhaps the most celebrated Canadian thinker ever. Not all readers may find that this text does indeed enable them to understand, or even to agree with, all that McLuhan posited. And some may feel a need to revisit some of his earlier texts. But this book does capture McLuhan in his prime, when he was—and intended to be—provocative, oblique, challenging. Now, twenty years after his death, we can see again why he was the thinker with whom all others in his day had to come to terms.

WORKS CITED

McLuhan, Marshall. *Understanding Me: Lectures and Interviews*. Eds. Stephanie McLuhan and David Staines. Toronto: McClelland & Stewart, 2003.

Stearn, Gerald, ed. *McLuhan: Hot and Cool*. New York: Signet, 1969.

SOPHIE-CARMEN ECKHARDT-GRAMATTÉ

Sonia and the Bear:
Madame Eckhardt-Gramatté Meets the
New Canadian Frontier

Whereto? Wherefrom? These words are a recurring motif in the letters and private musings of Dr. and Mrs. Eckhardt, two of the most storied immigrants ever to take up residence in the city of Winnipeg. In the fall of 1953, Dr. Ferdinand Eckhardt arrived from Vienna to take up his much-anticipated directorship of the Winnipeg Art Gallery. At his side was Madame Eckhardt, a European composer of some note, whose full name was the formidably hyphenated Sophie-Carmen Eckhardt-Gramatté (her friends were allowed to call her Sonia).

"Wherefrom," for the Eckhardts, was Vienna, a city of over-large chandeliers, haughty civil servants and incessant cold war intrigue. Vienna considered itself to be the undisputed world capital of music and Sonia Eckhardt-Gramatté had, after many years of determined effort, succeeded in becoming one of its leading contemporary composers. In 1950, she was the recipient of an Austrian state prize for her *Triple Concerto*, an honour that prompted one Viennese official to say: "Now you are no longer a Komponistin [female composer], you are a Komponist!"

This was a signal achievement for Sonia. Her entire life, to that point, had been characterized by her titanic struggle to achieve world-class recognition as a composer of contemporary twentieth-century music. That struggle was complicated by the fact that she was a woman, and because, in a strange irony of fate, she was also an astonishing virtuoso on two instruments, piano and violin. As a young woman living in Berlin, her early patrons, which included the Mendelssohn family, were happy to support her career as a concert prodigy, but not as a composer. It was 1916 and women, it was generally held, simply did not become composers, any more than they became conductors or politicians.

In 1920, Sonia married her first husband, Walter Gramatté, a young Berlin artist who fully supported her need to create music, despite their limited financial resources and the ill-health that plagued him throughout his own career. For the first time, she was able to concentrate on composing, and her works began to earn serious recognition among the musical cognoscenti of the Weimar Republic. Tragically, Gramatté's poor health led to his early death in 1929 from tuberculosis: the music was silenced for his grieving wife, who found herself unable to compose for several years. However, Sonia would eventually find solace in the attentions of a young art critic, Ferdinand Eckhardt, who had taken an interest in the graphics of Walter Gramatté and found himself even more taken with Gramatté's widow. Ferdinand pursued Sonia with his characteristic determination and the two were married in 1934.

Just as Sonia's musical ambitions began to awaken once more, the rise of the Nazi regime dealt her career a second devastating blow, as it did many artists' of the period. Joseph Goebbels, the infamous Minister of Propaganda, immediately set about skillfully fusing the arts and Nazi politics into a fascist polemic on patriotism. Sonia's music, indeed her identity as a female composer, fell outside the Nazi re-versioning of German culture. In 1939, Sonia and Ferdinand attempted to escape the onset of World War II by locating to Vienna, the city of Ferdinand's birth. But in the same year, Hitler rapidly annexed his native Austria under the iron grip of the National Socialist Party. Vienna's glitter was obscured by heavy bombing by the Allies during the final years of the war, a consequence of its ambivalent relationship with the Nazi leadership.

Nevertheless, the cultural predominance of Vienna reasserted itself with amazing speed after 1945. The brutal artistic repressions of the National Socialist regime were blown away in a fresh atmosphere of rigorous musical experimentation. Sonia placed herself firmly in the centre of Vienna's musical establishment and her career began to flourish once more. In 1948 and 1950, she was honoured with a number of nominations and awards for composition. There wasn't much time to savour her success, however. Three years later, at the age of fifty-four, Sonia would be forced to begin building her career all over again.

"Whereto" was Winnipeg, Manitoba, circa 1953. A steady sort of place—low-key, quiet, a great-place-to-raise-your-kids kind of city. Musical tastes ran to the classical repertoire, Mozart, Schubert, Chopin—nothing too terribly avant-garde. There were a few restaurants (Childs Restaurant at Portage and Main was de rigueur after a night of Gilbert and Sullivan or a religious revival meeting), and a fair assortment of night clubs, movie houses and bowling alleys.

There was also the Winnipeg Auditorium on Vaughan Street, a sort of all-purpose centre for dance performances, music recitals and wrestling matches alike. The Winnipeg Art Gallery of 1953 was rather infelicitously located in a hallway on the second floor of the same building. On those evenings when a big wrestling match was scheduled, all the artworks had to be taken down (presumably for fear they would somehow be shaken off the walls), and then reinstalled the next morning before the gallery opened.

For the younger set, there were movie houses and there was the Salisbury House, where you could go for a Nip and a coffee. But most people didn't have a lot of money and many of them pretty much stayed at home, listening to the radio or 78s, playing cards or socializing.

That's not to say, however, that the city's cultural leaders of the early fifties didn't have ambition. They wanted to give the citizens of Winnipeg something more by way of cultural diversion. Prominent members of the city's musical and artistic elite had begun actively developing a vision for the city—a vision that relied upon a broader, more international perspective of the arts. Part of their campaign would focus upon attracting individuals from outside the province, preferably outside the country, who could bring a degree of artistic sophistication and erudition that would provide a fundament for genuine cultural development and appreciation for the arts.

At this time, Dr. Ferdinand Eckhardt was an art educator at the Kunsthistorisches Museum (Austria's state art museum) and not particularly happy with the lack of opportunity for advancement. To his surprise, he received an invitation to consider the directorship of the Winnipeg Art Gallery. The invitation was tendered by Dr. Richard Hiscocks, a professor at the University of Manitoba, who was one of Ferdinand's many North American connections developed through the British Council in Vienna—connections Ferdinand had assiduously pursued after the end of the Second World War, despite the cold war paranoia that seeped into every communication with the West.

Dr. Eckhardt looked Winnipeg up in the dictionary because he had never heard of it before. Then, after a preliminary visit to the city, Ferdinand wrote to his wife: "The news from Hiscocks may indeed be very meaningful under the circumstances. But, let's not be excited too soon and let us think through and deal with everything calmly. If it is to be so and it should work out, I would view this purely as a foresight of fate, in which I have almost believed for some time." Ferdinand's letter went on: "Your suppositions are once again naturally very exaggerated. W. is not located in California, where the wonderful fruits come from, but in the north, in Canada, exactly halfway between the Atlantic and Pacific Oceans . . . it is not much bigger than Salzburg or Linz. I will write [Hiscocks] immediately, though in a very relaxed and calm manner, that I am interested in the matter, but that I have to first hear what exactly it is dealing with, and what the conditions are."

The conditions were ultimately acceptable. Sonia and Ferdinand left Vienna for Southampton, where they boarded the Mauretania bound for Montreal. From there, they travelled by train to Winnipeg. Although she had, at first, been excited by the rapid change in their circumstances and the potential for her husband's advancement, Sonia grew more uncertain and disconsolate with each passing mile. "Where are you taking me?" she said to Ferdinand, looking out the window at the rock-strewn landscape of the Canadian Shield rolling by. "This looks like the moon!"

Once Sonia and Ferdinand finally arrived in Winnipeg, the local intelligentsia were both intrigued and intimidated. Winnipeggers simply had never seen anything like these two: the tall, distinguished, silver-haired Ferdinand with his courtly Viennese manners, and the "passionate atom" that was the extraordinary Sonia, five feet tall with her shoes on. Her thrilling, husky voice tossed English, German and French all together in a high-speed blender of mispronunciations and mashed-up metaphors. Equally surprising was her loud, braying laughter, her powerful hands waving wildly, her furious energy, her fearsome temper and her childlike moments of charm.

It was also hard to miss Sonia's short-cropped hair, and the suit jackets and ties she wore with a distinctly masculine flair, in lieu of the feminine fifties silhouettes worn by most women. "There's a mad woman in town" was a general sentiment expressed in musical circles when she arrived. But then they heard her play, and those who knew something about music were astounded. "I was absolutely staggered by her technique," cellist Peggy Sampson later recalled. Former CBC music producer John Roberts put it another way: "She had a gift from God. You either have it or you don't. And she had it."

Sonia, for her part, was less impressed with her new surroundings, at least in the early years. Winnipeg was certainly not Vienna, and her forceful opinions about music and musicianship were not widely embraced by the locals. Her virtuosity could be terrifying because it was accompanied by an insistence upon the highest international standards, to which few could aspire. But perhaps most alienating of all was Sonia's relentless determination to have her own compositions performed in public—she had, after all, been fighting this battle her entire life and the timidity of western Canadian tastes wasn't going to stop her now. This occasionally led to uneasy encounters with musicians who found her works tremendously difficult to play—music written by a virtuoso for other virtuoso musicians to perform.

It must be said that some of Sonia's initial isolation was self-inflicted, but she nevertheless felt it keenly. Her diary entry of December 22, 1953, reads: "I am not at all happy in Winnipeg, when we should be very happy. This house becomes too solitary. It's but a work residence—the soul does not know where to take refuge." On the other hand, she now finally had the peace and quiet she needed to compose and after having suffered through a perpetual series of upheavals, both personal and political, Sonia began to appreciate that what appeared to her a backwater at first, could be a place for calm and unforced inspiration.

Ferdinand was also there for her, ever the consummate diplomat, smoothing over Sonia's ruffled feathers, glossing over a tactless or ill-considered remark (hers, mostly), perpetually ironing out the wrinkles in her relationships with Canada and Canadians. It was a job he never seemed to tire of, and to some people, it seemed clear that Sonia and Ferdinand were that rarest of couples, who saw one another clearly, honestly and completely, and who still loved what they saw.

Eventually, Sonia and Ferdinand settled into a little bungalow at 54 Harrow Street, which would soon become the centre of regular social and musical evenings, their Hausmusik concerts, as the Eckhardts called them, which were reminiscent of the gatherings they had held at their apartment in Vienna. Both Dr. and Madame Eckhardt were gregarious and generous hosts, entertaining their own intimate circle of friends with Viennese specialties like Wiener schnitzel and Apfelstrudel prepared by Ferdinand using secret recipes he smilingly refused to divulge.

In his dual roles as director of the Winnipeg Art Gallery and the Austrian honorary consul for Western Canada, Ferdinand was often obliged to host large groups of visitors. He and Sonia regularly crammed upwards of fifty to sixty people into the bungalow at 54 Harrow Street. This was made easier when they converted the basement into another space for entertaining, a bohemian rhapsody straight out of Berlin, circa 1927, replete with oriental kilims, Viennese crystal, black ceilings and even a wet bar built into one corner—one of their few concessions to Canadian customs.

Their chosen mode of transportation never varied during their years in Canada—they travelled everywhere in a Volkswagen Beetle. Like many women of her generation, Sonia left the driving to Ferdinand. They loved the freedom a car was able to provide, never forgetting the war years in Berlin and Vienna when fuel to heat one's home was impossible to find, much less fuel to drive an automobile. And they would pack carefully for their travels, as Sonia had learned to pack throughout a lifetime spent on the move through the capitals of Europe. Plates, knives, forks, shoes, shirts, purses, suitjackets, ties, handkerchiefs, correspondence, diaries, photographs and many other essentials—all were crammed into as many suitcases as it took. And often, it took many. Curator and friend Pat Bovey remembers watching the Eckhardts prepare for a trip, remarking that it was like going to the circus and watching twenty clowns pile out of a tiny car, except in reverse.

Once on the road, Sonia and Ferdinand explored many parts of the Canadian countryside, but one of their favourite destinations was the Rocky Mountains. On one trip, they stayed in Banff, and a photograph taken on that trip seems to say it all. It's summertime. Sonia is standing in front of a tall pine tree. She has combined her regulation suit jacket with a pair of rolled-up jeans and sports a jaunty pair of dark sunglasses. She looks casual, relaxed, completely unlike the self-conscious, serious composer of her many studio portraits. A few yards away from her stands a small black bear, a bear cub actually, and there's a curious resemblance somehow between the two. Sonia is completely intent on the bear, unafraid and smiling. She looks very much at ease with the situation—in fact, she looks very much at home.

In 1973, Sonia wrote Ferdinand a letter, one of many, many letters between them. The date was October 24th, the anniversary of the day they left Vienna to come to Winnipeg. "Mein Junge [my boy], 20 years ago we broke up our little home in Europe and came here to build a new little home. In spite of all the adversities that we have behind us, there are still things that were successful for which we should after all be thankful . . . we want only to hope that the strength that we'll need for the next years to come will be granted to us and the great love that binds us will without doubt help us in that. Love alone is one of the greatest strengths—a godly one. Your second self, dein kleiner Junge [your little boy]."

More than Just a "Spotlight":
Early Television in Winnipeg

O f the arts celebrated in this volume, television is the youngest, yet now the most widely disseminated and consumed. Although television is less than sixty years old as a North American phenomenon, no other medium so demonstratively confirms our contemporary globalized culture.

It is often assumed that from its earliest days television earned the enmity of social and cultural commentators; that when, for instance, Newton Minow referred in 1961 to American TV as "a vast wasteland," he was speaking not just about his own time but about television from its inception. However, just as a study of the early years of American television yields the evidence of sophisticated and even experimental forms of broadcasting, so the early years of the Canadian Broadcasting Corporation represent an era remembered for aesthetic potential and democratic reach.

A glance at the first years of television in Winnipeg reveals not just an opportunity to spin nostalgic anecdotes, but a chance to see how Winnipeg contributed to the cultural significance of this new medium.

Any summary of the development of television in Canada needs to begin with the impetus provided by the Massey-Levesque Commission, chaired by the future Governor General Vincent Massey, whose report issued in 1951 assessed the country's national culture and made fundamental recommendations. Massey, advised by Franklin Roosevelt not to let the mass media fall completely into private hands, and inspired by how British nationalist propaganda served Britain during World War II (also demonstrated by John Grierson's National Film Board of Canada during the war), recommended among other things the creation of a public television broadcasting service to be run by the Canadian Broadcasting Corporation, which had been founded in 1936.[1] Legislative action was swift: CBC television went on the air in Toronto in September 1952, followed by regional outlets in the following months, including Winnipeg on May 31, 1954.

"Winnipeg Gets TV"

If a special supplement to the *Winnipeg Free Press* entitled "Winnipeg Gets TV" (June 2, 1954) is a just indication, then television arrived in Winnipeg riding waves of both free enterprise hucksterism and cultural idealism. Nearly every page of the twenty-four-page supplement is anchored by advertisements for television sets in all makes and models, many paid for by the parent companies (RCA Victor, General Electric, DuPont), with the Winnipeg outlets printed on the bottom. Television sets were fairly expensive, but as early as this date one can see how models were pitched to a particu-lar consumer: the 17" table model showing a wrestling match sold for $239.95; the higher end 21" console model, featuring a classical violinist, retailed at $319.95. A complete home entertainment unit—21" television, radio and record player—cost $669.95.

While the eye may be pulled to the advertisements on these pages, the articles attracted more diverse readers. The latest innovation in home entertainment was also a gadget of sorts and a number of articles appealed to both the electronics buff and the confused first-time buyer who simply wanted to be the first on the block to own a set. There were pieces explaining adjustment of the set and antennae, one on the tele-vision set as a piece of furniture, another parsing a new vocabulary: *video* (from the Latin videre), *channel, ghosting* and *kinescope*. Other articles celebrated the television pioneers Guglielmo Marconi, Allen DuMont and the RCA team. Another asked "What Will TV Mean to Sport?" One article, assuring us that "Television Can Be Good for Your Eyes," was really a piece about the proper way to view the screen: darkness of the room, distance from the screen and posture. The *Free Press* cooking editor Philippa Gould offered a piece of advice both prescient and short-sighted about the behav-ioural effects of the new medium: "It is a wise homemaker who will arrange her living room so that TV and dinner can be enjoyed together. At least she should make this concession during the early days until the thrill of the entertainment form wears off a little."[2] Recipes for sandwiches, casserole dishes and salads were scattered throughout the supplement.

Perhaps responding to a cultural nationalism born of the Massey Report, Corporation bureaucrats were television advocates. J.R. Findlay, CBC Director for the Prairies, wrote in the supplement's lead article: "I would say that the state of society 30 or 40 years from now will be influenced to a very considerable extent by what is being projected into the homes of Canada. For this reason it seems essential that we produce a fair proportion of what people are going to see."[3] In a reprint of a lecture given at a television seminar in Toronto, Gilbert Seldes, then dean of American popular culture studies (author of *The Seven Lively Arts*), was also remarkably prescient. He suggested that as television absorbs more leisure time and challenges other media, it will not so much diminish conversation as become the subject of conversation. Seldes ends his thoughtful piece calling for television to "serve the genuine ends of democracy." He concludes by placing the onus on the consumers of the new medium: "If it [television] is to serve us, we must be sure that it serves us by disturbing our complacency as often as it lets us escape from our problems—that it makes us think as often as it makes us laugh."4

For six years beginning in June of 1954, Winnipeg was what economists term a "captive" as opposed to "competitive" market in television broadcasting: the CBC was the only show in town. CBWT broadcast local and national programs from its station at the corner of Young and Portage for a radius of eighty miles from the city. (The *Free Press* reported that reception was good following the initial broadcast, although Emerson was "snowy" and the signal faded in Gladstone.)

At first, local broadcasts consisted of news, interviews and commentary, and sports coverage. The first evening's schedule included a Manitoba government-spon-sored film, *Look to the Centre*, suggesting the government's awareness of the booster potential of the new medium. The station's signature show was *Spotlight*, a com-pendium of local news, weather and sports. The news was read by the authoritative Maurice Burchell. The weather was reported on and forecasted by avuncular Ed Russenholt, who would stand before a map of the country and end his segment by drawing a valentine in chalk over Manitoba, "the heart of the continent." "Cactus" Jack Wells (brother of Eric, editor of the *Free Press*'s rival, the *Winnipeg Tribune*), was a fan's sportscaster and an avid supporter of the Winnipeg Blue Bomber football team.

Evening programming following *Spotlight* consisted of shows originating from CBC Toronto, such as *CBC Concert, Window on Canada* and syndicated pickups from south of the border such as *Duffy's Tavern*, an early example of the CBC's predilection for picking mediocre American shows. A superior American-originated show and fondly remembered (not least for Richard Rodgers's stirring score) was the twenty-six-episode *Victory at Sea*, produced by NBC and detailing Allied operations in World War II. An early favourite among Canadian shows and one that proved a model for local variety shows in time was *Cross-Canada Hit Parade*. Beginning in October of 1955, Wally Koster, Joyce Hahn and guests such as Winnipeg's Giselle Mackenzie, backed by Bert Niosi's orchestra, would sing the popular songs of the day. (Viewers still recall how the song "Green Door" held position on the charts for weeks, spurring arrangers and set designers to invent innovative ways of keeping the tune fresh.)

Although CBWT programming for the first six years was dominated by Toronto-originated Canadian shows supplemented by American programs, a number of specials stand out in the schedule, often designated as "local drama" or "variety" and then by a title proper if its run was extended. It is these shows that indicate not only the way Winnipeg's local theatre, musical and dance talent found expression through the new medium, but how that medium was able to adapt to indigenous forms. A thorough study of Winnipeg television's early years would need a broader and deeper investigation of programming, not only in the cultural sphere but as well in areas such as current events, sports and agriculture, but I suggest the programs I describe below provide a fair impression of television's contribution to Winnipeg's cultural milieu in the 1950s.

CBWT Productions: Six Original Shows

The six shows I have chosen take a cross-section of what might broadly be called arts programming, including dance, music and theatre. They not only confirm the talent of Winnipeg performers, but the skill of the technical crews working in a new medium. The six shows were preserved on kinescope then converted to 16mm prints. The prints are documented and preserved in the Moving Images and Sound collection of the Provincial Archives of Manitoba.

In the *Free Press* supplement, Gordon Atkinson, the CBWT program director, ventured even further than J.R. Findlay in his expectations for the future: "If a truly Canadian culture is to be developed in Canada I firmly believe that it will have its bedroots in the plains of the prairies."[5] The artistic strength and diversity of the six presentations I discuss below indicate that Atkinson's words were not just inaugural rhetoric.

CBWT's production of Robert W. Service's *The Shooting of Dan McGrew*, adapted for the Royal Winnipeg Ballet by producer John Hirsch and choreographer Gweneth Lloyd has, as announcer Bob Wilson explains at the beginning of the show, a curious history. On June 8, 1954, just one week after the television station began broadcasting, a terrible fire erupted in the Times Building in downtown Winnipeg. While the event proved the readiness of the CBC's mobile news unit and made for riveting television, for property owners, including the ballet, it was a disaster. The dance company lost costumes, scenery and written choreography for most of its earlier works, including *The Shooting of Dan McGrew*, which had premiered at the Beaux Arts Ball at the University of Manitoba in 1950 (three years before the company received its royal charter). In staging the half-hour ballet for a television broadcast April 4, 1956, the RWB was reconstituting a work that had essentially been lost.

The ballet is staged for television with remarkable versatility and danced with verve. The set designed by Jack McCullagh reproduces a stylized version of a Klondike saloon, with a piano and a bar on either side of a backstage-located saloon door. Prospectors and bar girls sit at tables filling the space to the sides. Louise Meloney sets

Roger Fisher as Dan McGrew faces Alex Yenko as the gambler Black Jack with Marina Katronis as Lou looking on in the Royal Winnipeg Ballet's CBWT television production of Robert Service's *The Shooting of Dan McGrew*.

an initially desultory mood as she sings (deliberately off-key) of a gal who "was in her prime, once upon a time" and the bartender (a lithe Ted Paterson) yawns in response. But then the tempo picks up, the prospectors and the girls begin to dance and the bartender joins in. Soon the loudly dressed Dan McGrew (Roger Fisher) and Black Jack (Alex Yenko) are vying for comely but hard-looking Lou (Marina Katronis). This opening section makes witty use of props, including liquor bottles as trombones. Lloyd's choreography reaches a crescendo and the screen fades briefly to black, only to open up with snow falling blurrily in front of the camera and wind whistling on the audio track. The camera assumes an exterior view of the frosted rear door to the saloon and tracks forward as the stranger (RWB lead dancer Arnold Spohr) enters on wobbly feet. The initial impression is that he's nearly frozen, but as the camera halts to reveal the stranger now centre stage, it's evident he's still wearing snowshoes. The effect is comic, while not undermining the eerie effect produced by his bearded and crouched figure.

At about this point in his ballad Service writes: "His eyes went rubbering round the room, and he seemed in a kind of a daze, / Till at last that old piano fell in the way of his wandering gaze." Service's verse, popular in its day (the poem was published in 1907), but dated by the 1950s, finds apt dramatization in Spohr's slouch and fixation upon the piano. From here the poem temporarily plunges the reader into the wilderness, a segue the ballet cannot manage; the substitute, variations on the original steps, set to "Ta-Ra-Ra Boom De-Ay" (attributed to Henry J. Sayers), are less than captivating. In returning to the action of the poem's last stanzas—a shootout nicely rendered by flashes of gunfire on a pitch black screen and the sharp-eyed Lou taking the stranger's "poke" from his pocket—the ballet ends on a sharp, cynical turn. The whole piece is neatly bookended by Old Sourdough (Victor Murray) standing over a potbelly stove and taking a swig from a bottle, as he casts a glance at a portrait of Lou.

In addition to special programs, CBWT produced a number of musical variety shows. Though short-lived for the most part, shows such as *Let's Sing* and *Cabaret* were precursors of the songs of faith success *Hymn Sing*, while the country and western-themed *Saddle Songs* and *Rope Around the Sun* (with Stu Phillips) were tryouts for the popular *Red River Jamboree. Cabaret* was a variety show (the episode I viewed was broadcast January 26, 1956) recorded in a studio simulating a nightclub complete with tables occupied by well-dressed patrons visited occasionally by a cigarette girl. The genial host Marsh Phiminster opens with a few words, then introduces local singers Maxine Ware ("The Tender Trap") and Reg Gibson ("Rose Adieu"). Phiminster, who announces that Gibson is a new father, then discards his straight-arrow appearance and demeanour to impersonate a caricatured Italian newcomer for the comical "Canada, That's the Place for Me." For most of the show Mitch Parks's orchestra accompanies the singers offstage (Alvin Blye is that week's guest joining regulars Ware and Gibson), but some players are visible in the background as the ballroom dance duo of Spohr and Scott take the centre floor.[6] Then for an extended instrumental number the full orchestra is revealed, with Parks at the piano. Less slick than *Cross-Canada Hit Parade, Cabaret* proved a modest but smooth half-hour of nicely arranged current songs, pleasantly sung.

Unlike *Cabaret*, with its simulated nightspot, a variety special called *The Cab Calloway Show* was a CBWT mobile production, recorded at the Rancho Don Carlos nightclub and broadcast April 16, 1959. Warren Davis appeared briefly at the beginning to introduce Cab Calloway (then fifty-one years of age) before a not entirely attentive audience of middle-aged patrons seated at tables around Jose Poneira's orchestra. When Calloway burst onto the floor with "Jumpin' Jive" accompanied by five leggy young women in sequined dresses, a little bit of the Cotton Club seemed transported to Winnipeg.

The house orchestra for the CBWT series *Cabaret*: leader Mitch Parks, piano; Monty Levine, guitar; Ted Komar, accordion; Mel Bereskin, trombone; Jimmy Weber, saxophone; Paul Olynyk, bass and Harold Hunter, drums.

Following this opening number, however, Calloway essentially performed a solo show. Alternating ballads and up-tempo standards ("My Funny Valentine," "Black Magic" and "Stormy Weather") sometimes accented with a little soft-shoe, the veteran performer appeared to be going through the motions. Calloway concluded the show with his hits "St. James Infirmary Blues" and "Minnie the Moocher," on the latter inviting the audience to sing along and squeezing a few "hi de hoes" from self-conscious patrons whose faces could be glimpsed through the low-key lighting and cigarette smoke.

The archive sheet for the CBWT production entitled *Hometown* describes a musical drama with the following scenario: "A young man returns to his hometown to introduce his new wife. A shivaree is given by his friends." This description sent me to the new *Canadian Oxford Dictionary*, where a shivaree is defined as "a serenade of banging saucepans etc. to a newly married couple." Intrigued by the prospect of some authentic Canadiana, I viewed the kinescope print of the show (broadcast September 5, 1958) only to discover the slenderest of narrative gracing a string of pretty songs.

The opening credits to *Hometown* were charming: a scrolled sketch of the small town of Willowbend, a railway track and telephone line edged with stores and houses. But the show itself is a curiously mild song-fest, an indication perhaps that television

The James Duncan Singers on the set of *Hometown*.

was smoothing out the indigenous folk culture with the blandishments of American easy-listening music. The serenaders, among them Bernice Linney, Joan Karasevich, James Duncan and Herb Lothar, sing "Hello Young Lovers" and "Getting to Know You" from the popular musical *The King and I*, and the newlyweds smile cordially in response. The closest this shivaree comes to rambunctiousness is when a young woman feigns disappointment at being passed over and proceeds to remove the groom's wedding ring and snip his tie with a pair of scissors. But the rest of the chorus smooths over this brief rumpus with "Love and Marriage" and "Making Whoopee." The porch and yard set (suggestively designed by Stan Langtry to convey both town and surrounding country as in the credit design) becomes the setting for some second thoughts for the bride and the groom's tender song "Long Before I Knew You." *Hometown* emerges as a sweet but mild entertainment, its most intriguing aspect the new medium's reneging on the opportunity to preserve and revitalize authentic folkways.

CBWT appears to have committed its strongest creative energy during this period in the field of drama. I looked at two of the archives' several dramas. *The Man at the Window* by Mary Fowler (broadcast May 17, 1957) is a curious piece; on one level strained and awkward, but finally emerging as insightful and oddly moving. Fowler finds her premise in the Cornell Woolrich file: a thug (George Werier) stabs and robs a drunk (Gordon Pinsent, essentially a walk-on), then unceremoniously dumps the body in a garbage can. But before he and his partner (Des McCalmont) can flee, they catch sight of a man at the upper window of an apartment block overlooking the crime scene. Unbeknownst to them, the man is blind.

Actors Desmond McCalmont and George Werier on the set of *The Man at the Window.*

As the situation develops further, Fowler reveals she is less interested in the mechanics of suspense than in investigating the man's personality.

The action switches to the apartment interior where the blind man, Sam (Glynne Morris), is revealed as a self-absorbed composer who dismisses the offers of care by his daughter (Irene Kankova) and his caretaker (George Secord), arguing he needs to work on his music. With the man now alone, a perverse game ensues: the thug phones Sam pretending to be a police station desk sergeant trying to confirm the robbery. From Sam's confused response the robber remains uncertain about what to do but now both Sam and the partner become suspicious. Sam phones the police but is dismissed as a crank; the partner decides to accost the assumed witness. A struggle in the darkened apartment leaves the intruder beaten off but the blind man's desire for undisturbed solitude violated.

The play ends with another phone call: the daughter is as solicitous as before but her father continues to deny any need for comfort. Producer/director David Marcus-Roland effectively builds the tension by alternating tight facial close-ups with geometric compositions around sidewalk lampposts and apartment windows.

The effective set design was the work of Peter Kaczmarek. Successful as a crime story and as a sketch of urban alienation, *The Man at the Window* perhaps works best as an indictment of the insularity and moral blindness of the artist.

It should come as no surprise that John Hirsch's television production of Anton Chekhov's one-act play *The Anniversary* is as well-acted a piece of theatre as you might see on legitimate stages in the 1950s; what is striking is that this half-hour broadcast demonstrates the technical confidence of the early CBWT personnel, for this was the station's first drama, broadcast September 24, 1956.

As the critic Vera Gottlieb has explained, *The Anniversary* is a vaudevillian farce predicated on comic irrelevance usurping intended action.[7] On the afternoon of frantic preparations for a bank's anniversary, the chairman's wife Tatyana (Teresa Hughes) bursts into the office, interrupting the last-minute work of the fussy clerk Khirin (Murray Genens) and confusing the priorities of her self-centred husband Shiputchin (Victor Cowie). Already coming to a slow boil from his boss's interference, Khirin is able to deflect Tatyana to her husband, who must listen to her nattering gossip. At one point Tatyana claims the sofa at the centre of the room and recreates a train carriage and its passengers in a juicy but pointless story. Both men are further accosted upon the arrival of Mrs. Merchutkin (Adele Solovey), who has come to plead compensation

Teresa Hughes plays Tatyana and Victor Cowie plays Shiputchin in John Hirsch's production of Anton Chekhov's *The Anniversary*, CBWT's first televised drama.

on behalf of her husband, wrongfully dismissed by the War Office. She has of course come to the wrong office, but will hear none of Shiputchin's protestations.

All of these characters threaten to go beyond exasperating to be repulsive, but Hirsch's pacing of the action and the comic invention of the players dispel a negative response. Victor Cowie is especially superb, but this is necessarily an ensemble achievement. A crescendo of female persistence and male frustration leads to a climax of chaos and exhaustion. The play ends in a comic tableau: two delegates enter to announce the commencement of the jubilee only to find Shiputchin prone upon the sofa in the arms of a swooning Merchutkin; Khirin fixed in place, his work now a mess about him, looking as if he were about to strangle Tatyana. This is a wonderful piece of television theatre.

Six half-hour shows are but a small sample of the theatrical and musical programming that CBWT produced in its first seven years. The station also made a number of other dramas (plays by Art Zigouras and Alfred Harris, for instance) and sustained a ballet series for youngsters called *Toes in Tempo*. As well, the mobile unit televised an ice revue from the Winter Club, visited art classes at the University of Manitoba, and the reliable *Spotlight* was on hand for the opening of the Lionel LeMoine Fitzgerald show in Portage la Prairie. Behind the scenes on numerous shows not mentioned here were names familiar to the musical community in Winnipeg: Neil Harris, Bob McMullin and Eric Wild. Others deserving of mention whose names recur on the end credits of these and other programs are technical producer Don Robertson, cameraman Leo Herbert and Harry Saunders, responsible for audio.

End of an Era

In 1954, when television broadcasting started in Winnipeg, just 22 per cent of Canadian homes had a TV set; by the end of the decade 80 per cent of Canadian households made television a part of their home entertainment. In response to a western Canadian public envious of easterners who enjoyed more television options, including American network shows, the Bureau of Broadcast Governors licensed an independently owned station, CJAY, to begin broadcasting in Winnipeg in November of 1960. That year also saw the start of the CBC's French-language service from Winnipeg and the arrival of an American signal from Pembina, North Dakota.[8] CBWT would continue to produce original dance, musical and theatrical programs but the economics of culture were changing; Winnipeg was no longer a "captive" market but a "competitive" one.

In general the consumers of television in the early years were not unlike the audiences of the two nightclub-set shows described above: Winnipeg's middle class. They could afford the first TV sets and so the shows catered to their values and tastes.

As television culture became more widely consumed, shows attempted to cater to a younger and more multicultural audience. Information programming was given a high priority and so local news, weather and sports coverage was expanded. But local cultural productions became increasingly marginalized by national shows (produced out of Toronto, then Vancouver) and international (mostly American) imports. The consensus that seemed to govern the culture of the Massey Report era broke down. Television would become an ubiquitous presence in our lives, but its original focus on local productions, to which CBC Winnipeg made a significant contribution by tapping into the city's performing arts community, soon faded under pressure from the larger society.

My thanks to Gilbert L. Comeault, head of the Moving Images and Sound section of the Provincial Archives of Manitoba, who kindly arranged for me to view the early CBWT productions; to Benson Wincure, Executive Director of the Western Canada Pictorial Index, for permission to reprint the photographs that illustrate this essay; and to Gene Walz, my colleague at the University of Manitoba, whose writing and conversation on Canadian film and television are always entertaining and insightful.

NOTES:

1. Kate Taylor, "Marking the birth of a nation's cultural life" (*Globe and Mail*, April 6, 2002), R11.
2. Philippa Gould, "Timely Ideas For Snacks" (*Winnipeg Free Press*, June 2, 1954), 50.
3. J.R. Findlay, "Rapid Growth Seen For Canadian TV" (*Winnipeg Free Press*, June 2, 1954), 46.
4. Gilbert Seldes, "Noted Writer Gives Views On How To Live With Video" (*Winnipeg Free Press*, June 2, 1954), 55.
5. Gordon Atkinson, quoted in John Sifton, "CBWT Listings Show Wide Program Variety" (*Winnipeg Free Press*, June 2, 1954), 62.
6. Spohr and Scott were Royal Winnipeg Ballet dancers Arnold Spohr and Kay Bird, who used her married name when partnering with Spohr for this show.
7. Vera Gottlieb, *Chekhov and the Vaudeville: A Study of Chekhov's One-Act Plays* (Cambridge University Press), 1982.
8. Brad Oswald, ". . . And So Began Our Broadcast Day" (*Winnipeg Free Press*, May 30, 2004), B2.

JOHN HIRSCH

On John Hirsch:
An Observer's Footnotes

F irst, and always, there is the city he arrived in as an orphaned teenager who had survived the destruction of the Hungary and the ancient culture he was born into. No one could be more eloquent on Winnipeg as a home, as a place to make art, than John Hirsch. His adopted home remained at his core; it was, no matter where else he roamed, what Canada meant to him. He needed its continual invigoration. Its rich cultural mix provided that. It was his breath of life.

FOOTNOTE: True, I think, but often his faith isn't available so easily to some who want to live and work here. It's a reminder that, no matter the difficulty, Hirsch tended to make things seem easy.

Next, there is the first great phase of the career—as boy wonder. Hirsch wanted to work in the theatre, but Winnipeg didn't have much in the early fifties. By the end of the decade, it was a model of how the "first wave," as it has been called, in the Canadian theatre would develop. From his start in creating a puppet theatre which toured schools, to directing shows at the new Rainbow Stage, to the founding with Tom Hendry (an accountant with the then implausible wish to be a playwright in Canada) of the Manitoba Theatre Centre in 1958, the model, for better or worse, of the big regional theatres that now stretch across Canada, Hirsch achieved all by his late twenties.

FOOTNOTE: The legend proves true. There *was* an excitement about MTC as part of the community then. Its well-being, its growth, were important to the city's sense of itself. The "Centre" part was very deliberate, and Hirsch spoke of it often. The production of plays was to be one part of the theatre, but play development, a theatre school, actor training, and touring were important too. Looking now, we see many "centres" for all this activity; after the mid-sixties, MTC became, for all intents and purposes, a producer of plays. Hirsch's choice of plays, of course, reflected boldness with caution. We got *The Boyfriend*, but we also got *Mother Courage, Andorra*, and *The Hostage* and new Canadian plays as well. The *Mother Courage* production, with Zoe Caldwell, was at the centre of Hirsch's reign, but as an impressionable youth, I found it long and loud, and far preferred his *Threepenny Opera*, which was neither.

Then, we have Hirsch as wanderer, first to Stratford in the late sixties for a brief stint as associate artistic director. Stratford was inevitable for him. At MTC he had in some ways turned the theatre into a Stratford West; indeed there was talk at one time of MTC becoming its winter home. But there was a little too much love-hate in Hirsch's relationship with Stratford at this time. He had his successes there, including *The Cherry Orchard* with Kate Reid in 1965, and James Reaney's *Colours in the Dark* in 1967. This requires a note, since Hirsch had achieved something by convincing Stratford to actually commission a new Canadian play, and its success paved the way for a lot of new plays elsewhere, though that wasn't evident at the time. It attracted a new audience as well but, according to Hirsch, one Stratford board member told him that "those aren't the kind of people we want at Stratford." No wonder he left; certainly he felt out of place. That audience, by the way, later turned up at the Blyth Festival, which is precisely the kind of town Reaney describes in *Colours*.

So he wandered, mainly to New York, working at Lincoln Center and off Broadway, directing a wide repertoire, winning an Obie for his production of *AC/DC*. In a casual reading of some American critics of the period, you will find praise for his incisive, strong direction, but also criticism for being careful, albeit thorough, in the managing of a play.

FOOTNOTE: This seems fair and confirms my own experience with Hirsch productions over a twenty-year period. At their best, they provided excitement, engagement and a kind of ruthless energy. Like the man, his productions demanded a response. However, many shows were cool, proficient, as if he lost interest. Boldness with caution, I suppose.

He was ready for Stratford again when the job came free in 1973 but the search committee didn't call. Instead it was on to the CBC as Head of Drama, a job that by definition seems impossible. By this time he was long past boy wonder and already an elder statesman of the Canadian theatre, which shows how young the Canadian theatre is in many ways. The legacy of his CBC years? Mary Jane Miller in her exhaustive study of CBC television drama, *Turn Up the Contrast*, calls the Hirsch years a mixed blessing. Certainly television drama regained some ground, but he had to deal with cuts, which he fought strongly. The main achievement of those years, 1973–77, was his producing for posterity a great deal of the "second wave" of Canadian theatre and playwriting. These included the first television production of *Les Belles Soeurs* in either French or English, and famous theatre productions of the seventies such as *The Farm Show* of Theatre Passe Muraille, and Toronto Workshop Production's *Ten Lost Years*, among others: the list is impressive. However, according to Miller, "he had a repeatedly demoralizing effect on many in his team" (243). A colleague summed up Hirsch's legacy cordially as "tremendous messianic fervour." Miller offers "whirlwind" (244).

FOOTNOTE: This might be a polite way of reflecting on Hirsch's famous temper, manifested usually by scathing criticism, which emerged during the boy wonder years and never subsided. I saw it in action a few times; to me it seemed energy expended in order that he could recharge and concentrate. He would then forget the incident. This, of course, was no comfort to the one receiving the tongue-lashing. Above all, Hirsch provoked a response: the energy evoked as fierce a loyalty as the difficult side, if we can call it that, evoked discouragement and bitterness.

Stratford became his entirely in 1981 after a Byzantine struggle, best described in Martin Knelman's *A Stratford Tempest*. Hirsch himself was on the periphery of it; his appointment, though, resembled the crown prince restored, the inevitable playing out of a Canadian theatre history scenario. His years at Stratford were mixed. There were some great productions, including the 1983-84 *Tartuffe*; many were middling, a lot of them in his bold idea, cautious production mode. The unwieldy operation was bent into some kind of order—no easy task, as American critic Robert Burstein pointed out at the time. Still, in retrospect, his years in the killing job of artistic director seemed to be for the Festival like something waiting to happen. The Hirsch energy wasn't enough anymore to create magic.

After Stratford he went everywhere directing, teaching—just being the elder statesman he deserved to be. Then, with his untimely death, he passed into not only Canadian theatre history, but myth. This sounds grandiose, but wait.

If you are a Winnipegger, in your forties or older, and especially if, like me, you are involved in some capacity with the theatre here, then John Hirsch has had an impact on you. As presence, then as symbol, and, yes, as myth—and by 1967 he was already well on his way to being that in Winnipeg, since with few exceptions we didn't see his work after that, and nothing after the superb *Dybbuk* in early 1974. Hirsch was, simply, there. He dominated the minds of those who thought of making theatre here years after he left. Needless to say this has its disadvantages—enslavement to an ideal impossible to realize is one—but the one advantage is that his "example," as it was termed in the seventies, did focus energy and commitment in the community to build more and important theatre in this place, not the "somewhere else" where things were supposed to happen. Hirsch was potent as an example for the generation that followed him in the "second wave" of Canadian theatre, which was built on the dynamic and paradigm that Hirsch and Hendry created at MTC, but also against them. We sought to build something new. Whatever the results have been, to some extent, at least until recently, Hirsch hovered as the myth to embrace and match in terms of sheer work. If we have finally let him rest, then in a sense we have matured enough to place ourselves as his colleagues, not his unwilling acolytes, in the ongoing Manitoban and Canadian theatre story.

Is there one production to remember John Hirsch by? It would have to be *The Dybbuk*, which he adapted from S. Ansky's Yiddish classic. Martin Knelman in *A Stratford Tempest* puts it best: "Watching it, one could feel that John Hirsch had poured his entire life into this one production, finding the links between religion and theatre, between the old world and the new. *The Dybbuk* was his tribute to the vanished world that propelled him . . ." (23).

Here, then, is how we might remember John Hirsch. At his best, his productions were meant as acts of faith in theatre itself, where irreducible passion met bullying drive in the moral life of the play, and were offered to an audience to join in or not as it wished. Finally, as we come back to it, not only did a vanished world like that of *The Dybbuk* propel him, but, of course, Winnipeg and what he loved in it, propelled, compelled him, to carry energy into raucous creative motion. His love for this place, his belief in its ever-wakening potential for a dynamic artistic life, is what started John Hirsch and kept him going. He is, above all, ours.

WORKS CITED

Knelman, Martin. *A Stratford Tempest.* Toronto: McClelland & Stewart, 1982.

Miller, Mary Jane. *Turn Up the Contrast: CBC Television Drama Since 1952.* Vancouver: University of British Columbia Press, 1987.

A City Divided in Memory

You could, if you threaded a maze of hazards, reach Winnipeg from another continent by boat. It could be done with persistence and planning—a voyage that began in the High Arctic, found the brief season of open water in the ideal year when the weather allowed, traced the waterways, hugging the shoreline to avoid high winds, dodging the ice floes and slush that locked solid in the night, to the place where the water that flowed north from the Mississippi became the Red River and emptied into Lake Winnipeg and passed Norway House, then Wabowden, to the Nelson River, to York Factory and found the Hudson Bay. You could sail or paddle or steam against the current taking this journey in reverse and end, finally, at Winnipeg surrounded by wheat fields, in the middle of the continent, whether you measured it latitudinally or longitudinally. In the middle, by north, south, east or west, you'd be far from the edges of land. That's what the young Hungarian Jewish refugee John Hirsch thought, selecting Winnipeg as a safe haven so far from all coastlines as to absolutely guarantee sanctuary. Not accessible to German U-boats sliding up the Gulf of St. Lawrence in the night like eels, probing the possibilities of invading Canada, Winnipeg would be hard to surprise, would never be a chosen centre for occupation by an invading force whose entry would be no more stealthy than hundreds of wooden-wheeled Red River carts screeching their approach. Lookouts, if ever such things were necessary, would watch from the roof above the tenth floor of one of the city's skyscrapers and spot the invaders as soon as they left Regina coming from the west, or Kenora by the east. We were safe.

Nonetheless, the war shaped Winnipeg as it was given to me. My mother had brothers in uniform, one who did go overseas, but only because he was young and handsome and could sing so beautifully he could have made it a career and through these attributes, was held safe in spite of the work to which he was assigned, which had to do with blowing up airfields, and about this I understood no more. My father had volunteered and bad knees kept him at home but he earned the gratitude of the International Red Cross because he consistently donated blood until he was thanked and told he was too old to continue. His younger brother trained and was shipped to a camp on the West Coast and then the war ended. Others in the family served and came home. No one was hurt. No family members, even distant, in Europe, were taken by Germans. We suffered no immediate losses. But the war was present.

My father's father, who came to Winnipeg from Russia at seventeen with his family, had a plum tree in the garden of the house he lived in with my grandmother and he would make wine from the small red plums. During the war he traded his sugar ration coupons with family and friends for bottles of the wine when it was ready. But that was only an example of the war and not its real impact on the city.

When the war ended there were no revelations for Jews. Canada's reluctance to accept Jewish refugees while Europe burned and the Nazis proceeded with their evil plan was not something revealed later, in shame. Even in Winnipeg, in the centre of the continent, geographic security seemed insufficient and no one in the family that preceded me felt truly safe. Then it was over. If you lived in North America, if you didn't think about Hiroshima or Nagasaki, it seemed that sanity and evenness had been restored and with that, the future.

But after the war, in spite of all good plans for tomorrow, there remained a mantle of memory—for what had happened and the implications. Canada's national will had been to turn Jews away. In the world, a genocide had been planned and its goals, in large part, achieved. Goethe and Rilke and Beethoven and Schumann and Max Beckmann were German. Jews had also been German and had loved their country and its language and castles and wine and good doctors and fine old universities. Everyone was betrayed, here, and in Europe.

In Winnipeg, in my house, in my family and immediate milieu, it seemed the war never really ended in that it was over and gone. As persistent as the reconstruction and recovery that was necessary in Europe, its presence was sustained here too. As I think of it now, that was the honourable response. It hadn't been a hurricane with disorder and loss of property and even death for the hapless victims in its direct path. It was the biggest, most dreadful and unimagineable-but-realized event in the world's history and my parents assumed the weight of its gravity to the extent that they were able. They weren't morbid, just cognizant and responsible. The war, the Germans, the horror, the ovens, the heretofore unprecedented expression of anti-Semitism. Physically safe in Canada, certainly in Winnipeg, tucked all around by wheat fields, there was nothing to fear but knowledge, which, in this case, was indeed loss.

For all of my growing up years the war was felt in the vehemence of the discussions around our small table and at larger family gatherings, diminishing only latterly, but easily breathed into full flame by a commentary or newspaper article reporting anti-Semitic flare-ups in France or in Canada. Sitting little in a chair, I can remember, but not at the time with any understanding, the news of 1956 and the Hungarian uprising followed by an influx of refugees to Canada and my mother's profound bitterness, tinged with real hurt, that Canada welcomed the Hungarians just over a decade after the war when no Jews were allowed to enter, not even to save their lives. "And the Hungarians were the worst," she would say, not meaning their culture, or manners, or as individuals, but as anti-Semites. Then she'd correct herself and say that designation had been rightly earned by the Poles or Ukrainians. And my confusion, because people from middle Europe were so familiar, so like us. They were our season's ticket neighbours at the symphony, on a winter bus the scent of cooking that clung to their coats smelled like my paternal grandmother's kitchen, their voluble conversation—voices speaking at once over each other with excitement and pleasure—were like parties at home. Familiar enemies and friends, too familiar to trust, too similar to overlook. Not that my parents would ever have acted in any way impelled by these feelings. No one would have been turned away, no one hurt. But the burden of vigilance and memory was felt.

Winnipeg is divided in my memory not by its two rivers or railway tracks or the Francophone/Anglophone split we hadn't thought of until Pierre Trudeau's late sixties program of bilingualism and biculturalism. (In fact, what had he been thinking? In Winnipeg the situation had always been one of many more cultures than two.) Divided by being Jewish, or not. In kids' school language the terms were "Jewish and english" and I guess by this we were, without articulating it, acknowledging the founding first (immigrant) peoples of Manitoba—the Hudson's Bay factors and bookkeepers and the Red River settlers of Selkirk—people from the British Isles with a firm sense of their proprietorial interests. But really, the short-hand "english" meant not Jewish, or in other words, anyone who celebrated Christmas.

An outright discussion of these matters of memory, violence, discrimination and being apart and "other" didn't ever take place in any formal way that I can remember, and how are these thoroughly held convictions integrated in such a consensual manner? I know these views were held, and in some cases more closely held, by almost all of Winnipeg's Jewish community as it was in the 1950s and 1960s—vigorous, thriving, complete and separate.

With the prosperity that followed the war came the desire to stretch and play a little. Unwelcome at the private golf clubs and still seeking the security of a somewhat cossetted environment, the Jewish community started its own golf club and my parents—young, slender, full of energy and ready for sport—wore argyle socks and two-toned shoes and golfed with their canvas bags and wooden-shafted clubs. The Glendale Country Club was just west of the St. Charles Country Club where Jews were never allowed and are still only marginally welcome. In the winter there was curling, and the Maple Leaf Curling Club, in spite of its all-Canadian name, was the Jewish curling club. The YMHA had been started before the war, a response, if I correctly remember my father's telling it, to the notion that Jews were bookish sissies readily submitting to being walloped and set upon. As for the quotas limiting admission to medical school, to engineering societies, to other professional associations—there was nothing to do but wait.

Did Winnipeg look like this from outside the Jewish community, if anyone looked? Was the divide as apparent as it was shaping? At the time, in the midst of it, at its most necessary and formidable period when wounds were still raw and readily recollected, the divide was too broad to breach, from this side. More effective than a shunning, it kept you in and held you close. For a kid, with the exception of racially direct playground bullying and the sometimes frightening hoots and verbal threats on the walks home after school, inside was a comfortable place to be. When some kid, always bigger, or if smaller then in a group, hurled "Jew" at me, or us, it was only an affirmation.

Rich, stewy Winnipeg on the prairies with no mountain ranges to hold in the heat of old cultures when it was built, with no visible geographic impediments to halt growth, allowed all of this to mix and sift and settle. If it was necessary to slide-step sideways to make room for someone else, there was space and will to do it. Commodious place where small frictions guaranteed warmth and few sparks to flare into real danger. Small place as a locum for the trains to unload the cosmopolitan mix of arrogant, educated, greedy, unschooled, ambitious, hungry, hearty, eager, generous, close-fisted, nostalgic exiles who brought with them their most portable, valuable goods—their ideas. And here, in the middle, to make flourish new theatres, dance companies, paintings, books, music and schools.

I saw the Sadler Wells Ballet perform at the Playhouse Theatre when I was little. I heard Isaac Stern in concert at the Civic Auditorium and if the acoustics were bad I couldn't tell because I sat in the first row and watched the rosin fly off his bow. I saw Hal Holbrook as Mark Twain and believed it. Agnes de Mille, who was related to Cecil B., set *Brigadoon* on the Royal Winnipeg Ballet Company and I remember her glossy chignon. Sonia Eckhardt-Gramatté, widow of German Expressionist painter Walter Gramatté and wife of Ferdinand Eckhardt, who'd been brought to Winnipeg in 1953 to serve as the director of the Winnipeg Art Gallery, came to dinner at my parents' house. I'd be prepared to bet there was no one like her in Winnipeg, for people who ate roast beef on Sundays before dark and called it dinner, but to me she was familiar. She was short, maybe my height but I was still growing, her skin was suntan dark even though it was winter; her hair was black and short to her ears with a side part and bangs brushed stiffly to the side; her voice was husky and rough; I remember no make-up; she wore a black suit with a tailored jacket and straight skirt and a plain white blouse. She seemed fantastic. She was fantastic. She composed music that orchestras played, she played piano—a grand piano—she played violin. Her eyes were black. She loved Winnipeg, loved the light and never spoke of missing Berlin or Vienna.

John Hirsch came here from Hungary in 1947, fled here, alone, parents dead. He was beautiful, thin and elegant. My father's younger sister said all the girls swooned when they met him, a hero, a Jew who had survived, a genius, who later met Tom Hendry, who wasn't Jewish, was in fact "english," and together, in the late fifties, they created a theatre and produced plays that would be the model for regional theatres everywhere, did it here in Winnipeg, first near Portage and Main, the central juncture of this centred city and then, a few blocks over, built the Manitoba Theatre Centre's building designed by the architect husband of my aunt who'd swooned when Hirsch had first arrived. From Hungary. And I hear my mother's voice saying, "they were the worst . . .," but Hirsch was Hungarian, and Jewish, and the mixed ether of Winnipeg's history makes my head heavy, as heavy as it grew when I drank my grandfather's plum wine made with sugar no longer rationed, but still the wine was brought out with ceremony and a sense that even here, in Winnipeg, and now in better times, there were some things about which a person could never be sure.

DAVE WILLIAMSON

Reading and Reviewing Canadian Fiction in the Post-World-War-II Era

As I write this, a novel about a teenaged girl living in the fictional East Village, Manitoba (*A Complicated Kindness*, by Miriam Toews), is being snapped up in bookstores and discussed by book clubs almost as much as a glitzy American thriller (*The Da Vinci Code*, by Dan Brown). Canadian writers are not only enjoying international acceptance, they are winning such prestigious awards as the Booker Prize (Margaret Atwood and Yann Martel), the Pulitzer Prize (Carol Shields), and the National (US) Book Critics Circle Award (Alice Munro). The number of literary awards in Canada itself has increased dramatically. The *Globe and Mail* publishes a tabloid insert devoted to book reviews every Saturday, while the *Winnipeg Free Press* devotes three broadsheet pages to books every Sunday. If this is not a Golden Age for Canadian books and Canadian book criticism, then it is at least a Silver. Publishers and writers still complain, but consider the situation in the 1940s and 1950s, a period in which I was passing through childhood, adolescence and early manhood and somehow getting interested in writing.

In 1957, I read eight novels. For fifty years, I have kept a record of what I read. At the end of each year, I rank the books I have read in the previous twelve months. My first choice in 1957 was *Marjorie Morningstar*, by Herman Wouk. One of the books I read that year was *Peyton Place*, by Grace Metalious, a novel I had to smuggle out of the United States because it was banned in Canada. It had been a *New York Times* bestseller for over a year when I finally got my hands on it. But the most unusual book on my list in 1957 was *The Sixth of June*, by Lionel Shapiro. Why was it unusual? Because it was *Canadian*. Shapiro was born in Canada, lived and worked for many years in Montreal.

Most of the books I read in those days were American bestsellers, many in inexpensive (but hardback) book-club editions (about half the price of my regular-edition copy of *Peyton Place*, which cost a whopping $3.95). Shapiro's novel about D-Day in World War II had made it in the American market and that is why I came to hear about it. Even though many of us had a university education, working-class kids like me were not much aware of contemporary Canadian literature. We had had the poetry of Bliss Carman and E. Pauline Johnson forced upon us in grade school, but we had no inkling of, say, Douglas Durkin, whose 1923 novel about the Winnipeg General Strike, *The Magpie*, achieved some notoriety. Though my parents encouraged reading, there were not many books in the house.

Somehow—this remains a mystery to me—I got interested in books. For some reason, as early as grade six, I wanted to write a story of my own. I wrote something called "Arf Arf the Prairie Dog" (I was not exactly precocious) and the teacher, dear Mrs. Cloutier, read it out loud to the class in place of one of the regular published stories she normally read. When I think of it now, Mrs. Cloutier probably had a lot to do with kindling my interest in books.

Or was it one of my English professors? George Brodersen, who brought Chaucer's *Canterbury Tales* to life for me; ever since then, every time I see a woman who, like Chaucer's character The Wife of Bath, has a gap between her two front teeth, I recall Brodersen's assurance that it is a sign of lax morals. John Peter, the transplant-ed South African, who spent a whole fall urbanely teaching us Milton, convincing us that "the mind is its own place, and in it can make a Heaven of Hell or a Hell of Heaven." Lloyd Wheeler, who acted out portions of the five Shakespeare plays we stud-ied, though his voice came across more as Chicago con man than Stratford thespian. James Reaney?

I met James Reaney at university but did not get to know him until after gradu-ation, when I took a creative writing class from him in the evenings. Here at last was a real live Canadian writer. (John Peter emerged as a fiction writer, but not until well after he left Winnipeg. His first novel, *Along that Coast*, published in 1964, won the Doubleday Canadian Prize Novel Award.) I was vaguely aware that Reaney was a pub-lished poet. I likely heard that he had won the Governor General's Award for Poetry for his 1949 book, *The Red Heart*, but, despite Brodersen and Peter and, after them, Saunders (eighteenth century) and Stobie (nineteenth century), I did not feel com-fortable with poetry (the wretched rhyming thing I wrote for our grade eleven year-book notwithstanding). The *real* books were novels, I thought, and that is what I wanted to write. Reaney, it turned out, could be supportive of any kind of writing. When he gave the class an assignment to plan a novel and write one chapter of it, I went at it zealously. Reaney allowed me to write further chapters instead of the week-ly assignments he had everyone else do, and this work became the basis of my first novel (which, despite Reaney's best efforts, wasn't published till about seventeen years later).

Meanwhile, I met another writer who had almost overnight become the darling of the Canadian literary world. It was June 1957, and I had newly joined the Hudson's Bay Company as a management trainee. Like all HBC trainees, I had to spend some time in several different departments, learning the retail business. One of these could be of my own choosing, and I chose the Book Department. (Again, this affection for books asserted itself.) In those days, The Bay had a fine book department, second only to the one at Eaton's—there were precious few bookstores in Winnipeg and they were all inferior to what department stores had to offer. The Bay's Books manager was also in charge of Toys. He was more a toy man than a book man, and, when he received an invitation to the Governor General's Awards dinner, he asked me to go in his place. Staged by the Canadian Authors Association, it was held on June 27, 1957 at the Fort Garry Hotel. I was able to take my girlfriend, Janice, and, especially for the occasion, she gave me a copy of the book we already knew was the winner of the fiction prize: *The Sacrifice*, by Winnipeg's own Adele Wiseman.

This was my first glimpse of prize-winning prose writers—Wiseman, as well as Pierre Berton, who was receiving the non-fiction award for *The Mysterious North*. I approached Wiseman for an autograph. She was short, plump and friendly, and dressed in a strapless, floor-length gown. She opened the cover of my copy of her book and, seeing Janice's inscription to me, she wrote under it, "I hope this doesn't break up a beautiful friendship. Adele Wiseman."

At only twenty-eight years of age, Wiseman had won what was then Canada's top literary prize with her very first book. In the September 29, 1956 *Winnipeg Free Press*, a reviewer identified only as J.M.G. gave *The Sacrifice* a rave under the heading, "Greatness Achieved." "Her writing has the simplicity of greatness," the reviewer said. " . . . Winnipeg should be proud of this young woman, still in her twenties, who has written so powerful and so compassionate a story. . . . This is a great book—and proof that a Canadian can write fiction of the very highest order about his or her own country, about his or her own people." (This came eleven years before Expo 67, usually regarded as the turning point in our maturing as a nation. Canadian writers, publishers and critics began, in 1967, to gain confidence in our ability to produce worthy and lively literature.)

J.M.G. went on: "This is the kind of book which author Roger Lemelin called for recently when he challenged western writers and artists to tell the rest of the world about their country—a country rich in material. This, on the other hand, is not the kind of book which another Canadian author, Lionel Shapiro [author of the aforementioned bestseller *The Sixth of June*], called for when he said in a recent magazine article that the Canadian writer's place was not to write of his own country (which, we assume, Mr. Shapiro sees as rather dull) but to write of other peoples in the broader world—for who, he argues, can best interpret, with an unjaundiced eye, the Englishman, say, to the American or the American to the Englishman."

(The Ontario writer Leslie McFarlane would have agreed with Shapiro. In a kind of mentor-to-novice letter to me in 1967, he said, "Whatever you do with your new book, I'd suggest you don't make it too damned Canadian." Practising what he preached, McFarlane ghost-wrote the popular American Hardy Boys books.)

J.M.G. finally returned to the book he was supposed to be reviewing: "We would suggest that Mr. Shapiro should stick to his last and we hope that Miss Wiseman will stick to hers. Mr. Shapiro's facile pen will probably bring him considerable success with novels of the order of *The Sealed Verdict* and *The Sixth of June*. There is no doubt in my mind that Miss Wiseman's art is far deeper than his, that hers is never slick and never contrived. Miss Wiseman, although this is her first novel, is not a 'writer of promise' but rather a mature writer who has reached fulfillment. May we hope that *The Sacrifice* will be followed by more writing just as fine. We are confident that it will."

There was another novel about life in Winnipeg that appeared little more than a year after *The Sacrifice* and made a name for its immigrant author, John Marlyn. Though his book, *Under the Ribs of Death*, became popular and found its way onto Canadian Literature courses, the *Free Press*'s J.G. (was this J.M.G., who'd dropped the M, or someone else?) said in a November 30, 1957 review: "I would like to be able to say that this is an outstanding book—not only because of the author's Winnipeg connection, but mostly because some parts of it are so marvellously done. Unfortunately, the book as a whole is far from outstanding."

Neither meeting Adele Wiseman nor hearing about John Marlyn moved me to invest in Canadian books. Yet I, a Canadian, wanted to write one. And James Reaney was doing all he could to encourage me. He had a connection at the CBC and he arranged for one of the chapters I had written for his class to be read on the national literary program *Anthology*, along with a chapter from a novel by a fellow Winnipegger, John Parr. When relatives and friends living in other parts of Canada phoned to say they had heard my piece on CBC, I thought I was on my way.

The on-air reader's resonant voice made the most of my humble prose (eventually chapter nine in my first published novel, *The Bad Life*). That reader was Victor Cowie, one of the University of Manitoba's best-loved English professors. Over the years, Vic not only gave countless students a lasting love of literature, he wrote and produced a film, *And No Birds Sing*, and he became a much-in-demand actor in Canadian theatre and film. Shortly before his death in early 2004, he appeared in the Guy Maddin feature movie, *The Saddest Music in the World*.

Around the time of the *Anthology* program, Reaney talked about producing his own literary magazine. So devoted was he to seeing aspiring writers into print, he took lessons in typesetting. Those were the days of putting individual metal letters into rows in a flat frame called a chase. Without getting into the intricacies of letter-press printing, I must emphasize the difficulty of setting up the pages in groups, inking the metal, laying sheets of paper over it, and always being careful to keep everything squared off and straight and unsmudged. The process had to be repeated for every copy of every page. Reaney started his magazine, *Alphabet*, in 1960, and he published a new section of my class assignment in his fifth issue (December, 1962). That piece (chapter twenty-two in the eventual novel) was given the title "The Third Riel Rebellion" by Reaney and it appeared along with such varied fare as another John Parr chapter (from his novel *Jim Tweed*), an article by famed literary theorist Northrop Frye, and poetry by M.E. Atwood (who became better known as Margaret).

Meanwhile, Reaney was producing his own work. His book-long poem, *A Suit of Nettles*, appeared in 1958 and brought him his second Governor General's Award. In her *Winnipeg Free Press* book review, Margaret Stobie referred to Reaney as "our one real poet." She said, "*A Suit of Nettles* is fresh and alive; we don't often get anything as good as this. Let's rejoice in it." Stobie explained that the book is "made up of twelve eclogues, one for each month, after the manner of Spenser's *Shepherd's Calendar*. But where in Spenser's poem it is shepherds who carry on the dialogue, in Mr. Reaney's poem, it is geese—Canadian geese—for Mr. Reaney's first purpose is a satiric one." In January, 1959, the *Toronto Telegram* asked fourteen "Canadian personalities who we know read widely to name the books they enjoyed most in twelve months' reading." (It is a sign of those times that only one of the "personalities" was a woman, and, where the other thirteen were identified by name and occupation, she was identified as "Margaret Scott [Mrs. Wilfrid W. Scott]".) The people chose non-Canadian novels and biographies, except for Dr. Claude T. Bissell, president of the University of Toronto, who picked Reaney's *A Suit of Nettles*.

Yet neither Reaney's success nor his efforts on my behalf turned me toward Canadian books for reading material. In 1958, I read twelve works of fiction, all American, mostly recent bestsellers like *By Love Possessed*, by James Gould Cozzens; *Anatomy of a Murder*, by Robert Traver; and *Lolita*, by Vladimir Nabokov. My top three picks that year were Hemingway's *The Old Man and the Sea* (originally published in 1952), Salinger's *The Catcher in the Rye* (1951) and John Cheever's *The Wapshot*

Chronicle (1957). The main influence on my reading at the time was the *New York Times Book Review*, because, in The Bay's advertising office, where I worked, we subscribed to the fat Sunday edition of the *New York Times*. Even if Canadian books were written up in the *Winnipeg Free Press*, I never saw the articles, because our family was a *Winnipeg Tribune* family, and the *Trib* tended to have less coverage of books than the *Press*.

In 1967 (the year of Expo), a friend of mine, Dave Humphreys, asked me to write reviews for the *Albertan*, a Calgary newspaper for which he had become managing editor. Over the next few years, I developed a liking for expressing my opinion in print, and my reviewing horizons expanded to include *Alphabet, Books in Canada*, the *Winnipeg Free Press* and eventually, the *Globe and Mail* and *Prairie Fire*. More and more, the books I was assigned were Canadian, and Canadian novels began to appear in my Top Ten of the Year—Mordecai Richler's *Cocksure* in 1968, Richler's *St. Urbain's Horseman* in 1971, W.O. Mitchell's *The Vanishing Point* in 1973, Roch Carrier's *They Won't Demolish Me!* in 1974. Now, in 2005, having written over 800 book reviews and watched Canadian books become known all over the world, I look back with curiosity at the period that spawned my interest, as if discovering it for the first time.

Back in the 1940s, the books reviewed by the *Winnipeg Free Press* were mostly British and American. In September 1941, several short stories by British and American writers were being run in the newspaper's Saturday Magazine section, while book reviews were confined to a third of a page. On September 20, the books reviewed were *Strictly Personal*, a collection of essays by W. Somerset Maugham; *Is God Dead?*, an early entry in that debate by Newman Flower; *Death in High Heels*, a whodunit by Christianna Brand; and *The Firefighters of London in Action*, written and illustrated by members of the London Fire Brigade—a product of the Blitz.

In those days, there was no television, and the newspaper was the primary source of information. In the frantic 1940s, with war raging in Europe, one might have sought solace in books, and book reviews themselves could be calming. On September 27, 1941, thirteen books were reviewed and the featured volume was a novel, 1176 pages in length: *The Sun Is My Undoing*, by Marguerite Steen. The quaintness of F.A.M.'s prose was typical of the reviews of the time: "It is often the habit of reviewers to say that so and so has captured perfectly the feeling of such and such a period. It is quite obvious that unless one is able to project oneself, by means of some fourth dimensional gift, into the past, no such statement is possible. Few reviewers have this gift, so the best thing we can do, under the circumstances, is to remark that it seems to us that the feeling of the period is right. Such is the way with *The Sun Is My Undoing*." Take another look at those first three sentences. One could use them in any review about any book, and therefore they are quite meaningless. Instead of taking space to tell us the obvious, F.A.M. might have gotten on with telling us that the book seems to depict the period accurately. F.A.M. is also guilty of another sin of reviewers of the forties and fifties: the prose is dull. I hark back to advice given by English writer Auberon Waugh: "The first aim of a reviewer, as with anybody who writes, is to be read. You do no service to anyone if nobody wants to read you. Even if you fill your review with dirty limericks and anecdotes about your pets, you will have drawn somebody's attention to the book."

Proprietors of the *Free Press* Building sounded a siren on Monday, May 7, 1945, to signal the Allies' victory over Germany. Thousands of Winnipeggers took to the streets to celebrate. English author Anthony Powell has written (in volume three of his autobiography) that, on the night of VE-Day, "I was probably the only person in England . . . lying in bed reading the *Cambridge History of English Literature*." In much the same spirit, *Free Press* reviews that week dealt with books considerably removed from the war: *Jennifer's House,* by Christine Noble Govan (reviewer L.N.H. opened with "Stories of the south never lose their charm," assuming that the reader knew "the south" referred to the *American* southern states and confirming that the only literary south must be the *American* south—you see how brainwashed we were?); *The Complete Secretary,* by H.J. Russell (reviewer E.V.N. said, "Teachers and students of short hand will find this manual useful for dictation purposes"); and *Two Rapps,* an English novel by Dorothy Hewlett. (It was *de rigueur* in these reviews to refer to a female author as an "authoress," but never did you see the term, "writeress").

Of *Two Rapps,* reviewer A.C. said: "A somewhat mixed-up story of two sisters with the home of an English country clergyman as the setting. It is very light but the love stories of the two girls are interesting. The girls, sisters, are direct opposites. One is grave, the other gay. One is dreamy and egoistic and the other practical and kind-hearted. Some other very delightful characters will be found in the pages of this book." (A.C. deserves two raps on the knuckles, one for using the meaningless word "very" twice and the other for telling us redundantly that the "characters will be found in the pages of this book.")

On August 6, 1945, the atomic bomb was dropped on Hiroshima, marking a dramatic turn in the way countries might wage war. The threat of nuclear disaster was suddenly a grim reality. No sign of it in the *Free Press* book pages, however. Two days before Hiroshima, reviewer M.L.C. said that *In the Village of Vigar* by Duncan Campbell Scott "is a collection of superb vignettes of people in a French Canadian hamlet. There are now many Canadian books [!], but not many Canadian classics. It is our opinion that Mr. Scott's work may be placed in the latter category. To read it is an experience [!] and one which leaves the reader certain that Scott is one of the 'greats' in depicting the Canadian scene." (Note the use of "it is our opinion"—completely unnecessary since this is after all an opinion piece—and the use of the good old journalistic "our," as if M.L.C. were speaking for a whole group of folks—perhaps the newspaper's editorial board. Also, note the quotation marks around greats, which today would diminish the importance of the word and indicate that the reviewer does not really believe Scott is great.)

Five days after Hiroshima, the book featured by the *Free Press* was *Westward the River*, by Dale Van Every, a novel of life in Ohio found by reviewer L.N.H. to be "a swift-moving narrative that is extremely well-told."

Later that fall, as the Book-of-the-Month Club featured, in a quarter-page *Free Press* advertisement, Canadian Hugh MacLennan's novel *Two Solitudes* (offered with Glenway Wescott's *Apartment in Athens* for $3.75), the lead Book Section review dealt with *Philosophy of Business*, by University of Manitoba philosophy professor Rupert C. Lodge. Reviewer L.G.B. said Lodge was a Plato expert who examined "with a considerable degree of sympathy and insight, the philosophical status of the modern American businessman." One can only ponder what that means, but notice the key word "American."

Bill Stobie (my prof for nineteenth-century English) and his wife Margaret both reviewed regularly for the *Free Press* in the late forties and early fifties, often giving poetry more than its usual share of coverage. (No explanation of why the Stobies let their full names appear in the bylines, while so many other reviewers were identified only by initials.) On October 7, 1950, Margaret began a review of *Thy People, My People*, by Elizabeth Hoemberg, with: "In the summer of 1932, three young Canadians studying in Europe decided to investigate the strangely divided country of Germany. Mrs. Hoemberg and her sister were two of those Canadians, and this reviewer was the third." (A rather endearing lack of concern about conflict of interest here.)

In view of the explicit books and movies we are used to these days, it is amusing to read this September 13, 1952 comment by reviewer H.D. Ranns about *Love Is a Wound*, by (Mrs.) Worth Tuttle Hedden: "This is not in any sense a pleasant book. Its theme is not pleasant—that of a domestic triangle due to a frustrated woman, whose early life was repressive in character through the restlessness and cruelty of a step-grandmother with whom she lived." On October 11, 1952, in a feature review of Han Suyin's *A Many-Splendoured Thing*, J.A. questioned the taste shown in writing about a real love affair with a married man. A week later, in regard to *The Nymph and the Lamp*, by Canadian Thomas H. Raddall, R.N. said: "Prudes may shudder at the way Isabel sheds her inhibitions during her first confused year on the island, but the balance of tenderness and cruelty of love and hate reaches out to a level for a dramatic climax." (One hopes that the balance's reach did not exceed its grasp and find a different level.) Under the headline "Shocking!", an October 3, 1953 review by J.G. told of a British novel by George Miller, *Siesta*, in which an artist's painting of a nude woman creates a stir. The woman strongly resembles one of the respected married ladies in the community.

On February 7, 1953, The Bay advertised their men's made-to-measure suit sale (choice of all-wool serges, worsteds and gabardines, $46.95), while Eaton's suggested as "a charming Valentine gift," cotton eyelet slips, camisole style (with wide eyelet straps to cover her bra straps), for $2.98. There were forty individual movie theatres in Winnipeg and six drive-in theatres, featuring such all-American hits as *High Noon* (the quintessential American showdown flick, starring Gary Cooper) and *Francis Goes to West Point* (starring Donald O'Connor and Francis, the Talking Mule). By the lack of feature or lead-article treatment given to fiction—even American fiction—on the Book Page, one must assume that fiction was regarded by the *Free Press* (and other major dailies) as trivial. Much more importance (judging by the placement of the review on the page and the length of it) was given to books of non-fiction—biography, history, war, religion—such as *The Highland Constable: The Life and Times of Rob Roy MacGregor*, by Hamilton Howlett; or *Memories of Three Wars*, by the Viscount Dillon; or *The Glitter and the Gold*, by Cassandra Vanderbilt Balsan, former Duchess of Marlborough; or *A Bonnie Fechter: The Life of Ishbel Marchbanks, Marchioness of Aberdeen*, by Marjorie Pentland; or *The Bible in Canada*, by E.C. Woodley; or *Mary II, Queen of England*, by Hester W. Chapman; or *Period Piece: A Cambridge Childhood*, by Gwen Raverat. Many of the featured reviews were written by J.A. Stevenson. On September 12, 1953, the day Tommy Dorsey's sixteen-piece band appeared at Winnipeg's Rancho Don Carlos (with Jimmy Dorsey on sax), Stevenson's review of Charles A. Lindbergh's *The Spirit of St. Louis* said, "This book will have interest for airmen but few attractions for the general reading public."

Ahh, the fifties. The time of Perma-lift Stitched Cup bras ("with the lift that never lets you down"), Edsel cars ("They'll know you've arrived when you drive up in an Edsel"), movie ads featuring busty actresses (Jane Russell, Gina Lollobrigida, Elizabeth Taylor), and—in the American magazines that dominated the racks—cigarette ads that promised better taste, calmer nerves, scientific proof of mildness and "no song and dance about medical claims—we give you a treat instead of a treatment." In the *Free Press*, Canadian books were cited a little more often; on February 21, 1953, a novel by Ernest Buckler, *The Mountain and the Valley*, was given an understated but positive review by D.G.A., while L.Y. used only one evaluative word to describe a book of short stories called *Mike Mullins of Boston Crick*, by O.G.T. Williamson—"amusing." At the same time, Thomas B. Costain's novel *The Silver Chalice* was being serialized in the *Free Press*.

One October 31, 1953 item I found especially intriguing was G.M. Lacey's review of *Portrait of Jane*, by Frances J. Woodward. The book is a biography of Jane Franklin, wife of John Franklin, the man who led the ill-fated 1845 expedition in search of the Northwest Passage. Jane was a "valiant and talented woman" whose first love was Peter Mark Roget of *Thesaurus* fame. During the time (1838–43) in which her husband John was the second governor of Van Diemen's Land, which was eventually turned into the Australian state of Tasmania, she established herself as a social activist. (I became aware of her and the good work she did when, in 1997, I was a Visiting Fellow at Jane Franklin College in Hobart, Tasmania.)

By the mid-fifties, the *Free Press* was running the *New York Herald Tribune* best-seller list (exclusively American books, of course) on the Book Page every week. On September 7, 1957, the top three fiction works were *On the Beach*, by Nevil Shute; *Peyton Place*, by Grace Metalious; and *The World of Suzie Wong*, by Richard Mason; while the top three non-fiction books were Vance Packard's *The Hidden Persuaders*, Robert Paul Smith's *Where Did You Go? Out. What Did You Do? Nothing.*, and Bernard M. Baruch's *Baruch: My Own Story*.

It was the practice of the *Free Press* to run, in late November, an extra book page to commemorate "Young Canada Book Week." The newspaper would invite high-school students to send in reviews. On November 23, 1957, the third annual collection of these was published. Among the twelve reviews that appeared, one was written by Jim Lorimer, a grade eleven student at Winnipeg's Churchill High School, on *John A. Macdonald, The Old Chieftain—Vol. II*, by Donald Creighton; and another was written by Heather Robertson, a grade eleven student at Kelvin, on *The White and the Gold*, by Thomas B. Costain. Lorimer would become a Toronto-based publisher, while Robertson was destined to be a well-known novelist and biographer, both doing their part to strengthen, enrich and promote Canadian literature.

On August 30, 1958, while the movie version of *Peyton Place* was already playing in the local cinemas, the lead review on the Book Page concerned two Canadian novels. The reviewer P. McL. (Peter McLintock) called Robertson Davies's *A Mixture of Frailties* "unrealistic." He wrote, "The reader never for a moment gets the feeling that anybody like any of Mr. Davies's characters ever existed. They are strictly two-dimensional, and pulled about like puppets on strings for the amusement of the author and his readers." (*Fifth Business*, the novel that would clinch Davies's international reputation, did not appear until twelve years later.)

The second book McL. discussed was *The Well*, the first novel by Saskatchewan's Sinclair Ross since his highly regarded *As for Me and My House* appeared in 1941. McL. referred to that work as "the novel which best caught the feel of life on the prairies in the 1930s." He saw *The Well*, another treatment of Saskatchewan farm life in the thirties, as a worthy successor. But many critics agree with Roy St. George Stubbs, who wrote in the October 12, 1974 *Free Press* that Ross had failed to fulfill his early promise until thirty-three years later, with the appearance of *Sawbones Memorial*. There were two disappointments in between: *The Well* in 1958 and *Whir of Gold* in 1970. Adele Wiseman never did live up to reviewer J.M.G.'s pronouncement that she'd follow up *The Sacrifice* with something "just as fine." When, after moving to Toronto, she had difficulty writing a second novel and then finding a publisher, Margaret Laurence (also a former Winnipegger) had to intercede on her behalf. By then, Laurence had become a successful and popular novelist in her own right and she threatened to take her own work away from McClelland & Stewart if they didn't publish Wiseman's *Crackpot*. When M & S did publish it in 1974, Laurence not only wrote a lavish blurb for the jacket, she also shamelessly wrote a glowing review of it in the *Globe and Mail*. *Crackpot* was trashed by *Free Press* reviewer Tom Saunders: "Cliché piles on cliché, not only in expression but in action and in the delineation of character."

As the 1950s—that most innocent of the post-war decades—ended, there were signs of the coming sexual revolution. Vladimir Nabokov's *Lolita*, published in Paris in 1955, was allowed into North America in 1958, and D.H. Lawrence's long-banned 1928 novel, *Lady Chatterley's Lover*, appeared on our shores in 1959. The first of John Updike's *Rabbit* books—*Rabbit, Run*—was published in 1960. But at the same time, Canadian literature became liberated as well, and writers like Margaret Laurence challenged people's ideas of what could be written about. And the day would come when a Winnipeg-based writer like Carol Shields could gain an international following while writing from here, and she could say in *Prairie Fire*, "[Writers] need to live in a community that values what they do, and Winnipeggers do, I think, honour their writers, even when they don't always read them. Writers also need fellow writers around them so that they feel less lonely and odd and marginal and useless. It has been encouraging to me, always, to live among other Winnipeg writers."

That assignment I did for James Reaney in 1958 was published in 1975 as *The Bad Life*, but not before it ran into a small problem. Southern Manitoba (a part not far from Miriam Toews country) had not yet caught up to the world in sophistication. Friesens of Altona, Manitoba, the book printer that has grown to become one of the largest in North America, refused to print my book. According to my publisher, Joan Parr of Queenston House, they could not do it because it was a novel and therefore must contain some sex. (The sex was pretty mild even by the standards of those days, but it was there all right.) So Joan took it to Hignell's of Winnipeg. But there is a footnote to that story. Many years later, I was touring the Friesen plant, marvelling at the amazing changes that printing had undergone in the new computer age. I noticed that one of the books going through the many automated processes was a graphically illustrated history of sex. "A few years ago you turned down my tame novel," I said to my guide, the company president, "and now you do something as explicit as that? What changed?" He looked at me with a benign smile and said, "Grandfather died."

ADELE WISEMAN

Questionable Fathers and the Ghosts of Empire in Laurence, Wiseman and Blondal

Margaret Laurence, Adele Wiseman and Patricia Blondal graduated from United College in the 1940s, began their writing careers in mid-century and wrote novels set in southern Manitoba. Though these novels are all very much about family, they present, among their main characters, not one living, capable, admirable father. Each father figure is in some way questionable. Jason Currie in *The Stone Angel*, Gavin Ross in *A Candle to Light the Sun* and Abraham in *The Sacrifice* are domineering patriarchs tragically insensitive to the needs of the children under their sway. Niall Cameron in *A Jest of God* is an ineffectual ghost haunting the nether regions below the lives of Rachel and her mother. Christie Logan in *The Diviners* is an object of ridicule, an embarrassment to the young Morag, while Danile in *Crackpot* is penniless, helpless and blind, dismissed by his Jewish community as a fool. Almost without exception the surrounding fathers are no better, and fatherhood itself is called into question by the proportion of children without known fathers, including "No-Name" Lottie Drieser in *Stone Angel*, Hoda's David in *Crackpot*, and David Newman in *Candle*.

These are, admittedly, realist fictions in an ironic mode in which mothers might not fare well either, but the clear majority of mothers are sympathetically presented even in Laurence, where motherhood becomes a more central issue than fatherhood. All but one of the mothers of protagonists are dead at the outset of the actions or die prematurely. The protagonists who question themselves as mothers are seen as struggling gamely to overcome adverse circumstances. Mother figures thus raise a separate set of problems of marginalization, subjection and erasure that deserve, and are now being given, special study. The surprisingly consistent pejorative construction of fathers is puzzling. What does it signify? What does it tell us about these Manitoba novels?

Some of the answers may lie beyond these six novels. Fatherhood, like old Hamlet's ghost, assumes a "questionable shape" in much of Canadian fiction. In Western literary culture generally, the father, once revered as the ultimate source of meaning, value and being, has been represented with increasing ambivalence, especially since the mid-nineteenth century.[1] The devaluation of fathers in British and American fiction has already been studied as a progression leading to Donald Barthelme's savagely satirical *The Dead Father*, which presents the father as "Dead but still with us, still with us, but dead" (3).[2] Our questionable fathers must share some of the features of that general devaluation. For example, negative images of fathers and troubled filial relations inevitably invite Freudian interpretation, even for those who do not share Roland Barthes's belief that "every narrative leads back to Oedipus" (47). Little Freudian analysis has been done on our novels, though two of them all but demand it. Blondal was a reader of Freud[3]; one of her minor characters, Basil Waterman, is a Freudian psychoanalyst, and her protagonist, David, enacts a pattern that defines "the neurotic's family romance" in Freud's original essay on the subject. Freud describes a child who frees himself in imagination from his commonplace parents (or just his father) by replacing them with others of better birth. "He will make use in this connection of any opportune coincidences from his actual experience, such as becoming acquainted with the Lord of the Manor" (299). David does exactly this. His mother has married beneath her; daughter of the colonel of a British regiment, she has become pregnant and married the sergeant major to provide David with a father. David knows that Arthur Newman is not his father, and from a series of ambiguous circumstances he concludes that he must be the son of the town patriarch, Dr. Gavin Ross. The core of David's identity search through early youth is a campaign to win from the doctor an acknowledgement of kinship. Hoda's fatherless son in *Crackpot*, another David, is thrust into the same Freudian motif by a bit of cryptic nonsense in the note Hoda leaves with him on the steps of the foundling home: "a prince in disguise can make a piece of a prince" (158). Local gossips connect his birth to a recent visit by the Prince of Wales, Hoda encourages the confusion by leaving donations at the home "for the Prince," and the child is cruelly deluded by the attention that follows. A shadow of the same motif appears in *Stone Angel* when Hagar takes John to Vancouver, away from the low-class influence of his father, only to find he is distancing himself from Hagar the housekeeper by claiming to be a member of the family that owns the fine house she keeps. Since Freud identified this pattern specifically as the "neurotic's" family romance, the recurrence of this motif, like the figures of questionable fathers, is clearly symptomatic of problems in the identity search that traditionally becomes a search for the father.

Wiseman places David in a more directly Oedipal tension when he is brought to Hoda for sexual initiation, but that tension is more Sophoclean than Freudian, in that David, like Oedipus, is unaware that he is committing incest, and it is Hoda, like Jocasta, who must grapple with the moral dilemma. Again, this example involves a son rather than the daughters who are central to most of our novels and who do develop intense relationships with father figures. The little attention that has been paid to father-daughter relations in the works of Laurence and Wiseman has been in feminist critiques. But as Ursula Owen says in *Fathers: Reflections by Daughters*, feminists have available only two ways of writing about the father-daughter bond, a Freudian or an anti-patriarchal discourse,[4] and those writing on Laurence and Wiseman have generally chosen the anti-patriarchal. Thorough Freudian analyses remain to be done.

The fact that these questionable fathers are wrong in distinctly different ways may be a clue to their more local, specific significance. The difference between Jason Currie and Christie Logan can be seen as a progression: from powerful, overbearing patriarchs to socially powerless but loving and supportive fathers. There is also an intermediate generation in these novels, of failed and dying fathers, including Niall Cameron, Colin Gunn, Isaac, and Arthur Newman.[5] A similar progression can be seen in Wiseman's novels, from Abraham to Danile, and it, in turn, runs parallel to a progression Ruth Panofsky describes in her article "From Complicity to Subversion: The Female Subject in Adele Wiseman's Novels." The progression can thus be read as a movement toward feminist self-assertion, and one that may be more remarkable because it runs counter to the historical trend by redeeming the father morally as it deprives him of his overt authority. The later, marginalized fathers can thus take their places in a world establishing feminist values. Together, the evolving father figures can be seen to chart the development of a feminist narrative or, perhaps more accurately, a women's narrative in a process still haunted by ghosts of the patriarchy.

The first phase of this progression, found in *Stone Angel, Sacrifice* and *Candle*, is a direct assault on the patriarchy. The central fathers are cast as patriarchs in the full, traditional sense; like the Old Testament patriarchs, their earthly authority is somehow associated with divine will and power. Jason Currie places himself in a collegial relation with God in the minds of his children. As Hagar says, half-mockingly, "God might have created heaven and earth and the majority of people, but Father was a self-made man, as he himself had told us often enough" (17). In *Candle*, David is repeatedly suspected of making Gavin Ross his God; David's doppelgänger, Darcy Rushforth, for example, accuses him of thinking he is "the son of God" (252). Wiseman's Abraham is obsessed with the role his name implies as an agent of God's providence. To his neighbours he coyly points out the coincidence of his wife's name, Sarah, saying, "You see . . . we are not just anybody. . . . We will have strange events to distinguish our lives" (97). These fathers thus represent the Father, the ultimate source of meaning, value and being.

Our authors create these characters, however, as failed patriarchs, destructive, self-defeating and discredited in the action of the novels. Their misogyny, with its stifling effects on female characters, is too obtrusive to need discussion, but they are also shown as crippling their sons with their rigid, self-righteous demands and by denying them a father's recognition. Jason Currie is contemptuous of his sons, "graceful unspirited boys who tried to please him but rarely could," (7) preferring Hagar, who shows the grit to resist him. He is indirectly implicated in the death of his son Dan, who is pulled from the river and carried across town in thirty-below weather rather than taken to the nearest house because the children fear old Jason's displeasure. In the end, his "dynasty" is diminished to anecdotal memories of a pioneer family indistinguishable from the feckless Shipleys he so despised.

Gavin Ross inherits the dynastic ambitions of the town's founder, Sir Richard Rashleigh, when he marries Rashleigh's granddaughter, Christine, and moves into his great house. Childless after the drowning of their only daughter, Ross resists David's suit for recognition and directs his paternal ambitions instead toward his sister's son. As Christine reflects, "Darcy is somehow his heir to the future, son through some mystic union with Mary . . . " (215). His attempt to burden Darcy with the Ross family honour, like his rebuff to David, is obviously harmful, fuelling the arrogance and cynicism in which Darcy commits a senseless murder and goes to the gallows. Ross dies without heir or estate, but his failure is particularly signaled by the fact that David abandons his search for the patriarchal father-king-god, recognizing that his identity cannot be found through another or through the symbol Gavin Ross has become. As David concludes, "What man has a father?" (315)

Isaac overtaxes himself attempting to live up to Abraham's expectations, and, though he is skeptical about his faith, he brings on his early death by rushing into a burning synagogue to save the Torah. Abraham is himself destroyed by his delusional identification with his biblical namesake. In Laiah's apartment he imagines himself to be in "the completed circle, when the maker of the sacrifice and the sacrifice himself and the Demander who is the Receiver of the sacrifice are poised together, and life flows into eternity, and for a moment all three are as one" (178). Far from conducting a ritual that ensures the future and renews the faith of the tribe, Abraham is, of course, committing a cruel and blasphemous murder for which he is convicted, imprisoned and despised, his posterity diminished to grandson Moses, who, like his father, is scarcely even a believer.

In these novels the patriarchy, then, is represented as destructive even of its own ends, self-defeating because it devours its own young. On a larger scale, the sacrifice of the young in war becomes the central evidence of this patriarchal violence, and wars are everywhere. In *Crackpot*, Hoda's life is deeply involved in both world wars; in *Candle*, the patriarchs are frustrated because David cannot and Darcy will not go to war. And as Birk Sproxton has demonstrated, war is a pervasive presence in Laurence's work. All these patriarchal fathers fail, but the ghosts of patriarchy remain to haunt the outcomes. In *Candle*, for example, David's rejection of patriarchal succession seems absolute, but by marrying Ross's niece, Roselee, he joins a family in which the old doctor's values are revered, and he may be expected to sustain some shadow of the feudal order. The dead father may be with him yet. In a sense, Jason Currie is himself a ghost. Already dead in the narrative present of *Stone Angel*, he haunts Hagar's memories, attitudes, convictions and language. Hagar had been able to resist the living father, rebel against him and seek her own way, but as the Freudians have explained, the dead father is more powerful than the living, his laws internalized as conscience, or, as Hagar puts it, as "some brake of proper appearances" that has denied her "every good joy" she might have had (292). The crux of Hagar's narrative, toward which all her memories draw her inexorably, is her guilt at the death of her son John. In the fatal confrontation that precipitates his accident, it is with Jason's instilled prejudices that Hagar rejects John's marriage to the daughter of "No-Name Lottie," with Jason's voice that she dismisses their plans, saying, "You haven't got a nickel between you" (201), and with Jason's self-righteousness that she denies the young couple the use of her house and leaves John driving around in a desperate and drunken state.

Abraham's case is more problematic and has been complicated by two generations of critical response to *The Sacrifice*. The ending can be read as an endorsement of the old patriarch's values, and it certainly does confirm some of his values. After being haunted for years by the thought of his grandfather up on Mad Mountain, Moses feels resentment, even hatred, for what Abraham's crime has done to his life. But when Moses finally goes to the mountain to confront him, the old man confesses his sins, begs forgiveness, and establishes a bond of mutual love expressed in a handclasp: "their hands fused together—one hand, the hand of a murderer, hero, artist, the hand of a man." Moses feels himself "standing upright, with his grandfather leading him, as he always had" (345). To Panofsky and some other feminist critics, Wiseman is absolving Abraham of his guilt and licensing him to convey a patriarchal blessing on his grandson, maintaining the male continuity of his line.[6] It is argued that Wiseman thus aligns the moral world of the novel with Abraham's misogynist, patriarchal values, and this interpretation was encouraged by the conclusions of early male critics such as Donald Stephens that the death of Laiah was, indeed, a sacrifice necessary to the catharsis of the community.[7] The ghosts of patriarchy evidently haunt the critical discussion. And there is no denying that Abraham is in some sense redeemed, but are his values endorsed? In the scene before the murder, he clearly loses his argument with his daughter-in-law, Ruth, and he feels his beliefs severely threatened. After the murder, society condemns him and he condemns himself, renouncing his spiritual pride and taking responsibility for having "killed his sons." Abraham cannot form his bond with his grandson until, as Edna Froese says, he "returns to the moment of sacrifice and clearly repudiates his previous thinking" (21). Moses's perception of the hands further suggests the redemption of Abraham not as patriarch but simply as a man, a grandfather. Patricia Yaeger and Beth Kowaleski-Wallace, in *Refiguring the Father: New Feminist Readings of the Text*, offer this caution: "When feminist writers construe the father as a metaphor for patriarchy, we lose sight of the complexities of paternity and the paternal function" (xi). Wiseman's ending seems to be focused very deliberately on such complexities and on preserving the delicate distinction between the paternal and the patriarchal.

In *Diviners* and *Crackpot*, Laurence and Wiseman more decisively extricate fathers from the stereotypes of patriarchy. By any patriarchal standard, Christie Logan and Danile are contemptible failures as fathers: poor, ignorant and powerless. Yet they are able to provide Morag and Hoda with the fathering they need because, unlike the self-righteous, authoritarian patriarchs, they are understanding, loving and supportive. Perhaps most important, they are communicative; "questionable" in the best sense, they can be questioned by their children. In *Diviners*, Laurence unsettles conventional fatherhood, distributing its functions across a range of partial and surrogate fathers. Orphaned, Morag cherishes her dead father, Colin Gunn, idealized by memory and by her foster father, Christie. She loves Christie, but his status and his crudeness embarrass her, and she longs for a wider world. When she marries the cultivated English professor, Brooke Skelton, she is consciously rejecting her past and Christie, and, as she discovers, adopting another surrogate father. Thoroughly patriarchal, Brooke would keep her a child, deny her a chance to have children of her own, and stifle her creativity. When Morag asserts her independence it is by adopting Christie's colourful language and by deliberately choosing her childhood Métis lover, Jules Tonnerre, as the birth father for her child, Pique. And when Morag finally accepts her identity by recognizing the land of her ancestors, she describes it as "Christie's real country. Where I was born." (415) At the time of Christie's death she acknowledges him: "Christie—I used to fight a lot with you, Christie, but you've been my father to me" (420). Morag finally recognizes that Christie has provided her with the roots upon which her identity could grow.

Hoda, by contrast, remains in her father's home, and every crisis of her life is experienced in relation to his well-being and his approval. Hoda relies on the stability of Danile's love and on his blind faith to anchor her uncertain world. The relationship could be seen as a crippling dependence. In Freudian terms, the seductive father is most dangerous when he appears without power and in need. But when Hoda at last finds a mate in the holocaust survivor, Lazar, Danile urges her own independence upon her rejoicing in "How strange and wonderful it is that [Lazar] should come to us," yet insisting he is not advising her to marry: "I know some people think I'm a fool, and maybe I am, but I'm not such a fool as to try to tell you whom you should marry" (297). In a final dream where her conflicting desires are resolved, Hoda finds "a small Danny" by her side and wakes to realize "she had dreamed her daddy dead, and dreamed a child with his name" (304). The cycle of generations is thus restored and Hoda's world unified as it has not been since childhood. Danile and Christie have little of the patriarchal about them and, unlike the patriarchs, they achieve success as fathers.

The power of these later, post-colonial fathers to nurture and to liberate their daughters depends on more than love and understanding. Christie and Danile share a quality that is rare in prairie fiction: both are storytellers. Christie provides the orphaned Morag with his tales of Piper Gunn, about Morag's forebears immigrating heroically from the Scottish Highlands. Danile gives Hoda her myth of origins about being from a blessed union in which the most despised couple in the village is wed in a ritual to save everyone from the plague and is rewarded by being transported to the New World. Both daughters depend on these stories for security and stability in a disordered and potentially hostile world, and the fathers can present them at need. Both daughters at some point turn away from these stories in disillusionment. Morag, faced with the contending school histories and Jules's tales of "Rider Tonnerre," decides Christie's stories are not true. Hoda is simply bored by the repetition of Danile's stories. Both daughters, however, return to the parental stories in maturity, when they recognize their ritual value and poetic truth. In her darkest hour, despairing of being anything but harmful to her son, Hoda longs for the old stories, "the sequence, the rhythm of them, the inside secrets, . . . the feeling that they were true, and the truth had a terrible tenderness in it . . ." (258). Like some others in the community, she comes to at least entertain the thought of Danile as a "holy fool" or blind seer. Morag realizes that conflicting stories of the past simply demonstrate that there is no one story, that stories are created, and she sees that she must create her own, later spinning tales of Christie Logan and Lazarus Tonnerre for her daughter Pique.

The stories are essential as comfort and in providing the daughters with roots from which to grow, but they have a deeper value. Christie and Danile teach not only the tales but the telling. Hoda goes on to create her own tales—about the Prince of Wales, about finding acceptance in society, about claiming her son and drawing him into the family—and with these private fictions she holds together a fragile order in her shattered life. As Marcia Mack says, "Hoda survives through her belief in her own stories, through the manner in which she legitimizes her stories to herself. Stories heal her and create meaning out of her uncertain existence" (153). In a more explicit and overt way, Morag becomes a story-teller. Paul Hjartarson traces the process:

> Christie tells Morag the tales of her ancestors, of Piper Gunn "and his woman Morag," to open a space for her. . . . In bed later, Morag tells *herself* the "Tale of Piper Gunn's Woman." Having listened to Christie's stories, having heard herself named, Morag can, in turn, name herself, insert herself in the story, become herself the teller. . . . The story-telling empowers Morag both as a woman and as a speaking subject (51).

Morag goes on to write a series of novels which work through the phases of her growth to full, speaking subjectivity.

Both Laurence and Wiseman create fathers who are the keepers of the tribal legends, who communicate them to the next generation and who can pass on the gift of telling. That is, being powerless, they can demonstrate that even the marginalized can become speaking subjects and can create their own narratives embodying their own visions of order and value. Patricia Blondal did not live to create a later version of fatherhood, but in *Candle* there is a marginalized figure who mentors David and encourages him to write.[8] Gavin Ross's brother Ian, gassed in World War I, alcoholic and a closet homosexual, is the only adult of the "Father" class to offer counsel and understanding in what David remembers as "all the wonderful talking hours" (166). When Ian dies, his importance to David is suggested by Darcy's mocking telegram announcing "Holy Ghost gone" (229).

The importance of the gift of storytelling to the development of a women's narrative in these novels is confirmed by the absence of that gift among the earlier patriarchal figures. Gavin Ross is uncommunicative. Jason Currie has his "tales" but they are all about the Highlands, and they exclude Hagar, leaving her disconnected from her world, thinking: "How bitterly I regretted that he'd left and had sired us here . . ." (15). Abraham, too, presumes to be the keeper of the tribal legends, but his retelling of the Old Testament stories to Isaac and Moses is corrupted by his delusional identification with the biblical patriarch. Edna Froese, in her "Unbinding Isaac and God: Story as Promise in Adele Wiseman's *The Sacrifice*," offers a brilliant analysis of the way Wiseman traces Abraham's appropriation of sacred story as promise of greatness, fuelling his delusions and leading to the sacrifice of his sons and ultimately to murder. The power of narrative can be dangerous and destructive as well as creative.

With the emergence of positive father figures we can see that it is not fathers who are under attack in these novels so much as the symbolic Father, the system of order, values and laws with which the paternal function is identified, what Jacques Lacan calls the "name-of-the-father." And names are under intense pressure here, especially where the patriarchy is strongest. In each of the three earlier novels, the central action turns literally on the name of a father. In *Sacrifice* the fatal compulsion that drives the protagonist on to the tragic outcome arises entirely out of the name "Abraham," father of the Jews. In *Stone Angel*, the importance of fathers' names is signaled very early in the phrase "No-Name Lottie" as the epithet absolutely excluding the girl from society. Hagar herself is "haughty, hoity-toity, Jason Currie's black-haired daughter" (6). Ironically, Hagar later reflects that she has always been addressed by some man's name rather than her own "Hagar." She dismisses "Marvin" as a Shipley family name, "squat, brown names, common as bottled beer" (32), and the contrasting Currie and Shipley names define the struggle within Hagar between the earthiness to which she must descend and the social pretensions with which her father has imbued her. She tries vainly to insist that John is a Currie, fit to carry on her father's legacy, and, as we have seen, it is the protection of the Currie blood from marriage to No-Name Lottie's daughter that leads Hagar to the interference that precipitates John's death. The eventual resolution of Hagar's struggle is also signalled by the names "Currie" and "Shipley" on either side of the grave marker, with "nothing to pick and choose between them now," as Hagar says (306).

In *Candle*, the entire central action is quite explicitly the fatherless David's striving for a name and all that the name of a father implies. When Lilya envies his "royal name," he thinks "what good is a king's name to me when the king will not acknowledge me?" (177). When Gavin tries to burden his sister's son with the honour of the Ross family, Darcy's response is, "Uncle Gavin has poor eyesight, he can't see my father, my father's name, my father's house" (243). When David abandons his quest, he thinks of the letter his mother has left in trust for him, a letter he has thought would contain the secret of his paternity, and he reflects, "What name would he find? No name at all? What man has a father?" (315). The extent to which Blondal is questioning the full significance of the symbolic father, the name-of-the-father, is clear from Darcy's cynical comment to David: "There is no God, man, only the animal who coupled with mother" (294).

Fathers' names have a more benign function in *Diviners* and *Crackpot*. In the more patriarchal narratives, the name of the father binds the next generation to the law of the fathers. Isaac, like his biblical namesake, is bound; Hagar carries her chains with her. David is bound to Gavin's prescriptions for life. In the later novels the names of the post-patriarchal fathers signal rather the release of the daughters to move beyond the name-of-the-father to their own narratives. When Morag declares her ancestors, her home and her identity, and defines them in terms of a father's name, "Christie's country," she is released from a quest for European ancestors. She can take up her own (family) narrative as writer and mother in which, again, a father's name, "Tonnerre," is a catalyst for the release of Pique from Morag's control and into her own life's narrative, as the generations turn and the gift is passed on. Similarly, in Hoda's final dream, Danile's name signals her release into a new life with a new generation. With "small Danny" by her side she dreams "Danile was dead and gone the gift of knowing" (304). The turning of generations initiates a new narrative that moves beyond the father's name, the father's knowing, with Hoda as subject.

The ghosts in the fiction of Laurence, Wiseman and Blondal are identified with a patriarchal order quite specific to the time and place of these novels. All were set in a period extending from World War I through the Depression and World War II, a period in which Canada formally built its independence from a failing British Empire. All three of our authors studied at university in Winnipeg during World War II, which must have been a powerfully formative time in their development as writers. The novels were published in the fifties, sixties and seventies, during the rise of a revitalized feminism, a surge of nationalism, and a convergence of anti-centrist forces in Canadian culture and literature, including Prairie regionalism, growing racial and ethnic awareness, and official multiculturalism. All our authors contend with the colonial past, working to liberate their protagonists from what Laurence calls a "colonial mentality." With uncanny regularity, the ghosts of patriarchy are identified with imperial symbols, with kings, princes, knights and aristocrats. The opening line of *Candle*, when Gavin first addresses David, offers a striking example: "'Boy! Here,' the old man called and waited. 'The King is dead.'" (13). The decadent air of a dying monarchy pervades David's life as the "king" refuses to acknowledge him. Gavin himself labours under the mantle of colonial leadership that has descended on him from Sir Richard Rashleigh, while the pathetic last words of David's mother are "Tell him I was presented" (150). In *Stone Angel*, the self-destructive pride Jason Currie instills in Hagar is grounded in his ancient Highland clan and legitimized by the name of his father, Sir Daniel Currie.

The ghosts of empire linger in the later novels. Brooke Skelton in *Diviners* is a product of the British colonial service in India with a classic colonial mentality: "Trapped in a garden of the mind, a place which no longer has a being in external reality" (246). Hoda in *Crackpot* struggles in vain to fit herself into the imperialism of Miss

Boltholmsup, and her fantasy lover/husband, the Prince of Wales, haunts a major period of her life. Hoda's eventual liberation is signaled by her dismissal of such fantasies, seen in her references to "aging ex-princes" and "the trade-in value of an old empire in so-so condition" (287). It would be difficult not to identify the father figures in these novels with the fading colonial order on the prairies. The patriarchs of the earlier novels, including Abraham, belong to the last wave of a specifically European patriarchy to break on the shores of the New World. They join a host of patriarchs in prairie fiction bent on imposing their wills, their culture and their names on the new land, a land I earlier described as "unnamed country."9 The next fictional generation, the Niall Camerons and Colin Gunns, also join a wave of disappearing fathers suggestive of the lost paternal authority at the end of the imperial dream.

In Christie and Danile, Laurence and Wiseman create post-colonial fathers, marginalized and powerless but effective not only in redeeming fatherhood from its patriarchal excesses but in laying to rest the ghosts of empire. Their tribal legends transport their daughters spiritually to the New World and ground them solidly in their own place. The fathers' gift of the telling releases them from the imposed imperial narrative or meta-narrative and its names. They can take their own names, set down their own "title," as Morag says in the last line of *Diviners*, and they can struggle to create a new narrative that is more polyphonic, more inclusive in matters of race, ethnicity and class as well as gender. The fathers are not ultimately rejected, but they become ancestors, contained elements within that narrative of generations. Hoda passes on Danile's name, Pique takes the Tonnerre knife, Morag keeps the Currie plaid pin. Taken together, the evolving father figures can be seen more clearly as narrative elements with particular functions. They are not, after all, the fathers of autobiography or even of the more lyrical modes of imaginative literature. If we turn, for example, to Dennis Cooley's *Fielding*, or Tim Bowling's *The Witness Ghost*, or Margaret Atwood's *Morning in the Burned House*, we see more admirable fathers, more benign ghosts. And in Laurence's nearly autobiographical stories in *A Bird in the House* we see a more sympathetic construction of the paternal, even in Grandfather Connor. The ubiquitous questionable fathers have particular roles to play specifically in the fiction. Just as the natural imagery in earlier prairie fiction expressed the alienation of the invader-settler society imposing itself on the land, the questionable father seems to serve as a trope for a changing relationship to the past and to authority, to the familiar Canadian tradition of continuity, inheritance and culture.

Winnipeg in mid-century was the most likely locus for this post-colonial literary evolution. In the doubly colonized West, it was the original centre, with the deepest involvement in the imperial past and, at the same time, the longest experience of major cultural diversity. In the cultural capital and the only mature urban centre on the prairies, its writers could be expected to lead the way in shifting attention from the pioneer experience to the society that resulted from it—in effect, from the land to the imposed culture and the fathers who so often represent it. Fathers are, of course, infinitely suggestive wherever they appear in fiction, and in this first, groping exploration, I have hoped only to propose that some of their significance is specific to the time and place of these Manitoba novels.

NOTES

1. Robert Davis, *The Paternal Romance: Reading God-the-Father in Early Western Culture* (Urbana and Chicago: University of Illinois Press), 141.
2. For studies of British and American fiction, see, for example, Bueno et al., Davis, *The Fictional Father*, Sadoff; van Boheemen; Yaeger et al.
3. See Ricou, 59.
4. Cited in Yaeger et al., xiii.
5. The father has, in fact, such a minor part in the action that *A Jest of God* will be mentioned only occasionally in this essay.
6. See especially Pennee.
7. Pennee analyzes these early responses, 2.
8. *From Heaven With a Shout* (Toronto: McClelland & Stewart, 1962) was published later but written earlier than *Candle*. See Ricou, 71.
9. In *Unnamed Country* I examine the more general imposition of an imported cultural order on the Prairies. The names of the fathers are clearly a part of that process.

WORKS CITED

Atwood, Margaret. *Morning in the Burned House*. Toronto: McClelland & Stewart, 1995.

Barthelme, Donald. *The Dead Father*. 1975. New York: Farrar, Straus and Giroux, 2004.

Barthes, Roland. *The Pleasure of the Text*. Trans. Richard Miller. New York: Hill and Wang, 1975.

Blondal, Patricia. *A Candle to Light the Sun*. Toronto: McClelland & Stewart, 1960.

Bowling, Tim. *The Witness Ghost*. Roberts Creek: Nightwood, 2003.

Bueno, Eva Paulino, Terry Caesar, and William Hummel, eds. *Naming the Father: Legacies, Genealogies, and Explorations of Fatherhood in Modern and Contemporary Literature*. Lanham, Boulder, New York, Oxford: Lexington Books, 2000.

Cooley, Dennis. *Fielding*. Saskatoon: Thistledown Press, 1983.

Davis, Robert Con, ed. *The Fictional Father: Lacanian Readings of the Text*. Amherst: University of Massachusetts Press, 1981.

———. *The Paternal Romance: Reading God-the-Father in Early Western Culture*. Urbana and Chicago: University of Illinois Press, 1993.

Freud, Sigmund. "Family Romances." *The Freud Reader*. Ed. Peter Gay. New York: Norton, 1989, 297-300.

Froese, Edna. "Unbinding Isaac and God: Story as Promise in Adele Wiseman's *The Sacrifice*." *Canadian Literature* 181 (Summer 2004): 11-24.

Harrison, Dick. *Unnamed Country: The Struggle for a Canadian Prairie Fiction*. Edmonton: University of Alberta Press, 1977.

Hjartarson, Paul. "'Christie's Real Country. Where I Was Born': Story-Telling, Loss and Subjectivity in *The Diviners*." In *Crossing the River: Essays in Honour of Margaret Laurence*. Ed. Kristjana Gunnars. Winnipeg: Turnstone Press, 1988, 43-64.

Laurence, Margaret. *A Bird in the House*. Toronto: McClelland, & Stewart, 1970.

———. *A Jest of God*. 1966. New York: Knopf, 1970.

———. *The Diviners*. 1974. New Canadian Library. Toronto: McClelland & Stewart, 1989.

———. *The Stone Angel*. 1964. New Canadian Library. Toronto: McClelland & Stewart, 1968.

Mack, Marcia. "*The Sacrifice* and *Crackpot*: What a Woman Can Learn by Rewriting a Fairy Tale and Clarifying its Meaning." *ECW* 68 (Summer 1999): 134-58.

Panofsky, Ruth. "From Complicity to Subversion: The Female Subject in Adele Wiseman's Novels." *Canadian Literature* 137 (1993): 41-48.

Pennee, Donna Palmateer. "'The Hand of a Murderer, Hero, Artist, the Hand of a Man': Rereading Adele Wiseman's *The Sacrifice*." *ECW* 58 (Spring 1996): 1-14.

Ricou, Laurence. "Twin Misunderstandings: The Structure of Patricia Blondal's *A Candle to Light the Sun*." *Canadian Literature* 84 (Spring 1980): 58-71.

Sadoff, Dianne F. *Monsters of Affection: Dickens, Eliot and Brontë on Fatherhood*. Baltimore and London: Johns Hopkins University Press, 1982.

Schwartz, Nina. *Dead Fathers: The Logic of Transference in Modern Narrative*. Ann Arbor: University of Michigan Press, 1994.

Sproxton, Birk. "The Figure of the Unknown Soldier: Home and War in *The Fire-Dwellers*." In *Margaret Laurence: Critical Reflections*. Ed. David Staines. Ottawa: University of Ottawa Press, 2001, 79-100.

van Boheemen, Christine. *The Novel as Family Romance: Language, Gender and Authority from Fielding to Joyce*. Ithaca and London: Cornell University Press, 1987.

Wiseman, Adele. *Crackpot*. 1974. New Canadian Library. Toronto: McClelland & Stewart, 1978.

____. *The Sacrifice*. 1956. Toronto: Macmillan of Canada, Laurentian Library, 1968.

Yaeger, Patricia and Beth Kowaleski-Wallace, eds. *Refiguring the Father: New Feminist Readings of Patriarchy*. Carbondale: South Illinois University Press, 1989.

LAURIE RICOU

Patricia Blondal's Long Poem

As the past moves under your fingertips, part of it crumbles. Other
parts, you know you'll never find. This is what you have.
—*Timothy Findley,* The Wars

The papers of Patricia Blondal (1926–1959) were deposited in the Special Collections Division, University of British Columbia, in 1978. It is a small collection: seventy-six folders, all in one file box. As with any such collection—but perhaps here exaggerated by its confined size—the gaps frustrate, and tantalize. Only two letters from husband Harold to Blondal are preserved; none of Patricia's love letters are at UBC. The collection holds two fairly complete and amply revised transcripts of *A Candle to Light the Sun*, no manuscript of *From Heaven with a Shout*. Surely, much material remains to be located. Other parts we know we will never find.

For all its gaps, reading in this collection feels extraordinarily intimate. In the morning on my way to read in the Blondal papers, I call out, "I'm going to talk to Pat." But I would not think to say, anticipating other archival encounters at UBC, "I'm on my way to talk to Malc[olm Lowry] or Ethel [Wilson]." Maybe it's just a Brandon boy cherishing the Souris connection? Yet Mouse Bluffs, Blondal's fictional Souris, shudders in its intimacy. But nothing in the Blondal papers held at UBC is so intimate as the untitled poem here reproduced. We publish it for the first time, as transcribed by Pat's daughter Stephanie, unfinished and uncertain, in order to convey such intimacy. We're listening, as it were, to a woman talking to herself about her dying—and we can't quite catch it all.

The Blondal papers provide a set of contexts within which to read this last poem of drugged pain and large snow, a set of contexts that might suggest connections to the writers, and to the period in Manitoba's writing history, presented in this volume.

cold war

A Candle to Light the Sun is the raw, ambitious, crowded book that its author never saw between covers. It is not a war novel, but its psychic landscape trembles with the memory of one war and the haunting imminent beginning of another. In the novel, as in the poem, the reader senses panic—a form reeling in fear. I need to write my way through and beyond this fervour, Pat might be thinking. I need to do it in a hurry.

In what the archivist has labelled Blondal's "Character Notes," we are able to read the pre-novel, a quite simple set of discrete autobiographies, mostly in the first person, that are the palimpsest of *A Candle to Light the Sun*. On the wars and growing up in their bleak aftermath:

> **Darcy** Maybe we should have gone to war, all of us . . . Then we could have been brave, death-wishing and sadistic but we couldn't be; all we could do was sit in college and pretend (and I mean pretend like hell) that we approved of all those brave death wishing sadistic types off winning the lovely old war for us. . . . It would have spared us the brutal sanity with which we received it all and the brutal truth that sanity had no place in the world. (Box 1. Folder 17)

It may be an aspect of such "brutal sanity" that the intimate letters, if they existed, have not been found. Pat's letters to her father are closer to essays or tracts than to expressions of love, or questions of knowing. In the longest letter in the collection, she writes extensively within the climate of that other (cold) war that leaves her community in a "long open-eyed sleep":

> You see there is not one thing that Red Russia has done that our democracy has not done and done it better. Of course I don't conclude from that that we should immediately wage war on this educationally and socially inferior nation . . . on the contrary—hats off to the five year plan if it could do so much for that nation. But on no grounds should we invite them to bring their system of government here. (to Dad, December 1948. 1.3)

In part, I suspect this agony or paranoia rests in the familiar Canadian prairie motif—best unarticulated by Robert Kroetsch's *Seed Catalogue*—of an absence of war, of ghosts, of history. As Christine observes in the character note Blondal imagines for her:

> **Christine** The earth here is not yet rich with the dead. Will it ever be? Not in the old country sense, never. Because Henry Ford put America on wheels and Americans go away to die. (1.17)

Go away to die. Such going shakes the dream and recognition in Blondal's poem.

no way of talking

The paradox of intimacy in the Blondal papers—she calls her accumulated returned manuscripts and rejection slips "a box full of sadness" (1.2)—consists in some brutal sanity: she dwells on death and disease but as someone "consciously a cynic" (1.3). We read an obsession of avoiding. She really must be going.

In the papers Blondal speaks very little of cancer; a few hints rest in euphemistic evasions by others. A small exercise book is filled with notes about epilepsy, whose involuntary convulsiveness plays a thematic (and maybe formal?) role in *Candle*. But, moving under our fingertips, always the traumas that this last poem condenses.

> **Ian Ross** The essence of our existence is that each of us in this house is dead. (1.17)
>
> **Christine** Dr. can't tell her because i. he fears for her sanity ii. he has no way of talking to her now iii. he has no real desire to talk to her about it. (1.17)
>
> **Darcy** And even with ourselves there were honesties we never embarked upon. (1.17)

"When the world expands it hurts," writes Blondal in this poem. And a reader senses, in a poem so apparently frank, that even with herself there's an honesty not to be embarked upon. But, so furiously, repeatedly, is she *not* embarking upon it, that to read is to honour an explosion of trying. In the face of the brutal truth of "this cutting place," the *work* of writing—the furious accumulation of three novels, notes for others, a score of stories, fifty radio shows, a scattering of poems, almost all of it crammed into three or four years of "idiot intensity."

to be a woman

Although the United College novelists of the 1940s—Margaret Laurence, Adele Wiseman and Patricia—would go their separate ways, we can't help thinking of their similarities. Their writing against taboos, especially sexual taboos, their view of the thin promises of small towns (including north Winnipeg), their reaching, in their lives and writing, for the independent female. I wonder, for example, how much Pat shared her character Christine's view that the "principle of marriage [is] the soft prism" (1.17). "Take my feet, my eyes, whatever," the poet pleads, but "leave a woman." Yet in her best novel it is surely a young man, David Newman, who is the author's alter ego. Her character sketch of David in the archive cryptically asserts Blondal's own passion:

> he wants to write books; he doesn't talk of this to anyone for a long time; and then discovers talk very bad; (1.17)

Blondal's note for David (explicitly dated less than a year before her death) seems to me the best gloss on the Sherbrooke Street poem. It is perhaps "eminently female" in its recognition that "to be a woman is not enough":

> **David Newman 1958:** The need for love, for paying out the nedd [need] knowing it
>
> would never be returned has hung over my brain like a fugue. (1.17)

Recalling that she was once United College's "Freshie Queen," she imagines herself spending the rest of her life convincing the world "that I had something on my mind besides a lot of blond curls" (1.76). In the bewilderment of treatment, questions about her mother self, "about what makes you female," hang over her brain like a fugue.

free verse

Although she wrote few poems (there are only two in the Papers), Blondal is a poet's novelist. She makes frequent reference to her failure as a poet, repeating with rueful pleasure that her career as a writer began with "verse so free one might have called it abandoned (as indeed it should have been)" (1.76). But in 1959, in the year of her death, she abandons herself to verse just because it is so free.

The genre of "long poem," as we know from extensive commentary in Canadian criticism, is an odd form. It is odd, maybe especially because of its impurity, its ability to accommodate the unpoetic. So it is that Blondal writes her strongest poem (admittedly the extant examples are few) by failing to write a poem. It might, if in a distinctly different register, remind Canadian readers of Lampman's failure to revisit Tantramar, of Kroetsch up against it in *Seed Catalogue*, of Lionel Kearns reduced to citation in *Convergences*. Blondal writes documentary (and hence fits into Dorothy Livesay's lineage), recording the physical presence of hospital, inside and out, tracking the details of a treatment regime and response. She writes autobiography with a frank directness that deepens the fissures and creases in *A Candle to Light the Sun*. She writes to her loved ones what might be an apology and an explanation.

For all the trauma implied in our double framing of Blondal's poem, I would not want to forget her enthusiasm for the "street of delights" and her recognition of a "sweetness" however "gray." A crucial sweetness is that moment of human connection, perhaps her "sisterhood" with Beauregard (the name so obviously symbolic) that enables the poet, raging against the dying of the light, to find a love of going.

In her going is just the enthusiasm for language, the love of writing, that speaks intimacy. ". . . Too eccentric, too angular . . . too complicated and imagistic to go"

(Lambert Wilson to Blondal, June 7, 1957, 1.2). Blondal responds quickly to this rejection slip—"I have torn the prose apart"—but then adds, as if not quite convinced: "I suppose this is the danger inherent in experiment, one can develop so much individuality for its own sake that the result ceases to be communication and merely expresses the individual, perhaps distortedly" (Blondal to Lambert Wilson June 17, 1957, 1.2).

Angular, complicated, individual, distorted—the exchange with Wilson seems to summarize the clenched fluttering of the poem. Blondal stops to conjugate the verb of surgery, intones the will to live, expands the word as she feeds this disease of relentless, uncontrollable expansion. The real torment is the potential loss of mind—and this poem, unrevised, raw, unedited, not for publication, learns the word made flesh. Part of it crumbles. This is what you have.

NOTES

The original document is written in ballpoint pen on 8.5-x-11-inch paper, seven single sides. The transcription, including the order of the unnumbered pages, is by the author's daughter, Stephanie Blondal. She describes the piece as originally a "letter," or part of a letter, which she chose to understand as reading "more like a freeform poem." Underlining shows a combination of Stephanie's emphasis, and uncertainty about transcription. I have reviewed the transcription against a photocopy of the original and find no obvious variations; hence we choose to present here the version as best read by Stephanie, one that seems to represent the torment and possibly drugged state of someone whose handwriting was usually "neat" and "concise."

Thanks to the generosity of Dr. Rabbi Benjamin Herson, a duplicate photocopied set of these papers is now held by Patricia Blondal's alma mater, the University of Winnipeg (United College).

I would like to dedicate this commentary, with gratitude, to Stephanie Blondal and Joann Bishopric.

WORKS CITED

Blondal, Patricia. Papers. Special Collections Library. University of British Columbia.

———. *A Candle to Light the Sun*. Introduction by Laurence Ricou. 1960. Toronto: McClelland & Stewart, 1976.

Hunter, Catherine. "Underground in Winnipeg: Patricia Blondal's *A Candle to Light the Sun*." *Prairie Fire*. Special Issue: Winnipeg in Fiction, ed. Birk Sproxton (Summer 1999): 121-125.

Ricou, Laurence. "Patricia Blondal." *Canadian Writers 1920-1959 First Series*, vol. 68 of *Dictionary of Literary Biography*, ed. W.H. New (Detroit: Gale Research 1989), 29-32.

———. Introduction. *A Candle to Light the Sun*. By Patricia Blondal. Toronto: McClelland & Stewart, 1976.

Ricou, Laurie. "Twin Misunderstandings: The Structure of Patricia Blondal's *A Candle to Light the Sun*." *Canadian Literature* 84 (Spring 1980): 58-71.

PATRICIA BLONDAL

Transcribed from
Patricia Blondal's notes
Written in Montreal, 1959

I stood in Sherbrooke St.
            as the day died
Love pressed the quality of his mouth
            upon my days.
Before this day.
It was then dusk and warmth and large snow
<u>Feathering</u> thru the thickness of the hour
Street of delights
A world expanded, a brain exploded
To the limits, the <u>fullest beautie</u> of Sh. Street.
But up, beyond the hour, the doctor's office
Still the snow
And tears, for when the world expands it hurts.
A rage of tears against going
I knew, even then what they did not.
What I should have known from knee times
I really must be going.
From then the days piled up an agony <u>month</u>
Select <u>moments</u> like each <u>frail dream</u>
With <u>deliberate</u> exquisite precision
Will live & live & be lived till I leave

The night before they <u>shaved</u> my breast
While I lay fists clenched, the sweat pouring
Like <u>baptism</u> water over my hot unbelieving head
This, I said, is the worst.
But I knew even then
I really must be going
And in the morning, clogged with Demerol
Eyes fevevered [sic], saw the surgeon
All green & with a sad intensity.
I need your permission, he said, it was
                              a kindness.
And the lights, the big lights pressed down
                    like a <u>wind</u>
As pentothal blew my brain to silence
Someone in the drugged, pain <u>reddened</u> place
Screamed No! No! No!
Someone was <u>unable</u> to stop that voice
Moving about in slow morphine <u>sickness</u>
They bare the arm & plunge the
                              shaft into foreign parts
<u>Reeling</u> later into the light again, No!

They cut, they have cut, they were cutting
I lay once in my big warm puberty
                              bed
And counted ribs with slow loving fingers
Against the new budding breasts
And knew with delight I should soon
Never again be able to count those boundaries
<u>There</u> the supple growth of new woman
Twenty years ago.
I really must be going.
How <u>white</u>, how <u>raw</u> among the <u>lillies</u> [sic] time was.
To draw my loves, to show my world
That here resided, all <u>waiting</u> fresh, woman
Gave these as my mother self, with
Abundant love, to my pretty ones.
Saw the small, sweet smelling heads
Move, knowing, <u>hungering</u> to my breasts
To take life with strong little mouths
A new line of love from my body to <u>them</u>.
Now I count ribs once more
I really must be going.
Others, <u>Gwyne, Simpson</u> have rocked kingdoms
                              with it
I eminently female, feed the inward cancer
I am the hot, x ray fed, roentgen generation
Take my feet, eyes, whatever, leave a woman.

And I cross to the other side of the
                yellow lead glass
When I stop sweating & shaking weakly
<u>With</u> motion toward the bottom of the <u>hill</u>
When the scream, the tears, the terrible rage to smash
Will rest deeper in my throat than my teeth
Then I shall go, bewildered still to count my ribs
Take a small seat in a small bar beneath the hill
Go from <u>and to [word illegible] world</u>
And remember only one day and the gray sweetness
                        of Sherbrooke
A <u>fleetness</u> in red as rich as the order of my love
Then perhaps I shall love again, drink again,
                write again
But harder, because I have lost <u>NB</u> weight
Because I have been here to learn
I really must be going.

We must remove your ovaries they said
And the terrible No! began again
Where days before only a Yes! came to all
It is that thing which makes you female
Breasts, ovaries, estrogen, I was told,
Which feed these renegade cells.
No! And the corners of the <u>pale</u> green
                    room press down.
Save me. To be a woman is not enough
Save me. Have it all. Why should
              I cling
To <u>uselessness,</u> to tissue and members which
                serve worms.
The pain begins again & the gloom flocked room
Waits beyond the pentothal dark
High white beds, six, each a
              suffering woman
Tubes run out full of urine
Tubes run in full of saline or
             blood.

And they moan the <u>issue</u> of pain to the girl
Who moves with <u>starchy</u> speed
                         carrying the <u>tiny</u> Demerol blackness
A very small precious needle <u>comes.</u>
Are you leaving me here to die alone!
The woman in the far corner screams
Her agony is real, worse, it is augmented
                             by fear
Sister! Sister! May I have a needle?
Her eyes are gentle, the hypo
                     she carries is gentler
Her name is Beauregard, she is beautiful
My brain turns slowly to the dark like the
                  earth from the sun.
For the second time I start down the little <u>hill</u>
How to get out of this cutting place.
At night the nurses hurry by on
                    <u>rubber</u> feet
In the <u>solarium</u> Shell & Labatts look up

With <u>idiot intensity</u> to the <u>hill</u> hospital
A search light fans the air <u>ceaselessly</u>
And the searchlight is worst
It is a dead world, the place of that light
Unpeopled, where all the lights & machines
Continue a <u>brainless lifeless</u> function
In the cold <u>unfleshed</u> areas of our time
We are gone, <u>fade</u> out or phlogiston or cancer
Have destroyed the word made flesh
Alone I watch from the windows of the R. Vic
While the wind <u>howls</u> a counterpoint
Knowing I really must be going
There will be a day when all these men
The cutting men & the <u>sawing</u> men
Say, bless your stripped & severed self
To enter Montreal & live a while
When the x ray machine stops its silent rays
Stops its obscene octopus fleshings

ULRICH TEUCHER

Renegade Cells: Patricia Blondal's Last Poem

Susan Sontag noted in *Illness as Metaphor*, her famous cultural critique, that she thought it "unimaginable to aestheticize [cancer]" (1977, 18). Since then, many accounts of life with cancer have been written, covering the whole literary spectrum from self-help manuals such as Eric Gardiner's *How I Conquered Cancer* (1997) to popular accounts such as Liz Tilberis's *No Time to Die* (1998) and highly crafted books like Reynolds Price's *A Whole New Life* (1995) and Audre Lorde's *Cancer Journals* (1980). Nevertheless, one of the recurring statements in such narratives is that there seems to be no language to give voice to the terrors of life with cancer. Only a few writers have explored the artistic use of language and fictionalization in an effort to represent what seems unspeakable. For example, Winnipeg writer Wayne Tefs in his 2002 book *Rollercoaster: A Cancer Journey* includes a series of interchapters in which he constructs a dialogue between himself (or one of his personae) and his cancer. Poetry may be a particularly effective medium in which to address the unspeakable and, indeed, various writers, including Sylvia Legris (1995, 1996), Lorie Miseck (1997), William Matthews (1997) and Audre Lorde (1997), have tried to capture their experience in poetry, but perhaps no one has done so as evocatively as Patricia Blondal in her unpublished poem (1959).

It is part of the frightening mystery of the many different kinds of cancer that nobody experiences this illness in the same way. Some patients may have had painful symptoms for a while and the diagnosis confirms what they had feared all along. Others learn through a routine visit to the doctor that they have cancer and must have had it for a long time. In the latter case, it may be the treatment, not the cancer, that causes discomfort. Some have little difficulty talking about their experience and accept their lot, while others cannot acknowledge their diagnosis at first, let alone speak the "C-Word." The treatment of cancer is tolerated differently by different individuals, and not all treatments are hard to bear, but often they can take us to the limits of, and sometimes beyond, human dignity. There are periods of life with cancer and its therapy, sometimes extended, when patients can be overwhelmed with excruciating pains, signs and symptoms never felt before that cannot be compared, categorized and understood, eliciting visceral terrors. The sustained uncertainty of such sensations, the debilitating side effects of some therapies, the loss of parts of the body, particularly those that relate to our sexual image, the possibility of metastases and/or a relapse, and the threat of an early death can strip away last vestiges of control over one's life. All of these sensations, experiences and emotions may occur at the same time, competing at various levels, overwhelming, fragmenting and alienating a person from familiar notions of the body and self. It is this density of experience that seems incomprehensible and sometimes impossible to relate in language, and that some have identified as traumatic (e.g., Stacey 16).

The fragmentation of what once seemed coherent into a myriad of details, the sudden uncertainty of time, and the many sides of the question "what does it mean" and its proliferating answers can elicit an obsessive reflective re-evaluation of life, including reinterpretations of the past in the light of the new present. Quite understandably, many writers do not want to explore the depths of their countless terrors too deeply and their fellow patients—for whom such accounts are primarily intended— usually do not want to learn what else could go wrong as they themselves struggle to cope with cancer. Rather, writers want to demonstrate that one can make it "through the tunnel," that life will "continue on the other side," and that there are redemptive messages to be learned after all. And while writing can be therapeutic for some, recent trauma research shows that, for others, dwelling on a traumatic experience can add to its terror.

However, those who do write, in particular those who struggle hard to externalize what seems unspeakable, turn to language itself, to a variety of poetic tools that help draw attention to language and its many meanings, in order to approximate the confusing, overwhelming density of life with cancer. Ursula Maerz (2001) has identified a useful poetics of aestheticization with regard to historical trauma (the Holocaust) but her findings can also be applied to aestheticizations of other traumatic experiences, such as cancer. Maerz lists four literary instruments: tremendous attention to detail, extension of narrative time, inclusion of the narrator's reflection and an abundance of literary metaphors. Attention to detail subverts the systemic reduction of the individual; extension of time works against the efforts to destroy life and individual time; narrative reflection asserts freedom of movement in a space where movement is confined; and the use of metaphor asserts creative choice, in the face of annihilation (Maerz

2001). All these tools are available to poetry, too, and more. For example, staccato-like sequences of alliterations and/or linguistic stops, and the use of metre can enact and embody the frenzied chaos of a cancer patient's mind, thereby drawing the reader into the experience. These tools, artfully used, provide for a poetic testimony that can disentangle and approximate the personal experience of illness and trauma much more closely than factual autobiography, and provide deeper insights into the otherwise incomprehensible density of being with cancer. The following interpretation shows how some of these poetic elements are achieved in Blondal's poem.

Like so many accounts of cancer, Blondal's poem begins with a contrast, one that hardly could be more stark, and that returns in many images throughout the poem: what were days of new love and life on Montreal's Sherbrooke Street ("before this day") is now an image of foreboding death ("as the day died"). What was an experience of the density of life and pain and vulnerabilities of love ("a world expanded, a brain exploded"), where the world seems to reveal itself in a myriad of details, held together in boundless love, comes to a stop, evoked in the language of stops in "But up" ([b], [t], and [p]). The conjunction sets up the contrast to a density not of love but of death, away and above the life of Sherbrooke Street, in a doctor's office or the hospital on the hill. This is the density of life with cancer, itself "a world expanded, a brain exploded," fragmenting into countless details by the knowledge of impending death; images and phrases follow each other, in changing lengths and metres: "But up, beyond the hour, the doctor's office / Still the snow / and tears, for when the world expands it hurts."

As the days and moments now "pile [. . .] up an agony month," just as the phrases and images pile up in Blondal's poem, the narrator reorients herself, matching this life of days and moments with a desperate determination to subvert both her physical reduction—the removal of breasts and ovaries, and her psychological reduction—the loss of her femininity. She wants to make and count each moment her own, and make us read, and speak, and count, each individual syllable, repetition and alliteration of the lines that close the poem's introduction: "with deliberate exquisite precision / will live & live & be lived till I leave." The deliberate metre of these lines, slowing the reading, slows down and even stops narrative time, as the poem slows from "days," to the "thickness of the hour," to the double meaning of "still the snow," from "agony months" to "select moments," moments selected that the narrator now holds out against the uncertainty of time.

What seemed to have a certainty of meaning, just days ago, now, upon reflection, reveals its opposites: the love that "pressed the quality of his mouth upon my days" becomes the large surgery lights that "press down" on her. The ovaries that once provided new growth, to the narrator's children, and the breasts that helped feed new life, these very organs now feed another growth that will lead to death. The ribs, counted in early puberty before the onset of young budding breasts, can be counted once again—in the absence of breasts. What was light, "when time was white," now turns into the blackness of Demerol; what was a "Yes! To all," just days ago, is now a "No!" and resounds throughout the poem.

Treatment provides no relief, no safe haven in this poem; in fact, the metaphors of cancer and its therapy surpass each other in menacing intensity. The "inward" cancer grows from within, ever more threatening in its intangibility—and its origins. For "renegade cells," the poem's other metaphor for cancer, were once cells of life that have betrayed their birth and now bring death; etymologically, a "renegade" has deserted a cause. But the world of the hospital seems to be complicit in bringing on death. Set in an alien, lifeless moonscape where searchlights fan the air "ceaselessly," "with idiot intensity," the hospital is peopled by mostly nameless people in green, "they," the "cutting men & sawing men," the nurses who hurry "with starchy speed" on "rubber feet," and X-ray machines that produce "silent rays" and "obscene octopus fleshings." This imagery of Montreal's Royal Victoria Hospital in the late fifties is far from the life "down" in Montreal to which the narrator hopes to return, even for the life of one day. The metaphoric treatment of parts of Montreal as a destructive force calls to mind Blondal's aphorism in *A Candle to Light the Sun* about learning and the city, in this case, the city of Winnipeg. In *Candle*, Blondal writes, "Learning and the city: the one rotted religion; the other destroyed character" (155). The imagery of rot and destruction refers to a young man "destroyed" by moving to Winnipeg from the country, an imagery that is contained and controlled by the sentence pattern. Ironically, his destruction is metaphoric rather than literal. In the poem, Blondal sees destruction as both literal and from within, as in the image of "renegade cells."

Cancer is an experience through which patients often feel paralyzed, isolated and arrested in their imagined movement in life. The use of battle imagery, of envisioning cancer as an opponent who needs to be attacked through medical treatment and confronted in a patient's attitude, often serves to mobilize a patient's defences (the downside of the battle metaphor is that it is divisive, splitting the patient into both enemy and defendant). Cancer relaxation support groups may use other methods to re-mobilize patients, for example, as two or more therapists provide guided imagery and music from different corners of a room, and two assistants administer therapeutic touch to the head and feet of a patient at the same time, thereby gently "opening" the patient up. One of the most pervasive images in Blondal's poem is the knowledge that she "must be going"; this is not an image of arrest and paralysis, although at first there is a "rage of tears against going" that reminds us of Dylan Thomas's rage, inciting us to "not go gentle into that good night." But go we must, and the narrator reminds herself many times throughout the poem of what she has now learned: "I really must be going"; it may mean, most literally, that she wants to leave the hospital once treatment has ended, but it also means "going to and from this world," and not failing to visit a small bar in downtown Montreal on her way—and live, drink and write once more, even if only for a few days. The image of moving in and out of the world is reminiscent of the metaphor of the journey, another cancer metaphor that is almost as ubiquitous as the battle metaphor. However, the poem treats this metaphor to much more evocative imagery and ambivalence than linear, descriptive autobiographies often do. For the journey metaphor offers choice but no certainties except that the journey will take us from this world, when it becomes a "final journey."

World War II and the Holocaust have necessitated an exploration of the unspeakable (as the Maerz essay indicates). Adele Wiseman, like Blondal a graduate of United College, in *The Sacrifice* (1956) addresses issues often considered unspeakable. The most powerful scene has Abraham kill Laiah, and the language and sentence patterns show how the novelist filters horror through the screen language of sacred texts:

> Even as his arm leaped, as though expressing its own exasperation, its own ambition, its own despair, the Word leaped too, illuminating her living face, caressing the wonder of the pulse in her throat, flinging itself against the point of the knife. Life! cried Isaac as the blood gushed from her throat and her frantic fingers gripped first, then relaxed and loosened finally their hold on his beard. Life! pleaded Jacob as Abraham stared, horrified, into her death-glazed eyes. Life! chanted Moses as he smelled, sickened, the hot blood that had spurted onto his beard. Life! rose the chorus as the knife clattered to the ground, and the word rebounded from the walls and the floors and the ceilings, beating against the sudden unnatural stillness of the room, thundering in accusation against him. (304)

In these sentences, the experience is framed by the controlling devices of repetition, parallelism and anaphora, and the grammatically complete sentences themselves. In her poem, by contrast, Blondal breaks sentences, though the sentence of the life-journey is always inevitably present, like a dark undercurrent. As Blondal says in a letter to Lambert Wilson, "I have torn the prose apart" (June 17, 1957, quoted in Ricou).

These are just some elements from Blondal's poem that illustrate the use of poetic tools, particularly evocative in the tight space and imagery of a poem, as they convey the density of experience in living with cancer, its treatment and the knowledge of impending death—as well as the life to be lived until we leave.

WORKS CITED

Blondal, Patricia. *A Candle to Light the Sun*. Toronto: McClelland & Stewart, 1960.

Gardiner, Eric. *How I Conquered Cancer: A Naturopathic Alternative*. Houston: Emerald Ink, 1997.

Legris, Sylvia. *Circuity of Veins*. Winnipeg: Turnstone Press, 1996.

Lorde, Audre. *The Cancer Journals*. San Francisco: Spinster Ink, 1980.

_____. *The Collected Poems of Audre Lorde*. New York: W.W. Norton, 1997.

Maerz, Ursula. "Revolte und Requiem." *Die Zeit* 34 (August 16, 2001): 35.

Matthews, William. "Dire Cure." *Atlantic Monthly* (October 1997): 70-71.

Miseck, Lorie. "Self-examination." *Room of One's Own* 20.2 (1997): 76.

Price, Reynolds. *A Whole New Life: An Illness and a Healing*. New York: Plume–Penguin, 1995.

Sontag, Susan. *Illness as Metaphor*. 1977. New York: Vintage Books–Random House, 1979.

Stacey, Jackie. *Teratologies: A Cultural Study of Cancer*. London: Routledge, 1997.

Tefs, Wayne. *Rollercoaster: A Cancer Journey*. Winnipeg: Turnstone Press, 2002.

Tilberis, Liz. *No Time to Die*. Boston: Little, Brown and Company, 1998.

Wiseman, Adele. *The Sacrifice*. Toronto: Macmillan, 1956.

Underground in Winnipeg: Patricia Blondal's **A Candle to Light the Sun**

atricia Blondal's novel *A Candle to Light the Sun* contributes to literary history a fascinating, and unfortunately rather obscure, depiction of the city of Winnipeg as a universal site of modern, urban despair. The reader who looks for a recognizably "authentic" characterization of Winnipeg in this novel will be disappointed. Blondal is not interested, apparently, in putting the "real" Winnipeg on the so-called literary map, in celebrating its idiosyncrasies, in confirming or creating a sense of its individual identity. Instead, Winnipeg functions mainly as a source of symbolic images that reflect the hero's inner turmoil and map the landscape of his psychic journey.

In her study of Prairie literature, *Making It Home: Place in Canadian Prairie Literature*, Deborah Keahey argues that the literary concept of "place" in Canadian literature has relied heavily, and for too long, on aspects of the physical landscape. Canadian, especially Prairie, criticism, has long insisted that physical geography shapes character and theme and has sought by this method to identify definitive characteristics of Prairie literature. Perhaps this attitude partly accounts for the obscurity of Blondal's novel, especially the lack of attention to her depiction of Winnipeg, for few of her physical details are peculiar to Winnipeg, and therefore the novel provides the traditional critic of "place" with little to say. But there is more to the concept of "place" than physical detail. As Keahey states, "'place' can be a geographical location, but it can also be a symbolic, social, cultural, or psychic one." In Blondal's novel, Winnipeg is indeed a symbolic, rather than an actual, city. It is a city of the subconscious.

A Candle to Light the Sun tells the story of David Newman and his struggle toward self-awareness as he grows from a boy into a man. The novel is packed full of characters and storylines, not all of them fully developed, perhaps because Patricia Blondal died of cancer before the novel was published. It is therefore impossible to summarize the novel briefly. However, the most dramatic plot, and the one most relevant to Blondal's treatment of Winnipeg, involves David's intense and mysterious relationship with Darcy Rushforth. Darcy is David's childhood "summer friend" from Winnipeg who visits David's small hometown. At first, Darcy's hardened city attitude merely causes minor disruption in David's community. But as the novel progresses, Darcy is revealed as an evil influence who threatens to destroy David's life. In the first major crisis of the novel, Darcy persuades David to join him in an act of arson that results in the death of a baby. The boys' crime goes undetected and unpunished, but it forges a perverse bond between them. David, tormented by guilt, seems unable to separate himself from his partner in crime, even though Darcy is an obvious sociopath. At the novel's climax, Darcy kills again, but this time David abandons him to his inevitable fate: the gallows.

In *A Candle to Light the Sun*, the most vivid evocation of geographical place appears in the first half of the novel, when the characters are still living in the small town of Mouse Bluffs, Manitoba (most likely based on Blondal's home town of Souris). Blondal's vision of Mouse Bluffs is so powerful in its intensity that W.J. Keith once described the novel as "a hauntingly memorable, darkly effective *story of a small town*" (emphasis mine), even though almost half the novel, including its melodramatic climax, takes place in Winnipeg. The town's streets and businesses, its river and broken-down suspension bridge, its mansions, cottages, and hovels are all clearly described. More importantly, Blondal's depiction of the town's social codes and collective social consciousness is Faulkneresque in its authenticity.

But when the characters move to Winnipeg, Blondal seems to lose interest in the recreation of place, and the main action of the story becomes interior; the story seems to go "underground," in a sense, and proceeds to take place deep within the main character's psyche. As Laurence Ricou observes, Blondal's style undergoes a distinct shift: "the prose often seems less dense and more evasive in the later part of the novel. . . . In Mouse Bluffs the world . . . is primarily sensuous and portrayed in precise, yet suggestive images"; but in Book II, adds Ricou, when David moves to Winnipeg, he simultaneously moves "into the intellectual world of abstraction and concept."

Despite some modernist ironies, *A Candle to Light the Sun* is structured as a traditional quest myth. In the abstract realm of his own psychology, David fights his Goliath (Darcy, who represents the "dark side" of himself), and emerges as King. As a symbol, Winnipeg functions mainly as a kind of underworld—an immoral, dangerous and diseased space through which the hero must pass before his quest ends in (qualified) victory. (Ultimately, the novel's ending suggests, David will escape to begin his *real* life elsewhere—probably in England!)

The relationship between Mouse Bluffs and Winnipeg is, in many ways, highly conventional. Like all stories that follow a young character's move from a small-town childhood to maturity in the city, this novel presents the small town as a place of innocence and the city as a place of corruption. As a boy, David frequently hears the cautionary tale of Sholto Todd, a Mouse Bluffs boy whose unnamed "excesses" in the city led to his "ruin." Winnipeg, the place that spawned Darcy, is distant and vaguely menacing. The townsfolk's unsophisticated warnings about the city are ironically mocked: "Learning and the city; the one rotted religion; the other destroyed character." But in a double irony, this novel ultimately proves the townsfolk right.

David's move to Winnipeg coincides with his fall from grace, and Blondal is not subtle about it. The novel's narrative structure divides David's childhood from his manhood, and Mouse Bluffs from Winnipeg, in one clean and decisive stroke. Book I ends on the night of the fatal fire and the symbolically coincidental death of David's mother in Mouse Bluffs in 1939. At the beginning of Book II, David is already installed in his college dormitory in Winnipeg, and the year is 1942. The shift is abrupt; a gap of three years passes unnarrated, as if to emphasize the absolute nature of David's break from childhood. He has moved from town to city, and the country is now at war. In fact, the war follows the arson by one short week, suggesting that David's fall from grace, like Adam's in Genesis, symbolizes and precipitates the whole fallen world: "another week brought war and beside the enormity of war, death and burning dwindled to nothing; there was to be such a glut of death and burning." This close and clearly marked association between the city and these hellish images is further emphasized in a later scene in which David returns to his childhood home to find the doors locked, the windows boarded up, and "the apple tree beside the henhouse looked dead." In case the fire, the death of his mother, and the outbreak of World War II were not enough, the dead apple tree clinches it: David is forever exiled from Eden.

In contrast to her treatment of Mouse Bluffs, Blondal rarely provides detailed settings in the book's Winnipeg scenes. When she does use Winnipeg detail—the Assiniboine River, Winnipeg's elm trees, or specific street names—she tinges them with a sickly hue. At one of David's deepest moments of despair, he notes "the ragged top of a distant elm, limp and motionless, as if the intensity of the heat had glued its leaves." The inert tree, in the "blister" of the August heat, seems to represent the stagnancy of the whole city. The city is sluggish and greedy, feeding off the wholesome and natural production of the prairies:

> . . . this city was particularly dependent upon the crops, sweated and mopped and beefed
> and took in each other's laundry on a million-bushel scale; guilty because they did not

harvest or help with the harvest, they allowed weather reports to grow like parasites in their brains.

Winnipeg is an unhealthy place, as emphasized by a café scene in which even the juke-box has an air of dissipation:

> The food tasted of old tired grease; the two waitresses called one another and the tall soiled man "hon"; the recruiting poster on the wall, *Be a World Traveler at Twenty-one,* was covered with a yellow film of grease.
>
> No one glanced at David as he ordered, ate, smoked. It was what he wanted. No one came in and said, "Fine day." "Baby's over the colic." "Cookie Miles was bumped." The Wurlitzer thumped wearily over an old waxing of "My Devotion" and two airmen sneered at him as he paid his bill and went out.
>
> He strolled along Portage Avenue. He had never seen so many people in his life and under the neon and street lamps, they all looked as if they suffered cramps.

Despite its streets full of people, Winnipeg is a city of strangers, devoid of any sense of community. David remains an outsider. He develops no new friendships in any depth, but clings to his Mouse Bluffs companions: his childhood sweetheart Lilja, who has moved to the city, and the dangerously charming Darcy.

Darcy is David's guide to the city, and from Darcy's point of view, the city's major attractions consist of a generic house of prostitution and a series of superficial parties with "actors who can't act" and "writers who don't write." Although Darcy seems possessed of unlimited wealth, the bordello where he takes David is "a seedy middle-class clapboard house in a declining district," and it is even "crummier inside," with its "sad stuffy air," its "garish" decor and "vulgar" music. At the parties with these uncreative artists, the young men show "no trace of life's workings on them"; they are "shallow, no touch with anything but the moment's appetites." Like Eliot's hollow men, the young people of Winnipeg seem to exist in a "dry cellar." Winnipeg is a paralyzed city, where "overhead a network of wires clutched arthritically at the city, holding off the sky."

The rare scenes that mark Winnipeg as a distinct and original place occur mainly at the university, a location Blondal knew well. The book jacket states that Patricia Blondal graduated from the University of Manitoba in 1947, omitting the relevant fact that she actually graduated from United College. This is the downtown campus depicted in the novel, known to Winnipeggers today as The University of Winnipeg. Like David, Blondal (then Patricia Jenkins) published in the student paper, and like Lilja, she was elected Freshie Queen in 1943. The small campus and closely knit community of United College take on a claustrophobic atmosphere as Blondal transmutes them into the fictional Knox College. For example, the crowded, underground cafeteria contributes much to creating the dark, cramped atmosphere of David's college days:

> Alfredo's canteen was in the basement of Knox Hall. Against all the high dingy windows shrubs grew; even on bright days depressingly little light seeped through to war unpleasantly with the wire-covered drop lights. Students pressed against the hot-table, bickering genially, jostled past with books and coffee held high, wriggled noisily through the jam of chairs to join friends. The radio behind the counter blatted weather reports.

In this scene, Blondal draws on the physical details of the place to mirror David's depressed and confused state of mind. In reality, this cafeteria was "Tony's," in the basement of Wesley Hall. ("Tony's" exists to this day, though it has long since moved upstairs to a happier location.)

The university is a highly important place in David's development. It is a place he could never have entered without the financial support of Darcy's uncle Gavin, with whom David has a complex, ambivalent relationship. Gavin makes it possible for David to begin the studies necessary to fulfill his destiny as a writer, and then takes it all away again when he decides the Arts are impractical and refuses to continue David's tuition. Therefore the university, appropriately, symbolizes the life of David's mind, and the philosophical and intellectual realm he should be entering. But the campus, like the rest of the city, is corrupt.

Blondal reveals the general ambience on campus through the eyes of English Professor Paul Phillips, who tries, and fails, to reach out a helping hand to David. Phillips is concerned about the growing cynicism among the students as the war drags on, and thinks at one point: "It was as if they'd taken their youth underground." The students, like the other Winnipeggers, are superficial. Even when they manifest a form of rebellion, they are ineffectual and purposeless. Phillips observes that they "appeared to be against a great deal in a contemptuous way; for nothing."

Blondal provides brief glimpses into the actual city—Tony's cafeteria, Portage Avenue, the Winnipeg heat, the agricultural economy. On the whole, however, Blondal's Winnipeg is an enigma; its identity exists mainly as it is defined against David's home town. It is an empty space in the second half of the novel, a vacuum into which the hero plummets after he is cast out of Paradise. Perhaps it is even a form of hell. But it's a symbolic hell, with few specific details to distinguish it from the hell of any other modern, urban centre.

In one of his letters home, David admits to his own "lack of identity" and to "a larger concept that I began to develop soon after I left Mouse Bluffs. Lack of identity seems to be endemic to this country." Once out of Mouse Bluffs, David loses his bearings, and it is possible that his confusion about his own identity is the partial cause of the novel's failure to characterize the city of Winnipeg in any substantially identifiable way. After all, the story is told mainly (though not entirely) through his eyes.

But one suspects that the nebulous character of Winnipeg also reflects, at least in part, the author's mythological intentions. Blondal's lovingly detailed descriptions of Mouse Bluffs suggest that, to her, it was a real place; and Book I seems to promise the reader a truly "regional" novel. But in Book II, the novel turns away from geography to concentrate on its "universal" themes: the loss of innocence, the search for father and identity, the desire for redemption. Winnipeg, despite the occasional authentic detail, is mainly a place name; its details are made to serve as symbols of David's inner landscape. Thus, the novel ultimately resists the traditional Canadian reading that seeks to subsume all themes under the physical specifications of "place." It moves us from the regional to the subconscious realm, taking the concept of "place" under-ground. Winnipeg becomes a mythological site, freed from geographical reality, and Blondal, intentionally or not, moves her novel beyond the grasp of most studies of Prairie literature.

WORKS CITED

Blondal, Patricia. *A Candle to Light the Sun*. Toronto: McClelland & Stewart, 1960.

Bedford, A.G. *The University of Winnipeg: A History of the Founding Colleges*. Toronto: University of Toronto Press, 1976.

Keahey, Deborah. *Making It Home: Place in Canadian Prairie Literature*. Winnipeg: University of Manitoba Press, 1998.

Keith, W.J. "Novels in English 1940 to 1960." *The Oxford Companion to Canadian Literature*. Ed. William Toye. Toronto: Oxford University Press, 1983.

Ricou, Laurence. "Twin Misunderstandings: The Structure of Patricia Blondal's *A Candle to Light the Sun*." *Canadian Literature* 84 (1980): 58-71.

Exploring a Voice:
Patricia Blondal (1926–1959)

I n a letter to Pierre Berton, publisher Jack McClelland recalls his first meeting with Patricia Jenkins Blondal in early autumn of 1959. They had arranged to meet over lunch in Toronto's Royal York Hotel to discuss her writing. He says he was expecting what at the time was his mental picture of the typical woman Canadian novelist—middle-aged and dumpy—when a striking blonde woman in a powder-blue dress stepped off the elevator and introduced herself. By the end of the meeting, McClelland had accepted her manuscript for publication. Although he remembers sensing a desperate urgency on her part, he had no idea that she was terminally ill. Later, during what would be their final conversation, she told him that she wouldn't live to the end of the year, which he found difficult to believe. One month later, Patricia Blondal was dead.

Learning about this final exchange between publisher and writer was the beginning of a writing project I have been working on for the past few years. I often found myself reflecting on Patricia facing a young and certain death from breast cancer. Her knowledge of her impending death, and that she would never live to see her books, haunts me.

For several years, Patricia's life and writing occupied much of my spare time after they first engaged me professionally through my work at the Manitoba Writers' Guild. I remember taking the call from retired Rabbi Benjamin Herson. He was offering the Guild free access to his home in Arnes, just north of Gimli in Manitoba's Interlake: a little country house, isolated but close to a quiet highway, other farmhouses and Lake Winnipeg. Benjamin believed that this home was special. He had purchased it unexpectedly on a trip to Manitoba and felt that it should be designated a place where local writers could enjoy the serenity and have space for writing.

His only request was that the project be named after Patricia Jenkins Blondal, a young woman he had known briefly in 1944.

Many young Canadians were making their way through post-secondary studies. Benjamin's and Patricia's paths crossed at United College (now The University of Winnipeg). According to Benjamin, a wordless connection was made and though there wouldn't be enough time for that relationship to strengthen and develop, he believed that he and the other students were in the presence of a talented and intelligent young woman. One who, as he would learn decades later, was determined to develop her voice, write stories and publish books.

Not long after their first meeting, Benjamin abruptly left school due to a diagnosis of tuberculosis, which at the time was the leading cause of death for Canadians. Over his family's objections, he committed himself to a sanatorium in Ninette, Manitoba, but eventually returned to school after Patricia had already graduated. Once Benjamin graduated, he moved to the United States, where he married, had children and began work as a rabbi and educator. He explained to me that, while he had had a full life of love, children and work, every once in a while he wondered what had happened to that unique and spirited young woman who had engaged him in a way he couldn't understand.

The answer to that question came several decades later when a congregant came to him with an old novel that contained a character with the surname Herson. He realized that the book was written by his Patricia, and it was only then that Benjamin learned that she had died at the age of thirty-two. He decided he would try to learn everything that had happened to her from the time she graduated to the time of her death. He read as much of her work as he could and pored through her literary archives, which are housed at the University of British Columbia.

Benjamin had several conversations with Dr. Laurie Ricou, an English professor at UBC and longtime advocate of Patricia Blondal. Benjamin learned that Patricia had married Dr. Harold Blondal, had two children, Stephanie and John, and had begun a career as a writer and reporter for CBC. The family eventually relocated to Montreal and it was there that she and Harold (a cancer specialist) learned of her diagnosis. Patricia had a radical mastectomy and her ovaries removed as she underwent cancer treatment, such as it was in the fifties.

Once she realized she was dying, she left her husband and sent her children away to live with extended family so that they wouldn't see her deteriorate. I believe she also needed this time to do the writing that was so important to her. She completed her novel, *A Candle to Light the Sun*, in three months. In her final year, as she was driven to write as much as she could, she became romantically involved with another man who stayed with her until her death.

In an effort to track down anyone related to Patricia, I offered to play literary investigator, finding Patricia's sister-in-law, Joann Blondal, in Montreal, who led us to Patricia's daughter, Stephanie Blondal, in Toronto. After a year of exchanging phone calls and e-mails, a get-together of sorts was organized and Benjamin, Stephanie, Joann and Laurie had an opportunity to spend a morning at the Arnes home dedicated to the memory of Patricia. In November, 2002, *Globe and Mail* reporter Krista Foss wrote a lengthy feature article chronicling Benjamin's mission as well as the resurgence of interest in Blondal, which includes the possibility of Blondal's work being re-released, the creation of a biographical documentary and even feature film interest in her novels.

Benjamin's only desire was to pay tribute to a talented but forgotten Canadian writer whose work was out of print and no longer available to new readers. He believed *A Candle to Light the Sun*, a provocative story set in rural Manitoba and urban Winnipeg during the forties and fifties, deserved the designation of Canadian classic. My own interest, at first motivated by the establishment of the writers' retreat and spurred by Benjamin's determination to stake out what he believed to be Patricia's rightful place in literary history, eventually led to my writing poems about Patricia and fictional diary entries from her perspective during the final year of her life.

I remember reading *A Candle to Light the Sun* as a teenager and enjoying it partly because it was set in my home province of Manitoba and therefore seemed more real. Rereading it as an adult, I began to appreciate more fully Patricia's prose style and her ease and ability with language.

As a woman, I felt my connection to Patricia develop as I framed old photocopied photos of her and read the letters and notes she saved until the day she died. Somewhat obvious were the connections between us through our work as writers in Manitoba; less so were the shared interests in true and fictional mysteries, poetry, journalism, letter writing and travel, which I learned about through conversations with her family and by reading through her archives.

When I read Patricia's work, I imagine her as a young, highly sensitive girl quietly observing her community and the people around her. Her first novel caused a stir for many of the people of Souris, Manitoba, who were convinced that she had based her fictional town, Mouse Bluffs, and its inhabitants on them. Many people from her hometown felt that the book reflected negatively on them and one can assume that the sexual content (tame by today's standards but certainly provocative for the late fifties) was deemed too racy. I applaud her courage and her commitment to exploring those themes by making the main character male but at the same time giving her main female character a full range of emotion and desire at a time well before the sexual revolution.

As I approached my thirty-second birthday, I began to struggle with thanatophobia, an abnormal fear of dying or death, triggered by the 2001 terrorist attacks in New York, Washington and Pennsylvania. This anxiety manifested itself in a paralyzing fear of flying. Although I did seek treatment, this fear of death caused me to feel as Patricia may have felt more than forty years ago. I chose several paragraphs from her book and wrote poems around them, further strengthening my connection with Patricia's writing and her creative and emotional state during her final year.

Long after the Patricia Blondal Manitoba Summer Retreat for Writers was up and running, Benjamin and I developed a friendship. I shared his curiosity as to whether or not there was any meaning behind Patricia's choice of the name Herson for a character in her novel, particularly after I learned that until the late nineties, the alumni association at The University of Winnipeg had Benjamin Herson listed as deceased. Although he had returned to his studies after his convalescence and had graduated, he believes that in some circles of students, he may have been presumed dead.

Over time, I took the position that Patricia could have knowingly named a character in her book after him because she wanted to pay tribute in her own way to a young man she had barely known, but may have heard had suddenly died young. I believe it is beyond a coincidence that one her character Jacob has the same surname as Benjamin, because she seems to me to be the kind of writer who would have had the interest and taken the time to research the meaning of the names of the characters she created. She would have discovered that the Hebrew meaning of the name Jacob is the "supplanter, the man who replaced another" and that Benjamin means "son of the right hand." The biblical Benjamin was "Jacob's youngest son who carried out his father's wishes."

Because so much of what inspired me to write these poems came from conversations with Benjamin, it was easy for the writer in me to create a story based on his obvious love for Patricia. I wanted to embellish the scant memory of a bond that had transcended many decades and to suggest that she knew of his attraction and reciprocated it through her writing. I imagined Patricia spending time thinking about young death as she faced her own mortality, so I gave her a voice that contemplated longing and loss. Memories and how they shape our history or a story have become my main preoccupation as I complete my manuscript.

I am grateful to Benjamin for his gift of a space for Manitoba writers and his dedication to keeping the memory of Patricia Blondal alive. He believes that she possessed the talent and the potential to become one of Canada's most well-regarded authors, taking her place alongside many other writers of that time, including Hugh

MacLennan, Margaret Laurence, Gabrielle Roy and Irving Layton, whose praise for her writing can be found on the dust jacket of her novel.

While we will never know how many novels Patricia would have published or how bright her literary star would have shone had she survived, her work impressed Jack McClelland, who her read her entire manuscript in one evening and later told Pierre Berton, "This writer is interested in the raw meat of people and what makes them tick." Although their initial meeting may have been brief, he was not the only one who recognized her as a writer who would be read and remembered for years to come.

Note: The Manitoba Writers' Guild is a charitable, literary arts organization that provides programs and services for Manitoban writers of all genres and at all stages of their writing careers.

WORKS CITED

Foss, Krista. "Ghost Story." *The Globe and Mail*, November 28, 2002.

MacsKimming, Roy. *The Perilous Trade: Publishing Canada's Writers*. Toronto: McClelland & Stewart, 2003.

Royce Publications. *4004 Baby Names*. Toronto: Royce Publishing Company, 1983.

Henry Avenue! Where Are You Now That We Need You?: John Marlyn's *Under the Ribs of Death*

W hen John Marlyn's classic novel of ethnic Winnipeg was published in 1957, Henry Avenue in the city's North End, where the story is set, was alive with the energy of a dozen European nationalities, hating, loving and competing with each other. This is no longer the case, as the struggling world of the melting pot/mosaic that gave this part of Winnipeg its mythic character has evaporated into history, or at least, moved to suburbia. Reading *Under the Ribs of Death* today is an exercise in nostalgia, but more than that, it is an exercise in cultural anthropology because the past it describes is long gone and buried. Why is Henry Avenue no longer what it once was?

John Marlyn answers the question in a way when he describes the progress of the novel's protagonist, Sandor Hunyadi, from youth gang member to a respectable businessman a.k.a. Alex Hunter. Getting away from Henry Avenue and its ethnic working-class ghetto filled with "foreign names" was a desire instilled in every immigrant kid by parents, community and school. The flight from Henry Avenue toward the better reaches of Winnipeg society was the basic trajectory that education, white collar employment and intermarriage allowed. No more Henry Avenues; Academy Road, please.

Winnipeg also had a pre-immigrant history, a pre-railroad history as Fort Garry. The solemn gravesite of Louis Riel in front of the St. Boniface Cathedral testifies to that older past. But when Ottawa offered the West to homesteading, Winnipeg boomed and recreated itself in a multicultural mode. It was that mode that captured the creative imagination of the first half of the twentieth century and gave Winnipeg a mystique that it continues to draw on as a defining moment. Winnipeg and multiculturalism were synonymous until Toronto and Vancouver took over.

I came to Winnipeg as a child of three, the son of immigrant refugees who found their first home in the ethnic area just south of the greatest railway yards in the British

Commonwealth. In the fifties, when Marlyn was writing his novel, the Logan Street area west of Salter was a place of three- and four-storey brick factories, a steel fabricating plant, innumerable warehouses and easy access to Main Street with its ethnic businesses and its bazaar atmosphere. Without knowing it I grew up in Marlyn's novel, even though it was set in an earlier period.

Entering that novel now brings back the aromas, languages, streetcar noises, heavy winter clothing, and porch-sitting neighbours of my childhood. Back in the sixties, the venerable Prairie poet, Eli Mandel, described *Under the Ribs of Death* as an authentic depiction of Winnipeg's North End. Authentic then, but no more.

The past that Marlyn described so vividly is now bathed for us in the reflected glow of the sheaf-hugging Golden Boy atop the Legislature. It is a golden era of our imagination. In reality the sun has set on Marlyn's Chinese café at Logan and Main (for a short time my uncle owned just such a café in the same location); on the public steam baths where the protagonist's father works under the threats and heavy-handed orders of the owner, where friend and foe together rid their skin of its daily working-class sweat, grease and soot; on the old Salter Street steel bridge that trammed exhausted workers home; on Higgins Avenue and Jarvis and so on. The sun has set on all this and now only the moonlight of memory remains.

The streets in the novel describe a map of social geography, place names that jangled with ethnic energy and the attitudes of the old European world that its inhabitants remembered so well, a world where once they had status and prestige. Having lost it in the New World they dreamed of success for their Canadian-educated children. The price of that success, which came for so many, was the loss of the Old World. In the last lines of the novel, the self-created Alex Hunter, holding his son on his lap, has tears well up in his eyes. "He wiped them away," the author tells us, "and looked at his son and smiled and wept." Tears and laughter commingle as symbols of the immigrant experience—the tears of struggle and the heavy price paid for survival and the laughter of ethnic languages free from the daily grind of making headway in a foreign culture.

The terrain that Henry Avenue represents is one of simple joys and many heartaches. It is a social geography of poverty and seemingly endless economic struggle. But when Sandor takes the streetcar to River Heights to do some yardwork he enters a new landscape. "The boulevards ran wide and spacious to the very doors of the houses. And these houses were like palaces, great and stately, surrounded by their own private parks and gardens." He has arrived in paradise, the Garden of Eden that he aspires to inhabit. When he is asked what his name is, he stops being Sandor Hunyadi. He puts on an Anglo name, Alex Hunter, as the first step in assimilation.

In contrast to the lawns and flowers of River Heights there is a paucity of vegetation on Henry Avenue. The only flowers that Marlyn offers the readers are potted geraniums: "In window after window on Henry Avenue they stood, earthy and sturdy, throwing up leaves so that they might blossom and give their colour in lonely splendour. . . ." These geraniums grew out of pots on window sills in kitchens as signs of what could be afforded by working-class men crammed in rooming houses and families sharing dilapidated residences. The vegetable garden of the North End was a necessity, while the flower garden of River Heights was a luxury. Both the geranium in a small pot and the flowers bordering an expanse of lawn offered aesthetic values, but with different economic connotations.

At one point in the social geography of the novel, Sandor stands at the corner of Portage and Main, the crossroads of identity, which today is humanless because of its underground malled passageway, and he makes a decision about where he is going. He turns back down Main Street and heads for the North End, where he eventually creates a career for himself in insurance and uses his commissions to invest in real estate. That kind of scene is no longer possible for today's novelist of Winnipeg. The symbols have migrated with the city's transformation.

Main Street itself is pretty well denuded between City Hall and Logan. Even Selkirk Avenue, at the head of which stands the old Ukrainian hall where I used to go with my parents for cultural events and political gatherings, now lives a depleted existence. When I was a boy, my parents took me to old Dr. Reznowski, the Ukrainian-speaking physician who looked after us. His office on Selkirk Avenue was the epitome of ethnic success.

Of course, a city's social geography changes. New ethnic groups come into an area while the older ethnic groups leave. One wave follows another and often there is little time in between. On Pacific Avenue near Pinkham School, where I lived in the early fifties, there was an ethnic mix of English, Japanese, Ukrainian and Jewish people, and probably nationalities I didn't know. A long time after my family left for greener pastures in East Kildonan, the street became a bit of a slum, but then a decade later it was revived by working-class Portuguese immigrants who repainted and repaired the houses and made the whole street look honest again.

What hasn't happened in Winnipeg to these older inner-city neighbourhoods is gentrification. There hasn't been enough pressure on real estate or the kind of economic booms that make it feasible for rundown neighbourhoods to be reborn the way they have in cities like Toronto or Vancouver. So there is more downside than upside. The Third World immigration that has come to Winnipeg since the 1970s has been very poor and the increasing Aboriginal population, a Third World of its own, has only added to the expanding culture of the working poor. These migrations still await their John Marlyn.

So what's the point of reading *Under the Ribs of Death* forty years after its publication? Yes, it is well written; the characterization is strong; the plot has plausibility and the cultural flavour of European immigrant Winnipeg comes through on every page. *Under the Ribs of Death* is for Winnipeg what Mordecai Richler's *The Apprenticeship of Duddy Kravitz* and *St. Urbain's Horseman* are for Montreal—novels of place, of class, of white ethnicity. But this is not enough. In an interview (published in *NeWest Review*) with Walter Hildebrandt, poet, historian and former resident of Winnipeg, I described the meaning of the great divide between North and South in Winnipeg:

> South Winnipeg and the North End represent symbolically to me right-wing and left-wing thought. The very origins of my social, political and cultural thinking come from that dichotomy and the dialectic between one and the other. What I have been searching for since then is some way to synthesize those two worlds, to create a new element.

That I should spend my life writing a bridge between two distinct worlds, creating my own intellectual Arlington and Salter bridges, is an indicator of how powerful and disturbing the great gulf was. In the end I had to draw on the figure from St. Boniface, the French fact of Louis Riel, to symbolize a unifying idea or identity based on the concept of a new nation that could absorb the disparate elements into a unity. I called it the Métis Metaphor.

The relevance of such a concept depends on the continuing existence of ethnic and class struggle, of deep social divisions, of issues of race that seek resolution. Winnipeg continues to have such divisions, though the place names that point to them are different and the generations who stopped being Sandor Hunyadi and became Alex Hunter now live in what were once exclusive enclaves. When a writer reflects on who he is he reflects on how his childhood, family and urban universe moulded him. Each immigrant kid who grows up in Winnipeg is in his own way a Sandor Hunyadi, no matter what his race or nationality. The desire to belong, to be equal, to be recognised, not to be stereotyped, etc., are all motivations that drive the immigrant experience. It is a story of overcoming barriers, not once, but many times.

Whenever I visit Winnipeg I return to the old terrain like a droopy-eared bloodhound sniffing out a cache of bones. I drive over to Neptune's for smoked tulibee and to the nearby City Bakery for Winnipeg rye and delicious cinnamon buns. Between the two is a Native-owned co-op that sells freshly baked bannock, inexpensive pickerel and wild blueberries in season. In connecting with them I connect with my past and the deepest recesses of my personality.

Now that Winnipeg is an economic backwater, a self-sustaining ghost of its former rail-power self, it nurtures mythology. The myth of Winnipeg is contained, in part, in Marlyn's novel, and every time we enter it we keep that myth alive. It was a great defining moment in the city's history, one which it has yet to surpass. But as I drive the streets of my childhood today I realize that there are great new stories here awaiting their storyteller and that makes me happy. Winnipeg's divisions still have power to arouse the imagination.

In the period between the great flood of 1950 and the even greater one of 1997, Winnipeg changed its ethnic colours and yet stayed the same—fighting bitterly cold blizzards in winter, clouds of mosquitoes in summer and, of course, spring flooding. The human spirit that is galvanized by such a tough environment is one that offers a special gift to Canadian consciousness, just as John Marlyn's *Under the Ribs of Death* remains a special gift to Winnipeggers, wherever they live. As long as I live, its past will always be a present for me, living in memories and words. As for Henry Avenue, it is now a marker in my literary imagination. Whenever I need to remember who I am, I turn to Marlyn's Henry Avenue. No matter how far the immigrant journeys from Henry, no matter how deep he goes into his Alex Hunter persona, he will always carry around its tears and its laughter.

2006 Postscript: The ethnic reality of the North End persists, even for me. In the spring of 2006 the memorial for my mother's grave was purchased from a firm located at Selkirk and Main. My mother had spent her final months in a nursing home on Main Street, which is also the street where the funeral was held. When my father and I return from visiting her grave, we often stop at the Kalyna store on Main Street to buy a Ukrainian newspaper.

CHRISTIAN RIEGEL

Looking Home: Location and Dislocation in Margaret Laurence's **This Side Jordan**

This essay was born in the bright light of a microfilm reader in the Manitoba Legislative Library, where I had gone to seek signs of Margaret Laurence's ascendance as a writer from Neepawa into the wide world via Winnipeg. I was interested in the period that predated her renown, for soon after *The Stone Angel* was published in 1964 she was hailed as a singular creative force and was quickly acknowledged as a Manitoba great. But how was she seen in 1960, I wondered, when her first novel, *This Side Jordan*, was published? Amongst the many stories about the goings-on about town in the *Neepawa Press*—the high school theatre productions, the death of former residents long gone elsewhere, and local politics—I found a trace, but nothing more, of the writer who was to become the most important writer of her generation. I was looking for a sign that Laurence had perhaps been recognized as someone to look out for, and someone to be proud of, and that the locals were able to latch onto a good thing before the rest of the country took notice—I figured that the *Neepawa Press* might have an inside track on things.

Given that Laurence spent a number of years in Winnipeg, and that she was active as a journalist after her university days, I guessed that the Winnipeg papers at least would have paid some attention to the work of a new writer with a Manitoba heritage. Laurence was, after all, published by prominent publishers in Canada and England. But this was not the case at all. It is interesting to note, by contrast, that when Adele Wiseman's first novel appeared it was to great acclaim in her hometown of Winnipeg in addition to elsewhere in the world.

I emerged from the dark room with the microfilm readers and the bright light with a searing headache and one article from the *Neepawa Press* that recognizes her new novel, *This Side Jordan*. I also emerged with the sense that if I were to look to *This Side Jordan* I might recognize some of the ambivalent and contradictory signs of place and home that I saw in the mere traces of her existence that I found in the newspapers. If the home place constructed a writer in a fleeting way, was there perhaps some correlation with how the writer conceived of this idea of home? This, of course, before the novels that focused so definitely on her hometown and before she claimed Manitoba as the locus of her creative energy.

In his essay "Imaginary Homelands," Salman Rushdie writes about the idea of a home place in his imaginary and creative life. He begins the piece by discussing a photograph of his father's house in Bombay, a city that he has spent the larger part of his life away from: "It reminds me that it's my present that is foreign, and that the past is home, albeit a lost home in a lost city in the mists of lost time" (9). In the next paragraph, Rushdie considers the home place to be "reality" and his expatriate life to be "illusion." As he develops the idea of the home place, he reflects on how he feels in a position of loss in relation to the past and home and that writing is partially a reclamation of that home: "It may be that writers in my position, exiles or emigrants or expatriates, are haunted by some sense of loss, some urge to reclaim, to look back, even at the risk of being mutated into pillars of salt" (10).

We do not often think of Laurence as an exile or expatriate because we so solidly associate her with the growing awareness of Canada, within and without, in the 1960s, and we like to call her the mother of Canadian literature, and so on. But in so many ways, she was an *expatriate writer*, writing mostly while away from Canada, looking back to her home rather than out from it, and only reclaiming her place in this country after her greatest successes. To be sure, she returned to Canada periodically and wrote here (a draft of *The Stone Angel* was written in Vancouver in the early 1960s, for example), but we need to imagine a Laurence in her Hampstead apartment toiling to establish an income as a professional writer. A Margaret Laurence, indeed, who wandered the Heath, shopped on Oxford Street and later lived anonymously in an English country village. Or we need to imagine her, as she did herself in her African travel memoir *The Prophet's Camel Bell*, travelling and living in Africa: "There you go, rejoicing, as so you should, for anything might happen and you are carrying with you your notebook and camera so you may catch vast and elusive life in a word and a snapshot" (1). The figure that emerges cannot be further removed from many of the protagonists of her fiction (imagine Hagar marching around the Heath, perhaps swimming in the lady's pond). And of course, Laurence, like Morag, never returned to live in her Manitoba hometown. Later, Morag of course follows Laurence's trajectory, but she too looks to home and stays away. But Laurence fits Rushdie's profile of the writer who lives away and looks to home, to that "reality" that makes the fiction. The writing becomes, as Rushdie argues, a job of reclamation, an engagement of loss. This engagement, as becomes clear from her African and Canadian writing, is fraught with tension, for Laurence felt a dual tug to the homeplace;

she is emotionally compelled—and indeed burdened[1] —by the weight of her family losses which force a return to the territory of her past, but she also feels a need to reclaim the past in a more positive sense—there is a desire to look to the past as well.

Laurence herself comments on this form of gaining insight into home in *The Prophet's Camel Bell*, which appeared in 1963, when she notes that by going away, by travelling into the unknown and the alien, she was able to see herself more clearly; that is, the self that grew up and was formed by the small Manitoba town of Neepawa and then later shaped by Winnipeg. As she notes, "And in your excitement at the trip, the last thing in the world that would occur to you is that the strangest glimpses you may have of any creature in the distant lands will be those you catch of yourself" (1). The "vast and elusive life" she refers to earlier on the page, then, is one that ultimately reflects back to herself and by extension the place she came from.

In her essay "A Place to Stand On," published in 1970 in *Mosaic* and later reprinted in her book *Heart of a Stranger* (1976), Laurence explores the idea that her understanding of herself is deeply implicated in her writing about her past and her ancestry; that, indeed, "one way of discovering oneself . . . is through the explorations inherent in the writing itself" and that this discovery "involves an attempt to understand one's background and one's past" (1). She makes this same point in a *Maclean's* piece published in 1972 that also appears in *Heart of a Stranger*, "Where the World Began," when she asserts that her years growing up in Neepawa were elemental in shaping her perspective on the world. "Because that settlement and that land were my first and for many years my only real knowledge of this planet, in some profound way they remain my world, my way of viewing. My eyes were formed there" (237). But it is the going away, the writing as an expatriate, that allows her to recognize this vision. Her remarks about African writers are a clear sign that she has learned perspective—figured out what to write in the notebook she refers to in the opening passages of *The Prophet's Camel Bell*—by being away and by reading things that are quite alien to her childhood social context: "They have found it necessary . . . to come to terms with their ancestors and their gods in order to be able to accept the past and be at peace with the dead, without being stifled or threatened by their past" ("A Place" 2).

The expatriate writer is looking homeward with a longing that was perhaps not present when she lived there; an expatriate reclaiming a lost past through her writing and, most importantly, articulating a desire to remain attached to her home. But the first books the writer creates are not about the home place; are, in fact, about places alien to a small Manitoba town. How different from a prairie town can one get than, say, the "Weekend in Wyoming" nightclub in Accra, scene of the opening passages of *This Side Jordan*? The highlife band sings,

Fiyah, fiyah, fiyah, fiyah-ma,

Fiyah deah come—baby!

Fiyah, fiyah, fiyah, fiyah-ma,

Fiyah deah come—ah ah!

I went to see my lovely boy,

Lovely boy I love so well— (1)

And so, perhaps, the subject matter in fact contributes to the lack of recognition. The alien characters and cultures portrayed in the novel would have found little affinity with local readers and serve primarily to reinforce a sense of disconnection with the local place. The ambivalence locals felt at the portraits of Neepawa Laurence was later to provide in her Canadian novels was of another sort altogether and, of course, they paid attention to what she had accomplished—whether they liked it or not.

This Side Jordan is quite interesting, for a conflicted sense of home and away emerges. The only mention of the publication of *This Side Jordan* I could find in the Winnipeg papers or the *Neepawa Press* appears in the latter on January 27, 1961. The headline reads: "Vancouver Authoress Came From Neepawa: Has Novel on Africa Published." While origins are signaled, it is clear by the reference to Vancouver that the *Neepawa Press* felt no compunction to claim Laurence as a local other than by birth. A short article that delineates Laurence's connection to Neepawa appears under the headline along with a reprint of a review of the novel by Donald Stainsby in the *Vancouver Sun*. Why Laurence is not overtly claimed as a local is unclear, as the newspaper is rife with the minutiae of the town's residents—current and former. In the issues surrounding this one, one can find examples of obituaries on the front page of former residents (now residing in Phoenix, for example) and there is no doubt they are claimed for the homeplace.

What is curious about this short piece is that Laurence is identified as an outsider and simultaneously as originating as a local. Out of this arises a tension in the idea of a home place: if one is a Vancouver authoress one is not a Neepawa writer, and yet the tale of origins that is told beneath the headline asserts Laurence's claims to local status:

Born in Neepawa in 1926, she is the daughter of the late Mr. and Mrs. Robert H. Wemyss. Her grandparents, the late Mr. and Mrs. John Simpson, and the late Mr. and Mrs. John Wemyss, were prominent in the business and social life of the town during their many years of residence here.

Mrs. Laurence attended both Neepawa public school and high school. She edited the high school paper for two years.

Graduating in 1947 with a B.A. degree from United College, Winnipeg, she married Jack Laurence, a civil engineer, that same year. His work subsequently took them to England, British Somaliland and Ghana. They have two children, Jocelyn, eight, born in England, and David, five, born in Africa. They now live at 3556 West 21st Avenue, Vancouver, BC. (8)

The accretion of details emphasizes the duality of the headline, for Laurence is seen to be rooted in Neepawa, but she is fixed outside, with her various countries of residence, by her marriage, and by the birth of her children in foreign locations. The opening lines of the story point to this same duality, for one might come from "here" but one becomes an "authoress" elsewhere. The author is identified by two names that she did not carry when she lived in Neepawa: "Margaret Laurence, author of This Side Jordan, will be well remembered here as the former Peggy Wemyss." Wemyss is established as a "prominent" local name, through the place of her parents and grandparents in the community, but the new name is a sort of shedding of place, reinforced by her wide movements in the larger world outside Neepawa and by the fact that neither of her children is born in the place of her ancestry. In this consideration of Laurence as author, the article reinforces the sense of author-making as an activity that happens elsewhere, for Laurence becomes an "authoress" only by virtue of being a Vancouverite and not one of "us." When Laurence deliberately chose the formal "Margaret" over "Peggy,"[2] she unwittingly reinforced the impressions of the article that she had undergone a significant transformation from small-town "gal" to big-city "authoress."

When Adele Wiseman published The Sacrifice to great international and national acclaim a few years earlier, by contrast, she was heralded in a whole array of Winnipeg publications, from small weeklies to the largest newspapers. Even though the Vancouver Sun review of Laurence's first book was positive—Donald Stainsby writes, "You get the impression reading This Side Jordan, Vancouver writer Margaret Laurence's excellent first novel, that it all really matters, very much indeed, to the author. This is a rare thing, this controlled passion which is so happily evident in This Side Jordan"—Laurence's reception in general (and especially internationally) was significantly different from Wiseman's, however, and there would have been little reason for the Neepawa Press to lay claim to Laurence or to present her as anything other than a Neepawan by birth who went elsewhere to make good. It is noteworthy that none of the Winnipeg papers paid any notice to This Side Jordan, despite Laurence's earlier work as a journalist in that city.[3] As Lyall Powers points out in his biography, Alien Heart: The Life and Work of Margaret Laurence (Michigan State University Press, 2004), Laurence worked for the Westerner and the Winnipeg Citizen.[4]

We know from *The Prophet's Camel Bell* that Laurence realized that to travel, to be in a sort of exile—or at least to write as an expatriate—provided insight into the home place, and we know from her essays on the subject ("Where the World Began" and "A Place to Stand On") that Laurence recognized the home place as the primary originator of her imaginative vision. With hindsight it is possible to recognize that *This Side Jordan*, in its themes of origins, ancestry and identity, is an entry point for Laurence into the overt exploration of the home space that she undertook with her Manawaka fiction. The novel is rife with tensions of the old and the new, and with the effects of time and change on conceptions of the self in personal and other histories. I do not mean to suggest that *This Side Jordan* should be read as an analogue to the later work, or that the novel should be taken as a precursor to more *serious* later work, for I think the novel holds up well as an important insight into the shifting colonial world that Laurence encountered. However, *This Side Jordan* does signal Laurence's later figuring of the home place and space in her Manawaka work, even though in the novel she is not writing about her own home place.

This Side Jordan begins with contradiction. In the first line the reader encounters Johnnie Kestoe, white British example of colonialism, engaged in a contradictory act: "Johnnie Kestoe, who didn't like Africans, was dancing the highlife with an African girl" (1). Further, the music, the "Fire Highlife," signifies a dramatic shift from the old to the new, a rejection of tradition and the world and culture. This shift further defines the social changes that are present in the 1950s Ghana that Laurence fictionalizes in this novel. The "music was sophisticated. It was modern. It was new. To hell with rit-ual tribal dance, the drums with voices as ancient as forest" (1-2). This new music, fit-tingly, is played in a club with the name "Weekend in Wyoming," a place where the Europeans and the Africans come together to dance the highlife wholly unconscious of the colonial forces that have brought them together: "The dancers themselves did not analyse the highlife any more than they analysed the force that had brought them all together here" (2). Ultimately, the inherent contradictions of Ghanaian society as it encounters colonial pressures are exemplified by the dancers in the club. The old is inseparable from the new, Laurence's narrator tells us; its impulse is felt in the actions of the present even when the new attempts to reject the old.

And so it is in the description of Ghanaian society in the opening section of *This Side Jordan*. On the one hand, the old is rejected: "[T]he ancient drums could no longer summon the people who danced here. The highlife was their music. For they, too, were modern. They, too, were new" (2). On the other, the old is ever-present and insuperable:

> And yet the rhythms still beat strongly in this highlife in the centre of Accra, amid the
> taxi horns, just a few miles away, in Jamestown or Labadi, they pulsed through the drums

while the fetish priestess with ash-smeared cheeks whirled to express the unutterable, and the drummer's eyes grew glassy and still, his soul drugged more powerfully than the body could be. (2)

Clearly, the new culture encompasses the old, and as the society moves forward the new remains enmeshed with the old: "Into the brash contemporary patterns of this Africa's fabric were woven the symbols old as the sun-king, old as the oldest continent" (2).

This idea of the old and new intertwined in a paradox of presence and absence reminds us of Laurence's consideration of old and new in *The Diviners*, published in 1974. The famous opening line to the first section, "The River of Now and Then," is paradoxical and indicates metaphorically the co-presence of the old and the new: "The river flowed both ways" (11). For Morag Gunn, the protagonist, the contemplation of the river—what she terms "river-watching" (11)—is precursor to her imaginative and creative exploration of origins and identity. In some ways, *The Diviners* is centrally about the tensions inherent in the desire and need to look to the past, to live with the past in the present and somehow to find a way to cope with the weight of it.

There is one more element in the opening of *This Side Jordan* that prefigures Laurence's later exploration of her own home. The novel opens with an assertion of desire in the music being played: "The six boys were playing the Fire Highlife, playing it with a beat as urgent as love" (1). Underlying the move forward and back is desire, a desire for place, for location and rootedness, just as the musicians are moved by emotion to play. Desire is signaled in other ways too, for Johnnie Kestoe's dance is erotically charged: "Her . . . fleshy hips and buttocks swayed easily, and her big young breasts, unspoiled by children and only lightly held by her pink blouse, rose and fell as though the music were her breath" (1). This desire can be read as a trope for the desire for place, and that the creative expression of place must be rooted in deep desire, whether it is the sordidness of Johnnie's situation or the better understood desire for place and ancestry Laurence explores in the Manawaka fiction.

In reading through *This Side Jordan*, I want to move to a slightly different understanding of the African writing that situates the work in relation to the creative drive—a sort of compulsion indeed—that brought Laurence repeatedly back to her childhood and to her home place. We have predominantly read the thematic differences in the African and Canadian work, while sometimes noting some similarities, but it is important too to chart her work as an ongoing project of loss-reclamation, to echo Rushdie's assertions about his own expatriate writing. At the end of *This Side Jordan*, Nathaniel, the major African character in the novel, speaks to his newborn son and wishes that he will look to the future by figuratively crossing the river Jordan. "Joshua, Joshua, Joshua. I beg you. Cross Jordan, Joshua" (282). The future represented by crossing the river will be one free of the tensions of old and new announced at the beginning of the novel. For Laurence, the river can be read as another (earlier) version of the river of now and then, that paradoxical backward-and-forward-moving body of water that must be crossed in order for the future to become possible. To cross is a trope for active engagement of that paradox and, indeed, the beginning of that crossing is what Laurence undertook with the writing of her first Canadian novel, *The Stone Angel.*

The paradox of moving back to move forward is evident in the framing section of her short story cycle *A Bird in the House*, published in 1970, where the narrator Vanessa MacLeod describes her fraught connection to her grandfather's house in Manawaka. The house is both ancestral home and a place she occupied in her youth after the death of her father. Vanessa notes the importance of the Brick House in the opening story, "The Sound of the Singing": "That house in Manawaka is the one which, more than any other, I carry with me." For Vanessa, much like Rushdie in his assertion that the structures of the past are more easily reclaimed from afar, the house is a place to look back to and an object of memory: she sees the house as "part dwelling place and part massive monument" (11). With these thoughts, she sets in motion a series of stories that tell the major experiences of her childhood and the importance of the house and its people in her development. She also notes, at the very end of *A Bird in the House*, that it is not the physical house that catalyzes memory and story-telling. Rather its memory resides within her, as does her grandfather: "I had feared and fought the old man, yet he proclaimed himself in my veins" (191). Vanessa returns to Manawaka after a twenty-year absence to discover that the house is with her always even though it belongs to strangers now: "It was their house now, whoever they were, not ours, not mine. I looked at it only for a moment, and then I drove away" (191).

The stories she has just completed telling have become the structures for memory and for working over the past. But these stories, compelled as she is to tell them, contain a strong element of the desire to return to the home place. They are also testament to the necessity of returning there and even the impossibility of keeping away from the territory of home. As Birk Sproxton points out, the title of the story cycle suggests the weight of the past and home for Vanessa, for the title can be punned to read "a burden in the house."[5] The burden is the house itself and all the memories it "contains," and the burden is the inescapable memory-freight that Vanessa carries around with her for a lifetime. And so, there is paradox here too, for where there is the desire to return home—even if only through writing it—there is also loss that drives that revisiting.

Though Margaret Laurence appears only briefly in the consciousness of Neepawa with the publication of her first novel *This Side Jordan*, and not at all in Winnipeg publications, that lack of recognition is no sign of the book's importance. It is worth remembering that she was published in three countries simultaneously and by major publishers (Knopf in New York, Macmillan in London, and McClelland & Stewart in Toronto). One should not underemphasize the significance of a new writer being published in this major way, and one should not be swayed by the overwhelming response generated by her next five books, all set in Canada, to discount Laurence's achievement in getting her novel published as it was. There is no doubt she was considered a major talent by the three publishing houses and, while they expected her to carry on to a great career, there was no expectation, I am sure, that the next books would be set in a small and obscure fictional Manitoba town. One can surmise that, from the perspective of her London and New York publishers, the subject matter of *This Side Jordan* was an easier marketing project—with its links to world affairs—than her later work was to be. It is only, as the contemporary paucity of response to her work about anything outside of Canada and the strong response to her later Canadian work attest, when she writes of home that she is given legitimacy as a major writing figure in this country. Indeed, the tensions of home evident in *This Side Jordan* are ultimately reciprocated by the community of her birth and youth. To look home, as she did throughout her writing career, was to engage with a dual sense of location and dislocation, to feel desire and compulsion, and to know that the past needed to be examined in all its pain and joy. As she says in "Where the World Began," Neepawa was to her "A place of jubilation and of mourning, horrible and beautiful" (237).

NOTES:

1. See my discussion of *A Bird in the House* below as well as note 3.
2. Lyall Powers points out that the change to Margaret occurs with the publication of *This Side Jordan*. He quotes Laurence in a letter to Adele Wiseman (January 22, 1961): "Peggy I hated, so I have killed her off" (163).
3. Though *This Side Jordan* is not reviewed in Winnipeg, in the July 1, 1961 edition of the *Winnipeg Tribune*, Colin Godbold writes of Laurence's (spelled "Lawrence" in the article) winning two awards from the Canadian Authors Association, and notes that she is in Winnipeg to visit old friends at United College and that she is a graduate. He interviews her about her novel as well as one she is currently working on (*The Stone Angel*). Laurence is identified as being born in Neepawa and that she is now writing about Canada. And so, with external acclaim, Laurence begins to rise to prominence in the province of her birth.
4. See especially Powers's discussion in chapter 4, "Citizen Peg." See also Donez Xiques's discussion of Laurence's newspaper career in "Early Influences: Laurence's Newspaper Career," which appears in *Challenging Territory: The Writing of Margaret Laurence*. [See also Noelle Boughton's essay in this present volume. Ed.]
5. Birk pointed out this pun and its potential to me in his editing of this paper. My discussion of *A Bird in the House*, in *Writing Grief: Margaret Laurence and the Work of Mourning*, looks at how Vanessa labours through her grief in the writing of her stories—another form of burden.

WORKS CITED

Dempsey, Elsie. "Vancouver Authoress Came From Neepawa: Has Novel on Africa Published." *The Neepawa Press* (January 27, 1961): 8.

Laurence, Margaret. *A Bird in the House*. 1970. New Canadian Library. Toronto: McClelland & Stewart, 1990.

———. "A Place to Stand On." In *Heart of a Stranger*. 1-7.

———. *The Diviners*. 1974. New Canadian Library. Toronto: McClelland & Stewart, 1988.

———. *Heart of a Stranger*. 1976. Seal Books. Toronto: McClelland & Stewart, 1988.

———. *The Prophet's Camel Bell*. Toronto: McClelland & Stewart, 1963.

———. *This Side Jordan*. 1960. New Canadian Library. Toronto: McClelland & Stewart, 1989.

———. "Where the World Began." In *Heart of a Stranger*. 237-44.

Powers, Lyall. *Alien Heart: The Life and Work of Margaret Laurence*. Winnipeg: University of Manitoba Press, 2003.

Riegel, Christian, ed. *Challenging Territory: The Writing of Margaret Laurence*. Edmonton: University of Alberta Press, 1997.

Riegel, Christian. *Writing Grief: Margaret Laurence and the Work of Mourning*. Winnipeg: University of Manitoba Press, 2003.

Rushdie, Salman. "Imaginary Homelands." In *Imaginary Homelands: Essays and Criticism 1981-1991*. London: Granta Books, 1992.

Stainsby, Donald. "This Side Jordan." *The Neepawa Press*. Rpt. of *The Vancouver Sun*. (January 27, 1961): 8.

Time, the Paper Fan and the Villanelle: Form and Forcefulness in **The Stone Angel**

A poem should not mean
But be.
— Archibald MacLeish, "Ars Poetica" (1926)

In the ordinary or popular sense of the term, poetry is language in which expression of the qualities of experience is felt to predominate greatly over statement concerning its uses.
— Frederick A. Pottle, "What Is Poetry?" (1941)

The *Stone Angel*, Margaret Laurence's first Canadian novel, was not published or even written before 1960, the closing year of the period with which the essays of this collection are concerned. More than any of her African writings, however, it is permeated with imaginative responses to some of that period's most influential writers, and it embodies some of its most vital critical concerns and insights.

When the second edition of George Sampson's *Concise Cambridge History of English Literature* appeared in 1961, the most heavily promoted and seriously discussed feature of it was the updating of the 1941 edition with a new chapter entitled "The Age of T.S. Eliot" by R.C. Churchill. When Eliot gave some readings at Yale in 1946, people who had lined up long before the doors of the huge auditorium were opened had to be turned away, and the atmosphere inside could be characterized only as worship in the cathedral. (And Eliot's worshippers were not all devout Anglo-Catholics. I remember vividly a fellow honours English undergraduate at the University of Toronto, who shall remain nameless because he went on to become a distinguished academic, lined up beside me in a Canadian Officers Training Corps platoon in 1941 while we stood silently at attention, awaiting inspection by a senior Canadian general. He kept trying to sneak peeks at his newly arrived copy of the latest of Eliot's *Four Quartets* in his greatcoat pocket while muttering *St. James Infirmary*

Blues under his breath. When the general was within two or three paces, my friend whispered hoarsely, "Say, Walt, what's all this jazz about the Incarnation?")

Especially for a decade or so after 1946, Dylan Thomas was the most popular poet writing in English. Probably no other poet has read his own poetry more excitingly, and through his broadcasts and recordings Thomas thrilled hundreds of thousands who had never thought that there was anything in poetry beyond Edgar A. Guest. Even today the thirst for *A Child's Christmas in Wales* and *Under Milk Wood* has not been slaked for multitudes who had equated poetry with rhyming verse.

The reputation and the influence of prominent writers have changed in the past forty years, but so has the prevailing concept of what literature is. As my favourite graffito says, "All generalizations are false," but it is true that most of my teachers and professors, brilliant and sensitive as most of them were, tended to approach literature through history, biography, ideas, themes, influences, sources and analogues, versification and so on. (I have encountered more than one less profitable approach in recent years.) But throughout the 1940s and for a few years beyond, Archibald MacLeish's closing lines of "Ars Poetica," "A poem should not mean / But be," became the triumphant war cry of teachers, critics and writers who insisted that while a work of literature rises out of personal and social experience and a sense of tradition, and embodies themes, overt or concealed, and while it is expressed through plot, characterization, imagery, metrical patterns, irony, paradox and so on, it achieves its significance only in a successful amalgam of these and countless other, often indefinable, but real, elements.

In 1938 Cleanth Brooks and Robert Penn Warren published their first edition of *Understanding Poetry*, which went on through many revisions, spawned *Understanding Fiction* and *Understanding Drama* and inspired almost every other "introduction to literature" text for decades. While Brooks was also a superb biographical and historical scholar and Warren was a prize-winning novelist, they focused on the way language reconciles the ironical, paradoxical, often antithetical, meanings embodied and expressed in forceful writing and on the creative dynamics in the multiple effects of imagery and versification. Brooks, in the final chapter of *The Well Wrought Urn* (1947), argued that reducing any poem (or other work of creative writing) to a paraphrase betrays the poem as poem, and is an act of heresy. About the same time, W.K. Wimsatt, Jr. and Monroe Beardsley's essays "The Intentional Fallacy" (1946) and "The Affective Fallacy" (1949) argued convincingly that the essence of a work of art or literature cannot be judged by a documented knowledge of the author's intention, nor by any report of how the work affects an individual reader.

To today's reader, the New Critics may be passé, but they do provide the context in which *The Stone Angel* was written and in which it is profitably read.

The Stone Angel was Margaret Laurence's favourite among her novels (see, for example, *Dance* 165-66). Paradoxically, it was the novel that, over two decades, seemed to give her the most uneasiness, especially about the appropriateness and plausibility of a pervasive structural device that she characterized as "the coincidence of present happenings touching off—conveniently—memories in sequence . . . probably straining credulity" ("Gadgetry or Growing" 57).[1]

I find this concern surprising for two reasons. The first is that most readers of the novel and most audiences and reviewers of James W. Nichol's superbly faithful stage adaptation, which uses the same actor to portray Hagar from six to ninety without change of makeup or costume,[2] have not shared Laurence's uneasiness about strained credulity, but rather have responded to the convincing presentation of the reality of the past in the present, both as memory with which one can be rampant (*Stone Angel* 5), and as experience of the timeless unity of past and present. The second reason is that at least four years before Laurence's first public expression of this uneasiness, she had rejected any view of the novel on which such uneasiness seems to be based.

In a letter to her former teacher at United College, Professor Robert N. Hallstead, dated January 15, 1965, just weeks after the publication of *The Stone Angel*, Laurence says:

> It seems to me that the traditional novel, with its God's-eye view and its certainty of
> what reality is, is no longer possible. *The only alternatives at the moment seem to be: the*
> *"poetry" novel, by which I don't mean anything poetic in the conventional sense, but only a*
> *knowing use of symbolism, an absolutely concise use of language, and an ability to write on*
> *at least 2 levels simultaneously* [italics added],[3] or the "tragi-comic" novel—which is
> where I find myself at this point [writing *A Jest of God*]. I think the first may be, in the
> end, the better form—but not one which anyone would voluntarily dare; either it comes
> compulsively or it does not. . . .

Many times Laurence repeated the story of how Hagar came into her mind, uninvited, and became "insistent" (see, for example, *Dance* 155), and how the form of the novel came with her: "I decided I couldn't help it. That was the way the story was coming out" (156). It came out using a chronological flashback device that, in one form or another, is at least as old as the *Odyssey*.[4] With each subsequent novel Laurence experimented with different modifications and refinements of the device and constantly tried to assess their appropriateness and effectiveness. But she could not do anything else with *The Stone Angel*, and its lasting success proves the appropriateness of the form. What she repeatedly considered the improbability of an apparently mechanical device is convincingly appropriate to the experience of the teller. It is also one of the vital sources of the power of the novel and one of the major means of developing Laurence's central themes about time.

Hagar's words "when time has folded in like a paper fan" (90, but first mentioned on 31) present an explicit image of the splintering of linear experience or narrative into shrinking, alternating sectors, with the fragmentation of the conventionally coherent picture in the creation of new and surprising and converging near-parallels, the elimination of expected distances between past and present, beginning and end, birth and death, and with extremes and differences being brought together until they are melded. Yet the opened fan with its continuity of linear form and the closing fan with its fragmentations, juxtapositions and compressions are the same artifact. "Like a paper fan" is a simile that would spring naturally to the mind of someone who had been sent, full of resentment, to a finishing school for young ladies in Toronto (42). The paper fan is also an effective image of the structure of a novel that begins in a cemetery with an old woman's memory of a child speculating about a memorial to her dead mother and ends with a nonagenarian remembering her baby's first breath just before she draws her own last.

The epigraph to *The Stone Angel* consists of the final two lines of Dylan Thomas's villanelle: "Do not go gentle into that good night. / Rage, rage against the dying of the light." Since the 1890s, poetry editors have not been overwhelmed by the submission of villanelles, although theatre audiences are still delighted when Cyrano de Bergerac can compose and recite one while finishing off his opponent in a duel, with versification as sophisticated as his swordplay and footwork. (I can think of only one other attempt by Thomas to use the form—"Request to Leda,"[5] which the poet omitted from his *Collected Poems*.) But "Do not go gentle" reverberates throughout *The Stone Angel*. Right up to and including her very last gesture, Hagar will not go gentle into that good night. Protesting violently on page after page against the indignities she suffers from the erosion of her mental, physical and emotional control and against the loss of her loved ones, and rudely impatient with everyone on whom she must depend increasingly and humiliatingly, she continues to rage against the dying of the light. Hagar complains about her brother Matt's dying so quietly: "I found this harder to bear than his death, even. Why hadn't he writhed, cursed, at least grappled with the thing?" (60).

Arbitrary form in "Do not go gentle" operates in the same way as does the fan structure in the novel. The five tercets and the quatrain, employing only two rhymes and a rigidly arbitrary sequence, with the repeated lines incrementally reinforcing the individual hammer blows, far from robbing Thomas's poem of emotion, instead discipline and intensify the emotion, creating a more painful impact than many simpler, apparently more "natural" expressions of grief might have done. Changing contexts give identical words and phrases different meanings, even different grammatical functions. (The first and third lines are repeated as the final two lines of the poem, and the imperative "Do not go gentle" of the first tercet and the concluding quatrain becomes a simple assertive in the second and fourth tercets.) The words "good night" mean something different in each of their four appearances. The splendidly vivid strobe flashes of whole life patterns of utterly dissimilar human beings are compressed with violent suddenness into the relationship of the speaker and his father in a climax that has been building since the opening line. The essence of the experience of both father and son is intensified in this concentration of human experience into inescapable awareness of life and mortality. Thousands who have wept openly when reading or hearing the poem have been unaware of any "artificiality" of form or any straining of credulity.

Similarly, the violent contrasts and the reinforcements of the shards of Hagar's experience that are driven into each other by the apparently mechanical juxtaposition of past and present, and the repetition of the same or similar words or images in new contexts, conveying new meanings and intensifying old ones, give the novel much of its force, without our being disturbed by the mechanics.

When the young nurse says to Hagar: " . . . you've had those years. Nothing can take them away" (284), and eight pages later Hagar says: "Oh, my two, my dead. Dead by your own hands or by mine? Nothing can take away those years" (292), no reader is likely to complain of coincidence or repetition. When Hagar watches the children playing on the beach at Shadow Point (187-89), she remembers John and Arlene playing house (203-09). When Hagar's discussion with Lottie (213) recalls the crushing of the baby chicks in the town dump (27-28), it does not strain our credulity for Murray F. Lees's story of Donnie's death (232-34) to trigger Hagar's suppressed memory of John and Arlene's deaths (238-42). On the contrary, the immediate reinforcement of shared bereavement and guilt adds poignancy to both stories and moves Hagar and us towards what Aristotle called *peripeteia*, the always unexpected and surprising reversal of just about everything.

This structure, moreover, illuminates the mystery of time embodied in Hagar's experience. I find it impossible to read *The Stone Angel* or even to think of it without feeling the shaping of Hagar's experience by the words and phrases of T.S. Eliot's *Four Quartets*. I find it equally impossible to read *Four Quartets* without feeling that a multitude of phrases, lines, even extended passages are inevitably relevant to Hagar's experience. I remember discussing *Four Quartets* with Laurence in the summer of 1946 not long after the complete volume was available and long before Hagar had begun to invade Laurence's consciousness, but I am implying nothing about sources, merely recognizing intertextuality. Perhaps the finest fruit of intertextuality is the enjoyment of an awareness that the echoes and reverberations one senses between two works have deepened and enriched one's understanding and appreciation of both works, an awareness that has extended the significance of both.

The opening scene of *The Stone Angel*, the cemetery (3-5), for example, intentionally or not, seems to parody the rose-garden of "Burnt Norton" (117-18), which clearly echoes much of Frances Hodgson Burnett's *The Secret Garden* (see Barton). Instead of the "leaves . . . full of children, / Hidden excitedly, containing laughter" (*BN* 118), the children in the Manawaka cemetery are openly laughing at the inscription for sad Regina Weese (*SA* 4). Eliot's stately presences, "dignified, invisible, / Moving without pressure, over the dead leaves" (118) could be echoed by Laurence's "prairie bluffs . . . walked through only by Cree with enigmatic faces and greasy hair" (5).

Reid MacCallum has argued that for each poem of *Four Quartets* to be a quartet, it must contain and respond to the voices of the other three poems, even though some of them were not written until years later. "Hazardous assertions, certainly . . . Yet the doctrine of time's redemption which the *Four Quartets* expound in incomparable poetry, may, for all that, be confirmed in the very tissue of its verses" (161). The unity of Laurence's Manawaka fiction needs no further demonstration, but there is no doubt that the impact and significance of this opening scene are enriched by the reverberation of these Cree with enigmatic faces throughout *The Fire-Dwellers*, "The Loons," several essays and especially *The Diviners*.

In words already quoted, Hagar wonders if the deaths of John and Arlene can be reversed. "Oh, my two, my dead. Dead by your own hands or by mine? Nothing can take away those years" (292). She wonders if the "Twenty-four years [with Bram] . . . scoured away like sandbanks under the spate of our wrangle and bicker" (116) can be taken away or changed. Can a stone angel grow a new wing? she speculates "snappishly" (280). She muses: " . . . I'd finally accept the necessity of the sedative to blot away the image of Bram's heavy manhood. . . . I'd waken, sometimes, out of a half sleep and turn to him and find he wasn't beside me, and then I'd be filled with such a bitter emptiness it seemed the whole of night must be within me and not around or outside at all. There were times when I'd have returned to him, just for that" (160). She concludes: "I can't change what's happened to me in my life, or make what's not occurred take place" (160).

Perhaps human beings have always wondered why time is the only dimension in which it seems impossible to change direction. In "Burnt Norton" Eliot says:

What might have been is an abstraction

Remaining a perpetual possibility

Only in a world of speculation.

What might have been and what has been

Point to one end, which is always present. (117)

In the preceding lines he has just said: "If all time is eternally present / All time is unredeemable."

But as William Blissett was one of the first to point out sensitively and perceptively in 1946 (115), and as Reid MacCallum developed the thesis so excitingly in 1949 (rept. 1953), the "text"—homiletically speaking—for *Four Quartets* is Paul's injunction to the Ephesians: "See then that ye walk circumspectly, not as fools, but as wise, redeeming the time, because the days are evil" (5:16-17), an injunction repeated in Colossians 4:5. Modern English versions have blunted the challenge of all earlier versions in Greek, Latin, French and English up to about 1900, by changing "redeeming the time" to "buying up the opportunity" (Ferrar Fenton), "making the most of the time" (RSV and NRSV), "Use the present opportunity to the full" (NEB), and so on, thus removing the apparent absurdity of the original Greek (that was maintained literally in versions up to the King James) of "buying back," "ransoming," "rescuing." The newer renderings abandon the mystical conviction that lies at the heart of *Four Quartets* and the concept that the past can be changed, that the future is not determined, that human beings have freedom and can take responsibility.

As not only Blissett and MacCallum, but many other commentators have taken pains to warn, and as Brooks insisted, extracting philosophical themes from poetry such as that of *Four Quartets*, poetry that is musical, not only in its texture but in its formal structure, may approach vandalism. Nevertheless, while listening to the music, with the constant echoing and picking up of the "voices" of all four quartets as one reads each of them in sequence, one cannot help recognizing, in the long grey sagas of despair, the moments of freedom, of exultation:

The release from action and suffering, release from the inner

And the outer compulsion, yet surrounded

By a grace of sense, a white light still and moving,

Erhebung without motion, concentration

Without elimination, both a new world

And the old made explicit, understood

In the completion of its partial ecstasy,

The resolution of its partial horror. ("Burnt Norton" 119)

> But to apprehend

The point of intersection of the timeless

With time, is an occupation for the saint—

. . . .

For most of us, there is only the unattended

Moment, the moment in and out of time . . . ("The Dry Salvages" 136)

But for all of us, the purpose and the destination are clear:

And the end of all our exploring

Will be to arrive where we started

And know the place for the first time. ("Little Gidding" 145)

The Stone Angel, with the constant juxtaposition of past and present, within seg-ments as well as between them, presents the inexorable consistency of human charac-ter, the irretrievability and unchangeability of the past, and the futility of trying to halt the erosion of time. Jason Currie's erection of the stone angel, "bought in pride to mark [his wife's] bones and proclaim his dynasty, as he fancied, forever and a day" (3) links him with the ancient Egyptian pharaohs and with the "fledgling pharaohs in an uncouth land" (3). But the proclaimed dynasty is no more permanent than that of the snow angels the children make (81). Within decades the "pouting marble mouth and the full cheeks" are desecrated with lipstick (179), and the statue is toppled over on her face among the hated peonies (178). When it is re-erected and cleaned, it is in constant danger of toppling over again, and it no longer serves Jason Currie's purpose. The stone now bears beside Currie the name of the man who was not good enough to touch his daughter. The young caretaker, "raised in South Wachakwa," cannot tell the difference between the two names (306).

In *A Bird in the House* Vanessa MacLeod eventually recognizes her human kinship with Grandfather Connor: "I had feared and fought the old man, yet he proclaimed himself in my veins" (*Bird* 207), but it is hard for Hagar to admit or retain a similar recognition. When Bram relieves "hisself . . . against the steps of Currie's Store," Hagar takes it as a desecration of her father's store and an attack on his pride, but does not accept it as a response to her own (115). The constant repetition of her father's pride and tyranny in Hagar's behaviour is a depressing motif, which seems predestined to continue.

In spite of the kindness and helpfulness of so many people, Hagar's view of human destiny is epitomized by the juxtaposition of cemetery and dump:

> Above Manawaka, and only a short way from the peonies drooping sullenly over the graves, was the town dump. Here were crates and cartons, tea chests with torn tin stripping, and the unrecognizable effluvia of our lives, burned and blackened by the fire that seasonally cauterized the festering place. Here were the wrecks of cutters and buggies . . . purchased in fine fettle by the town fathers and grown as wracked and ruined as the old gents, but not afforded a decent concealment in earth. (26)

One thinks of Eliot's words:

> Feet rising and falling.
> Eating and drinking. Dung and death. ("East Coker" 124)
> Ridiculous the waste sad time
> Stretching before and after. ("Burnt Norton" 122)

Eventually Hagar and we, in Eliot's words, "arrive where we started / And know the place for the first time" ("Little Gidding" 145). After cruelly bullying Mr. Troy into singing "Old Hundredth," Hagar realizes "so forcefully, so shatteringly," that she must always have wanted "simply to rejoice," but has been enslaved by her pride. This miraculous, "unattended" *anagnorisis*, as Aristotle would call it, or recognition scene, and the experiences that immediately precede it and follow it, constitute the most moving sequence in the novel (291-93).

In *A Jest of God* Rachel has a similar anagnorisis as, trying to recall the *Miserere*, "the penitential Psalm *par excellence*" (McNeile 358), she says, "I do not know how many bones need be broken before I can walk. And I do not know, either, how many need not have been broken at all." Struggling to remember the words she has known since childhood but that had never meant anything to her before, she goes on immediately to quote Psalm 51:8: "*Make me to hear joy and gladness, that the bones which Thou hast broken may rejoice*" (201). She now has buoyant confidence that she still has life ahead of her in which she will rejoice. Her running feuds with her mother, her colleagues, her community and with God, against whom her outbursts have been documented persistently throughout the novel, have been resolved in her new vision of herself and her heretofore imprisoning experience. Aware of the relentless ticking of her biological clock, she knows that one way or another she will have children, even if she could not have Nick's child.

Stacey MacAindra, Vanessa MacLeod and Morag Gunn have comparable experiences of grace. Their novels or stories are what Laurence meant by "tragi-comic novels." Hagar's is tragic.

Tragically, Hagar has her *anagnorisis* after fifty-five more years of breaking and being broken than Rachel had, and she has time for two victories only—the "joke" with the bedpan (298-301) and the "lie" to Marvin (304), which we know to be the truth, even if Hagar does not. Both are huge victories in contrast with such painfully recalled incidents as her refusal to "play mother" to her dying brother Dan (24-25), her casual ignoring of Bram's cut-glass decanter with the silver top (51) and her recognition of its Bacchic potential too late (62), but cruelly insignificant in contrast with her realization of the loss of "Every good joy I might have held, in my man or any child of mine or even the plain light of morning, of walking the earth, all . . . forced to a standstill . . . "(292).

Like Lear, like Macbeth, like Oedipus, Hagar has prided herself on seeing, but the reader has known from the opening paragraphs until almost the end that she has been doubly blind to herself and to the values most important in her universe. Time for Hagar and for all these tragic protagonists is redeemed in that they finally break through to a new perspective on their whole lives and their universe and see them afresh or for the first time, with the reassurance that they are in touch with reality at last. But time is tragically unredeemable in that while these heroes gain insight and freedom, and at least our forgiveness, kingdoms are still gored, wrongs to others are still undone, wounds are not healed. Nothing can bring back or take away those years.

As Hagar, wakened from her cocoon (306), wrests "the glass, full of water, to be had for the taking," and the novel ends with the words "And then—"(308), there is little point in debating whether this is the same wilful Hagar, still rudely, impatiently rebuffing those who are trying to help her, still refusing to go gentle into that good night, or the miraculously reborn Hagar at last seeing and reaching for what she really wants, the water of life.

She is both.

That is what is so reassuring and so devastating.

The form of the novel leaves us no alternative.

NOTES

A different version of this article was presented at the Margaret Laurence Symposium at the University of Ottawa, April 30, 1994. I thank Dr. Neil Besner and Dr. Birk Sproxton for suggesting that the ideas in that paper might be relevant to this collection.

1. See also, for example, Laurence, "Ten Years' Sentences," *Canadian Literature* 41 (1969), 14 (rept. New, 20-21); Michel Fabre, "From *The Stone Angel* to *The Diviners*: An Interview with Margaret Laurence" [1981], in Woodcock, 204. Also Laurence, *Dance on the Earth*, 156.
2. I have seen the Prairie Theatre Exchange production, starring Shirley Douglas as Hagar, directed by Michael Springate, in Winnipeg, on March 4, 1993, and October 27, 1994. Both Winnipeg runs were completely sold out, and the Ottawa run at the National Art Centre, November 22 to December 10, 1994, was extended a full week because of the demand.
3. See a paper I wrote years before seeing this letter, entitled "Margaret Laurence: Novelist-as-Poet" (Coger, 3-16), which I presented at the conference on "Margaret Laurence: Her Life and Work," at Brandon University on August 10, 1988. It concludes: "In terms of Frederick Pottle's definition, Margaret Laurence in her fiction has written little but poetry."
4. An example is Terry Waite's autobiography, *Taken on Trust*, in which the author interleaves memories of his life prior to being taken hostage in Beirut with experiences of his captivity, both series in chronological order, and brings them to the point at which "The outer and inner journeys have at last met . . ." (205).
5. "Request to Leda: Homage to William Empson," *Horizon* (July 1942): 6.

WORKS CITED

Barton, Ruth. "T.S. Eliot's Secret Garden." *Canadian Notes and Queries* 31 (229), no. 4 (1984): 512-14.

Bible. King James Version (1611), Ferrar Fenton (1903), Revised Standard Version (1953), New English Bible (1970), New Revised Standard Version (1989).

Blissett, William. "The Argument of T.S. Eliot's *Four Quartets*." *University of Toronto Quarterly* 15 (1946): 115-126.

Brooks, Cleanth. *The Well Wrought Urn*. New York: Harcourt, 1947.

Brooks, Cleanth, and Robert Penn Warren. *Understanding Poetry*. New York: Holt, 1938.

Burnett, Frances Hodgson. 1911. *The Secret Garden*. Illus. Michael Hague. New York: Holt, 1987.

Coger, Greta M.K. McCormick, ed. *New Perspectives on Margaret Laurence: Poetic Narrative, Multiculturalism, and Feminism*. Series: Contributions in Women's Studies, Number 154. Westport, CT: Greenwood, 1996.

Eliot, T.S. *The Complete Poems and Plays 1909-1950*. New York: Harcourt Brace, 1952.

Laurence, Margaret. *A Bird in the House*. Toronto: McClelland & Stewart, 1970.

———. *A Jest of God*. Toronto: McClelland & Stewart, 1966.

———. "Gadgetry or Growing: Form and Voice in the Novel." *The Work of Margaret Laurence*. Ed. John R. Sorfleet. *Journal of Canadian Fiction* 27 (1980): 54-62.

———. Letter to Robert N. Hallstead, January 15, 1965. Unpublished ts. University of Winnipeg Library, Winnipeg.

————. "Sources." New, *Margaret Laurence* 12-16.

————. *The Stone Angel*. Toronto: McClelland & Stewart, 1964.

MacCallum, Reid. *Imitation and Design and Other Essays*. Ed. William Blissett. Toronto: University of Toronto Press, 1953.

MacLeish, Archibald. *The Human Season: Selected Poems 1926-1972*. Boston: Houghton, 1972.

McNeile, A.H. "The Psalms." *A New Commentary on Holy Scripture Including the Apocrypha*. Ed. Charles Gore et al. London: SPCK, 1929.

New, William, ed. and intro. *Margaret Laurence*. Series: Critical Views on Canadian Writers. Toronto: McGraw-Hill Ryerson, 1977.

Pottle, Frederick A. *The Idiom of Poetry*. Rev. ed. Ithaca: Cornell University Press, 1946.

Sampson, George. *The Concise Cambridge History of English Literature*. 2nd ed. With a chapter on "The Age of T.S. Eliot" by R.C. Churchill. Cambridge: Cambridge University Press, 1961.

Thomas, Dylan. *Collected Poems 1934-1952*. London: Dent, 1952.

Waite, Terry. *Taken on Trust*. Toronto: Doubleday, 1993.

Wimsatt, W.K. Jr. *The Verbal Icon: Studies in the Meaning of Poetry*. New York: Noonday, 1954.

Woodcock, George, ed. *A Place to Stand On: Essays by and about Margaret Laurence*. Western Canadian Literary Documents Series 4. Edmonton: NeWest, 1983.

The Green Room

for Dave Robertson

I have an old paperback with my childhood signature (the circle over the i in Margie) and my childhood address on it. It has been chewed by one of our dogs back then, in the 1960s. It's *An Actor's Handbook*, by Konstantin Stanislavsky; an alphabetized series of statements on aspects of acting. Under **U**, we find the following:

UNBROKEN LINE

Our art . . . must have a whole, unbroken line . . . that flows from the past, through the present, into the future. . . . It is only when [an actor] comes to a deeper understanding of his part and a realization of its fundamental objective that a line gradually emerges as a continuous whole. Then we have the right to speak of the beginning of creative work.

On the stage, if the inner line is broken an actor no longer understands what is being said or done and he ceases to have any desires or emotions. The actor and the part, humanly speaking, live by these unbroken lines, that is what gives life and movement to what is being enacted. . . . A role must have continuous being and its unbroken line. (154)

Stanislavsky repeatedly points out that Art is not Life. But the passage quoted above lends itself to analogy. In a lifetime, there are periods of discontinuity when we experience a painful lack of rhythm and purpose, a depressing rupture of drive, desire, motivation, emotion. Working as a writer, it's easy to feel disempowered, colonized, without a role to play, partly because there's such a small audience. It can happen on a personal and on a larger cultural scale, one or both. Unbroken is a powerful word. So is its counterpart: broken.

But in Stanislavsky's offhand assumption, that we are speaking "humanly," we may find everything that sustains us through the quixotic desire to work in the arts.

Elsewhere, Stanislavsky speaks of "the life of a human spirit" which it is the actor's task to recreate and to affirm, however darkly; we do this, he points out, through simple repetition, through hard work. When I read this again, a paperback issued in 1963, I unearth the tremendous—in some ways almost grotesque—good fortune of growing up in Winnipeg in the 1960s. I'm fifty-two years old now, and have had time to experience "broken" times. Remembering the sixties, the Manitoba Theatre School, the good fortune of reading Stanislavsky, serves more than nostalgia; it offers a chance to focus on the unbroken lines.

The city I grew up in was itself dialectic. Anti-Semitism was a structural principle of many institutions, insidious and persistent (think of the Manitoba Club, the St. Charles Country Club and the Winter Club for just a few examples). The South and North Ends were split along ethnic and political lines, thesis and antithesis. One synthesis was the Manitoba Theatre School and the Manitoba Theatre Centre. Physically, at the centre: the Dominion Theatre was very near the corner of Portage and Main. ("Theatre 77" was seventy-seven steps from Portage and Main.) Physically, in the rather tormented body of John Hirsch, an immigrant, a survivor of the Holocaust, a brilliant and courageous man, from what I've learned, and the seminal figure in the creation of professional theatre in Winnipeg.

I was a ten-year-old geek in red stretch pants, hair painfully curled by my beautiful mother the night before and pinned with a barrette, a plastic fragment of the family escutcheon, and, with my little sister, shown how to ride northeast on the Academy Road bus on Saturday mornings, and later on Wednesday nights, and later still as I grew older, nearly every day of the week, down to Portage and Main to go to Theatre School. The school was in a wonderful, mouldy old building half a block up Portage East. It was enormously exciting. I met my first Communist there. He was twelve years old. He was from "the North End." Real, I thought, real. I was always timid and bewildered, but Theatre School was my hockey, my religion, my life.

The theatre teachers who seemed to have emerged from the Atlantic, from Europe, from England, from the War, filtered out through the 1950s into Winnipeg: three Brits—David Barnett, David Latham, Roberta Dolby—and later a Canadian, Colin Jackson. These were teachers of strange magnitude. They knew so many interlinked things, the difficulties of theatre more than matched by the difficulties of living, and they treated us with challenging, respectful diffidence. I don't think anyone ever told us our work was "good." Yet in such an environment, we could take outrageous risks in losing our precarious dignity. In my case, I felt all too serious about acting. (My little sister was funny and got all the paying gigs.) But I'm very grateful to these teachers for letting me be so, responding with a fairly straight face, with what I thought was a *gnomic smile*. In a life there are only a few major teachers, and David

Barnett in particular was certainly of great importance in mine—and in the lives of many other people who would go on to make a life in theatre.

Are there unbroken lines in a life? Only in theatre? Only in theatrical roles? Maybe, in some amoral, chance-driven way, not only in theatre, not only in roles. The extremity, the cruelty of the war moved into the sweater sets of intelligent women at home with babies in Winnipeg, their husbands perhaps rather mum on the subject of their recent past. "History"? What a bizarre concept. We have to make it up and sustain the invention, to save "the life of a human spirit."

Unbroken Line #1

I've been trying to write a play called "Thirst." In November 2003, Theatre Projects Manitoba with the Manitoba Association of Playwrights—marvellous, small organizations devoted to new play development—organized a five-day workshop so that I could hear an early draft of my play.

In these first drafts, I'd written a character with some of the verbal cadences of my father, who is now eighty-four. I've never written my dad into anything before, and it felt as invasive as I'd always thought it would. But I read it at a festival with my father present, and it was fine, and the portrait has stayed, altered over countless consecutive exponents or drafts. The character who was like my father has become a character in the play, a function of that play.

Arne MacPherson directed the workshop, and he hired Dave Robertson to play Art, the character initially inspired by my father. Dave Robertson had been working in theatre in Winnipeg since those first early days. When I was on the Academy bus, he was working in the first professional theatre Winnipeg would see. Here is some of what happened.

Dave was at home and got a call from John Hirsch. Hirsch was directing Arthur Miller's *Death of a Salesman*, which at that time, in 1958, was a fairly new piece, having premiered in New York in 1949. Hirsch had had "an altercation" with the actor playing Biff (brother of Happy—who was being played by Gordon Pinsent), and would Dave come down and read for the part. This was halfway through the rehearsal of a difficult, heartbreaking play. Dave had had no training in theatre, in movement or voice or stagecraft. He got the part.

> BIFF: Pop! I'm a dime a dozen, and so are you!
>
> WILLY, *turning on him now in an uncontrolled outburst*: I am not a dime a dozen! I am Willy Loman, and you are Biff Loman!

Biff starts for Willy, but is blocked by Happy. In his fury, Biff seems on the verge of attacking his father.

BIFF: I am not a leader of men, Willy, and neither are you. You were never anything but a hard-working drummer who landed in the ash can like all the rest of them! I'm one dollar an hour, Willy! I tried seven states and couldn't raise it. A buck an hour! Do you gather my meaning? I'm not bringing home any prizes any more, and you're going to stop waiting for me to bring them home!

WILLY, *directly to Biff*: You vengeful, spiteful mutt!

Biff breaks from Happy. Willy, in fright, starts up the stairs. Biff grabs him.

(Act II)

Imagine playing that role, your first on stage, directed by John Hirsch. How did he control his voice, how did he not hallucinate the thing, overact, strangle his lines along with Willy Loman?

John Hirsch had rented the Dominion Theatre for the run. The city had to recalibrate after that. This was high-stakes theatre, born on its feet. The Winnipeg Little Theatre joined with Hirsch and became the Manitoba Theatre Centre. Dave said it happened very quickly, "in a burst of energy, and then John was gone . . ." (to Toronto, to head CBC Drama there, and to many places—to Stratford, as artistic director).

Dave Robertson went on to do a number of shows with Hirsch, and he would eventually become "a general manager sort of guy" at Rainbow Stage and, for twenty years, would work in radio and television production at the CBC. He and his wife, Viola Busday (a dancer, and a teacher with the Royal Winnipeg Ballet, where she was known as Mrs. Robertson), directed musicals for the University of Manitoba Glee Club (*Guys and Dolls, Kiss Me Kate, Bye Bye Birdie, My Fair Lady*). "It was tough to make a go of it," Dave said. "You were always banging your head against the wall, very tough trying to get things done." Without working wages, actors had to hold a job and rehearse at night. Everything changes, everything stays the same: the people who work in theatre in Winnipeg today, who live here, raise a family, do without, subsidize our culture with their own bones and blood.

I never met Hirsch. I remember his shows though. I remember the posters at Theatre School, and the mysterious effect they had on us, a dawning awareness of something serious and purposeful in theatre. *Mother Courage, The Caucasian Chalk Circle, The Playboy of the Western World, Volpone* (Dave played Voltore, the vulture), mixed up with a bit of "commercial" stuff such as *A Streetcar Named Desire*. Hirsch programmed but could not bring himself to direct, *The Diary of Anne Frank* (he hired a director from New York). Dave describes Hirsch as a man "on the edge," shattered by his experiences in the war, "an emotional bundle." I know that Hirsch's drive to create powerful theatre, his compulsion to produce plays that challenge our complacency and intellect, filtered through to the dusty black-painted floors of Theatre School.

I: Inner Ardour

Anything you do on the stage with coldness inside you will destroy you because it will encourage in you the habit of automatic, mechanical action, without imagination.

What can be more effective, fan your ardour, excite you inwardly, than an imaginary fiction which has taken possession of you?

. . . One cannot be cold when working in art. . . . You have to possess a certain degree of inner warmth. (Stanislavsky 79)

Unbroken Line #2

For the workshop for "Thirst," Arne MacPherson hired John Bluethner to play the role of Art's weak-willed son, Jeremy. John and I were at Theatre School together long ago. I remember his voice and his wildly energetic mind. As a teenager he directed *Macbeth*, sometime around 1969, when the school had moved out of Portage Avenue East and into the Warehouse Theatre. I played an old woman in that production. I was about seventeen years old. I'm sure I was riveting. I had a tendency to hallucinate my roles, stumble around and drip characterization.

Bluethner is one of many talented people who "stayed in theatre." (When he was about fourteen years old he played one of those standard Boys in John Hirsch's production of Max Frisch's *Andorra*, wide-eyed over all "the f#'s in rehearsal.") After *Macbeth*, and with David Barnett, he did the music of Brecht's *Caucasian Chalk Circle*. Later, he did a MFA at York. (Now he teaches at Collège universitaire de Saint-Boniface, and directs and acts too.)

We went for lunch, Bluethner and I, and listed some of the people who started out as kids at the Manitoba Theatre School: Tom Diamond (theatre and opera director), Sam Malkin (professional actor), Leslee Silverman (artistic director of Manitoba Theatre for Young People). Elizabeth, Liz, my funny and better-looking sister, who got all the gigs, took the Academy bus with Nancy Palk (actor, and director of the highly successful Soulpepper Theatre Company, in Toronto). In the summer of 1967, Liz and Tom Diamond, at eleven years of age, were hired to play eight-year-old kids in some well-intentioned "educational" drama. (Lizzy, the little con, made $457, an ungodly sum; says it was the best pay she's ever had, all things considered; came with lunch.)

Bluethner and I also talked about the strange hazards of acting. At York, he learned to survive improv. It's true that coldness will destroy you, but so will heat. Sometimes improvisations and "warm-ups" spring you into actions without consequence, smack you into the wall like chewed gum. Learning to improvise requires the follow-through, developing the instincts for the "unbroken line" without a second thought, and without self-consciousness. It's a paradox of the actor that he needs something like a super-ego, a carapace that he doesn't own, that lets him perform in all transparency. Sometimes—and I found this very frightening—you have to go away and be there at exactly the same time.

We did a lot of improv, Bluethner and the others. Dave Robertson and the adults, they did a lot of improv too. It was the dawning of the age of improv; dawn till dusk; from when I was in elementary school through to first-year university when I went to study acting at the University of Alberta, lived with draft "dodgers," smoked hash early one morning before a voice class for which I'd forgotten to prepare a monologue, improvised Lady Macbeth's speech, which as I recall begins with "I have given suck . . .," got a scathing review from my fellow classmates (philistines, education students taking theatre as a "subject") and grew so abruptly and permanently afraid of acting that I became a writer.

But as a kid, under the challenging pedagogy of David Barnett, we investigated Restoration theatre—leading me to a lifelong fascination with those punkish plays. Colin Jackson tried to introduce us to *Antigone*. I hadn't a clue what any of this was all about, but it was big, infinitely resonant if not completely in tune. We did a Brian Friel play called *Lovers and Losers*, directed by a teenaged Susan Ferley, who went on to become artistic director of the Globe Theatre in Regina. My partner (it was a two-hander) was Jim Sutherland, with whom I've since lost touch. Jim was a handsome, very nice guy, serious. Friel is a great writer, and the play would swell up and overwhelm us. Jim left these performances by the back door out to the lane, weeping. I wept in the green room.

We spent a great deal of time lying on that dusty black floor, *relaxing*. Another contradiction of the actor's work: relaxation *exercises*. Stanislavsky said, "You cannot . . . have any conception of the evil that results from muscular spasms and physical contraction." David Barnett—British, rumpled, wore a "muffler," would eventually go out to the University of Alberta and head the drama department there—walked around us while we splayed out and he'd pounce on a stiff ankle, a pretentious face and cry out "Relax!"

We played many theatre games. Dave Robertson remembered games too, under Hirsch's direction; one where they would stand in a circle and pass an object around, and each person was required to give a verbal response to the object. These games are exhausting. You must learn *not* to think; you must respond *honestly*. You might be holding a warm shoe in your hand, but you must not act.

We were in Theatre School to learn to split the infinitive, to *not act*. After one performance, when I finally learned something about listening, and before going off to Edmonton to study and "become an actor," David Barnett guardedly congratulated me on my recent work, and said, "That was the only professional performance you will ever give in your life." This kind of thing was common with David: he is intuitive and blunt. And he was right.

Unbroken Line #3

My mother and father would take Liz and me to the Dominion Theatre to see the plays. And one of the plays was written by a Canadian, by a woman, Ann Henry. *Lulu Street*. It was about the 1919 Winnipeg General Strike. It was about us. Or them. It was about us as them.

Stories told by Canadians about the epiphanic moment when one sees one's own life represented artistically in the space, the stage, the page, traditionally reserved for British and American material, these are worn yarns and have become trite. But the moment itself can be honoured. I remember the collision, a surge of stubborn, serious ambition. Dave Robertson tells me that Ann Henry had to fight to get that play produced here. Yes. Okay. Fight.

Lulu Street was produced at MTC in March 1967, directed by Eddie Gilbert. (John Hirsch would direct it in Lennoxville, Quebec in 1972.) It's about the experiences of the strikers, and Ann Henry deployed the counter-dynamics, the conflict, within that constituency. The play is not only about class struggle; it portrays the costs of idealism, especially the costs in comfort and safety to those people inspired by the Social Gospel in that period.

If I remember it correctly, the set was Spartan and spare, a naturalistic function that also focused our attention on the characters' pain. Though I've written about the 1919 Strike in two novels and one play, I didn't read *Lulu Street* until last week, preparing to write this essay. It's weird to see that *Lulu Street* formed cadences similar to those I tried to follow in my play "Fox," though I was writing about the conflict the Social Gospel created in the lives of the Winnipeg "establishment." I wonder how much of Henry's play crept into some adolescent cerebral crevice.

From *Lulu Street*:

ALBERT: Yes! Woodsworth, Ivens, Heaps, Bray. All of them! Dragged out of their homes! And they've broken into the Labour Church and the Ukrainian Hall. Taken all the papers. The men want you to go down there, Matthew. Talk to them. What'll I say? What'll I tell them? (Act II)

This event has echoed through our cultural history. My dad drove a British sports car at that time, a red MGB, and Liz and I would have been stuffed into the tiny backseat going home. I was thirteen years old. I didn't know, then, that my grandfather had acted as counsel against the strikers, and I don't remember talking about it on the way home—though we may well have done so and I was distracted by the idea of Ann Henry writing a play rather than worrying over my inherited complicity in social injustice. I don't remember the ride home. But I do know that *Lulu Street* confirmed in me my self-appraisal as a thorough fraud. It wasn't that my parents were rich—they weren't, they were struggling with a big family—but they certainly weren't poor and my childhood was privileged in ways both material and emotional. I wasn't a member of the "ruling class." My sense of failure grew out of the production values, the aesthetics of *Lulu Street*: the absence of self-consciousness, of distractions, of narcissism.

I was a fraud. I kept going, interested in the peculiar fact that shyness can make you pigeon-toed. I did a lot of relaxation exercises, and muddled through. This was the time of Larry Zolf, and it seemed to me that Zolf was the only kind of human who could break through Canada's colonial arts scene. A North End Jewish guy. No matter how hard I try, I just can't be Larry Zolf. Alas.

So I wrote about self-consciousness, distractions and narcissism. And it's no longer an issue. The non-profit writing life has taken care of it: I've been kicked out of class. "I'm one dollar an hour, Willy!"

The immigrants from northern Europe, the Jewish community, and the assorted offspring from all over town I met in improvs (like the one in the rowboat, where you're all sinking and dying of thirst and sunstroke) broke the surface of the colonial Dominion. That's what happened. Without this surge of energy, which we may say was epitomized in John Hirsch, we might never have achieved the republic of funk, might not have detected the (occasionally congestive) heart of dusty old Winnipeg, a place where the Old World rippled up to take air, like some scarred Leviathan.

M: Magic If

From the moment of the appearance of [the *Magic*] *If* the actor passes from the plane of actual reality into the plane of another life, created and imagined by him.

In order to be emotionally involved in the imaginary world which the actor builds on the basis of a play, in order to be caught up in the action on the stage, he must believe in it. . . . This does not mean he should give himself up to anything like hallucination, . . . quite the contrary. . . . He does not forget that he is surrounded by stage scenery and props. . . .

The secret of the effect of *If* [is] that it does not use fear or force. (Stanislavsky 94)

Unbroken line #4

After the workshop for "Thirst," I more or less asked Dave Robertson if he would be my friend. I asked him out for coffee, to speak about the early days of MTC. When I went to meet him, I was astonished at how much affection I felt at seeing him. He'd played the role that was my father, that was not my father. We'd had most of a week working in the "magic if," the space of special circumstance. He was a gentle man with that curious bravery an actor demonstrates in the smallest gesture. He died in September 2004. I wish people wouldn't do that. I wish that wouldn't happen.

Theatre productions can go dreadfully awry. It's a volatile, pressurized few weeks, and when things go wrong, the people involved are particularly vulnerable, largely because you are working with imagination and memory, perhaps the most personal aspects of a life. It can also be the occasion of deep and abiding affection.

We're working with recombinant forms in countless ways. We're moved by strange occurrences because they are familiar. That's why this word "history" is so weird and problematical. That's why the memory of Dave Robertson in the coffee shop will always surprise me; recognition is the biggest surprise of all.

Somewhere the serious adolescents are improvising a lifeboat on the black floor of a rehearsal hall. They are lost at sea. They must help one another survive. One by one they succumb to thirst. Delirious, they tell the survivors about their childhood, the luck and the injustices and the unjust luck. None of them die. Oh, sure they die. But in the play. In the play.

WORKS CITED

Henry, Ann. *Lulu Street*. Vancouver: Talonbooks, 1975.

Miller, Arthur. *Death of a Salesman*. 1949. New York: Penguin, 1976.

Stanislavsky, Konstantin. *An Actor's Handbook: An Alphabetical Arrangement of Concise Statements on Aspects of Acting*. Ed. and trans. Elizabeth Reynolds Hapgood. 1936. New York: Theatre Arts Books, 1963.

Contributors

Born in Winnipeg (1926), ARTHUR ADAMSON taught English literature and creative writing at the University of Manitoba and has published poetry and art criticism. He is also a visual artist; *Arthur Adamson—A Celebration*, a book of selected paintings, was published by J. Gordon Shillingford (2006).

PATRICIA BLONDAL was born in 1926 and grew up in Souris, Manitoba. She studied at United College, graduating with a BA in 1947. She was an active CBC broadcaster in Winnipeg in the early 1950s before moving to Montreal with her husband, cancer researcher Harold Blondal. Her novel *A Candle to Light the Sun* (McClelland & Stewart, 1960), a frank and impassioned study of small-town Manitoba, was published after Blondal's death from breast cancer in November 1959.

NOELLE BOUGHTON is a former Manitoban now living in Toronto. She worked in both Winnipeg and Toronto as a journalist and communications consultant before recently returning to full-time writing. Her spiritual biography, *Margaret Laurence: A Gift of Grace*, will be published by the Canadian Scholars'/Women's Press this year.

DI BRANDT has published five books of poetry and four books of critical and creative non-fiction. Her most recent poetry title is *Now You Care* (Coach House Books 2003) and her latest essay collection is titled *So this is the world & here I am in it* (NeWest Press Writer as Critic series 2006). She has collaborated extensively with artists in other media, including the poetry/song cycle *Awakenings*, featuring her poetry and that of Dorothy Livesay, and music by Carol Ann Weaver and Rebecca Campbell (CD 2003). She was recently appointed Canada Research Chair in Creative Writing at Brandon University.

JACK BUMSTED is a fellow of St. John's College and a professor of history at the University of Manitoba. He is also president of the Manitoba Historical Society. He currently researches and writes almost exclusively on the cultural history of Winnipeg and Manitoba.

DENNIS COOLEY, a founding editor with Turnstone Press, is an editor, poet and critic. He is especially interested in Prairie writing, about which he has written and which he has taught on many occasions, including several times in Germany. He has edited two anthologies of Prairie poetry, *Draft* (Turnstone Press, 1981) and *Inscriptions* (Turnstone, 1992). His latest books include a collection of Dracula poems, *seeing red* (Turnstone, 2003), and country music (Kalamalka Press, 2004). Forthcoming in 2006 are a chapbook, a collection of selected poems, and a long poem, *the bentleys* (University of Alberta Press), which plays freely off of Sinclair Ross's *As For Me and My House.*

HOWARD CURLE was born, raised and continues to live in Winnipeg. He remembers vividly the summer of 1954 when his father, who worked in television sales at Eaton's department store, brought home the first television set on their block. Today, he teaches film studies at the University of Manitoba. He co-edited (with Steve Snyder) *Vittorio De Sica: Contemporary Perspectives* (University of Toronto Press, 2000).

CHRISTOPHER DAFOE was born in Winnipeg in 1936 and now divides his time between his apartment in Vancouver and his cottage on Lake Winnipeg. He is the author of *Dancing Through Time: The First Fifty Years of the Royal Winnipeg Ballet* (Portage and Main Press, 1990), *Winnipeg, Heart of the Continent*, a history (Great Plains Publications, 1998) and *The Molsheim Meadowlark,* a fictional biography (Great Plains, 2000). His essays have been included in a number of anthologies and he edited *The Beaver*, a Canadian history magazine, from 1985 to 1997.

An accomplished pianist, composer and critic, CHESTER DUNCAN (1936-2002) taught in the English department at the University of Manitoba, where he specialized in criticism and the poetry of W.H. Auden. For many years he wrote program notes for the Winnipeg Symphony Orchestra and gave talks on CBC's *Critically Speaking* and *Passing Show*. His collection of essays, *Wanna Fight, Kid?*, appeared in 1975 (Queenston House).

SCOTT ELLIS has been a railroad brakeman, fruit picker, show groom, Fuller Brush salesman, steelworker and professional malingerer. He lives in Winnipeg and has published poetry, fiction and criticism in various venues.

ARIEL GORDON is a Winnipeg-based writer and editor. In spring of 2006, her poems appeared simultaneously on buses in Alberta and Manitoba. Her collaboration with composer David Raphael Scott, "Tranquility and Order," recently had its world premiere at the Westminster United Church as part of the Winnipeg Symphony Orchestra's 2006 New Music Festival and via the airwaves as a part of a live broadcast of CBC Radio's *Two New Hours*.

DICK HARRISON is a professor emeritus from the University of Alberta, where he taught English, American and Canadian literature for twenty-eight years, specializing in fiction of the North American Wests. He is best known for *Unnamed Country: The Struggle for a Canadian Prairie Fiction* (University of Alberta Press, 1977). The present essay is part of a wider investigation of questionable fathers in western fiction he has begun under the working title "The Name of the Father." Harrison now lives on British Columbia's Sunshine Coast.

CATHERINE HUNTER is a poet, novelist, critic and editor who teaches English literature and creative writing at the University of Winnipeg. Her most recent book is the crime novel *Queen of Diamonds*, forthcoming from Ravenstone, an imprint of Turnstone Press.

PAULA KELLY is a Winnipeg writer/director whose most recent feature-length documentary *Appassionata: The Extraordinary Life and Music of Sonia Eckhardt-Gramatté* premiered on CBC's *Opening Night* in 2006. The European premiere of *Appassionata* took place at the Rome Music Documentary Festival in September, 2006. Her previous documentary, *The Notorious Mrs. Armstrong*, was winner of three Manitoba Blizzard Awards in 2003, for best direction, writing and editing, and received a Gemini nomination for best editing. Her article "Looking for Mrs. Armstrong" (published in *The Beaver* magazine) was nominated for two Western Magazine Awards in 2003.

Educated at Winnipeg's United College, MARGARET LAURENCE (1926-1987) travelled in Africa in the 1950s. She subsequently wrote several books out of her African experience, including the novel *This Side Jordan* (1960), followed by *The Tomorrow-Tamer and Other Stories* and *The Prophet's Camel Bell*, both in 1963. In 1964 *The Stone Angel*, the first book of five in the Manawaka series, which concluded with *The Diviners* in 1974, was published simultaneously in London, Toronto and New York.

JACK LUDWIG has published three novels, *Confusions* (McClelland & Stewart, 1963), *Above Ground* (Little, Brown and Co., 1968) and *A Woman of Her Age* (McClelland & Stewart, 1973). His fiction and non-fiction have been published in numerous magazines and anthologies in Canada, the USA, the UK, including *Prize Stories: The O. Henry Awards, Best American* [sic] *Short Stories*, etc. He also took time out to write several non-fiction books including *Five Ring Circus* (Doubleday, 1976), about the Montreal Olympics, *Hockey Night in Moscow* (Doubleday, 1972) and *Games of Fear and Winning* (Doubleday, 1976).

ROBYN MAHARAJ is a Manitoba-based literary arts administrator, freelance writer and poet. Her poetry, book reviews and profiles have appeared in various literary journals and publications including *Prairie Fire, Dandelion, Contemporary Verse 2, Zygote,* the *Winnipeg Free Press* and *Prairie books NOW*. Two of her poems were published in *Spider Women*, an anthology published by J. Gordon Shillingford in 1999. Robyn is co-founder of the Winnipeg International Writers Festival and has worked for the Manitoba Writers' Guild since 1992. She has completed her first poetry manuscript, "Missing Patricia," dedicated to Patricia Blondal. Robyn is currently co-writing a local true-crime, non-fiction manuscript.

CARSON McCANCE grew up in Winnipeg. After living, studying and working in Vancouver, Halifax and London, England, he returned to his home town, and now lives and works near the intersection of Portage and Main.

DAWNE McCANCE grew up crossing Portage and Main. She is a professor and editor at the University of Manitoba, has published widely, and recently contributed to the beautiful chapbook *Three Days in Spain*.

GEORGE MELNYK is a cultural historian who teaches Canadian studies at the University of Calgary. He was raised in Winnipeg and educated at the University of Manitoba. In addition to his books on Canadian writing and film, he has published four books of essays, in which his upbringing in Winnipeg plays a vital role.

ROBERT MILLS was born and raised in Winnipeg, and left there in 1972 to pursue graduate studies at the University of Alberta. After teaching at the Universities of Prince Edward Island and British Columbia, he returned to Alberta. He lives in Edmonton and teaches Shakespeare and eighteenth-century literature at Red Deer College.

LAURIE RICOU was born and raised in Brandon. In the 1950s, for him, Winnipeg was the impossibly remote, strange and exotic "big city." Then it was the home of the Guess Who and CKY. When he moved to another big city, Toronto, he discovered that

Winnipeg was the literary centre of the country. Ever since, he's been trying to figure out where region is.

CHRISTIAN RIEGEL teaches Canadian literature, genre studies and contemporary poetry at Campion College at the University of Regina. His recent books are *Writing Grief: Margaret Laurence and the Work of Mourning* (University of Manitoba Press, 2003) and *Response to Death: The Literary Work of Mourning* (University of Alberta Press, 2005).

RORY RUNNELLS is coordinator of the Manitoba Association of Playwrights, drama editor of *Prairie Fire*, and has produced numerous plays at the Winnipeg Fringe Festival and elsewhere.

A former student of Marshall McLuhan, JIM SCOTT is currently an instructor at Red Deer College. His creative work has been shortlisted for a National Magazine Award and for a CBC Literary Award. He has also published articles on his mountaineering experiences, as well as a guidebook to the Rocky Mountain backcountry.

WALTER SWAYZE is professor emeritus of English, The University of Winnipeg, and a fellow of United College. Eighteen years after retiring he still actively enjoys life and literature.

MARGARET SWEATMAN's most recent novel, *When Alice Lay Down with Peter*, won the Rogers Writers' Trust Fiction Prize, the Carol Shields Winnipeg Award, the Margaret Laurence Award for Fiction, the Sunburst Award for Canadian Literature of the Fantastic and the McNally Robinson Book of the Year Award. She is a playwright and poet, and performs with jazz and new music ensembles. Most recently she won a Genie Award for Best Song in Canadian Film, with composer Glenn Buhr.

ULRICH TEUCHER is assistant professor in the Culture and Human Development Program in the Department of Psychology at the University of Saskatchewan. His work connects the humanities and social sciences and examines the epistemological foundations for work across cultures and disciplines. In his interdisciplinary and cross-cultural doctoral dissertation in psychology and comparative literature, entitled "Writing the Unspeakable: Metaphors in Cancer Narratives," Teucher established a "therapeutic psychopoetics" of metaphor in cancer discourse.

MEEKA WALSH is the editor of *Border Crossings*, an award-winning international art magazine. She has contributed essays to catalogues published in Canada and the United States and her short fiction has been published in a number of anthologies. Her books include *Ordinary Magic*, a travel memoir, and *The Garden of Earthly Intimacies*, a collection of short stories. She has also edited *Don Reichert: A Life in Work* and *The Body, Its Lesson and Camouflage: The Photographs of Diana Thorneycroft*. She served on the board of the National Gallery from 2001 to 2005 and is a member of the board of Winnipeg's Plug In ICA. In 2003 she was awarded the Lifetime Achievement Award by the Western Magazine Awards Foundation.

GENE WALZ, professor of film studies at the University of Manitoba, has recently edited two books: *One Man's Documentary: A Memoir of the Early Years of the National Film Board* by Graham McInnes (University of Manitoba Press, 2005) and *Canada's Best Features* (Rodopi, 2002), a collection of fifteen essays on Canadian films. Previous publications include the award-winning *Cartoon Charlie: The Life and Art of Animation Pioneer Charles Thorson* (Great Plains Publications, 1998), and a book on François Truffaut. He has written several film scripts, one of which, *The Washing Machine*, he directed for CBC-TV; he also wrote and produced *Birding for Kids* for PBS.

TRICIA WASNEY's background is in film, literature, visual art and landscape architecture. Her work explores notions of memory, place and human experience in the landscape, combining writing with visual art practices. It has been published in *Contemporary Verse 2* and in several essay anthologies. Tricia developed, and currently manages, the new public art policy and program for the City of Winnipeg through the Winnipeg Arts Council.

MARGARET A. WIGMORE teaches in the English department at the University of Regina and has been doing research on the work of Margaret Laurence for a number of years.

DAVE WILLIAMSON is the author of more than 750 book reviews that have appeared in various newspapers and magazines over the past thirty-five years. He has published four novels, a collection of short stories and a memoir, *Author! Author! Encounters with Famous Writers* (Great Plains Publications, 2000). He collaborated with Carol Shields on a stage play called *Anniversary*. He lives in Winnipeg, where he was dean of Business and Applied Arts at Red River College until his retirement in February, 2006.

NOTES

The following were previously published in *Prairie Fire* magazine:
"Surrational Dreams: A.E. van Vogt and Mennonite Science Fiction" by Scott Ellis (15.2); "On John Hirsch: An Observer's Footnotes" by Rory Runnells (17.3); "Underground in Winnipeg: Patricia Blondal's *A Candle to Light the Sun*" by Catherine Hunter, "North Main Car" by Jean Margaret Laurence, "Henry Avenue, Where Are You Now That We Need You? John Marlyn's *Under the Ribs of Death*" by George Melnyk (under the title "Henry Avenue! Where Are You When We Need You?"), "Jack Ludwig's Winnipeg: Cold City, Warm People" by Robert Mills, "*North Main Car*: A Context" by Margaret A. Wigmore (all in 20.2); "The Riverworlds of Jack Ludwig: An Interview" by Ariel Gordon (21.4).

The poems by Chester Duncan on pages 50 and 51 appear courtesy of Mark Duncan, copyright Mark Duncan.

Photographs on pages 40, 134, 186, 234, 256, 280, 300 courtesy The University of Manitoba Archives & Special Collections, The Winnipeg Tribune Collection.

Photograph on page 80 by Robert Lansdale.

Photograph on page 110 by G.N. Louise Jonasson. Book courtesy Chester Cuthbert. Front cover of *Reflections of A.E. van Vogt: The Autobiography of a Science Fiction Giant, with a complete bibliography*. Cover design: Cary Bradley. Published by Fictioneer Books, 1975.

Photograph of Birk Sproxton by Mark Sproxton.

Every effort has been made to locate holders of copyright for photographic material contained herein. If you have any information pertaining to such copyright not already credited here, please contact the publisher immediately.

ABOUT THE EDITOR

Birk Sproxton was born and raised in Flin Flon, a town named after a fictional character, and has spent many years puzzling about writing and place. In a longpoem, *Headframe:* (Turnstone Press, 1985) and its sequel, *Headframe: 2* (Turnstone, 2006), a novel, *The Red-Headed Woman with the Black Black Heart* (Turnstone, 1997) and a memoir, *Phantom Lake: North of 54* (University of Alberta Press, 2005), he explores the fabled mining town in Manitoba's Shield country. *Phantom Lake* won the Manitoba Historical Society's Margaret McWilliams Award for Local History and the Grant MacEwan Alberta Author Award of $25,000. His edited books also address issues of place. *Trace: Prairie Writers on Writing* (Turnstone, 1986) and *Great Stories from the Prairies* (Red Deer Press, 2000) have proven to be essential works in the Prairie literature archive. In 1999 he edited a book-length special issue of *Prairie Fire* titled "Winnipeg in Fiction: 125 years of English-Language Writing." Sproxton has lectured and read across Canada and, recently, in Berlin. He currently divides his time between the Alberta greenbelt and a house on Lake Winnipeg.